Essentials of Microeconomics

Essentials of Microeconomics

Edited by
Luis Bender

Willford Press
www.willfordpress.com

Published by Willford Press,
118-35 Queens Blvd., Suite 400,
Forest Hills, NY 11375, USA

ISBN: 978-1-68285-773-1

Cataloging-in-Publication Data

Essentials of microeconomics / edited by Luis Bender.
p. cm.
Includes bibliographical references and index.
ISBN 978-1-68285-773-1
1. Microeconomics. 2. Economics. I. Bender, Luis.
HB172 .E87 2020
338.5--dc23

For information on all Willford Press publications
visit our website at www.willfordpress.com

WILLFORD PRESS

Contents

'reface

e branch of economics which studies the behaviour of firms as well as individuals in aking decisions regarding the allocation of scarce resources is known as microeconomics. also studies the interactions among these individuals and firms. One of the primary goals microeconomics is to examine the market mechanisms that establish relative prices among ods and services along with the allocation of limited resources among alternative uses. e failure of markets to produce effective results is also analyzed under microeconomics. ere are several key areas which are studied under microeconomics such as demand, pply and equilibrium, measurement of elasticities, consumer demand theory, theory of oduction, and cost of production. The extensive content of this book provides the readers th a thorough understanding of microeconomics and its fundamental elements. It is an sential guide for both academicians and those who wish to pursue this discipline further. will also help new researchers by foregrounding their knowledge in this branch.

e information contained in this book is the result of intensive hard work done by searchers in this field. All due efforts have been made to make this book serve as a mplete guiding source for students and researchers. The topics in this book have been mprehensively explained to help readers understand the growing trends in the field.

vould like to thank the entire group of writers who made sincere efforts in this book and y family who supported me in my efforts of working on this book. I take this opportunity thank all those who have been a guiding force throughout my life.

Editor

1

he relationship between employees' ompetences and the consequences and ıanner of exercising emotional labour (EL)

ıieszka Springer[1], Karolina Oleksa[1]

STRACT Many job posts require one to display emotions specified by organisational standards. Such work is referred to as emotional labour (EL) and consists in producing particular emotional reactions in contacts with a customer as well as suppressing the actual emotional reactions that could be seen negatively by the other party. An employee may cope with such work by choosing one of two strategies: surface acting or deep acting. Emotional labour has various consequences, and professional burnout is among the negative ones. The objective of the article is to review the literature concerned with the exercise and the consequences of EL and analyse the relationship between surface and deep acting and the level of professional burnout among selected professional groups (N=297). Furthermore, the authors examine the correlation between an employee's competences and their preferred style of EL and assess the moderating role of competences in negative consequences of EL. Analyses confirm that the persons characterised by surface role-playing display a higher level of professional burnout; however, no correlation is found between deep role-playing and lower professional burnout. Analysis of the coefficients of correlation demonstrates no significant correlation between an employee's competences and deep acting, whereas a statistically significant correlation is discovered between competences and the surface strategy. The higher the competences, the less likely the employee will exercise surface acting. Verification of the last hypothesis reveals that people with a higher level of competences who follow the surface strategy in terms of faking emotions are characterised by a lower level of professional burnout than employees with lower competences.

Y WORDS: emotional labour, surface role-playing, deep role-playing, professional burnout, professional competences

[1]SB University in Poznan, the Institute of Management, Poland

1. Introduction

The practical experiences of employees show that work is more and more commonly connected with displaying a certain type of emotion (Ashforth & Humphrey, 1995; Hochschild, 2009). Organisations dictate to employees how to react emotionally with standard behaviours in relations with customers, specifying the manners of greeting, servicing standards, and complaint handling (Grandey, 2000). Such practices often cause the employees to find themselves in a situation where the emotions they feel do not correspond to the emo-

rrespondence concerning this article should be addressed to: **nieszka Springer**, WSB University in Poznan, the Institute of ınagement, ul. Powstańców Wielkopolskich 5, 61-895 Poznań, land. E-mail: agnieszka.springer@wsb.poznan.pl tions they display (Morris & Feldman, 1996; Szczygieł, Bazińska, Kadzikowska-Wrzosek, & Retowski, 2009). Such work can give rise to both positive consequences, e.g., taking pride in or having high satisfaction with work (Jin & Guy, 2009), and negative consequences connected with emotional exhaustion (Seery & Corrigall, 2009), professional burnout (Babakus, Yavas, & Ashill, 2011; Jin & Guy, 2009), or lower commitment or absence from work (Chau, Dahling, Levy, & Diefendorff, 2009). Enterprises that introduce behavioural standards regulating emotional reactions hope to produce positive effects such as customer satisfaction and loyalty as well as increased organisational revenue (Hwa, 2012) but underestimate the negative consequences of the phenomenon. The difficulty in evaluating the potential negative consequences of emotional labour arises from the existence of multiple moderating variables related to both persons and organisations. This analysis is focused on identifying the role of selected variables related to persons, including employees' competences. Until now, in addition to the most commonly analysed influence of emotional intelligence on the consequences of emotional labour (Rathi, 2014), research has stressed the role of personality variables (Brook, 2013), reaction styles (Groth, Hennig-Thurau, & Walsh, 2009; Judge, Woolf, & Hurst, 2009), effects (Judge et al., 2009), and the system of values (Diefendorff & Gosserand, 2003). Identification of these variables is of immense importance in cognitive terms and contributes to a better understanding of the nature of a reaction, but it does not offer many possibilities for application in the practice of human resource management. The authors, however, see such a chance in indicating the dependencies between competences and the consequences of EL, as competences are more and more commonly used in recruitment, evaluation, or development of employees. Thus, the objective of the article is to indicate the role of competences in coping with emotional labour.

2. Theoretical basis for the study

2.1 Emotional labour

Looking after the client is a significant element of running a business; therefore, employees are required to meet numerous demands in terms of displaying emotions. An example is work as a client adviser, which requires an employee to adopt a positive attitude towards the client and to use impeccable manners and body expression to mask feelings and emotions that might negatively influence the client's opinion. Arousing and experiencing emotions is dependent on various social factors, and people generally strive to feel emotions that are in compliance with a given social situation and accepted norms (Hochschild, 1979). This is particularly visible in professional life (Ashforth & Humphrey, 1995; Grandey, 2000; Hochschild, 2009) and in consequence employees endeavour to moderate their emotions adequately according to organisational requirements. Management of emotions as an element of one's role at work is referred to as emotional labour – which means that employees must show or suppress given feelings to create the impression that will evoke a desired state of the client's mind (Hochschild, 2009). Emotional labour is mainly the domain of employees in the service sector, as they represent the company in contacts with clients and interact frequently with clients (Hochschild, 2009; Morris & Feldman, 1996; Rafaeli & Sutton, 1990). However, emotions are also a significant part of work in the public sector, e.g., in public administration bodies where the level of bureaucratisation seems to be correlated with suppression of emotions (Vigoda-Gadot & Meisler, 2010), and among people working in professions that require a certain relation to be built with a client, high moral standards to be demonstrated, and services to be of high quality, e.g., doctors, psychologists, nurses, or teachers (Bajcar, Borkowska, Czerw, & Gąsiorowska 2011, p. 11). Various determinants may influence display of emotions, not only organisational requirements but also particularities of the client, such as their age, gender, or even social status (Rafaeli & Sutton, 1990).

Analysing the spectrum of factors determining emotional labour, it may be concluded that it is an element that is present to some extent in any profession; however, some professions require particular devotion to emotional labour, which prompts employees to adopt a strategy of emotion regulation. Hochschild (1979) presumes that workers may achieve this in two ways: by deceiving others in playing an appropriate role or by convincing both others and oneself of genuine experience of the required emotions. These strategies are respectively referred to as surface acting and deep acting or role-playing (Hochschild, 1979). Sur-ace acting consists in limiting emotion management o exclusively displaying an emotion without experincing it. A shop assistant will smile at a demanding ustomer while masking irritation, and a prison guard vill show power and dominance with verbal expresion and posture while in fear of a prison riot. In both ases, the employees merely camouflage their true feelngs. Deep acting is more complex than surface acting, s in deep acting an employee puts effort into feeling he emotion that is appropriate in a given situation.

Emotion management through surface and deep cting brings about various consequences, both positive and negative (Grandey, 2000). Research demontrates that surface acting is correlated with the sense of tiredness and isolation because it requires greater energy to correct feelings and constantly monitor and nask one's emotions (Brotheridge & Grandey, 2002; Gradney, 2000; Hülsheger & Schewe, 2011). Furthernore, in comparison to deep acting, surface acting reates greater difficulty in maintaining positive emoions in the face of stress provoked by the discord beween true and presented feelings, which is reflected by a higher level of exhaustion and a less positive assessnent of one's own work (Totterdell & Holman, 2003). Emotional labour is also correlated with the level of authenticity of emotion – surface acting lowers the evel of authenticity, whereas research has shown no such correlation in the case of deep acting (Hülsheger & Schewe, 2011). As Brotheridge and Gardney (2002) conclude: although both surface and deep acting allow employees to express the emotions desired by the organisation, the physiological state produced by the actual emotions felt remains, which may negatively influence employee health and level of stress. The effect of such influence may be the emergence of professional burnout in an employee affected by emotional labour (Babakus et al., 2011; Brotheridge & Grandey, 2002; Grandey, 2003; Hochschild, 2009; Hülsheger & Schewe, 2011, Hwa, 2012; Jin & Guy, 2009, Maslach, Schaufeli & Leiter, 2001; Seery & Corrigall, 2009, Zapf, Seifert, Schmutte, & Mertini, & Holz, 2001).

2.2. Negative consequences of emotional labour – professional burnout

The phenomenon of professional burnout has been studied since the 1970s. It has been discussed mainly in the context of service professions following the cultural transformations in the 1960s, when clients started to demand greater care, empathy, and emotional input from employees but did not reciprocate their efforts, which amplified the feeling of exhaustion and lack of appreciation (Schaufeli, Leiter & Maslach, 2009). It is believed that because of the article by Herbert Freudenberger – one of the pioneers in research on burnout – this set of symptoms acquired the name professional burnout (Sęk, 2004, p. 7). Dynamic development of the concept of professional burnout took place owing to the research and publications of the American psychologist Christina Maslach, among others, who not only created a theoretical model of burnout but also co-authored a tool serving to measure it. Maslach and Jackson (1984) defined professional burnout with a three-factor model including a psychological syndrome of emotional exhaustion, depersonalisation, and lower opinion of one's personal achievements, which may appear in people working with other people. They call the sense of emotional overburdening accompanied by a simultaneous shortage of emotional resources emotional exhaustion. Depersonalisation is negative and often seen in reaction to people who are usually clients or subordinates of the person suffering from professional burnout, whereas a low opinion of one's personal achievements is related to a low opinion of one's competences and successes at work (Maslach & Jackson, 1984; Maslach et al., 2001). Another researcher, Demerouti, Bakker, Nachreiner and Schaufeli (2001) proposed a model of professional burnout consisting of two dimensions: exhaustion, i.e., general tiredness, bad mood, and fear in reaction to organisational stress, and loss of commitment, i.e., withdrawal from one's work owing to difficulty in meeting professional requirements.

Professional burnout seems to be a threat to any employee because the factors causing this syndrome to emerge are varied and common. However, practice demonstrates that some professional groups are more susceptible to burnout, e.g., where employees maintain contacts with other people, such as clients, patients, and subordinates (Jenkins & Maslach, 1994; Schaufeli et al., 2009). Among the factors correlated with the level of professional burnout are emotional stressors resulting from working with people, including, among others, the requirement to show or suppress some emotions and be empathic towards the client (Maslach et al., 2001; Zapf et al., 2001). Variables related to emotional labour partially correspond to organisational variables that are stressors influencing professional burnout, e.g., emotional labour is connected to time pressure placed on establishing positive relations with clients (Zapf et al., 2001). In such cases, the manner of coping with emotional labour, i.e., reacting through surface or deep acting, may be seen as a determinant of the symptoms of professional burnout. The two styles interact differently with each of the three factors contributing to burnout: the syndrome of emotional exhaustion, depersonalisation, and lower opinion of one's personal achievements.

Research has confirmed the hypothesis that surface role-playing coexists with emotional exhaustion, whereas there is no such relation in the case of deep acting (Grandey, 2003; Hwa, 2012; Judge, Woolf & Hurst, 2009; Morris, Feldman, 1996; Seery & Corrigall, 2009). Although deep acting requires energy to be put into feeling the desired emotions, it lowers the emotional distance between the state one experiences and the one that is presented and additionally correlates with a greater number of authentic, positive reactions from the clients, which is rewarding for the employee engaged in emotional labour (Gardney, 2003). Furthermore, surface role-playing coexists with distancing oneself from the client – people who mask their true emotions and portray other emotions begin to treat the client like an object, which makes it easier for them to feign emotions (Brotheridge & Gardney, 2002). Such distancing from the client and deception through expressed emotions may cause negative feelings towards oneself, which indicates that surface acting is significantly correlated with a lower opinion of one's achievements and decreased commitment towards the organisation (Brotheridge & Gardney, 2002; Hochschild, 2009; Zapf et al., 2001). Based on analysis of the relevant literature, the authors put forward two hypotheses concerning professional burnout and the manner of acting in emotional labour:

H1: People who adopt the strategy of surface acting in emotional labour show a higher level of professional burnout.

H2: People who adopt the strategy of deep acting in emo tional labour show a lower level of professional burnou

Because the syndrome of professional burnout bring about serious consequences for the psychological an physical balance of an employee, which affects the effectiveness and the success of an organisation, it i worth analysing the factors that might reduce the negative influence of the stressors and other consequence arising from emotional labour. The authors presum that such factors can be employees' competences whose application may allow effective management o one's emotions in the workplace.

2.3. Employee Competences

Competences have been present in the practice an theory of human resource management for over 40 years. In understanding the significance of competences seen as the internal potential of an employee the publications by D. C. McClelland and his followe R. E. Boyatzisa have been groundbreaking (Boyatzis 1982; 2008; McClelland & Boyatzis, 1980; McClelland, 1973). These authors first stress the relationship between an employee's effectiveness in a given pos and his internal predispositions. Boyatzis defines competences as "*the potential, existing within the human, leading to such a behaviour that helps to satisfy the requirements at a given post*" (Boyatzis, 1982, p 18). Competences are most commonly treated as a collection of three components: knowledge, skills and attitudes (Kossowska & Sołtysińska, 2002; Sidor-Rządkowska, 2006; Thierry, Monod, & Sauret, 1994 p. 90); however, they may also include motivation, personality traits, values, self-esteem, and social role (Spencer & Spencer, 1993). As Dubois and Rothwel put it, defining competences moves towards including each trait of an individual that allows them to achieve the expected results in a given post (Dubois & Rothwel, 2008, p. 32). In the present analysis, competences are treated as a collection of knowledge, skills, and attitudes, whereas personality traits or motivation are rather the conditions for building and manifesting competences and not the competences themselves.

The American approach to competences focuses on universal models of the most effective managers and person-related conditioning of effectiveness, while the British approach focuses on analysis of the requirements of a profession or a job post (Boak & Coolican, 2001; Garavan & McGuire, 2001, p. 150). This paper adopts the American approach. However, analyses are not merely limited to examination of managers; the authors are interested in the way employees engaged in emotional labour operate. Because various professions are considered in the study, analyses are carried out for basic competences that are used by a person regardless of their professional role (Filipowicz, 2004, pp. 19-38). Owing to the availability of a great variety of lists and models of competences (Filipowicz, 2004; Oleksyn, 2006; Wood, 2006), we have decided to adopt the model of competences making use of six clusters of competences (Springer, 2011).

The basic competence clusters singled out by Springer (2011) are as follows: dominance, focus on information, being organised, focus on emotions, focus on analysis and the use of facts, and imaginativeness and openness. Dominance is a factor encompassing employee traits where the key characteristic is influencing others. It also includes prognostic skills connected with diagnosis and evaluation of the market. Focus on information is sending and receiving messages and skills related to acquisition of information, including data obtained with the use of modern information and communication technologies. Focus on emotions is sensitivity to emotions felt by co-workers and clients. Imaginativeness and openness refers to a non-standard and innovative approach to tasks. Being organized is chiefly about technical skills that are necessary in everyday work.

Competences are becoming increasingly common in organisations and in the practice of human resource management, and the systems based on work posts are increasingly abandoned in favour of systems based on competences (Sienkiewicz & Trawińska-Konador, 2013). Human resource management based on competences is an approach that not only integrates different areas of HRM that despite of integrating different areas of managing employees, also takes into consideration their individual predispositions of employees (Dubois & Rothwel, 2008, p. 26).

This indication of the influence of competences on employee effectiveness has become the basis for two research hypotheses.

H3: There is a statistically significant correlation between an employee's competences and the strategy governing emotional labour.

H4: In a group of employees following the surface strategy of emotional labour, a lower level of professional burnout is present among employees with higher competences.

3. Research Methodology

The study was conducted in 2015 and 2016 on a sample of 297 employees. Sample selection was purposive and carried out on the basis of professional contacts of the researchers; the sample was composed of people engaged in work meeting the criteria of emotional labour: employees had direct contact with clients, exerted influence over their clients' emotional reactions, and were bound by rules of displaying emotions. All the respondents completed three questionnaires; some of them received the questionnaires directly from the researcher, while others by electronic means. The study was conducted on employees whose work was a mission, that is, it required taking care of others and offering help, as well as employees whose work was not a mission. The first group comprised 160 people (teachers and policemen) and the second 136 people (tradesmen and services providers). The average job seniority was 13 years, and the average job seniority at the current post was 10.3 years. Nearly 70% of the respondents were women, which reflects the general dominance of this gender in such professions teachers and sellers (the structure of the group under examination is provided in table 1).

Three tools were used to conduct the study: the Scale of Surface and Deep Emotional Labour (SPGPE) (Finogenow, Wróbel & Mróz, 2015), Oldenburg Burnout Inventory (OLBI), (Demerouti, Bakker, Vardakou, & Kantas, 2003), and the Questionnaire of Self-Assessment of Competences (Springer, 2011). The manner of role-playing – surface or deep – was measured with the SPGPE questionnaire. This is the Polish version of the revised Emotional Labour Scale (ELS) developed by Brotheridge and Lee (2003). The tool consists of three subscales; two are related to surface acting and are called hiding feelings and faking feelings, and the third one is concerned with deep acting (Finogenow et al., 2015). The questionnaire is composed of nine state-

Table 1. Structure of the group under examination according to gender, age, and education

		Size	%
Gender	Female	205	69.3%
	Male	91	30.7%
	Total	296	100.0%
Age	18-26	79	26.7%
	27-35	87	29.4%
	36-45	53	17.9%
	46-55	66	22.3%
	Above 55 years old	11	3.7%
	Total	296	100.0%
Vocational education	Junior high school	13	4.4%
	Secondary	71	24.0%
	Higher	212	71.6%
	Total	296	100.0%

ments regarding activities during a typical day at work. The respondents are asked to estimate on a five-point scale (ranging from "never" to "always") to what extent they agree with a given statement.

Professional burnout was measured with a translated OLBI questionnaire developed by Demerouti and her co-workers (Demerouti et al., 2003) OLBI encompasses the affective, physical, and cognitive aspects of exhaustion. The questionnaire measures two dimensions: exhaustion and lack of commitment. Each subscale contains four items phrased positively and four phrased negatively (Demerouti et al., 2003). The questionnaire is composed of 16 statements regarding feelings and behaviours related to work. The respondent determines the level to which they agree with a given statement on a four-point scale from "completely agree" to "completely disagree". The Polish adaptation of the test was made by Teresa Chirkowska-Smolak (in press) on a group of 664 respondents.

Evaluation of competences was performed with a self-assessment questionnaire composed of 36 descriptions of various skills of an employee. These skills were grouped into a model consisting of six basic competences characteristic of various areas of professional operation. Employees evaluated all the items on a 5-point scale from 1: "I absolutely cannot do it" to 5: "I can do it really well".

4. Research results

Eleven variables are analysed in the study, three of which characterized emotional labour, two professional burnout, and six competences. The reliability of all the scales is verified with the Cronbach's alpha coefficient, indicating the integrity of the adopted tool. The coefficients for all the adopted scales have satisfactory values and are comparable to the results obtained in other studies (see table 2). Simultaneously, all the variables obtained in the scales under analysis have a normal distribution.

The respondents are characterised by a similar level of deep emotional labour and score in the scale of hiding feelings. The scores in the scale of faking feelings are a little higher. It is worth stressing that the results describing emotional labour and the mean, and the

Table 2. Evaluation of the reliability of the adopted scales with the Cronbach's alpha coefficient

Scale	Number of items	Cronbach's alpha
Deep acting	3	0.66
Surface acting – hiding emotions	3	0.79
Surface acting – faking emotions	3	0.64
Lack of commitment	8	0.64
Exhaustion	8	0.75
Dominance	9	0.84
Being organized	6	0.76
Focusing on information	6	0.73
Focusing on emotions	5	0.68
Analysis and use of facts	6	0.77
Imaginativeness and openness	4	0.72

differences in professional burnout are similar to the ones obtained in other studies carried out on Polish workers with the use of the same tools. The situation is slightly different when it comes to competences, as in this case the mean results are a little higher and differences are lower than those in research using the same tools conducted on a representative sample of people working in the Wielkopolskie Voivodeship. The above score is, however, amply justified and results from the structure of the sample under examination, where 70% of the respondents are people with higher education. Indeed, earlier research showed that education is a variable that significantly differentiates the level of competences.

Analysis of the interdependencies among the variables under analysis (see table 3) shows no correlation between the deep strategy of emotional labour and the indicators of professional burnout, while the surface strategy does show influence on professional burnout.

With the median score in individual scales of emotional labour adopted as the point of division, assessment of the significance of differences in terms of an employee's lack of commitment and exhaustion has been performed. T-test confirms that people with a higher level of surface acting (in the contexts of hiding and faking emotions) are also marked by a higher level of professional burnout. No such correlation has been found concerning deep acting (see table 4).

The above results confirm the first hypothesis that people who adopt the surface strategy of emotional labour display a higher level of professional burnout. At the same time, no grounds have been found to support the second proposed hypothesis that people exercising a higher level of deep acting show a lower level of professional burnout.

Another question asked in the paper concerns the influence of one's competences on the way emotional labour is handled. Analysis of the coefficients of correlation demonstrates no dependencies between employees' competences and the intensity of deep acting. Simultaneously, there is a statistically significant correlation between competences and surface acting observable in many cases. It is thus worth highlighting that this relation is inversely proportional, and hence the higher the level of competences, the less likely the employee will undertake surface acting. Comparison of employees with low and high levels of competences within a given competence cluster (with the median of the obtained scores as the point of division) reveals that employees who are highly organized, focused on

Table 3. Descriptive statistics and r-Spearman's correlation coefficients for the variables under analysis

			Coefficients of correlation										
Variables	**M**	**SD**	**1**	**2**	**3**	**4**	**5**	**6**	**7**	**8**	**9**	**10**	**1**
PG	2.85	0.810	1										
PP hiding	2.82	0.809	.082	1									
PP faking	2.49	0.781	.139*	.628**	1								
Lack of commitment	2.38	0.448	-.060	.308**	.273**	1							
Exhaustion	2.48	0.447	-.055	.274**	.251**	.657**	1						
Dominance	3.59	0.589	.034	-192**	-.077	-.122*	-.101	1					
Being organizededed	3.90	0.572	.032	-.154**	-.102	-.125*	-.191**	.655**	1				
Information	3.85	0.642	.013	-.125*	-.044	-.032	-.077	.655**	.580**	1			
Emotions	3.98	0.573	.017	-.097	-.066	-.161**	-.133*	.638**	.615**	.536**	1		
Facts	3.88	0.574	.024	-.188**	-.145*	-.153**	-.194**	.700**	.727**	.632**	.704**	1	
Openness	3.81	0.647	.103	-.156**	-.083	-.096	-.044	.715**	.574**	.618**	.675**	.693**	1

Note: *p<0.05 , **p<0.01

Table 4. Analysis of the significance of differences among the mean scores in the scale of professional burnout amon the subgroups under examination.

Independent variable	**M1**	**SD1**	**M2**	**SD2**	**t**	**df**	**two-tail significar**
	high deep acting		low deep acting				
Lack of commitment	2.3324	.46768	2.4288	.42297	-1.863	293.376	0.063
Exhaustion	2.4449	0.4524	2.5087	0.4414	-1.228	293.739	0.221
	PP-hiding – high		PP-hiding – low				
Lack of commitment	2.5122	0.4290	2.2550	0.4313	5.142	292.855	0.000
Exhaustion	2.6075	0.4576	2.3529	0.4018	5.072	283.054	0.000
	PP-faking – high		PP-faking – low				
Lack of commitment	2.4676	0.4528	2.3011	0.4309	3.231	285.591	0.001
Exhaustion	2.5522	0.4489	2.4084	0.4366	2.785	287.526	0.006

le 5. Level of significance of the differences in terms of hiding and faking emotions among employees with high and levels of competences from a given cluster

npetence cluster	PP – hiding	PP – faking
ninance	.143	.430
ng organized	.042	.198
rmation	.001	.075
otions	.440	.236
s	.004	.012
nness	.009	.161

le 6. Level of significance of the differences between the mean scores in the scales of professional burnout and the cted groups of employees.

alysed variables	Employees with low competences		Employees with high competences	
	Lack of commitment	Exhaustion	Lack of commitment	Exhaustion
ep acting	0.031	0.190	0.649	0.832
face acting – ing feelings	0.000	0.001	0.002	0.001
face acting – ing emotions	0.004	0.007	0.043	0.128

information and analysis of facts, imaginative and open hide their emotions less frequently. At the same time, employees with higher focus on analysis and use of facts are less likely to fake their emotions during contacts with clients.

Considering the results of the above analyses, which indicate that competences are correlated with the strategy of emotional labour to a limited extent, it has been decided that the third hypothesis, that competences influence the way emotional labour is exercised, can only partially be supported. As research demonstrates, competences exert influence on hiding emotions exclusively.

The last research question is concerned with the moderating influence of competences on the emergence of the negative effects of emotional labour. Two groups of employees have been singled out for that purpose: the groups of people with lower (N=147) and higher (N=178) levels of competences. The analysis reveals that the negative consequences of surface acting, namely lack of commitment, are less common among employees with higher competence levels. Simultaneously, the level of competences determines whether faking emotions will bring about negative consequences in the form of professional burnout. The analysis confirms that people with a higher level of competences who follow the surface strategy by faking emotions are characterised by a lower level of professional burnout than employees with low competences. It is worth stressing that putting effort into faking emotions has negative consequences such as professional burnout regardless of the level of an employee's competences (see table 6).

Analogously to hypothesis 3, the above results only allow partial acceptance of hypothesis 4, that in the group of employees exercising surface acting in emotional labour, those with higher competences show lower levels of professional burnout. This hypothesis may only be supported with regard to surface acting through faking emotions.

5. Discussion of the results

The objective of this study was to verify four hypotheses regarding correlations among the variables: deep and surface acting in emotional labour, the level of professional burnout, and the level of competences. First, the correlations between surface and deep role-playing and the level of professional burnout were examined. In accordance with the results of international research (Gardney, 2003; Hwa, 2012; Judge et al., 2009; Morris, & Feldman, 1996; Seery & Corrigall, 2009; Totterdell, & Holman, 2003), analyses have demonstrated that surface role-playing is correlated with a higher level of professional burnout, whereas there is no such correlation in the case of deep acting. As initially presumed, surface acting requires greater effort to be put into correcting feelings and monitoring one's emotions, which influences the sense of exhaustion that is a component of burnout (Brotheridge & Grandey, 2002; Gradney, 2000; Hülsheger & Schewe, 2011). Moreover, surface acting requires maintaining distance from clients and deceiving them though the expression of appropriate emotions, which results in lower commitment to doing one's job (Brotheridge & Gardney, 2002; Hochschild, 2009; Zapf at al., 2001). Studies have not confirmed the existence of a correlation between deep acting and a lower level of professional burnout, although such an opinion can be found in the relevant literature (Gardney, 2003; Hülsheger, & Schewe, 2011).

Second, the hypothesis that an employee's competences differentiate the style of emotional labour (i.e., surface or deep acting) was verified. Six competence clusters were singled out in the study, and tests were performed to determine whether these clusters differentiate the selected style of emotional labour. Analysis of the coefficients of correlation demonstrated no dependencies between employees' competences and deep acting. It was particularly surprising to find that there is no significant correlation between competences connected with application of emotions, which is inconsistent with previous research that indicated that emotional intelligence influenced deep acting (Rathi, 2014). Simultaneously, a statistically significant correlation was noted between competences and the adoption of the surface strategy – the higher the level of competences, the less likely the employee would undertake surface acting. The above result may arise from the fact that persons characterised by a higher level of competences have greater self-confidence, are thus less worried about the consequences of displaying their emotions, and resort less often to hiding or faking emotions.

The final hypothesis assumed that employees with higher competences experience fewer negative consequences of emotional labour. The analyses that were conducted revealed that people with a higher level of competences that follow the surface strategy by faking emotions are characterised by a lower level of professional burnout than employees with a lower level of competences. It has simultaneously been proven that putting effort into faking emotions has negative consequences such as higher professional burnout regardless of the level of an employee's competences.

The above result may arise from the effort that employees must put into maintaining positive emotions in the face of stress caused by a discord between the actual and presented states of mind, which, independently from other variables, increases the sense of exhaustion and lowers the opinion of one's own work (Totterdell & Holman, 2003).

6. Conclusions and recommendations

The obtained results show that surface acting in emotional labour coexists with a higher level of professional burnout. This has serious consequences for employees and the company because professional burnout involves lower commitment to one's work and higher exhaustion, which usually results in decreased effectiveness. It is thus worth analysing the organisational requirements that cause employees to hide or fake emotions. Analysis of competences and confirmation of the existence of correlations between higher levels of individual competence clusters and lower levels of hiding or faking emotions may hold practical implications for the recruitment process. During recruitment for the posts where emotional labour is a must, it is worth checking the candidate's competences in individual competence groups. It is also worth considering the possibility of training employees engaged in emotional labour to develop given competences and prevent professional burnout. The authors are aware of the limitations of the presented study, which are concerned with the selection and size of the sample and the use of self-assessment to diagnose the level of competences. This study uses a self-reporting tool, which means that evaluation of competences might have been subjective and dependent, e.g., on the level of self-esteem or the respondent's experience. To verify the research results, it is advisable that the sample of the respondents be increased and more objective methods be used to diagnose employee competences. Analyses may also be carried out based on a division of the respondents in terms of job type, e.g., related to education or trade. This would allow analysis of the manner of coping with emotional labour, the level of professional burnout, and the competences of employees in a given profession.

References

Ashforth, B. E., & Humphrey, R. H. (1995). Emotion in the workplace: A reappraisal. *Human Relations*, 48(2), 97–125. http://dx.doi.org/10.1177/001872679504800201

Babakus, E., Yavas, U., & Ashill, N. J. (2011). Service worker burnout and turnover intentions: Roles of person-job fit, servant leadership, and customer orientation. *Services Marketing Quarterly*, 32(1), 17–31. http://doi.org/10.1080/15332969.2011.533091

Bajcar, B., Borkowska, A., Czerw, A., & Gąsiorowska, A. (2011). *Satysfakcja z pracy w zawodach z misją społeczną. Psychologiczne uwarunkowania* [Job Satisfaction in professions with social mission. Psychological determinants]. Gdańsk: Gdańskie Wydawnictwo Psychologiczne.

Boak, G., & Coolican, D. (2001). Competencies for retail leadership: accurate, acceptable, affordable. *Leadership & Organization Development Journal*, 22(5), 212–220. http://doi.org/10.1108/EUM0000000005675

Boyatzis, R. E. (1982). *The competent manager: A model for effective performance.* New York, NY: John Wiley & Sons.

Boyatzis, R. E. (2008). Competencies in the 21st century. *Journal of Management Development*, 27(1), 5–12. http://doi.org/10.1108/02621710810840730

Brotheridge, C. M., & Grandey, A. A. (2002). Emotional labor and burnout: Comparing two perspectives of "people work". *Journal of Vocational Behavior*, 60(1), 17–39. http:/doi.org/10.1006/jvbe.2001.1815

Brotheridge, C.M., & Lee, R.T. (2003). Development and validation of emotional labour scale. *Journal of Occupational and Organizational Psychology*, 76(3), 365-379. http://dx.doi.org/10.1348/096317903769647229

Brook, P. (2013). Emotional labour and the living personality at work: Labour power, materialist subjectivity and the dialogical self. *Culture & Organization*, 19(4), 332–352. http://doi.org/10.1080/14759551.2013.827423

Chau, S. L., Dahling, J. J., Levy, P. E., & Diefendorff, J. M. (2009). A predictive study of emotional labor and turnover. *Journal of Organizational Behavior*, 30(8), 839–862. http://doi.org/10.1002/job

Chirkowska-Smolak, T. (in press). Polska adaptacja kwestionariusza do pomiaru wypalenia zawodowego OLBI (Oldenburg Burnout Inventory), [The Polish adaptation of Oldenburg Burnout Inventory] Studia Oeconomica Posnaniensia, 5.

Demerouti, E., Bakker, A. B. , Nachreiner, F. , & Schaufeli, W. B. (2001) The job demands- resources model of burnout. *Journal of Applied Psychology*, 86(3), 499-512. http://dx.doi.org/10.1037/0021-9010.86.3.499

Demerouti, E., Bakker, A. B., Vardakou, I., & Kantas, A. (2003). The convergent validity of two burnout instruments: A multitrait-multimethod analysis. *European Journal of Psychological Assessment*, 19(1), 12-23. http://doi.org/10.1027//1015-5759.19.1.12

Diefendorff, J. M., & Gosserand, R. H. (2003). Understanding the emotional labor process: a control theory perspective. *Journal of Organizational Behavior*, 24(8), 945–959. http://doi.org/10.1002/job.230

Dubois, D. D., & Rothwel, W. J. (2008). *Zarządzanie zasobami ludzkimi oparte na kompetencjach [Competency-based human resource management]*. Gliwice: Wydawnictwo Helion.

Filipowicz, G. (2004). *Zarządzanie kompetencjami zawodowymi* [Management based on professional competence]. Warszawa: PWE.

Finogenow, M., Wróbel, M., & Mróz, J. (2015). Skala Płytkiej i Głębokiej Pracy Emocjonalnej (SPGPE) - adaptacja narzędzia i analiza własności psychometrycznych [Deep acting and surface acting scale (DASAS) - Adaptation of the method and analysis of psychometric properties]. *Medycyna Pracy*, 66(3), 359-371. http://dx.doi.org/10.13075/mp.5893.00168

Garavan, T. N., & McGuire, D. (2001). Competencies and workplace learning: Some reflections on the rhetoric and the reality. *Journal of Workplace Learning*, 13(3-4), 144–164. http://doi.org/10.1108/13665620110391097

Grandey, A. A. (2000). Emotional regulation in the workplace: A new way to conceptualize emotional labor. *Journal of Occupational Health Psychology*, 5(1), 95–110. http://doi.org/10.1037//1076-8998.5.1.95

Grandey, A. A. (2003). When "the show must go on": Surface acting and deep acting as determinants of emotional exhaustion and peer-rated service delivery. *Academy of Management Journal*, 46(1), 86-96. http://dx.doi.org/10.2307/30040678

Groth, M., Hennig-Thurau, T., & Walsh, G. (2009). Customer reactions to emotional labor: The roles of employee acting strategies and customer detection accuracy. *Academy of Management Journal*, 52(5), 958–974. http://dx.doi.org/10.5465/AMJ.2009.44634116

Hochschild, A. (1979). Emotion work, feeling rules, and social structure. *American Journal of Sociology*, 85(3), 551-575. http://doi.org/10.1086/227049

Hochschild, A. R. (2009). *Zarządzanie emocjami. Komercjalizacja ludzkich uczuć [The Managed heart: Comercialization of Human Feeling]*. Warszawa: PWN.

Hülsheger , U. R., & Schewe, A. F (2011). On the costs and benefits of emotional labor: A meta-analysis of three decades of research. *Journal of Occupational Health Psychology*, 16(3), 361-389. http://doi.org/10.1037/a0022876

Hwa, M. A. C. (2012). Emotional labor and emotional exhaustion: Does co-worker support matter? *Journal of Management Research*, 12(3), 115–127. http://search.proquest.com/openview d3042ca6da7d85f05fc3c66159079f5a/1?pq origsite=gscholar&cbl=55395

Jin, M. H., & Guy, M. E. (2009). How emotional la bor influences worker pride, job satisfaction, an burnout: An examination of consumer complain workers. *Public Performance & Managemen Review*, 33(1), 88–105. http://doi.org/10.2753 pmr1530-9576330104

Jenkins, S. R., & Maslach, C. (1994). Psychologica health and involvement in interpersonally de manding occupations: A longitudinal perspective *Journal of Organizational Behavior*, 15 (2), 101 127. http://dx.doi.org/10.1002/job.4030150202

Judge, T. A., Woolf, E. F., & Hurst, C. (2009). Is emo tional labor more difficult for some than for oth ers? A multilevel, experience-sampling study *Personnel Psychology*, 62(1), 57–88. http://doi org/10.1111/j.1744-6570.2008.01129.x

Kossowska, M., & Sołtysińska, I. (2002). *Szkolenia pra cowników a rozwój organizacji* [Employee training and organizational development]. Kraków: Oficy na Ekonomiczna.

Maslach, C., & Jackson, S. E. (1984). Burnout in or ganizational settings. In S. Oskamp (Ed.), *Applie Social Psychology Annual: Applications in Orga nizational Settings* (Vol. 5, pp. 133-153). Beverly Hills, CA: Sage.

Maslach, C., Schaufeli, W. B., & Leiter, M. P. (2001). Job burnout. *Annual Review of Psychology*, 52, 397-422 http://doi.org/10.1146/annurev.psych.52.1.397

McClelland, D. C. (1973). Testing for competence rather than for „intelligence". *The American Psychologist* 28(1), 1–14. http://dx.doi.org/10.1037/h0034092

McClelland, D. C., & Boyatzis, R. E. (1980). Opportunities for counselors from the competency assessment movement. *Journal of Counseling and Development*, 58(5), 368- 372. http://doi org/10.1002/j.2164-4918.1980.tb00415.x

Morris, J. A., & Feldman, D. C. (1996). The Dimensions, antecedents , and consequences of emotional labor. *Academy of Management Review*, 21(4), 986–1010. http://doi.org/10.5465/AMR.1996.9704071861

Oleksyn, T. (2006). *Zarządzanie kompetencjami. teoria i praktyka* [Competency-based management. Theory and practice]. Kraków: Oficyna Ekonomiczna.

Rafaeli, A., & Sutton, R. I. (1990). Busy stores and demanding customers: How do they affect the display of positive emotion? *Academy of Management Journal*, 33(3), 623–637. http://doi.org/10.2307/256584

Rathi, N. (2014). Impact of emotional intelligence and emotional labor on organizational outcomes in service organizations: A conceptual model. *South Asian Journal of Management*, 21(4), 54–71. https://www.econbiz.de/Record/impact-of-emotional-intelligence-and-emotional-labor-on-organizational-outcomes-in-service-organizations-a-conceptual-model-rathi-neerpal/10010519710

Seery, B. L., & Corrigall, E. A. (2009). Emotional labor: links to work attitudes and emotional exhaustion. *Journal of Managerial Psychology*, 24(8), 797–813. http://doi.org/10.1108/02683940910996806

Sęk, H. (2004). *Wypalenie zawodowe. Przyczyny i zapobieganie* [Professional burnout. Causes and prevention]. Warszawa: Wydawnictwo PWN.

Sidor-Rządkowska, M. (2006). *Kompetencyjne systemy ocen pracowników* [Competency- based employee appraisal systems]. Kraków: Oficyna Ekonomiczna.

Sienkiewicz, Ł. & Trawińska-Konador, K. (2013). Koncepcja zarządzania zasobami ludzkimi w oparciu o kompetencje [Concept of competency-based human resource management]. In Ł. Sienkiewicz (Eds.), Zarządzanie zasobami ludzkimi w oparciu o kompetencje : Perspektywa uczenia się przez całe życie [Competency-based human resource management : lifelong learning perspective] (pp. 7-18). Warszawa: Instytut Badań Edukacyjnych.

Schaufeli, W. B., Leiter , M. P., & Maslach, C. (2009). Burnout: 35 years of research and practice. *Career Development International*, 14(3), 204-220. http://dx.doi.org/10.1108/13620430910966406

Spencer, L. M., & Spencer, S. M. (1993). *Competence at work: Models for superior performance*. New York, NY: John Wiley & Sons.

Springer, A. (2011). Problemy definiowania i klasyfikowania kompetencji pracowników [Problems of defining and classifying employees' competence]. *Zeszyty Naukowe Wyższej Szkoły Bankowej w Poznaniu*, 34, 249–260. http://jml.indexcopernicus.com/search/article/1437537

Szczygieł, D., Bazińska, R., Kadzikowska-Wrzosek, R., & Retowski, S. (2009). Praca emocjonalna w zawodach usługowych - pojęcie, przegląd teorii i badań [Emotional labor in service work- theory and research review]. *Psychologia Społeczna*, 3(11), 155- 166. http://www.spoleczna.psychologia.pl/pliki/2009_3/Szczygiel_PS_2009_3.pdf

Thierry, D., Monod, N., & Sauret, C. (1994). *Zatrudnienie i kompetencje w przedsiębiorstwie w procesach zmian [Employment and competence in enterprise during change process]*. Warszawa: Poltex.

Totterdell, P., & Holman, D. (2003). Emotion regulation in customer service roles: Testing a Model of Emotional Labor. *Journal of Occupational Health Psychology*, 8(1), 55–73. http://dx.doi.org/10.1037/1076-8998.8.1.55

Vigoda- Gadot, E., & Meisler, G. (2010). Emotions in management and the management of emotions: The impact of emotional intelligence and organizational politics on public sector employees. *Public Administration Review*, 70(1), 72-86. http://doi.org/10.1111/j.1540-6210.2009.02112.x

Wood, R. (2006). *Metody rekrutacji i selekcji pracowników oparte na kompetencjach [Competency-based recruitment and selection]*. Kraków: Oficyna Ekonomiczna.

Zapf, D., Seifert, C, Schmutte, B, & Mertini, H., Holz, M. (2001). Emotion work and job stressors and their effects on burnout. *Psychology in Health*, 16(5), 527-545. http://doi.org/10.1080/08870440108405525

Self-employment, Knowledge and Economi Growth: An empirical study for Latin American countries

Víctor M. González Sánchez[1]

ABSTRACT

There has been a numerous amount of economic research carried out which has aimed at identify the factors that could contribute positively to economic growth. The economic literature available this matter appears to acknowledge that entrepreneurship is one of the elements that could p tively contribute to this growth. Among other factors, both entrepreneurship and knowledge are g erally considered to play an important role regarding this macro-economic goal. Bearing this in mi the positive bond that exists between both of them, which also contributes to economic growth a improvements in welfare, is increasingly analyzed in the different economic studies available.

The goal of this paper is to empirically analyze the existing relationship between econor growth, knowledge and entrepreneurship within the context of Latin American countries dur the period 2001-2016. For this purpose, the self-employment variable has been used as an emp cal proxy of entrepreneurship. In general, the availability of reliable statistical information on ent preneurship is quite limited especially in the case of the Latin American countries. Consequen this is one of the reasons why there is a lack of unanimity as to the application of one dataset or other to measure entrepreneurship in the analysis. Therefore, although it is true that there is cert disagreement regarding the use of the aforementioned empirical proxy, there are, however, seve references in favor of the use of self-employment statistics in the analysis of entrepreneurship.

In order to do so, first of all we study the existing link between economic growth and cert determining factors such as public expenditure, investment, human capital, knowledge and ent preneurship. Afterwards, we analyze the effects on entrepreneurship caused by such factors as, example, unemployment, taxes and education (as a proxy of knowledge).

KEY WORDS: self-employment, entrepreneurship, knowledge, economic growth, unemployment, taxes, educati

[1] Department of Applied Economy, UNED – National University of Distance Education, Spain

1. Introduction

Entrepreneurship is one of the elements that could positively contribute to economic growth. This may be observed in a number of different studies such as th of González-Sánchez (2015), Hunt (2012), Korez-Vi and Tominc (2016) Nissan, Galindo Martín and M ndez Picazo (2011) and Van Stel (2006). On the ba of this original idea (Schumpeter, 1934), the econon literature increasingly analyzes the improvement the population's well-being which occurs due to t relationship between entrepreneurship and econon

Correspondence concerning this article should be addressed to: **Víctor M. González Sánchez**, Department of Applied Economy, UNED – National University of Distance Education, Madrid, Spain. E-mail: vgonzalez@cee.uned.es growth. In this respect, if a positive link is shown to exist between both of them, it will be necessary to analyze other factors that may, either positively or negatively, affect entrepreneurship. In this work, despite the lack of unanimity found in the economic literature, self-employment has been used in the analysis to measure entrepreneurship in the Latin American countries.

The importance of analyzing entrepreneurship in Latin America can be observed in different publications such as Brenes and Haar (2012). This book examines the perspectives of Latin American entrepreneurs within the new global environment. It also studies cases of various countries in the region belonging to different economic integration agreements such as Mercosur or the Pacific Alliance. Likewise, Lora and Castellani (2014), among other factors, also analyze entrepreneurship in this region from the perspective of policies to promote entrepreneurship as an important vehicle for social mobility in Latin America, as well as the steps to eliminate any limitations that hinder entrepreneurship. Ríos (2017) mentions the importance of reinforcing the environment of entrepreneurship in Latin America to make the most of all of its potential as well as its natural advantages. At the same time, he indicates that this would help the region to be far better prepared to attract quality FDI.

In order to evaluate the possible effects on economic growth, this work has considered other variables besides entrepreneurship, which are also expected to have a positive effect on such growth in Latin American countries. These variables include: public expenditure, investment and human capital. Subsequently, the analysis focused on factors which, either positively or negatively, influence the entrepreneurial activity. In this case, after discarding other variables relating to infrastructure and the use of information and communication technologies, the study concentrated on: unemployment, taxes and education (as a proxy of knowledge).

In short, the main goal of this work is to empirically analyze a number of countries in Latin America, on the one hand, and the relationships that exist between public expenditure, investment, human capital and entrepreneurship with economic growth; and, on the other hand, to assess how unemployment, taxes and education affect entrepreneurship, measured through the self-employment variable.

Among other things, as Cáceres and Cáceres (2017) indicates, the need and importance of this work is based on the fact that particularly in Latin America, self-employment is a means of subsistence in response to unemployment, economic stagnation, and inequality of opportunity.

2. Economic Growth and Self-Employment: Theoretical framework

This work empirically analyzes the relationships between public expenditure, investment, human capital and entrepreneurship and economic growth, in line with other previous studies that associate entrepreneurship with economic growth (Nissan et al., 2011). On the basis of the results obtained, the effects on entrepreneurship caused by unemployment, taxes and education indicators are also analyzed.

In consonance with the author's previous works (González-Sánchez, 2015), this paper uses the self-employment variable as an estimation of entrepreneurship to measure its relationship with economic growth. Therefore, it seems necessary to begin with a brief analysis of the different points of view in the economic literature available, which are both against and in favor of such use. Accordingly, as the availability of reliable statistical information regarding entrepreneurship is limited, especially in the case of the Latin American countries analyzed in this work, there is no unanimity in the literature when the analysis uses certain data to measure entrepreneurship. Some authors like Bjuggren, Johansson and Stenkula (2010) or Hurst and Pugsley (2010), among others, are against using self-employment as a synonym for entrepreneurship. Others, such as Sanandaji (2011), state that it is inaccurate to consider self-employment as an appropriate measure of entrepreneurship, as not all entrepreneurs are self-employed and vice versa, although at the same time he acknowledges that the proxy most commonly used is self-employment. In any case, the alternative variables normally proposed by critical authors regarding the use of self-employment as a proxy, do not provide homogeneous data for the Latin American countries analyzed in this paper.

Conversely, there are also numerous works where the data uses self-employment as an empirical proxy for entrepreneurship. These papers include, for example, Cagetti and De Nardi (2006), Djankov,

Ganser, McLiesh, Ramalho and Shleifer (2010), Evans and Leighton (1989), Faggio and Silva (2012 & 2014), Folta, Delmar and Wennberg (2010), Kitao (2008), Margolis (2014), Paulson, Townsend and Karaivanov (2006) or Schuetze and Bruce (2004). Following this line in the literature, as mentioned above, this work uses self-employment as a proxy for entrepreneurship.

In the economic literature, it is also possible to find various works that analyze, from different points of view, the link between self-employment, entrepreneurship and economic development in Latin American countries. Among others, Cáceres and Cáceres (2017), Cortés Aguilar, García Muñoz and Moro-Egido (2013), Eversole (2003) or González, Cunningham and Maloney (2010).

Economic Commission for Latin America and the Caribbean data shows that Ecuador, with a growth of self-employment of 10.9%, Panama (6%), and Chile (5.5%), were the countries that experienced the largest growth of self-employment in 2016 in Latin America. Likewise, for the purpose of this work, Economic Commission for Latin America and the Caribbean- International Labour Organization (ECLAC-ILO, 2017) shows that Peru and Colombia (members of the Pacific Alliance as Chile) also grew in self-employment but in a less significant way. Peru is one of the countries in the region with the largest growth of self-employed workers in 2016 (4.4%), while Colombia did not have a significant growth in self-employment (2.3%), although the decrease in job creation was more significant. In this sense, according to ECLAC-ILO (2017), self-employment has become an alternative source of income creation for many workers who have lost their jobs, or for new workers who try to compensate the income losses of their households.

As mentioned above, at least in the case of the Latin American countries analyzed in this paper, no significant effects on entrepreneurial activity have been found regarding the indicators relating to infrastructure and the use of information and communication technologies. Therefore, as in the author's previous works carried out for European countries, the empirical study has focused on the three factors that seem to significantly influence the evolution of self-employment in the countries of Latin America: unemployment, taxes and education (as a proxy of knowledge).

In the first case, there is no single focus in evaluating the relationship between unemployment an entrepreneurship. Accordingly, the positive influence between both factors takes place when the increase in unemployment also leads to an increas in self-employment, which is known as the "refuge effect" (Audretsch, Carree & Thurik, 2001). In thi sense, Cáceres and Cáceres (2017) conclude for th case of some Latin American countries, that mal self-employment increases as male unemploymen increases, but it does not apply to female unemployment. In addition, male self-employment decrease when economic growth increases. However, the literature has also identified cases where the relationship between unemployment and self-employment i negative, which is known as the "Schumpeter effect (Audretsch & Thurik, 2000). That is, when entrepreneurship increases, a reduction in unemploymen may also occur (Schumpeter, 1934).

In the second case, disparity is common on reviewing the literature that analyzes the relationshi between taxes and entrepreneurship. Schuetze an Bruce (2004) asserted that economic theory suggest that a country's tax system may have complex an ambiguous effects on the level of entrepreneurship In addition, empirical studies have shown in practic the lack of unanimity that was predicted by theory Accordingly, as shown in the work by González-Sánchez (2015), many studies have found that higher tax rates lead to higher rates of entrepreneurial activity (Bruce, 2000; 2002). Conversely, there are studies that showed how reductions in personal tax rates could reduce the level of entrepreneurial activity. Nevertheless, other studies question these results (Cullen & Gordon, 2002) and other works indicated that it is not possible to find a clear consensus regarding the influence of taxes on self-employment (Moore, 2003).

Thirdly, the effect that education may have on economic growth generally has significant presence in the literature (Barro, 1991). As asserted in González-Sánchez (2015), precisely one of the ways whereby education can influence economic growth, is through entrepreneurship. The relationship between education and entrepreneurship may be considered in terms of two interrelated pathways: the education of business owners and the average educational level of the local labor market. Both points of view have been analyzed by the literature, which has found significant links between markets with a higher educational level that show more educated entrepreneurs, in addition to discovering a marked association between the education of business owners and the success of small companies (Doms, Lewis & Robb, 2010).

The importance of education, as regards entrepreneurship, is also clear when certain authors point out that the effects of education on entrepreneurship may be even more significant than the effect it has on employees. Accordingly, Van der Sluis, Van Praag and Van Witteloostuijn (2007) empirically analyzed the returns to education for the entrepreneurs and employees and concluded that they are significantly higher for the former than for the latter. That is, despite the fact that investment in education does not specifically seek to achieve results through graduates that become entrepreneurs, having greater average education levels amongst the population does seem to encourage entrepreneurship.

3. Empirical Analysis

This work has jointly analyzed two groups of Latin American countries. Four of them belonging to a regional economic integration agreement associated with the Atlantic coast of the continent, Mercosur, and the other four belonging to the integration agreement which is geographically closer to the Pacific Ocean, the Pacific Alliance. The Common Market of the South (Mercosur) is a process of regional integration created in 1991 initially by Argentina, Brazil, Paraguay and Uruguay. Although not included in this work, Venezuela was incorporated later on. The economic and development initiative between Chile, Colombia, Mexico and Peru to create the Pacific Alliance began in 2011. The purpose is to obtain a representative sample of the Latin American countries that represents the region's geographical, economic and political diversity.

The study has included the following countries: Argentina, Brazil, Paraguay and Uruguay (Mercosur members) and Chile, Colombia, Mexico and Peru (Pacific Alliance members), during the period between 2001 and 2016. The estimation method is Ordinary Least Squares using a multiple regression model of constant coefficients. Accordingly, it is assumed that the resulting coefficients are the same for each of the countries included in the sample.

Compiling the data from the eight countries considered during the period 2001-2016 has allowed the models to be analyzed in a panel format with 128 observations. As it is a study relating to Latin American countries, the data used come from different sources as ECLAC (2018), ILO (2018), OECD (2017) and UNESCO (2018).

To examine the relationships mentioned in the sections above, we should attempt to compare the following hypotheses:

H1: Public expenditure, investment and human capital have positive effects on economic growth.
H2: Entrepreneurship has a positive effect on economic growth.
H3: Unemployment has a positive effect on entrepreneurship.
H4: Taxes have a negative effect on entrepreneurship.
H5: Education has a positive effect on entrepreneurship.

The contrast of the two initial hypotheses, H1 and H2, is carried out by the following equation:

$$\ln (y)_{it} = \beta_0 + \beta_1 \ln (PE)_{it} + \beta_2 \ln (I)_{it} + \beta_3 (HK)_{it} + \\ + \beta_4 (EI)_{it} + \varepsilon_{it} \qquad (1)$$

Equation 1 corresponds to GDP growth, where y is the dependent variable gross domestic product (GDP). The independent variables are public expenditure (PE), investment (I), human capital (HK) and the entrepreneurship indicator (EI). To define the EI, the study used the data on the proportion of self-employed workers in each country in relation to their labor force as a reference. The International Labor Organization (ILO) provides this data regularly.

H1 establishes that public expenditure, investment and human capital have positive effects on economic growth. The positive influence that both investment (Auerbach, Hassett & Oliner, 1994; Madsen, 2002) and human capital (Engelbrecht, 2003) have on economic growth is generally accepted in the economic literature. While the effect that the PE variable has on GDP is the subject of more controversy. Accordingly, as asserted by Nissan et al. (2011), some studies claim that expansive fiscal policies end up negatively affecting economic growth as a consequence of the crowding-out effect that leads to a drop in investment (Alesina & Rodrik, 1994). Other studies point in the opposite direction and defend the positive effects of PE on economic growth through different aspects (Saint-Paul & Verdier, 1993).

Table 1. Regression results for GDP equation

Variable	Coefficient	P-value
Constant (β_0)	2.3328	0.000
PE	0.3932	0.000
I	0.4020	0.000
HK	0.1264	0.000
EI	0.0418	0.002

R^2 (adjusted)=0.997

Source: Adapted from "CEPALSTAT Indicators Database." by ECLAC (2018). Available at http://estadisticas.cepal.org/cepalst WEB_CEPALSTAT/estadisticasIndicadores.asp?idioma=i; "ILOSTAT – ILO Database of Labour Statistics" by ILO (2018). Availak at https://www.ilo.org/global/statistics-and-databases/lang--en/index.htm

H2 proposes that entrepreneurship has a positive effect on economic growth. The link between both variables has been analyzed in numerous studies such as: Acs and Audretsch (2010), Audretsch, Keilbach and Lehmann (2006), Braunerhjelm (2010), Box, Lin and Gratzer (2016), Holcombe (1998), Kritikos (2014), UNCTAD (2004), Van Stel, Carree and Thurik (2004) or Wennekers and Thurik (1999). In this respect, there are numerous studies in the literature that broadly accept the positive connection between entrepreneurship, in this case measured through the self-employment proxy, and economic growth. Among others, we could mention Blanchflower (2000), Carree, Van Stel, Thurik and Wennekers (2002; 2007) and Goetz, Fleming and Rupasingha (2012).

The results corresponding to the first two hypotheses are shown in Table 1. On the one hand, the effect of the three variables compiled in H1 is positive regarding economic growth. Furthermore, they are significant. That is, public expenditure, investment and human capital show direct effects on GDP in the group of countries analyzed during the period 2001-2016. On the other hand, the fact that, according to the premise of H2, the EI shows a positive effect and the fact that it is significant supports the idea of a direct relationship between self-employment and economic growth in Latin America.

Other works, such as Ilie, Cardoza, Fernández and Tejada (2018) or Terjesen and Amorós Espinosa (2010), analyze entrepreneurship in Latin America based on gender. Minniti (2010) analyzes the relationship between female entrepreneurship and economic activity while Bullini Orlandi (2017) tries to explain the current difficulties that women encounter when identifying themselves as entrepreneurs.

Among the Latin American countries analyzed in this paper, the analysis has been carried out by differentiating between men and women. Traditionally, it seems that in this region there exists more relative weight in entrepreneurship associated with men than with women. As a result, if the analysis differentiates between men and women, the level of significance of the results obtained allows them to be accepted from a statistical point of view in both cases. Nevertheless, as shown in Table 2 and Table 3, from a data perspective on male self-employment, not only is it significant but even slightly more than with respect to the overall data regarding women. This result seems to suggest that entrepreneurship is a phenomenon with greater male weight in the countries analyzed in this paper.

The equation used to contrast the rest of the hypotheses proposed is as follows:

$$\ln(\delta)_{it} = \beta_0 + \beta_1 \ln(UPL)_{it} + \beta_2 \ln(TX)_{it} + \\ + \beta_3 (EDU)_{it} + \varepsilon_{it} \quad (2)$$

Equation 2 is an entrepreneurship equation (δ) with self-employment data. In accordance with the funda-

e 2. Regression results for GDP equation – Male

Variable	Coefficient	P-value
nstant (β_0)	2.3289	0.000
	0.3960	0.000
	0.4008	0.000
	0.1191	0.000
	0.0506	0.000

djusted)=0.997

ce: Adapted from "CEPALSTAT Indicators Database." by ECLAC (2018). Available at http://estadisticas.cepal.org/cepalstat/_CEPALSTAT/estadisticasIndicadores.asp?idioma=i; "ILOSTAT – ILO Database of Labour Statistics" by ILO (2018). Available tps://www.ilo.org/global/statistics-and-databases/lang--en/index.htm

e 3. Regression results for GDP equation – Female

Variable	Coefficient	P-value
nstant (β_0)	2.3995	0.000
	0.3872	0.000
	0.4083	0.000
	0.1342	0.000
	0.0289	0.021

djusted)=0.997

ce: Adapted from "CEPALSTAT Indicators Database." by ECLAC (2018). Available at http://estadisticas.cepal.org/cepalstat/_CEPALSTAT/estadisticasIndicadores.asp?idioma=i; "ILOSTAT – ILO Database of Labour Statistics" by ILO (2018). Available tps://www.ilo.org/global/statistics-and-databases/lang--en/index.htm

mental purpose of this study, variables relating to unemployment (UPL), taxes (TX) and educational level (EDU) are included. The unemployment measurement used for the Latin American countries refers to "open urban unemployment" (ECLAC, 2018), which measures the total number of unemployed people aged over 15. This is the most homogeneous variable available for the countries which are analyzed in this paper.

The variable relating to taxes refers to "total tax revenue as percentage of GDP" (OECD, 2017). As the influence that taxation may have, regarding the decision to become self-employed, does not take place immediately, this work includes a two-year time-delay in the variable relating to taxes.

The independent variable used in this work to measure the educational level of Latin American countries refers to the number of "graduates from tertiary education" (UNESCO, 2018). This variable is used as a proxy of the level of educational as well as the level of knowledge. In other words, the evolution of the population with university studies is used to evaluate its influence on entrepreneurship. Furthermore, in order to expand the analysis to a gender perspective, both overall data and data relating to men and women separately have been used.

Table 4. Regression results for entrepreneurship equation

Variable	Coefficient	P-value
Constant (β_0)	-1.6239	0.055
UPL	0.5465	0.005
TX	-0.6422	0.003
EDU	0.9248	0.000

R^2 (adjusted)=0.929

Source: Adapted from "CEPALSTAT Indicators Database." by ECLAC (2018). Available at http://estadisticas.cepal.org/cepalstat/WEB_CEPALSTAT/estadisticasIndicadores.asp?idioma=i; "ILOSTAT – ILO Database of Labour Statistics" by ILO (2018). Available at https://www.ilo.org/global/statistics-and-databases/lang--en/index.htm; "Revenue Statistics in Latin America and the Caribbean 2017" OECD (2017).

The results corresponding to equation 2 are shown in Table 4. As may be seen, in accordance with H3, unemployment has a positive effect on entrepreneurship and shows a significant, direct relationship with self-employment. This demonstrates the major positive influence that unemployment has on the development of entrepreneurship in the Latin American countries analyzed, measured through the self-employment proxy. Other works have already pointed to the direct, positive influence of unemployment on entrepreneurship (Highfield & Smiley, 1987; Remeikiene & Startiene, 2009; Reynolds, Miller & Maki, 1995).

Furthermore, H4 predictions are fully met. The level of total tax revenue in Latin American countries has a negative effect on entrepreneurship. This result coincides with the conclusions of the author's works carried out on a group of European countries (González-Sánchez, 2015). Therefore, in compliance with what could be expected from an economically logical point of view: the greater the level of taxation the lesser the predisposition for an increase in the volume of entrepreneurs measured through self-employment.

A summary of the literature that links education and entrepreneurship can be seen in Van der Sluis, Van Praag and Vijverberg (2008). The positive relationship between education and entrepreneurship as considered in H5 is also met in the case of the Latin American countries analyzed. The relationship is the clearest and most straightforward within the variables analyzed, and compares to the idea that the greater the level of higher education a country has the more positive effect it produces on the level of entrepreneurship in the country's economy. This also applies to Latin America.

The analysis of equation 2 concludes with the differentiation of data between men and women. Accordingly Table 5 and Table 6 show the results of differentiating according to gender in the unemployment influence, taxes and education on entrepreneurship. It is interesting to observe that that the provisions of H3, H4 and H5 are also met, and the level of significance is also fully valid.

Comparing the results according to gender, regarding the Latin American countries analyzed, the influence of the variable relating to the countries' educational level on the entrepreneurial level is greater among men, while among women, unemployment and taxes affect entrepreneurship to a greater extent.

4. Conclusions

One of the main conclusions of this work is that Latin America falls in line with the results obtained in previous studies referring to other geographical areas and more developed economies. That is, a positive, significant relationship is shown to exist between public expenditure, investment, human capital and entrepreneurship with economic growth.

Furthermore, both from a global perspective and from differentiating the analysis according to gen-

le 5. Regression results for entrepreneurship equation – Male

Variable	Coefficient	P-value
onstant (β_0)	-2.1804	0.009
PL	0.5160	0.006
[illegible]	-0.6134	0.004
DU	0.9311	0.000

djusted)=0.934

rce: Prepared by the author on the basis of information from ECLAC (2018), ILO (2018), OECD (2017) and UNESCO (2018).

le 6. Regression results for entrepreneurship equation – Female

Variable	Coefficient	P-value
onstant (β_0)	-2.4927	0.009
PL	0.6017	0.006
[illegible]	-0.6959	0.004
DU	0.9171	0.000

djusted)=0.913

rce: Prepared by the author on the basis of information from ECLAC (2018), ILO (2018), OECD (2017) and UNESCO (2018).

der, the variables that most clearly influence self-employment (as a proxy of entrepreneurship) are unemployment, taxes and education (as a proxy of knowledge).

In the first case, the effect that unemployment has on entrepreneurship is both positive and significant. That is, an increase in unemployment in Latin American countries causes a growing trend towards self-employment. As asserted by Audretsch et al. (2001), it coincides with the so-called "refugee effect", whereby the increase in unemployment causes a growing search for professional opportunities as an entrepreneur. This takes place regardless of gender, although maybe to a greater extent among women. It could be said that this result is in line with Cáceres and Cáceres (2017) when they affirm that self-employment is a manifestation of a historical framework of inequality of opportunities and low taxation, which gives rise to a persistent poverty trap.

In the case of the second variable, although the literature is not unanimous, the results demonstrate that the effect of taxes on entrepreneurship complies with the foreseeable negative influence. That is, on the basis of the analysis carried out in eight Latin American countries between 2001 and 2016, it is shown that an increase in a countries' tax level negatively affects the increase in the number of self-employed in an economy.

Finally, the positive influence exerted by a country's overall educational level on entrepreneurship in Latin America, coincides with the results of numerous theoretical and empirical works carried out previously. This link is verified and clearly significant both from a global perspective and when the analysis is accomplished by differentiating both men and women. In all cases, the improvement in education positively influences the volume of self-employment, although it occurs slightly more among men than among women.

References

Acs, Z. J., & Audretsch, D. B. (Eds.). (2010). Handbook of Entrepreneurship Research. An Interdisciplinary Survey and Introduction (2nd ed.). New York, NY: Springer.

Alesina, A., & Rodrik, D. (1994). Distribution policies and economic growth? Quarterly Journal of Economics, 109, 465–490.

Audretsch, D. B., Carree, M. A., & Thurik, A. R. (2001). Does Entrepreneurship Reduce Unemployment? (Tinbergen Institute Discussion Paper, No. 01-074/3). Tinbergen Institute. Retrieved from http://hdl.handle.net/10419/85927

Audretsch, D. B., Keilbach, M. C., & Lehmann, E. E. (2006). Entrepreneurship and Economic Growth. Oxford, UK: Oxford University Press.

Audretsch, D. B., & Thurik, A. R. (2000). Capitalism and Democracy in the 21st Century: from the Managed to the Entrepreneurial Economy. Journal of Evolutionary Economics, 10, 17-34.

Auerbach, A. J., Hassett, K. A., & Oliner, S. D. (1994). Reassessing the social returns to equipment investment. Quarterly Journal of Economics, 109(3), 789-802.

Barro, R. J. (1991). Economic growth in a cross section of countries. Quarterly Journal of Economics, 106(2), 407–443.

Bjuggren, C. M., Johansson, D., & Stenkula, M. (2010). Using Self-employment as Proxy for Entrepreneurship: Some Empirical Caveats (Working Paper No. 845). Research Institute of Industrial Economics. Retrieved from http://www.ifn.se/wfiles/wp/wp845.pdf

Blanchflower, D. G. (2000). Self-employment in OECD countries. Labour Economics, 7, 471–505.

Box, M., Lin, X., & Gratzer, K. (2016). Linking Entrepreneurship and Economic Growth in Sweden, 1850–2000. In D. Bögenhold, J. Bonnet, M. Dejardin, & D. Garcia Pérez de Lema (Eds.), Contemporary Entrepreneurship: Multidisciplinary Perspectives on Innovation and Growth (pp. 31-49). Cham: Springer.

Braunerhjelm, P. (2010). Entrepreneurship, Innovation and Economic Growth - past experience, current knowledge and policy implications (Working Paper No. 224). Centre of Excellence for Science and Innovation Studies. Retrieved from https://www.diva-portal.org/smash/get/diva2:484894/FULLTEXT01.pdf

Brenes, E., & Haar, J. (Eds.). (2012). The Future of Entrepreneurship in Latin America. London, UK Palgrave Macmillan.

Bruce, D. (2002). Taxes and Entrepreneurial Endurance: Evidence from the Self-Employed. National Tax Journal, 55(1), 5-24.

Bruce, D. (2000). Effects of the United States Tax System on Transitions into Self-Employment. Labour Economics, 7(5), 545-574.

Bullini Orlandi, L. (2017). Am I an Entrepreneur? Identity Struggle in the Contemporary Women Entrepreneurship Discourse. Contemporary Economics, 11(4), 487-498.

Cáceres, L. R., & Cáceres, S. A. (2017). Self-employment in Latin America. Journal of Developing Areas, 51(3), 33-49.

Cagetti, M., & De Nardi, M. (2006). Entrepreneurship, frictions, and wealth. Journal of Political Economy, 114(5), 835-870.

Carree, M., Van Stel, A., Thurik, R., & Wennekers, S. (2002). Economic development and business ownership: an analysis using data of 23 OECD countries in the period 1976–1996. Small Business Economics, 19, 271–290.

Carree, M., Van Stel, A., Thurik, R., & Wennekers, S. (2007). The relationship between economic development and business ownership revisited. Entrepreneurship and Regional Development, 19, 281–291.

Cortés Aguilar, A., García Muñoz, T. M., & Moro-Egido, A. I. (2013). Heterogeneous self-employment and satisfaction in Latin America. Journal of Economic Psychology 39, 44–61

Cullen, J. B., & Gordon, R. H. (2002). Taxes and Entrepreneurial Activity: Theory and Evidence for the U.S (Working Paper No. 9015). National Bureau of Economic Research. Retrieved from https://www.nber.org/papers/w9015.pdf

Djankov, S., Ganser, T., McLiesh, C., Ramalho, R., & Shleifer, A. (2010). The Effect of Corporate Taxes on Investment and Entrepreneurship. American Economic Journal: Macroeconomics, 2(3), 31-64.

Doms, M., Lewis, E., & Robb, A. (2010). Local labor force education, new business characteristics, and firm performance. Journal of Urban Economics, 67, 61–77.

ECLAC. (2018). CEPALSTAT Indicators Database. Available at http://estadisticas.cepal.org/cepalstat/WEB_CEPALSTAT/estadisticasIndicadores.asp?idioma=i

ECLAC-ILO. (2017). Employment Situation in Latin America and the Caribbean. Labour immigration in Latin America. Retrieved from https://repositorio.cepal.org/bitstream/handle/11362/41371/1/S1700341_en.pdf

Engelbrecht, H. J. (2003). Human capital and economic growth: cross-section evidence for OECD countries. Economic Record, 79, 40-51.

Evans, D., & Leighton, L. (1989). Some Empirical Aspects of Entrepreneurship. American Economic Review, 79(3), 519-535.

Eversole, R (2003). My Business Pays Me: Labourers and Entrepreneurs among the Self-Employed Poor in Latin America. Bulletin of Latin American Research, 22(1), 102-116.

Faggio, G., & Silva, O. (2012). Does Self-Employment Measure Entrepreneurship? Evidence from Great Britain (Discussion Paper No. 109). Spatial Economics Research Centre. Retrieved from http://eprints.lse.ac.uk/57919/

Faggio, G., & Silva, O. (2014). Self-employment and entrepreneurship in urban and rural labour markets. Journal of Urban Economics, 84, 67-85.

Folta, T. B., Delmar, F., & Wennberg, K. (2010). Hybrid Entrepreneurship (Working Paper No. 825). Research Institute of Industrial Economics. Retrieved from http://www.ifn.se/wfiles/wp/wp825.pdf

Goetz, S. J., Fleming, D. A., & Rupasingha, A. (2012). The Economic Impacts of Self-Employment. Journal of Agricultural and Applied Economics, 44 (3), 315–321.

González, P. A., Cunningham, W., & Maloney, W. F. (2010). The Decision to Become Informal Self-Employed in Latin America. In H. S. Esfahani, G. Facchini, & G. J. D. Hewings (Eds.), Economic Development in Latin America (pp. 62-72). London, UK: Palgrave Macmillan.

González-Sánchez, V. M. (2015). Factors Promoting Entrepreneurship in European Countries: Unemployment, Taxes, and Education. Journal of Promotion Management, 21(4), 492-503.

Highfield, R., & Smiley, R. (1987). New Business Starts and Economic Activity: An Empirical Investigation. International Journal of Industrial Organization, 5, 51-66.

Holcombe, R. G. (1998). Entrepreneurship and Economic Growth. The Quarterly Journal of Austrian Economics, 1, 45-62.

Hunt, S. D. (2012). Understanding the Drivers of Economic Growth: Grounding Endogenous Economic Growth Models in Resource-Advantage Theory. Contemporary Economics, 6(4), 4-8.

Hurst, E., & Pugsley, B. (2010). Non Pecuniary Benefits of Small Business Ownership (Working Paper). University of Chicago. Retrieved from https://conference.nber.org/conferences/2010/SI2010/ENT/Hurst_Pugsley.pdf

Ilie, C., Cardoza, G., Fernández, A. & Tejada, H. (2018). Entrepreneurship and Gender in Latin America, Social Science Research Network. Available at https://ssrn.com/abstract=3126888 or http://dx.doi.org/10.2139/ssrn.3126888

ILO. (2018). ILOSTAT – ILO Database of Labour Statistics. Available at https://www.ilo.org/global/statistics-and-databases/lang--en/index.htm

Kitao, S. (2008). Entrepreneurship, Taxation and Capital Investment. Review of Economic Dynamics, 11(1), 44-69.

Korez-Vide R., & Tominc P. (2016). Competitiveness, Entrepreneurship and Economic Growth. In P. Trąpczyński, Ł. Puślecki, & M. Jarosiński (Eds.), Competitiveness of CEE Economies and Businesses (pp. 25-44). Cham: Springer.

Kritikos, A. S. (2014). Entrepreneurs and their impact on jobs and economic growth (IZA World of Labor, 8). Institute of Labor Economics. Retrieved from https://wol.iza.org/uploads/articles/8/pdfs/entrepreneurs-and-their-impact-on-jobs-and-economic-growth.pdf

Lora, E., & Castellani, F. (Eds.) (2014). Entrepreneurship in Latin America: A Step Up the Social Ladder? Washington, DC: Inter-American Development Bank.

Madsen, J. B. (2002). The Causality between Investment and Economic Growth, Economics Letters. January, 74(2), 157-163.

Margolis, D. N. (2014). By Choice and by Necessity: Entrepreneurship and Self-Employment in the Developing World (Discussion Paper No. 8273). Institute of Labor Economics. Retrieved from http://ftp.iza.org/dp8273.pdf

Minniti, M. (2010). Female Entrepreneurship and Economic Activity. The European Journal of Development Research, 22 (3), 294–312.

Moore, K. (2003, December). The Effects of the 1986 and 1993 Tax Reforms on Self-Employment. Paper presented at the Ninety-Fifth Annual Conference on Taxation. Orlando, FL.

Nissan, E., Galindo Martín, M. Á., & Méndez Picazo, M. T. (2011). Relationship between organizations, institutions, entrepreneurship and economic growth process. International Entrepreneurship and Management Journal, 7, 311–324.

OECD. (2017). Revenue Statistics in Latin America and the Caribbean 2017. Retrieved from http://dx.doi.org/10.1787/rev_lat_car-2017-en-fr

Paulson, A., Townsend, R., & Karaivanov, A. (2006). Distinguishing Limited Liability from Moral Hazard in a Model of Entrepreneurship. Journal of Political Economy 114(1), 100-144.

Remeikiene, R., & Startiene, G. (2009). Does the Interaction between Entrepreneurship and Unemployment Exist? Economics and Management, 14, 903-911.

Reynolds, P., Miller, B., & Maki, W. R. (1995). Explaining Regional Variation in Business Births and Deaths: U.S. 1976-1988. Small Business Economics, 7(5), 389-707.

Ríos, G. (2017). Innovation and Entrepreneurship in Latin America, EU-LAC Newsletter 11/2017, 7-8.

Saint-Paul, G., & Verdier, T. (1993). Education, democracy and growth. Journal of Development Economics, 42(2), 399–407.

Sanandaji, T. (2010). Self-Employment Does Not Measure Entrepreneurship. Chicago, IL: The Institute for Industrial Economics, University of Chicago.

Schuetze, H., & Bruce, D. (2004). Tax policy and entrepreneurship. Swedish Economic Policy Review, 11, 233–265.

Schumpeter, J. A. (1934). The Theory of Economic Development, Cambridge, MA: Harvard University Press.

Terjesen, S., & Amorós Espinosa, J. (2010). Female Entrepreneurship in Latin America and the Caribbean: Characteristics, Drivers and Relationship to Economic Development. The European Journal of Development Research, 22(3), 313-330.

UNCTAD. (2004). Entrepreneurship and Economic Development: The EMPRETEC Showcase. Retrieved from https://unctad.org/en/docs/webiteteb20043_en.pdf

UNESCO. (2018). UIS.Stat Database. Available a http://data.uis.unesco.org/

Van der Sluis, J., Van Praag, M., & Vijverberg, W. (2008). Education and entrepreneurship selection and performance: A review of the empirical literature. Journal of Economic Surveys, 22(5), 795-841.

Van der Sluis, J., Van Praag, M., & Van Witteloostuijn, A. (2007). Why are the returns to education higher for entrepreneurs than for employees? (Discussion Paper No. 3058). Institute of Labor Economics. Retrieved from http://repec.iza.org/dp3058.pdf

Van Stel, A. (2006). Empirical Analysis of Entrepreneurship and Economic Growth. International Studies in Entrepreneurship 13. New York, NY: Springer.

Van Stel, A., Carree, M., & Thurik, R. (2004). The effect of entrepreneurship on national economic growth: An analysis using the GEM database (SCALES-paper N200320). EIM Business and Policy Research. Retrieved from http://papers.econ.mpg.de/egp/discussionpapers/2004-34.pdf

Wennekers, S., & Thurik, R. (1999). Linking Entrepreneurship and Economic Growth. Small Business Economics, 13, 27-55.

3

conomic News and Household Decisions

.Vinokurov[1,2], A.A. Medved[1], L. A. Mierin[1]

STRACT This paper is devoted to the role of information context in the dynamics of consumption/savings decisions. The deviations from the traditional model of rational expectations are investigated, and the hypotheses of the «rational inattention» are tested. The basis for the study was a selection of news from the major Russian TV channels for 2006-2016. This news available to ordinary households in Russia was analyzed. News was defined as negative or positive with special program tools of sentiment analysis. It was found that increased uncertainty (the spread of positive and negative news) leads to the choice of consumption to the detriment of savings, which then reduces the investment base of the economy. The authors analyze the connection of the tonality of news and its changes with the real business cycle. The authors found that the information cycle with some lag correlated with the cycle in consumption/savings decisions in the Russian Federation. The authors conclude that the concept of rational inattention is more acceptable for this case. Based on the study, recommendations are offered for adjusting public policy.

Y WORDS: cycles, information imperfectness, bounded rationality

b State University of Economics (UNECON), Russia; [2] HSE, Russia

1. Introduction

In this paper, we investigate the impacts of economic news on households' decisions concerning income distribution for consumption and savings. Our research is based on the concepts of bounded rationality and information imperfectness. Real-life households make their decisions in an imperfect information environment, and they are unable to use all the relevant information (even if it were available) due to time limits and/or bounded cognitive capacity. Therefore, an outline of the informational context of the household`s decision-making is desirable.

We assume that the decision-making mechanism is as follows. When obtaining and processing becomes costly, according to the concept of rational inattention (see par. 2), people ignore some amount of information and make the choice between consumption and savings with some error. The tonality of economic news obtained from TV channels is the most available and has no processing costs. Therefore, we can suppose that this information should be the bases for decision-making, and more information leads to a lower probability of deviation from the optimal consumption and savings levels.

Our economic news sample is built upon news broadcasted by main Russian TV channels and covers the period from 2006-2016. The Russian case is characterized by the strong trust of households to the TV news (see par. 3) from the major federal channels that have a large audience reach in Russia. Thus, economic TV news and its impacts on households' decisions can be an indicator of the information background for households' decision-making. This news usually does

rrespondence concerning this article should be addressed to:
\. **Medved**, SPb State University of Economics (UNECON), s-sia, St.-Petersburg, 197375, Glavnaya, 31-2, 208. E-mail: ımedved@mail.ru

not need specific skills or knowledge to be understood. Moreover, we suppose that people perceive news according to sensitive saturation, which is why we evaluated the tonality of news.

For measuring the amount of information obtained through the tonality of economic news, we use the Shannon concept (growth of information means the reduction of uncertainty). Our analysis has two steps. First, we check the Granger causality between the cycle of information growth and the dynamics of savings as the disposable income ratio. After that, we build a model of the «bounded rational household» whose decisions depend on the amount of information obtained and test this model with the «Generalized method of moments». We found that the cyclical component of information growth (isolated with the Butterworth filter) causes the cycle of households' savings ratios in the sense of Granger causality. The model of representative household behavior based on the concept of rational inattention predicts the following situation: the less information that is processed, the more likely that the non-optimality of the decisions and the realistic discount rate where the household consumes more than would be optimal will be. The GMM test of this model was satisfactory.

In the next paragraph, we provide a brief review of the related literature. In section 3, we describe the data and test the Granger causality. In section 4, we build a model of the interaction between household decisions about consumption/savings and the amount of information obtained and then check it with the GMM.

2. Related Literature

Three streams of literature are related to our research. First, we examine works on the impacts of bad and good news on the financial markets, especially on the foreign exchange market. Then, there is a body of research on households' savings under income uncertainty. Finally, the literature on rational inattention plays an important role for our theoretical intuition in this paper.

Mainly, the efficient market hypothesis is tested in the first stream of literature. That is, since the efficient market should absorb all available relevant information, the effects from news should be in the form of good or bad "surprises" about economic activity. It was shown (in the case of the U.S.) that only a few macroeconomic parameters ("surprises" about them) could have an impact on the stock exchange (Flannery & Protopapadakis, 2002). However, most of the studies report that economic news affects volatility rather than stock returns. M. Evans and R. Lyons showed that the effects of foreign exchange are mostly not through direct price adjustment but to a great extent are the results of changes in order flow volatility (Evans & Lyons, 2008). On the other hand, there are cross-border spillovers from economic "surprises", mostly from the U.S. news abroad. Nonetheless, in fact, the significance of such spillovers depends on the magnitude of bilateral trade (Caporale & Spagnolo, 2012; Singh, Nejadmalayeri, & Lucey, 2013) or is connected with periods of world financial crises (Caporale, Spagnolo, & Spagnolo, 2016; 2017). Notably, the psychology of financial market participants could provide its effect. For example, L. Fang and J. Peress found that simple coverage by the media could affect stock returns, even if there is no genuine news that is transmitted (Fang & Peress, 2009).

It should be mentioned that unlike in this research, we use the linguistic estimation of tonality of the whole text of news messages, while previous works usually only analyzed headlines that were classified as "good" or "bad". Therefore, while information background is usually characterized by the ratio of "good" headlines, we are able to operate with the average tonality of news or its variance. Moreover, we can estimate the amount of information (in the Shannon sense) on this basis.

The second stream of the related literature is the literature about how uncertainty influences households' decisions about disposable income. Here, uncertainty is usually treated in "statistical" way that is not like information received from media but is like the variance of income or some accidents such as elections or reforms. In fact, competing reasons affect savings. Precautionary motives make households save more when income is not predictable enough. On the other hand, uncertainty about returns on investments leads to lower savings. It was theoretically shown that the result depends on what is more salient for a decision-maker's attention: income stability or returns on savings (Miao, 2004). Indeed, the investigation of the dramatic rise of savings in China during the 2000s (Chamon, Liu, & Prasad, 2010) or the rise in savings during the German general elections in 1998 (Giaazzi & McMahon, 2012) showed that such sources of ıncertainty (like structural changes in the economy, ension reform, change of the political elite, etc.) pro-oke more savings and less consumption. It seems to ontradict to the idea that risk-aversion should lead to lecreased savings. In fact, these findings address the hreat to lose the current level of well-being, which ould play the role of a reference-point in the process f decision-making. In more general situations, risk-version leads to rather weak decreases of consump-ion as a reaction on bad news, whereas consumption ncreases significantly when the news is good (Bow-nan, Minehart, & Rabin, 1999). R. Thaler, regarding he behavioral aspects of decisions about pension in-urance plans, stated that the mere shift of the empha-is from the current to an alternative plan could result n more switches from one plan to another (Benartzi & Thaler, 2007; Thaler & Benartzi, 2004).

In this literature, the reactions to the dynamics of conomic conjuncture and possible threats are inves-igated but not the question about how households orm their knowledge about it and how they operate based on the available information. For our purposes, we need to build a model that captures the effect of nformation processing on the savings ratios in dispos-ıble income.

In our research, we rely on bounded rationality or, nore precisely, procedural rationality intuition. That s, individuals balance the probability of an incorrect decision with the cost of accurate decision-making. Recently, the concept of rational inattention was pro-posed as an approach to the formalization of such a type of bounded rationality. The main idea of the approach is that an individual solves the optimiza-tion task such that the more accurate decision (greater probability of correct decision) demands more in-formation (interpreted as the reduction of the initial Shannon entropy of decisions), the processing of which is costly. This view relies on H. Simon's works (Simon, 1976; 1978), and the precise formalization of the concept is due to C. Sims (Sims, 2003; 2006; 2010). The features of this optimization lead to the greater probability of mistakes in a particular direction, while the reduction in information processing costs makes decisions closer to ones that are built upon rational expectations. This leads to important implications for macroeconomic policy. While the view of "new clas-sics" imposes the neutrality of money, an individual re-action on monetary stimulus is only due to imperfect information (Lucas, 1972; Sargent & Wallace, 1976). Therefore, rational inattention demonstrates informa-tion problems more straightforward (Martins & Sin-igaglia, 2009.) and reveals some effects of monetary policy (Alvarez, Lippi, & Paciello, 2015). In particular, it was shown that due to costly information processing, a representative household counts very little for the dy-namics of the real interest rate during a business cycle. Therefore, the interest rate has little impact on house-holds' short-run decisions, while the price level has a significant effect (Maćkowiak & Wiederholt, 2015).

However, in these studies, the amount of informa-tion to be processed in order to make the optimal decision was given exogenously with respect to the information environment of the representative house-hold. Therefore, changes in this environment could not have an influence on the decisions. Thus, the mac-roeconomic policy also does not affect the decisions through this channel. However, it seems plausible that, for instance, the unexpected decisions of government or monetary authorities will be reflected by the growth of uncertainty in economic news from media, which would consequently change the decisions of the repre-sentative household. As we hope, our approach could capture this effect, and we address this issue in the dis-cussion.

3. Methodology and results: Information and Saving Ratio Cycles

In this section, we assess the Granger causality be-tween the cyclical components of information growth and savings in the disposable income ratio. We start with the characteristic of the sample and the specifica-tion of the information measure that we use. Then, we turn to the problem of causality.

3.1 Sample and Descriptive Statistic

It is difficult (if not impossible) to consider all infor-mation and processing costs that influence a house-hold's decisions. To make a proxy for the informational conditions of a household's decision-making, it is nec-essary to find appropriate messages that are commonly known and sufficiently cheap to process. With these messages, we use the attitudes toward economic news that are given by leading Russian television media. The case of Russian television media is quite convenient, since they have excessively large trust and audiences compared to Internet news, the radio or newspapers. Moreover, three federal TV channels accumulate significantly larger audiences than the other channels that offer economic news. For instance, according to the Russian Center for the Public Opinion Study, which is the most well-known center for investigating public opinion in the Russian Federation (www.wciom.ru), the rating of trust for the TV news in the most recent decade was not less than 50 %, compared to less than 20 % for Internet news. Meanwhile, the absolute outsider is foreign TV news, newspapers, magazines and so on, whose index of trust lies deep in the area of negative values. In 2017, according to Mediascope research agency (mediascope.net), the audience of these channels was 98.5 % of Russia's population and more than 50 million viewers in the CIS and Baltic countries. At present, the main Russian TV companies (VGTRK, ORT, and NTV) either through their «nationalization» or by transferring ownership to affiliated financial and industrial groups, are under the control of the authorities.

On the other hand, the attitudes toward translated economic news are something that lies at an emotional level, and understanding it is a great deal easier than insight into the economic meaning. Therefore, information about attitudes is very cheap information. Together with large audiences and trust, it allows us to expect that most households process this information received from federal TV channels.

We form the sample as follows. The three federal TV channels of 1tv, "Russia 1" and NTV were analyzed. For the period from January 2006 to September 2016, we aggregated the monthly economic messages. To be precise, for every channel in every month, we randomly picked three days. Then, we took the texts of all messages for these dates that were labelled with tag "Economy" from the websites of the channels. To measure the attitude of the author of a message toward a reported news story, we applied sentimental analysis of the text of the message. To realize such analysis, we used the analyzer provided by Eureka Engine (http://eurekaengine.ru). This analyzer measures positive and negative attitudes in a text. The differences between them were used as a measure of attitude as a whole.

Then, we conducted the same analysis with another text analyzer Repustate (Repustate.com). The reason was that the Eurika Engine counts for the economic context of a message, while Repustate provides estimations based on common vocabulary. By doing this, we would like to ensure that it is not a very strict assumption that the representative household takes the economic background of a news story into consideration.

As a result, 6 071 messages were analyzed (1 13[illegible] from 1tv, 2 860 from "Russia 1" and 2 089 from NTV). For every month, we estimate the average attitude and dispersion. Then, we compared them with the normal distribution with a zero average and dispersion equal to 0.35 for Eureka Engine (attitude estimates for particular messages were not greater than 1.75 in the absolute value, and 0.35 is roughly a dispersion of normal distribution in the interval [-1.75; 1.75]). For Repustate, we respectively compared the average and dispersion with zero again (0.09 was roughly the dispersion of the normal distribution in the interval [-0.95; 0.95], which is the interval of obtained values of tonality). The reason for this comparison is to ensure that the observed attitudes are not actually "white noise". We present the results in Table 1.

The average tonality of economic news estimated with Eureka Engine over 55 months (42.6 % of months in the sample) significantly deviated from zero (according to Student's t-test with a 5 % level of significance). When we correct the average for different quantities of news provided by different channels and take average of the average tonalities of each TV channel, then the 66-month period (48.1 %) significantly deviates from zero. Surprisingly, the results for the estimations, made with Repustate, considerably differ. Less than a quarter of months in the sample have an average tonality of news during them significantly different from zero.

Thus, operations with the average tonality of economic news are risky, since such analysis is sensible to the assumption about whether the representative household could account for the economic background of received news.

In contrast, the dispersion of economic news significantly differs from the dispersion of the corresponding normal distribution for estimations based on the Eureka Engine and those based on Repustate. This was le 1. Number of months when the average mood of news and the dispersion are significant

	Number of months when the average mood significantly differs from zero.	%	Number of months when the average dispersion significantly differs from the normal distribution.	%
eka Engine	55	42.6	122	94.6
eka Engine (corrected)	62	48.1	122	94.6
ustate	30	23.3	125	96.9
ustate (corrected)	31	24.0	125	96.9

the case in 122 months (94.6 %) for the Eureka Engine estimations and in 125 months (96.9 %) for the Repustate estimations (again, according to the Student's t-test with a 5 % level of significance). As could be seen, there is almost no difference between the different estimations. Hence, for more a careful analysis, we should use the dispersion of the tonality of economic news rather than its average tonality.

This conclusion is not unexpected. From the point of view of Shannon information theory, information is a reduction of entropy, and a continuous distribution entropy (or differential entropy for this case) is directly associated with dispersion. Therefore, the next step was to estimate the information associated with a diminished (with respect to the normal distribution) dispersion of attitudes toward economic news.

We consider information as the reduction of entropy from the level corresponding to the normal distribution to the entropy of the normal distribution with dispersion equal to the attitude of economic news within a month. That is:

$$I_i = \frac{1}{2}\ln\left[\frac{s_i^2}{\sigma_i^2}\right], \qquad (1)$$

where I_i is the amount of information translated in month i, s_i^2 stands for the unbiased variance of the normally distributed variable with dispersion equal to 0.35 for the Eureka Engine and 0.09 for the Repustate estimations, and σ_i^2 stands for the dispersion of the attitudes of economic news messages in i months.

Based on formula (1), we could retrace the information dynamics and identify some stylized facts about it. First, there is a remarkable high frequency of fluctuations in the information. For example, Figure 1 shows how information changes over time. We could see that notable changes in information occur from one month to another.

On the other hand, we hardly could find any trend in information dynamics. It could be seen more clearly from Figure 2 where a trend in the information growth rate was isolated with the Hodrick-Prescott filter (λ = 14400). Here, the trend of the growth rate is stable, thus implying constant information growth in the long run, and it is close to zero.

The same features of information dynamics are common to other estimations, such as those corrected with respect to different numbers of economic news in the programs of different TV channels and/or estimations obtained with Repustate.

3.2 Granger causality between information and saving ratio cycles

In this subsection, we estimate the relationship between cycle components of information growth and savings in disposable income ratios. For this analysis, we exclude from disposable income the household mandatory payments, and we eliminate from savings cash and foreign currency remaining in the hands of households. By doing so, we hope to avoid the transactional motive of saving and the mere speculative attempts of households realized by the short-term buying and selling of foreign currency.

We use the Butterworth filter (with the order of the filter equal to 8 and the cutoff frequency equal to

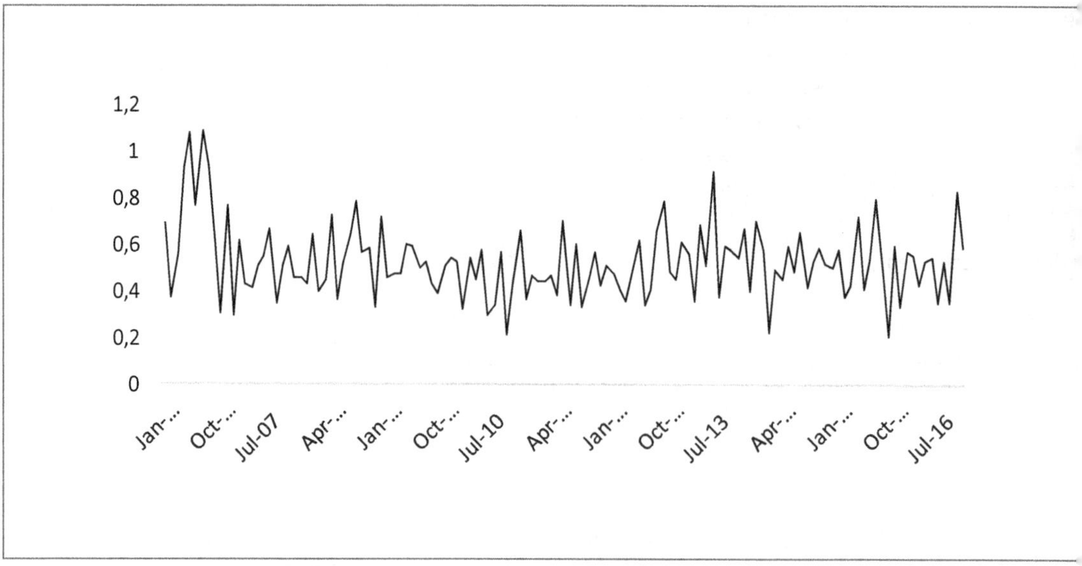

Figure 1. Information dynamics (Eureka Engine estimations)

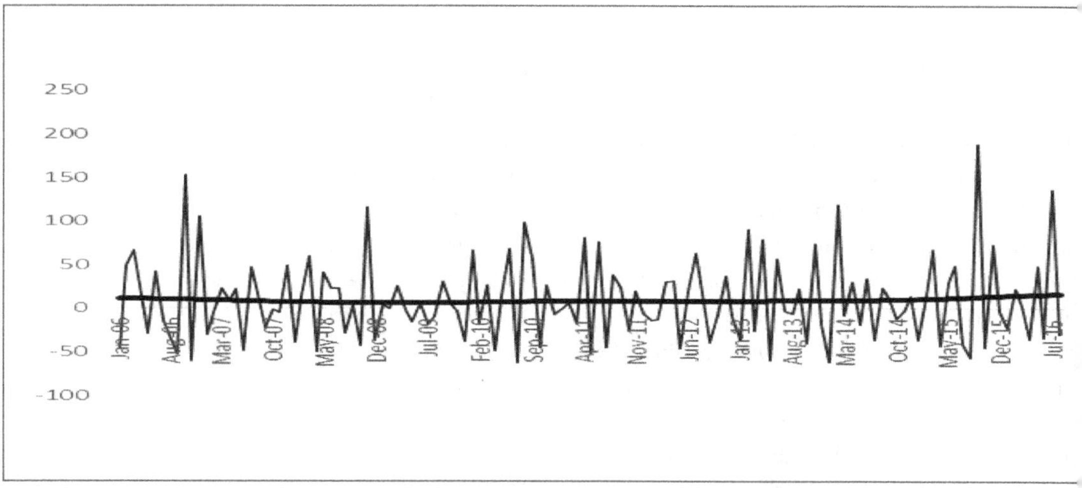

Figure 2. Information growth rate with the Hodrik-Prescott filter (λ = 14400), Eureka Engine estimations

67) to isolate the cyclical components of information and savings ratio dynamics. The reason is that the Hodrick-Prescott filter with the standard parameter λ that is usually used for business-cycle analysis is able to detect any cycle in information growth rate dynamics (see Figure 2). The other reason is that we would like to isolate a cycle from a dynamic that is high-frequency itself and, in the case of the savings ratio, lies in pre-established limits. The Butterworth filter has a maximally flat frequency response that is useful for our goals. Moreover, it could be seen as a variation of the Hodrick-Prescott filter (Gomez, 2001). The characteristics of the obtained trends for the estimations based on Eureka Engine can be seen in Figure 3.

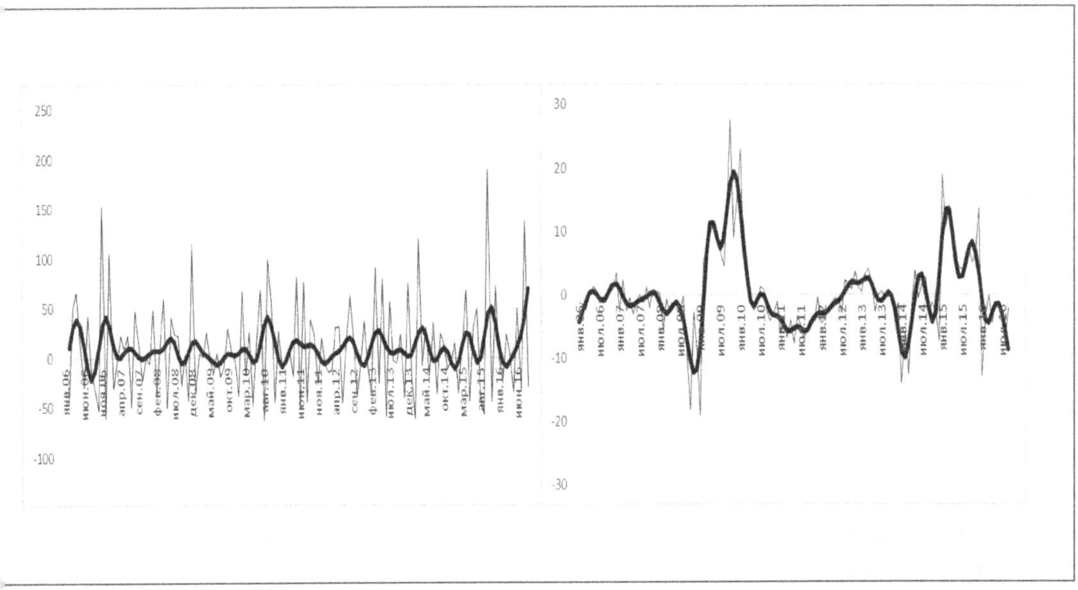

ure 3. Information growth rate (left), the savings in disposable income ratio (right), and the dynamics with trends ck lines) isolated with the Butterworth filter (n = 8, cutoff frequency = 67)

First, we check whether the information growth cycle causes the savings ratio cycle in the Granger sense. That is, we estimate

$$\left(\frac{Sav}{Inc}\right)_t = \sum_{x=1}^{12}\left[\alpha_{t-x}\left(\frac{Sav}{Inc}\right)_{t-x} + \gamma_{t-x}\varepsilon_{t-x}\right] + \varepsilon_t, \qquad (2)$$

where $\frac{Sav}{Inc}$ is the cyclical component of savings to disposable income ratios and ε is an error.

Then, we compare equation (2) with the following equation and check whether it brings a sufficient improvement to the regression:

$$\left(\frac{Sav}{Inc}\right)_t = \sum_{x=1}^{12}\left[\alpha_{t-x}\left(\frac{Sav}{Inc}\right)_{t-x} + \beta_{t-x}Inf_{t-x} + \gamma_{t-x}\varepsilon_{t-x}\right] + \varepsilon_t, \quad (3)$$

where *Inf* stands for the cyclical component of the information growth rate.

The null hypothesis is that Inf_{t-x} are redundant variables. The Wald test has shown that with *p-value = 0.04*, the null hypothesis is rejected. That is, the information growth cycle does cause cyclical changes in the savings to disposable income ratio.

For further analysis, we analyzed how the informational growth cycle arises in its turn. It is attractive to link this cycle to any characteristics of macroeconomic indicators' dynamics. Since the main problem for a household is to distinguish between the real and nominal parameters of the current macroeconomic situations, the movements of real indicators should increase the certainty of decisions, while the movement of nominal (mostly monetary) indicators should increase their uncertainty. We estimated the autoregressive model as:

$$Inf_t = \sum_{x=1}^{12}\left[a_{t-x}GDP_{t-x} + b_{t-x}M2_{t-x} + c_{t-x}e_{t-x}\right] + e_t, \qquad (4)$$

where *Inf* is the cyclical component of the information growth rate, GDP is the cyclical component of the GDP growth rate, *M2* is the cyclical component of the M2 growth rate, e is the error, and a, b and c are the regression coefficients. All cyclical components were isolated with the Butterworth filter. The dates for GDP and M2 were obtained from the official Russian statistics and were seasonally adjusted.

The best specification of equation (4) shows that the coefficients for all errors are statistically significant, and some coefficients for the lags of GDP and M2 growth rates' cycles were also statistically significant (see Table 2; to save space, we present only the values of a and b).

Table 2. Estimation of equation (2)

	Value	St. error
a(t-1)	6.8443***	1.9043
b(t-5)	3.9877**	1.9171
b(t-9)	- 13.5684***	2.1997
b(t-11)	- 15.0659***	2.3819

** 5 % significance level, and *** 1 % significance level. All c values are significant at the 1 % level and lie in the inte [- 29.3322; - 0.3311]. c(t-5) and c(t-6) have the highest absolute values. $R^2 = 0{,}999$

Using the results of the estimation of equation (4), we determined the unexpected component of the information growth rate cycle as an error in the regression (e_t). Now, we return to the Granger causation and estimate

$$\left(\frac{Sav}{Inc}\right)_t = \sum_{x=1}^{12}[d_{t-x}Sav_{t-x} + g_{t-x}e_{t-x}] + \varepsilon_t, \qquad (5)$$

where e is the error from equation (2), and *d* and *g* are regression coefficients.

The result of the estimation of equation (5) shows that all values of d are significant at the 1 % level and are in the interval [- 28.1875; - 0.7214]. Additionally, the most absolute values were for d(t-5)-d(t-7). Excluding e(t-x) with the insignificant g(t-x), we found that only g(t-11) is statistically significant at the 1 % level (g(t-11) = 0.0265 with standard deviation 0.0074). $R^2 = 0.989$, and the Wald test denies the null-hypothesis of g(t-11) = 0 with p = 0.0001 ($\chi^2(1) = 14.6796$). Therefore, we could conclude that unexpected deviations in the information growth rate cycle cause the savings to the disposed income ratio.

Again, additional information increases savings, which corresponds to our leading hypothesis. However, some information is not determined by GDP or M2 dynamics. Possibly, this information could be seen as "pure" information that does not follow statistical reports.

Our findings could infer political implementations that could be partially related to the macroeconomic policy of "new classics" and could be partially seen as an alternative to this policy.

The part of the information that is unconditional on GDP and M2 decisions affects (with lag) households' decisions about consumption and savings. Therefore, macroeconomic policy should count for such influence, since it could lead to over- or underinvestment. When this unconditioned part of information grows, it is possible to neutralize it by increasing the other part of the information growth cycle through (according to (4)) a current decrease in M2 growth or an increase in GDP growth (if it is possible through budget and fiscal policy). If the GDP growth rate falls, the M2 growth rate should also be decreased, and vice versa.

However, manipulations of M2 growth could affect savings and reduce interest rates, which in turn would stimulate economic growth. An increase in GDP growth could ceteris paribus reduce the amount of information in addition to that produced by the GDP and M2 dynamics. Then, households will decrease their savings in future periods, which would increase the interest rate, constrain further economic growth, and so on. Therefore, a cyclical dynamic is produced.

However, the best evidence for such logic was obtained through the Butterworth filter, which restrains the absolute value of the described effects. Most of the savings per income ratio fluctuations fall in the trend, while the cyclical component is relatively small.

4. The Model: Rationally Inattentive Household and Decisions about Consumption and Saving

In the previous section of our work, we found the causality between the cyclical component of information growth and the savings ratio. In this section, we try to substantiate the impact of information with a model hat shows the decision-making about consumption and savings in an explicit way.

4.1 Baseline Model

We suppose infinitely living rationally inattentive consumers, which seek to maximize their overall utility:

$$u = \int_0^\infty \int_0^\infty \beta^t p(c(t))dc(t)dt \tag{1}$$

where:

β is the discount factor, c(t) is the consumption in period t, u(c(t)) is the utility of consumption, and (c(t)) is the probability of choosing the amount of consumption c(t) in period t.

A «rationally inattentive» entity maximizes their general utility by means of establishing p(c(t)) for each amount of consumption c(t) in every period subject to the following constraints:

a) Budget constraint:

$$E\dot{a}(t) = a(t-1)r(t) + w(t) - \int_0^\infty p(c(t))c(t)dt \tag{2}$$

where a(t) is the assets retained by the entity in period t, r(t) is the interest rate, and w(t) is labor income in the period t.

b) Information constraint:

$$I(t) = H + \int_0^\infty p(c(t))\ln(p(c(t))dc(t) \tag{3}$$

where H is the initial entropy of decision-making that is determined by the prior probability c(t) (that is, $H = -\int_0^\infty p_0(c(t))\ln(p_0(c(t))dc(t)$ where $p_0(c(t))$ is the prior probability to choose the amount of consumption that equals c(t)), and I(t) is the information available in period t that is set as the reduction of the initial entropy H.

c) Probability constraint:

$$\int_0^\infty p(c(t))dc(t) = 1 \tag{4}$$

By solving the dynamic optimization problem, we obtain the following:

Definition 1. The entity is rationally inattentive if the decision concerning consumption leads to the maximization of the utility function (1) subject to constraints (2)-(4).

Proposition 1. Ceteris paribus, the rationally inattentive entity chooses the amount of consumption c(t) in period t with a probability:

$$p(c(t)) = \frac{\exp(\frac{\beta^t u(c(t)) - c(t)\exp(r(t)t)}{\kappa(t)})}{\int_0^\infty \exp(\frac{\beta^t u(c(t)) - c(t)\exp(r(t)t}{\kappa(t)})dc(t)} \tag{5}$$

Proof. The rationally inattentive entity seeks to maximize the utility determined by formula (1) subject to (2)-(4). Then, the Hamiltonian is as follows:

$$H = \beta^t u(c(t))p(c(t)) +$$

$$-\lambda(t)\left[a(t-1)r(t) - w(t) - \int_0^\infty c(t)p(c(t))dc(t)\right] +$$

$$-\kappa(t)\left[H - \int_0^\infty p(c(t))\ln p(c(t))dc(t)\right] - v\left[\int_0^\infty p(c(t))dc(t) - 1\right],$$

where *κ(t)* is the costs of processing a unit of information in period *t*.

By applying the Pontryagin principle, we obtain

$$p(c(t)) = \exp\left[\frac{\beta^t u(c(t)) - \exp(r(t)t)c(t)}{\kappa} - 1 - \mu\right].$$

Then, using condition (4), we reach result (5).

Definition 2. A path of consumption is the sequence c(0), c(1), …, (c(t)), c(t+1), …, that is, for each c(t) and c(t-1) on the path of p(c(t)) = p(c(t-1)).

Quite straightforward, from Proposition 1, the following can be stated:

Proposition 2. On the path of non-zero consumption for each c(t), β, and c(t-1)

$$\frac{\beta^t u(c(t)) - c(t)\exp(r(t)t)}{\kappa(t)} = \frac{\beta^t u(c(t-1)) - c(t-1)\exp(r(t-1)t)}{\kappa(t-1)} \tag{6}$$

It seems noteworthy that according to (6), greater information processing costs (κ) result in fewer savings with realistic discount and interest rates. It is an important deviation from the rational expectation approach, according to which a decision-maker

Table 3. GMM estimations

	I	II	III
β	0.99672 (0.00182564)	0.997323 (0.000513351)	1.00088 (0.000478386)
θ	-8.86833e-05 (0.000235572)		−0.00413666 (0.00332837)
k	20.2327 (4.84185)	23.4219 (5.27175)	
Q[TQ]	6.52982e-007 [8.29287e-005]	2.25561e-012 [2.88718e-010]	0.0837819 [10.6403]
χ^2	8.29287e-005	2.88718e-010	10.6403

is indifferent about a direction of his/her mistake. In our case (i.e., the rational inattention approach), a decision-maker would prefer to deviate from the optimum toward greater consumption than toward greater savings.

4.2 Testing the baseline model with GMM

In our research, the information transfers to the entity through the free channel federal economic TV news. We assume that the information ($\widetilde{I}(t)$) received through this channel reduces the information processing costs according to the function $\kappa(t) = \widetilde{I}(t)^{-k}$.

By allowing t=1 for adjacent periods t and t-1 and applying the CRRA utility function, we can infer the following function for the GMM estimation.

$$E_t = \left[\left(\beta\frac{c(t)^{1-\theta}}{1-\theta} - c(t)\exp(r(t))\right)\widetilde{I}(t)^k + \right.$$
$$\left. -\left(\frac{c(t-1)^{1-\theta}}{1-\theta} - c(t-1)\right)\widetilde{I}(t-1)^k\right] = 0 \qquad (7)$$

We estimate three parameters: the discount factor β, the risk aversion θ and the elasticity of information processing costs based on the affectivity of federal TV channels' economic news $\widetilde{I}(t)$ - *k*. Note that, unlike in the previous section, we use all consumption (corrected for the changes in the price level) and not its ratio to disposable income. For the interest rate (*r*), we use the interest rate on 1-year deposits.

We present the results for the estimations of news tonality based on Eureka Engine in Table 3. Here, the direct estimation of equation (7) is presented in column I. Column II presents the estimations with the assumption of no constant risk aversion, i.e., $\theta = 0$. Column III contains the valuations of the parameters of the standard consumption capital-asset-pricing model (CCAPM).

We see that according to the GMM criterion and the Sargan-Hansen J-test, the rational inattention model of the representative households' decisions better fits the data than the CCAPM. The risk-averse parameter θ is insignificant in both models (columns I and III). Moreover, when θ is allowed to be zero, we obtain even better results. Then, instead of the non-plausible interpretation of the insignificance of θ in the way of the risk-neutrality of the household, we could suggest that the level of risk aversion is generated by information that is available from economic news and broadcasted by TV channels.

Additionally, we find verification for our hypothesis that with realistic discounts and discount rates, rationally inattentive households prefer to make a mistake toward greater than optimal consumption. Indeed, a discount rate equal to 1 is a great deal larger than the interest rate on bank deposits. In this case, from formula (7), it follows that more information leads to less consumption.

5. Conclusions

To draw conclusions, we stipulate the following findings from our analysis:

- The information growth cycle does cause the savings ratio cycle;
- The information growth cycle is mainly determined by economic growth and the M2 growth cycle, and the remaining part of the information growth cycle also affects savings;
- Rational inattention assumption predicts higher probability of mistakes toward higher consumption (with plausible interest and discount rates); and
- GMM estimation confirms the prediction and obtains better results than the rational expectations model.

We can also make fundamental conclusions for modern economics:

- The information factor plays an important role in the process of households' decision-making about the distribution of disposable income between consumption and savings.
- The information growth cycle does cause the savings ratio cycle. The information growth cycle is mainly determined by economic growth and the M2 growth cycle, but the remaining part of the information growth cycle also affects savings.
- With the increasing uncertainty of the information environment, households prefer the strategy of risk avoidance and make choices in favor of consumption.
- The behavior of households confirms the concept of «rational inattention».
- The disregard of the information factor in the state policy can cause its ineffectiveness.

References

Alvarez, F. E., Lippi, F., & Paciello, L. (2015). Monetary shocks in models with inattentive producers. *The Review of Economic Studies, 83*(2), 421-459.

Benartzi, S., & Thaler, R. H. (2007). Heuristics and biases in retirement savings behavior. *Journal of Economic Perspectives, 21*(3), 81-104.

Bowman, D., Minehart, D., & Rabin, M. (1999). Loss aversion in a consumption–savings model. *Journal of Economic Behavior & Organization, 38*(2), 155-178.

Caporale, G. M., & Spagnolo, N. (2012). Stock market integration between three CEECs. *Journal of Economic Integration, 27*(1), 115-122.

Caporale, G. M., Spagnolo, F., & Spagnolo, N. (2016). Exchange rates and macro news in emerging markets (Working Paper No. 5816). Center for Economic Studies & Ifo Institute. Retrieved from https://www.econstor.eu/bitstream/10419/130433/1/cesifo1_wp5816.pdf

Caporale, G. M., Spagnolo, F., & Spagnolo, N. (2017). Macro news and exchange rates in the BRICS. *Finance Research Letters, 21*, 140-143.

Chamon, M., Liu, K., & Prasad, E. S. (2010). Income uncertainty and household savings in China (Working Paper No. 10289). International Monetary Fund. Retrieved from https://www.imf.org/external/pubs/ft/wp/2010/wp10289.pdf

Evans, M. D. D., & Lyons, R. K. (2008). How is macro news transmitted to exchange rates? *Journal of Financial Economics, 88*(1), 26-50.

Fang, L., & Peress, J. (2009). Media coverage and the cross-section of stock returns. *The Journal of Finance, 64*(5), 2023-2052.

Flannery, M. J., & Protopapadakis, A. A. (2002). Macroeconomic factors do influence aggregate stock returns. *The Review of Financial Studies, 15*(3), 751-782.

Giavazzi, F., & McMahon, M. (2012). Policy uncertainty and household savings. *The Review of Economics and Statistics, 94*(2), 517-531.

Gomez, V. (2001). The use of Butterworth filters for trend and cycle estimation in economic time series. *Journal of Business & Economic Statistics, 19*(3), 365-373.

Lucas, R. E. (1972). Expectations and the neutrality of money. *Journal of Economic Theory, 4*(2), 103-124.

Maćkowiak, B., & Wiederholt, M. (2015). Business cycle dynamics under rational inattention. *The Review of Economic Studies, 82*(4), 1502-1532.

Martins, G., & Sinigaglia, D. (2009). Real business cycle dynamics under rational inattention (MPRA Working Paper No. 14089). University Library of Munich, Germany. Retrieved from https://mpra.ub.uni-muenchen.de/14089/1/MPRA_paper_14089.pdf

Miao, J. (2004). A note on consumption and savings under Knightian uncertainty. *Annals of Economics and Finance, 5*(2), 299-311.

Sargent, T. J., & Wallace, N. (1976). Rational expectations and the theory of economic policy. *Journal of Monetary economics, 2*(2), 169-183.

Simon, H. A. (1976). From substantive to procedural rationality. In T. J. Kastelein, S. K. Kuipers, W. A. Nijenhuis, & G. R. Wagenaar (Eds.), *25 years of economic theory* (pp. 65-86). Boston, MA: Springer.

Simon, H. A. (1978). Rationality as process and as product of thought. *The American Economic Review, 68*(2), 1-16.

Sims, C. A. (2003). Implications of rational inattention. *Journal of Monetary Economics, 50*(3), 665-690.

Sims, C. A. (2006). Rational inattention: Beyond the linear-quadratic case. *The American economic review, 96*(2), 158-163.

Sims, C. A. (2010). Rational inattention and monetary economics. In B. M. Friedman & M. Woodford (Eds.), *Handbook of Monetary Economics* (Vol. 3, pp. 155-181). New York, NY: Elsevier.

Singh, M., Nejadmalayeri, A., & Lucey, B. (2013). Do US macroeconomic surprises influence equity returns? An exploratory analysis of developed economies. *The Quarterly Review of Economics and Finance, 53*(4), 476-485.

Thaler R. H., & Benartzi S. (2004). Save more tomorrow: Using behavioral economics to increase employee saving. *Journal of political Economy, 112*(1), 164-187.

4

.ocation Theory and Multi-Criteria)ecision Making: An Application of he MOORA Method

llem K. M. Brauers[1,2]

3STRACT The first systematic research on Location Theory dates back to 1826. Quantitative approaches came much later. On the supply side extensive Input-Output Tables can be mentioned and on the demand side the optimization by Multi-Criteria Decision Making. The advantages of Input-Output Tables for location opportunities on a regional and urban basis have to be emphasized, whereas the link is made between Input-Output and Multi-Criteria Optimization. MOORA, Multi-Objective Optimization by Ratio Analysis, is composed of two methods: Ratio Analysis and Reference Point Theory and responds to the different conditions of robustness needed for optimization. This approach attempts to localize in an optimal way a certain project facing different indicators, criteria or objectives sometimes originating from different groups or individuals. Here however type and importance of objectives and alternatives were only simulated. The real stakeholders to be considered are rather the national and local authorities, the contributing firms and their personnel. In the production sphere consumer sovereignty was only indirectly involved. If consumers, via consumer organizations and trade unions, were directly involved, other claims could emerge. The simulation used was limited in its applications. Clearly if this simulation has no practical consequences, it still provides a learning experience with the use of the MOORA Method in its double composition.

EY WORDS: **Location Theory, Input-Output Analysis, MOORA, MULTIMOORA, Objectives, Alternatives, Simulation, Ratio Analysis, Reference Point Method**

)epartment of Economics, University of Antwerp, Belgium; [2] Vilnius Gediminas Technical University, Lithuania;

1. Quantification in Location Theory

1.1. The Beginning

In 1826 Von Thünen wrote the first systematic work on Location Theory in his publication on the "Isolierte Staat", (translated by Wartenberg, 1966). For the first time he remarked that transportation costs may correct the Comparative Costs of Ricardo. However, real quantification came much later by Input-Output Analysis (Leontief, 1936; 1941) and Multi-Criteria Decision Making (MacCrimmon, 1968; Roy, Benayoun, & Sussman, 1966).

Nevertheless one should be aware that there is considerable confusion and overlapping with Regional and Urban Economics. For instance Voogd (1983) treats urban and regional planning, but he also includes Location Theory. For instance he presents an evaluation for potential sites for new housing (p. 239).

orrespondence concerning this article should be addressed to: **/illem K. M. Brauers**, Department of Economics, University Antwerp, Prinsstraat,13, 2000 Antwerpen, Belgium. E-mail: illem.brauers@uantwerpen.be

Location Theory has a supply side and a demand side. The supply side provides an inventory of location possibilities for production and distribution. It is assumed that the supply side is supported by extensive Input-Output Tables with many sectors and sub-sectors. The demand side, in turn, is characterized by many criteria or objectives specifying the demand more effectively.

1.2. Location Theory on Basis of Input-Output Tables

An Input-Output Table forms the basis of the Input-Output Theory with, vertically, all the materials, services and value added necessary for the production of an industrial or service sector and, horizontally, all the clients. The table is the most interesting for the choice of a location of an enterprise when the table shows a large number of sectors and a limited area of application such as regions and urban centers.

Isard was the first to introduce empirical results of Regional Input-Output Analysis as a model of a Space Economy (Isard). Brauers composed Input-Output Tables for the three Belgian Regions: Flanders, Wallonia and Brussels (1973; 1980). The more an I/O model is extensive, the more corresponding location theory will be valuable. At this point, China is the most advanced at this moment. For example, a model on water supply uses a simulation period ranging from 2012 to 2025 including more than 80 mathematical functions with 8828 variables and 7878 constraints (Ke et al., 2016).

Urban location is another example of Input-Output application, such as a study for Stockholm (Artle, 1959). Still another Input-Output study concerns the harbor city of Antwerp with a large concentration of chemical industry (Van Straelen, Puuylaert, & Brauers, 1964). Finally has to be mentioned the construction of a new port for the export of natural gas in Algeria, known as the port of Arzew. The government decided that the port would come between Oran and Algers. An Input- Output pre-study was made to measure the social and economic impact on the whole region (Brauers & Hurt, 1975).

The support of an authority for a well defined project is another example at the supply side of location. This support would be observed if, for instance the Thai government were to ask for the construction of a new seaport in the Gulf of Thailand. Any construction firm can subsequently introduce its project.

1.3. Demand side of Location Theory

Up till now, locations were considered attractive for an investment. Next will be to find the best location but for a given project. In both cases, advice has to be given for selection among several options and consequently for an optimal choice. Each project will be characterized by several criteria and these criteria have to be fulfilled in an optimal way.

A single criterion-objective is not advisable for any planning. It could be General Well-being, but what does it mean? If general well-being is the top objective, economic welfare, individual well-being and sustainable development could be the objectives. At that level measurability is still absent but not at a lower level such as income and employment for economic welfare; public goods, life expectancy and security for individual well-being and abatement of water, air and noise pollution and rationing of natural resources at the sustainable development level. Therefore a Method of Multi-Criteria has to be chosen.

1. 4. Six Conditions to complete a Study on Multi-Objective Optimization

A Study on Multi-Objective Optimization needs the presence of six conditions:

1) the choice of objectives (criteria)
2) number of objectives at least two
3) the choice of alternative solutions at least two
4) normalization of the units of the objectives
5) importance of the objectives
6) all stakeholders are involved. The whole operation could be made by one person, such as an expert, but an expert is not considered to be neutral. One decision maker like a captain of industry will focus on his own objectives. In certain industrial countries the large companies are obliged to have directors in the board of directors from outside the company. Even this group of decision makers will adhere to their own limited objectives. Rather all stakeholders, which mean all persons interested in a certain issue, have to be found, which may present a difficult issue. The choice of stakeholders will take place in a Nominal Group Technique exercise (Brauers & Lepkova, 2003). Contrary to Delphi, convergence is

le 1. Decision Matrix Composition

	Obj. 1	**Obj. 2**	**..........**	**Obj. i**	**...........**	**Obj. n**
rnative 1	X_{11}	X_{21}	....	X_{i1}	....	X_{n1}
rnative 2	X_{12}	X_{22}	....	X_{i2}	....	X_{n2}
....	......	....	....	....	....	....
rnative j	X_{1j}	X_{2j}	....	X_{ij}	....	X_{nj}
......	......	....	....	......	....	....
rnative m	X_{1m}	X_{2m}	....	X_{im}	....	X_{nm}

not aimed at, but final voting is used in the Ameliorated Nominal Group Technique. In this way, the Nominal Group Technique could be considered as exploring any idea about objectives, advisable for a preliminary version of Delphi, where convergence could be reached regarding the list of objectives. Delphi and the Ameliorated Nominal Group Technique are explained in Brauers, (2004), with Dalkey and Helmer (1963) as basis for the first one and Van de Ven and Delbecq (1971) for the second.

In a simulation exercise the author takes the place of the stakeholders.

The method MOORA is selected given its robustness in realization of the six conditions.

2. MOORA Method (Multi-Objective Optimization by Ratio Analysis) applied for the Location of a Project

2.1. Decision Matrix

Multiple Objective Optimization will count at least two objectives and two alternative solutions.

A **Decision Matrix** assembles raw data with vertically numerous objectives, criteria (a weaker form of objectives) or indicators and horizontally alternative solutions, such as projects.

2. 2. Horizontal reading of the Decision Matrix

The Additive Weighting Procedure (MacCrimmon, 1968), which was called SAW, Simple Additive Weighting Method by Hwang and Yoon (1981, p. 99) starts from the following formula:

$$Max\ x_j = w_1 x_{1j} + w_2 x_{2j} + \cdots + w_i x_{ij} + \cdots + w_n x_{nj} \qquad (1)$$

$$\sum_{i=1}^{i=n} w_i = 1 \qquad (2)$$

creates a Super-Objective on basis of the sum of weights = 1

Weights: mixture of normalization and importance. What is what?

Numerous Numbers of objectives would ask for many, many weights, how to choose? It is impossible to fix weights for a huge number, like 20, of objectives or criteria.

2.3. Vertical Reading of the Decision Matrix

SAW reads the Decision Matrix horizontally. Reading vertically means creating **Dimensionless Measurements,** i.e. there is no longer a need for Normalization and no more problems with the number of objectives.

Consequently of the 5 problems, only 3 remain:

i. choice of objectives
ii. importance of objectives
iii. choice of alternative solutions.

The vertical reading of the Response Matrix is applied in the Ratio Analysis of MOORA and in the Reference Point Methods.

2.4. Ratio Analysis of MOORA (Multiple Objectives Optimization by Ratio Analysis)

Simple averages are inconsistent as they may change the sign and even lead to non-sense results. A study of 2006 showed several other solutions (Brauers & Zavadskas, 2006) with this conclusion being the best one:

$$x_{ij}{}^{*} = \frac{x_{ij}}{\sqrt{\sum_{j=i}^{m} x_{ij}^{2}}} \quad (3)$$

with no problem for the number of objectives and with all objectives of the same importance leading to:

$$y_j{}^{*} = \sum_{i=1}^{i=g} x_{ij}{}^{*} - \sum_{i=g+1}^{i=n} x_{ij}{}^{*} \quad (4)$$

i = 1,2,…,g, objectives to maximized

i = g+1, g+2,…, n objectives to minimized

$y_j{}^{*}$= alternative j concerning all objectives and showing the final preference.

2.5. Second Part of MOORA: the Method of Reference Point

Which Reference Point has to be chosen?

1) ***Maximal Objective Reference Point***
   Suppose 2 points: A (100,20) and B (50,100)
   Dominating coordinates r_m***(100;100)***
   or in general $\{r_m\} = \{r_1, r_2, \ldots, r_n\}$
2) ***Utopian Objective Reference Point***
   is farther away than the Maximal Objective Reference Point
3) ***Aspiration Objective Reference Point*** is closer than the Maximal Objective Reference Point.

The most general synthesis of the Reference Point is the Minkowski Metric (Minkowski, 1896, 1911):

$$Min.M_j = \left\{ \left\{ \sum_{i=1}^{i=n} (r - x_{ij}^{*})^{\alpha} \right\}^{1/\alpha} \right\} \quad (5)$$

with M_j = Minkowski metric for solution j

r = reference point each time with its ith coordinate

x^{*}_{ij} = objective i of solution j

$\alpha = 1$ → **Rectangular**

For two attributes or objectives leads to ∞ solutions:

$$Min.M_j = (r - x_{1j}^{*}) + (r - x_{2j}^{*}) \quad (6)$$

In order to come to a single solution VIKOR introduces **Significance Coefficients**: *s*, which the authors (Opricovic & Tzeng, 2004, p. 452) call wrongly weights (see above):

$$(s_i r_i \quad - \quad s_i x_{ij}{}^{*}) \quad (7)$$

$\alpha = 2$ → **Euclidean** → ∞ solutions

$$Min.M_j = \left\{ \left\{ \sum_{i=1}^{i=n} (r - x_{ij}^{*})^{2} \right\}^{1/2} \right\} \quad (8)$$

In order to come to a single solution TOPSIS, originally using Euclidean distances (Hwang & Yoon, 1981, p. 132), introduces **Significance Coefficients**: *s*, which the authors call wrongly weights (Hwang & Yoon, 1981, p. 133).

The Euclidean Distance Metric, characterized by three attributes, is represented by radii of concentric spheres, with the reference point being the center.

This convex outcome does not produce evidence of optimality for non-convex manifolds possible for *more than three attributes.*

$\alpha = 3$

negative results are possible if some co-ordinates of the alternatives exceed the coordinates of the Reference Point, possible with an ***Aspiration Objective Reference Point.***

It is also not clear if non-convex manifolds will eventually have a chance for optimality.

The same for the case with $\alpha > 3$ and following.

Continuing in that direction, difficulties arise in imagining further outcomes. Therefore Tshebycheff sees the best fit in the Max.-Min. Norm with $\alpha \rightarrow \infty$ (Chebyshev, 1947; Karlin & Studden, 1966, p. 279).

Only one distance per point, viz. the largest one away from r_i, is kept in the running. Finally, the smallest outcome is chosen. This outcome is similar to a chain that is only as strong as its weakest link.

The Minkowski metric becomes then the Tchebycheff *Max - Min Metric:*

$$\underset{(j)}{Min} \left\{ \underset{(i)}{max} \sqrt[2]{(r_i - x_{ij}{}^{*})^{2}} \right\} \quad (9)$$

r_i = the ith co-ordinate of the reference point
x_{ij}^*= the dimensionless measurement of objective i for alternative j
i = $1,2......n$; n the number of objectives or attributes
j = $1,2.....m$; m the number of alternatives

2.6. *Only the importance of an objective in comparison to the other objectives still has to be solved.*

With MOORA the introduction of importance coefficients does not change the result (see Appendix A).

Two alternative solutions are possible

- The introduction of exponents (see Appendix B), which is not very advisable because the increase is exponential:
  - with the importance coefficients the increase is as follows for two: 2; 4; 6; 8; 10 etc.
  - instead for exponents for two: 2; 4; 8; 16; 32 etc.
- The introduction of sub-objectives:
  - for instance instead of given an importance coefficient of 3 to pollution three kinds of pollution, each with their own criteria are introduced.
  - The importance coefficient 2 of employment is compensated by the introduction of objectives direct and indirect employment.

3. Two Applications of Location Theory with the use of MOORA

Location Theory has many possible applications. Two simulations are presented: one concerning the location of a Department Store (Brauers & Zavadskas, 2008) and one on the location of a container terminal in a seaport (Brauers, 2013).

3.1. *Simulation Exercise*

The studies are limited to simulation exercises. Contrary to many other definitions, simulation is defined in this study in a rather broad sense. Gordon, Enzer and Rochberg (1970, p. 241) give the most complete description of simulation as mechanical, metaphorical, game or mathematical analogs. These authors conclude that simulations: "are used where experimentation with an actual system is too costly, is morally impossible, or involves the study of problems which are so complex that analytical solution appears impractical".

The simulations explained here and based on MOORA are acceptable as no other multiple objective method based on dimensionless measures studied the problem, neither in reality nor as a fictive example.

3.2. *Location of a Department Store*

The problem posed is a problem of location theory: where to install department stores? There are several objectives for a department store: the turnover, either with deepening of the home market or with penetration abroad; the profitability and productivity aspects; government support; increasing employment level and Value Added and eventually a positive influence on the Balance of Payments. In addition, support is needed of the personnel, the trade unions, the shareholders and the clients. All these stakeholders like to enjoy an optimum position, as well.

In order to better define an objective, we have to focus on the notion of *Attribute*. For instance, if the objective to be maximized concerns the generating of new employment, the attribute could be: guaranteeing at least 1,000 new jobs over a certain period. An attribute should always be measurable.

Assume a number of mutually competitive alternatives, called here *Projects,* facing the attributes and objectives. A simulation for a large department store takes into account four projects, called A, B, C and D. First the alternatives have to pass a filtering stage. Afterwards an optimization method is used, namely MOORA.

All the stakeholders together decided on a hard constraint on the Internal Rate of Return of 12% and Project D did not reach that rate. On the contrary, projects A, B and C passed all the constraints. Project A expands less in the domestic market, but rather in one country of Southern Europe and in one country of Eastern Europe. This expansion means a higher risk ratio, mainly because import prices for these countries will rise more than their domestic and export prices, which means a deterioration of the terms of trade. Project C is more interested in the domestic market. Project B expands in the domestic market and in another large industrialized country, but is in fact mainly situated between the two other projects. In other words, projects A and C take more extreme positions than B. After examining the available information none of the remaining projects seems to dominate the others for all objectives simultaneously.

The following objectives were proposed:

- Entrepreneurial economics

1. NPV MAX
2. IRR MAX.
3. Payback Period MIN.
4. Taxes min. Subsidies (incl. para-fiscal) MIN.
5. Penetration Domestic MAX.
6. Penetration International MAX.
   6.1. Other Industrialized Country MAX.
   6.2. Country Southern Europe MAX.
   6.3. Country Eastern Europe MAX.
7. Deterioration Terms of Trade possible MIN.

- Macro-economics

1. Direct Employment (national) MAX.
2. Indirect + Secondary Employment (national) MAX.
3. Gross VA MAX
4. Positive influence Balance of Payments MAX.

The filtering process excluded Project D already, but kept Projects A, B and C in the running. In the final test on the given data and with MOORA, project C is excluded as expanding only in the domestic market. In this study, the common sense of investment remains: "you must not put all your eggs in one basket", or in other words spread your risks. Moreover, the possibilities of growth in the domestic market concerning department stores are very restrained in Western Europe. Therefore, Project A, expands mainly in foreign countries, whereas Project B expands in the domestic market and abroad. In fact, Project B brings a midway solution between A and C with no extreme positions of its responses to the objectives. Finally, MOORA will chose Project B as solution.

3.3. *The Location of a Container Terminal in a Seaport*

The "Annals of Operations Research, Vol. 2020 of 2013" give all calculations made by MOORA concerning the Location of a Container Terminal in a seaport.

On this subject no other studies are known that are based on Multi Criteria Decision Making. Adler (1967) explains in detail Cost-Benefit in transportation and Coto-Millán, Pesquera and Castenado are the editors of a book on Essays on Port Economics (2010), consisting of nineteen papers using Cost-Benefit Analysis for an economic evaluation of the feasibility of building new ports or enlarging existing ones. Furthermore, Cost-Benefit presents a materialistic approach, whereby for instance unemployment and health care are degraded to monetary items. People are more likely to be solution minded rather than objective-oriented. Cost-Benefit Analysis is a product of this way of thinking.

A developing country or a transition economy wishes to install a container terminal of at least 500,000 TEU.

Five alternatives are proposed.

The first alternative, *Project A*, consists of the installation at a riverside port, 100 km inland, but the installation is on the river itself, capable of receiving large container ships. The possibility to bring large container ships so far inland is an important advantage of this project, reflected in the willingness of the ship owners to pay high demurrage and local taxes for this solution. The installation remains, however, part of a tidal harbor.

Project B possesses the same advantages as project A, belonging also to a riverside port, but installed behind locks. This project also means fewer problems with low and high tide, but investment costs are higher, given the necessity to foresee locks and docks.

Project C is located at a seaport immediately near the sea, but behind locks, which means fewer tidal problems, but again with considerable investment costs.

Project D consists of a terminal also immediately near the sea but in open docks i.e. without locks. This means fast delivery of the goods but with a severe problem of salinity, caused by the open dock system at the seaside.

Project E consists of a container terminal on an island in the sea, meaning fast delivery of the goods. However investment costs are extremely high translated into high depreciation costs for the island.

Seven objectives or criteria have to be fulfilled: two for *micro-economics*; three for *macro-economics* and two for *consumer sovereignty* (Brauers, 2013, pp. 13-14).

The Filtering Stage in Seaport Planning

- Project D is excluded from the side of the national government, as the degree of saltiness is too high.
- Project E is rejected on basis of prohibitive investment costs. In this way only projects A, B and C remain in the running.

Nevertheless in China instead of the extension of the seaports at the seaside like Shanghai, already used intensively, one could think of an inland seaport with the advantages described above. Suppose that there is an nterest for a seaport in industrial Wuhan. The fact that ea ships could come far inside China is an important .dvantage. Indeed Wuhan is located approximately ',400 km inland on the Chang Jiang River (Yangtze), which flows directly in the East China Sea without passing Shanghai.

The bottlenecks are rather of a technical nature. If a city such as Wuhan seeks to become an inland seaport, together with other industrial regions along the river, different existing too low bridges have to be changed and the course of the Chang Jiang River (Yangtze) has to be corrected. Nevertheless other expensive alternative investment opportunities in the country have to be taken into account too (Adler, 1967). Perhaps a choice has to be made, for instance to abandon the also cost-intensive project of a New Silk Road.

Ranking Stage in Seaport Planning

A ranking of alternatives (projects) is derived from the objectives per alternative. However, before considering a ranking, the problem has to be solved if one alternative does not dominate all the others for all objectives. The ranking only takes place for a set of non-dominated alternatives. Neither projects A, B or C is dominating completely, which means that a ranking has to bring the solution.

A summary of the ranking of the two MOORA methods was made on view. If there would be no unique classification at that moment, other additional methods could bring support. First of all, we thought of another method also based on dimensionless measurements, namely the Full Multiplicative method. Brauers and Zavadskas made this link under the name of MULTIMOORA. As MULTIMOORA consists of 3 approaches an Ordinal Dominance Method will bring the final ranking (Brauers & Zavadskas, 2010a).

Nevertheless the simulation side of the example has to be stressed.

The final ranking for Projects A, B and C which passed the Filtering Stage is derived from the simulated numbers as given in: Table 3 of Brauers, *Annals of Operations Research,* Vol. 2020 of 2013 p. 15.

The ranking is then as follows for the two methods:

1. Project A, namely a container terminal at a riverside port on the river itself;
2. Project B, viz., a container terminal at riverside port behind locks;
3. Project C, viz., a container terminal near the sea behind locks. Previously, projects D and E were already excluded:

4. Is There No Link Possible between MOORA and Input-Output for Application in Location Theory?

Is it possible to make a link between MOORA and Input- Output for Location Theory but only to show the location possibilities? The answer is positive. The exercise was made for Tanzania on basis of an updated 2002 Input-Output table (Brauers & Zavadkas, 2010b). It was shown that for 2002 and the following years, light industry under the form of a sugar factory and a cotton mill has to be promoted on the first place. This finding is understandable, as Tanzania possesses a comparative advantage in cotton and sugar.

Secondly, tourism and the construction of new roads is classified. Intensified promotion of tourism is handicapped without a network of new roads. This new roads program needs more imports, counterbalancing the balance of payments surplus of tourism revenues. Two tendencies exist. On one side, Tanzania could follow the example of Kenya in the promotion of tourism. On the other side, the status quo could be maintained with respect for the wildlife in the national parks. Moreover, the quietness of the tribes in the interior is also guaranteed. Reform of agriculture comes on the third place and finally heavy industry could be promoted under the form of a steel plant and a new hydro-electrical power station.

5. Conclusion

If Location Theory was somewhat theoretical in the beginning, it became more quantitative at the supply side with Input-Output Tables and by Multi-Criteria Optimization at the demand side.

For a researcher in multi-criteria decision making the choice between many methods of Multi-Criteria Optimization is not easy. We intended to assist the researcher with several guidelines to make an effective choice. In order to distinguish the various multi-criteria methods from each other we used a qualitative definition of robustness whereby the most robust multi-objective method has to satisfy different conditions.

MOORA, Multi-Objective Optimization by Ratio Analysis, composed of two methods: Ratio Analysis and Reference Point Theory, which starts from the previous found ratios, responds to the different conditions of robustness.

Two simulations of Location Theory illustrated the MOORA research. The suggested planning followed the MOORA method with its two parts, the Ratio System itself and the Reference Point part. As we are only concerned with a simulation, we determined the type and importance of the criteria and the alternatives ourselves, instead of the stakeholders concerned. Being in the production sphere consumer sovereignty was only indirectly involved. Nevertheless the authorities were also taken as the legitimate representatives of the consumers. If consumers, via consumer organizations and trade unions, would be directly involved perhaps other claims could still emerge.

The simulations were limited in their application. Even if the simulation has no practical consequences, in any case it provides a learning experience with MOORA in its double composition.

References

Adler, H. A. (1967). Sector and Project Planning in Transportation (Occasional Paper No. 4). International Bank for Reconstruction and Development.

Artle, R. (1959). Studies in the Structure of the Stockholm Economy: Towards a Framework for Projecting Metropolitan Community Development. Stockholm: Business Research Institute at the Stockholm School of Economics

Brauers, W. K. M. (1973). Input Output Analyse-Instrument van de Regionale Economie in België [Dutch for: Input-Output Analysis of the Regional Economy of Belgium]. Leuven: Center for Economic Studies, University of Leuven.

Brauers, W. K. M. (1980). *The Belgian Experience in Interregional Input-Output Table.* Leuven: Center for Economic Studies, University of Leuven.

Brauers, W. K. M. (2004). *Optimization methods for a stakeholder society. A revolution in economic thinking by multiobjective optimization.* Boston, MA: Kluwer Academic/Springer.

Brauers, W. K. M. (2013). Multi-objective seaport planning by MOORA decision making. *Annals of Operations Research, 206*(1), 39-58.

Brauers, W. K. M., & Hurt, M. A. R. (1975). *Impact du Pôle Industriel d'Arzew sur l'Environnement Oranais* [Impact of the Industrial Zone of Arzew o the Region of Oran]. Boumerdes, Algeria: INPED

Brauers, W. K. M., & Lepkova, N. (2003). The application of the nominal group technique to the business outlook of the facilities sector of Lithuania over the period 2003–2012. *International Journa of Strategic Property Management, 7*(1), 1–9.

Brauers, W. K. M., & Zavadskas, E. K. (2006). Th MOORA method and its application to privatization in a transition economy. *Control and Cybernetics, 35*(2), 445–469.

Brauers, W. K. M., & Zavadskas, E. K. (2008). Multi Objective Optimization in Location Theory wit a Simulation for a Department Store, *Transformations in Business & Economics, 7*(3), 163-183.

Brauers, W. K. M., & Zavadskas, E. K. (2010a). Projec Management by MULTIMOORA as an Instrument for Transition Economies, *Technological an Economic Development of Economy, 16*(1), 5-24 https://doi.org/10.3846/tede.2010.01

Brauers, W. K. M., & Zavadskas, E. K. (2010b). Robustness in the MULTIMOORA Model, The Exampl of Tanzania, *Transformations in Business and Economics, 9*(3), 67-83.

Chebyshev, P. L. (1947). *Complete Collected Works* Moscow: Academy of Science of the U.S.S.R.

Coto-Millán, P., Pesquera, M. A., & Castenado, J (Eds.). (2010). *Essays on Port Economics.* Heidelberg: Physica-Verlag Heidelberg.

Dalkey, N., & Helmer, O. (1963). An Experimental Application of the Delphi Method to the us of Experts. *Management Science, 9*(3), 458-487 https://doi.org/10.1287/mnsc.9.3.458

Gordon, T. J., Enzer, S., & Rochberg, R. (1970). An experiment in simulation gaming for social policy studies. *Technological Forecasting,* 1(3), 241-261 https://doi.org/10.1016/0099-3964(70)90027-X

Hwang, C. L., & Yoon, K. (1981). Multiple attribute decision making: Methods and applications: A state-of-the-art survey. Berlin: Springer.

Isard, W. (1951). Interregional and Regional Input-Output Analysis, a Model of a Space Economy, *Th Review of Economics and Statistics,* 33(4), 318-328 http://dx.doi.org/10.2307/1926459

Karlin, S., & Studden, W. J. (1966). *Tchebycheff systems with applications in analysis and statistics.* New York, NY: Interscience.

Ke, W., Sha, J., Yan, J., Zhang, G., & Wu, R. (2016), A Multi-Objective Input–Output Linear Model for Water Supply, Economic Growth and Environmental Planning in Resource-Based Cities. *Sustainability, 8(2)*. https://doi.org/10.3390/su8020160

Leontief, W.W. (1936). Quantitative Input and Output Relations in the Economic System of the United States, *the Review of Economic Statistics, 18*(3), 205-125.

Leontief, W. W. (1941). *The Structure of American Economy, 1919-1939*. New York, NY: Oxford University Press.

MacCrimmon, K. R. (1968). *Decision Making among Multiple Attribute Alternatives. A Survey and Consolidated Approach*, Santa Monica, CA: Rand Corporation.

Minkowsky, H. (1896). Geometrie der Zahlen [Geometry of Numbers]. Leipzig: Teubner.

Minkowsky, H. (1911). Gesammelte Abhandlungen [Collected Essays]. Leipzig: Teubner.

Opricovic, S., & Tzeng, G. H. (2004). Compromise solution by MCDM methods: a comparative analysis of VIKOR and TOPSIS. European Journal of Operational Research, 156(2), 445-455. https://doi.org/10.1016/S0377-2217(03)00020-1

Roy, B., Benayoun, R., & Sussman B. (1966). *ELECTRE*. Paris: Société d'Economie et de Mathématique appliquées.

Van de Ven, A. H., & Delbecq, A. L. (1971). Nominal versus interacting group processes for committee decision making effectiveness. *Academy of Management Journal, 14*(2), 203–212.

Van Straelen, R., Puylaert, L., & Brauers, W. K. M. (1964). Tableaux Input-Output pour l'Arrondissement d'Anvers [Input-Output tables for the district of Antwerp]. Antwerp: Centre d' Etudes pour l'Expansion d'Anvers, *Mededelingen*.

Voogd H. (1983). *Multicriteria Evaluation for Urban and Regional Planning*. London, UK: Pion.

Wartenberg, C. M. (1966). *Isolated State*. New York, NY: Pergamon Press.

Appendix A

Table. A MOORA Simulation Lithuanian Sustainable Development (2006-2012)

a - Matrix of Responses of Alternatives on Objectives: (x_{ij})

Yearly figures	1. Inflation (in %) MIN.	2. Increase Public Debt (% GDP) MIN.	3. Def.Public Budget (% GDP) MIN.	4. Unemploym. (in % labor force) MIN.	5. Increase real wages in% MAX.	6. Shop time (in weekly hours) MIN.	7. Increase GDP (in%) MAX.	8. Minus % Energy consumpt. MAX (a)	9. CO2 ton/cap. MIN.	10. Other Pollution MIN.
EMU	2	3	3	17	3	38	6.88	7.3	8.53	2
EEU	4	1.9	1.9	8.3	1	40	7	7.3	8.53	2
Secession	3	1	1	12	2	45	5.5	0.5	8.70	4
Totals	9	5.9	5.9	37.3	6	123	19.38	15.1	25.756	8

b - Sum of squares and their square roots

Projects										
EMU	4	9	9	289	9	1444	47.3344	53.29	72.692676	4
EEU	16	3.61	3.61	68.89	1	1600	49	53.29	72.7609	4
Secession	9	1	1	144	4	2025	30.25	0.25	75.69	16
sum of squares	29	13.61	13.61	501.89	14	5069	126.5844	106.83	221.14358	24
square roots	5.38516481	3.68917335	3.6891733	22.4029016	3.741657387	71.19691	11.250973	10.3358599	14.870897	4.898979486

c - Objectives divided by their square roots and MOORA

											sum	rank
EMU	0.37139068	0.813190	0.8131903	0.75883028	0.801783726	0.533731	0.61150	0.70627892	0.5733346	0.40824829	-2.1523502	2
EEU	0.74278135	0.515021	0.5150205	0.370488	0.267261242	0.5618221	0.6221684	0.706279	0.5736036	0.40824829	-2.091276	1
Secession	0.55708601	0.271063	0.2710634	0.5356449	0.534522484	0.6320499	0.4888466	0.04837527	0.5850353	0.816496581	-2.596695	3

d - Reference Point Theory with Ratios: co-ordinates of the reference point equal to the maximal objective values

ri	0.37139068	0.271063	0.2710634	0.37049	0.801783726	0.533731	0.62217	0.70627892	0.5733346	0.40824829

e - Reference Point Theory: Deviations from the reference point

											max.	rank m
EMU	0	0.54213	0.5421269	0.38834	0	0	0.01067	0	0	0	0.5421269	2
EEU	0.37139068	0.243957	0.2439571	0.000000	0.534522484	0.0280911	0.00000	0.000000	0.000269	0	0.5345225	1
Secession	0.18569534	-	0	0.16516	0.267261242	0.0983189	0.13332	0.65790365	0.0117007	0.40824829	0.6579037	3

le. A MOORA Simulation Lithuanian Sustainable Development (2006-2012) with increase in real wages x 2 (n°5)

latrix of Responses of Alternatives on Objectives: (x_{ij})

s	1. Inflation (in %) MIN.	2. Increase Public Debt (% GDP) MIN.	3. Def.Public Budget (% GDP) MIN.	4. Unemploy. (in % labor force) MIN.	5. Increase real wages in% MAX.	6. Shop time (in weekly hours) MIN.	7. Increase GDP (in%) MAX.	8. Minus % Energy consumpt. MAX (a)	9. CO2 ton/cap. MIN.	10. Other Pollution MIN.
	2	3	3	17	6	38	6.88	7.3	8.53	2
	4	1.9	1.9	8.3	2	40	7	7.3	8.53	2
sion	3	1	1	12	4	45	5.5	0.5	8.70	4
	9	5.9	5.9	37.3	12	123	19.38	15.1	25.756	8

ım of squares and their square roots

ts										
	4	9	9	289	36	1444	47.3344	53.29	72.692676	4
	16	3.61	3.61	68.89	4	1600	49	53.29	72.7609	4
sion	9	1	1	144	16	2025	30.25	0.25	75.69	16
f es	29	13.61	13.61	501.89	56	5069	126.5844	106.83	221.14358	24
e roots	5.3851648	3.6891733	3.6891733	22.402902	7.483314774	71.19691	11.250973	10.33586	14.870897	4.8989795

bjectives divided by their square roots and MOORA											sum	rank
	0.3713907	0.813190	0.8131903	0.7588303	0.801783726	0.533731	0.61150	0.7062789	0.5733346	0.4082483	-2.1523502	**2**
	0.7427814	0.515021	0.5150205	0.370488	0.267261242	0.5618221	0.6221684	0.706279	0.5736036	0.4082483	-2.091276	**1**
sion	0.557086	0.271063	0.2710634	0.5356449	0.534522484	0.6320499	0.4888466	0.0483753	0.5850353	0.8164966	--2.596695	**3**

eference Point Theory with Ratios: co-ordinates of the reference point equal to the maximal objective values

	0.3713907	0.271063	0.2710634	0.37049	0.801783726	0.533731	0.62217	0.7062789	0.5733346	0.4082483

eference Point Theory: Deviations from the reference point											max.	rank min.
	0	0.54213	0.5421269	0.38834	0	0	0.01067	0	0	0	0.5421269	**2**
	0.3713907	0.243957	0.2439571	0.000000	0.534522484	0.0280911	0.00000	0.000000	0.000269	0	0.5345225	**1**
sion	0.1856953	-	0	0.16516	0.267261242	0.0983189	0.13332	0.6579037	0.0117007	0.4082483	0.6579037	**3**

Appendix B

Table. A MOORA Simulation Lithuanian Sustainable Development (2006-2012) with increase in real wages with exponent 2 (

a - Matrix of Responses of Alternatives on Objectives: (x_{ij})

Yearly figures	1. Inflation (in %) MIN.	2. Increase Public Debt (% GDP) MIN.	3. Def.Public Budget (% GDP) MIN.	4. Unemploy. (in % labor force) MIN.	5. Increase real wages in% MAX.	6. Shop time (in weekly hours) MIN.	7. Increase GDP (in%) MAX.	8. Minus % Energy consumpt. MAX (a)	9. CO2 ton/cap. MIN.	10. Other Pollution MIN.
EMU	**2**	**3**	**3**	**17**	**9**	**38**	**6.88**	**7.3**	**8.53**	**2**
EEU	**4**	**1.9**	**1.9**	**8.3**	**1**	**40**	**7**	**7.3**	**8.53**	**2**
Secession	**3**	**1**	**1**	**12**	**4**	**45**	**5.5**	**0.5**	**8.70**	**4**
Totals	**9**	**5.9**	**5.9**	**37.3**	**14**	**123**	**19.38**	**15.1**	**25.756**	**8**

b - Sum of squares and their square roots

Projects										
EMU	4	9	9	289	81	1444	47.3344	53.29	72.692676	4
EEU	16	3.61	3.61	68.89	1	1600	49	53.29	72.7609	4
Secession	9	1	1	144	16	2025	30.25	0.25	75.69	16
sum of squares	29	13.61	13.61	501.89	98	5069	126.5844	106.83	221.14358	24
square roots	5.38516481	3.68917335	3.6891733	22.4029016	9.899494937	71.19691	11.250973	10.3358599	14.870897	4.898979486

c - Objectives divided by their square roots and MOORA

											sum	rank
EMU	0.37139068	0.813190	0.8131903	0.75883028	0.90913729	0.533731	0.61150	0.70627892	0.5733346	0.40824829	-2.0449966	**1**
EEU	0.74278135	0.515021	0.5150205	0.370488	0.101015254	0.5618221	0.6221684	0.706279	0.5736036	0.40824829	-2.257522	**2**
Secession	0.55708601	0.271063	0.2710634	0.5356449	0.404061018	0.6320499	0.4888466	0.04837527	0.5850353	0.816496581	-2.727157	**3**

d - Reference Point Theory with Ratios: co-ordinates of the reference point equal to the maximal objective values

ri	0.37139068	0.271063	0.2710634	0.37049	0.90913729	0.533731	0.62217	0.70627892	0.5733346	0.40824829

e - Reference Point Theory: Deviations from the reference point

											max.	rank m
EMU	0	0.54213	0.5421269	0.38834	0	0	0.01067	0	0	0	0.5421269	**1**
EEU	0.37139068	0.243957	0.2439571	0.000000	0.808122036	0.0280911	0.00000	0.000000	0.000269	0	0.8081220	**3**
Secession	0.18569534	-	0	0.16516	0.505076272	0.0983189	0.13332	0.65790365	0.0117007	0.40824829	0.6579037	**2**

5

)eveloping a Digital Co-Creation Assessment /lethodology

›nika Mačiulienė[1], Aelita Skaržauskienė[2], Dick Botteldooren[3]

3STRACT Digitally enhanced public open spaces are ideal environments for the social innovations to emerge due to the involvement of the entire community and ICT (Information and Communication Tools) in knowledge creation and aggregation. This research paper presents an early-stage methodological digital co-creation assessment framework that considers a variety of aspects to transform public open places into co-created spaces: socio-cultural contexts, multi-stakeholder perspective, diversity in needs, incentives for participation of different groups and cooperation capabilities. The framework incorporates these aspects and proposes a suitable community-wide co-creation model employing the creative, innovative and cooperative applications of ICT. The assessment methodology is developed using a pragmatic mixed-method research design where the theoretical framework summarizes current research progress on the topic and the expert interviews allow to condense the complex and multi-dimensional realities for decision-makers seeking social innovations in the public spaces. The methodological assessment framework presented in this paper strengthens the scientific evidence regarding the potential of co-creation in developing social innovations and provides a managerial framework for developing co-creative initiatives.

:Y WORDS: Co-Creation, Public Spaces, ICT, Social Innovation

/lykolas Romeris University, Lithuania;
ilnius Gediminas Technical University, Lithuania;
ihent University, Belgium

1. Introduction

Urban social innovation is a rapidly growing priority for countries everywhere with increasingly urbanized world's population. Public spaces play a vital role in urban democracy and inclusiveness since they enable collective usage and reflection. Martinus (2014) explores the public opens spaces (POS) as platforms strengthening the social capital networks and supporting social innovation systems. The author suggests that "there is an economic and policy imperative to better understand the design, location and user perception aspects of urban space as determinants of user attraction" (Martinus, 2014, p. 44). This research paper presents an early-stage methodological framework that considers a variety of aspects in transformation of public open places into co-created spaces: socio-cultural contexts, multi-stakeholder perspective, diversity in needs, incentives for participation of different groups and cooperation capabilities. The framework incorporates these aspects and proposes a suitable community-wide co-creation model employing the

›rrespondence concerning this article should be addressed to:
onika Mačiulienė. Mykolas Romeris University, Lithuania.
mail: maciuliene@mruni.eu

creative, innovative and cooperative applications of ICT (Information and Communication Technologies). The article is a part of the C³PLACES project (www.c3places.eu) which focuses on developing the strategies and tools to increase the quality of public open spaces through the use of digital tools by positively influencing co-creation and social cohesion effects. The C³PLACES generates knowledge and know-how to use the co-creation approach in order to merge the ICT with the functions of the public spaces.

2. Literature review

One of the ways to make the open public spaces more attractive and inclusive is the use of innovative digital technologies. Digitization may lead to modern bottom-up initiatives where the citizens and civic organizations voluntarily lend their talent and resources to help the public entities in solving social problems and enhancing the quality of life. Similarly, Stewart-Weeks (2010, p. 83) suggests that "citizens are increasingly willing and able to translate their day-to-day experience into ideas, preferences and insights that can become powerful resources for innovation". The co-creative approach is intrinsically user-oriented because it helps the people and organizations to promote their own decisions, develop capacities for open-ended social innovations, rather than invites citizens to participate in existing initiatives (Mačiulienė, 2018). However, the multiple studies on co-creation (Bason, 2015; Bulc, 2012; Brabham, 2009; Franz, 2015; Mulder, 2012; Mulder & Stappers, 2009), digital tools (Baldersheim & Kersting, 2012; Cheliotis, 2015; Certomà, Dyer, Pocatilu & Rizzi, 2017; Poplin, 2012) and their application in developing POS as separate subject lack a holistic perspective. The concept of digital co-creation itself is rarely clearly defined and operationalized. In response to the issues discussed herein, following sections demonstrate the relevance of ICT urban social innovations through development of digital co-creation assessment methodology.

3. Research Methodology

The development of the assessment methodology adopts a pragmatic mixed-method research design illustrated in Figure 1 and discussed in the following sections. Typically, the assessment criteria research is conducted through statistical analysis in order to demonstrate the multicollinearity of individual indicators. However, according to Hoelscher, Mildenberger & Bund (2015) concepts with multidimensional outcomes benefit from a mixed research strategy combining the theory (top-down approach) with experts' knowledge (bottom-up approach) in order to minimize the risk of overlooking dimensions. Here, the theoretical framework summarizes the current research progress on the topic and the empirical evidences allow to condense the complex realities for decision-makers seeking social innovations in public spaces.

The first step in designing the methodology was to build a theoretical framework. The analysis of the previous research efforts captured the theoretical influences and provided the basis for the selection and combination of framework dimensions. Lester (2005, p. 458) states that theoretical framework "provides a structure for conceptualizing and designing research studies. In particular, a research framework helps determine the principles of discovery and justification allowed for creating "new knowledge" about the topic under study (this refers to acceptable research methods)". Hence, the framework allowed to structure the further discussion and provided a theoretical rationale behind the evaluation tool.

The second step of the process was the expert interviews. The theoretical frameworks provide an interpretative approach to the social reality and empirical investigations are needed to test their consistency with the reality (Jabareen, 2009). Based on the literature review, we hypothesize that a set of dimensions are influencing the digital co-creation outcomes. However, there may be different configurations and additional preconditions. The in-depth knowledge provided by the experts on the key evaluation points is particularly suited for broadening the theoretical framework. Nine purposively sampled semi-structured face-to-face expert interviews were conducted to check and improve the theoretical model. During the research, 9 experts – in urban planning (4 experts), digital tools (2 experts) and co-creative initiatives (3 experts) – have been selected to be interviewed based on the professional experience, knowledge and the affiliation. The C3PLACES project collects data and information on designated POS in Belgium (Ghent Public Space Living Lab), Italy (Milano Living Lab), Lithuania (Vilnius Aukštamiestis Living Lab) and Portugal (Lisbon: Alvalade Living Lab) in order to develop the strategies

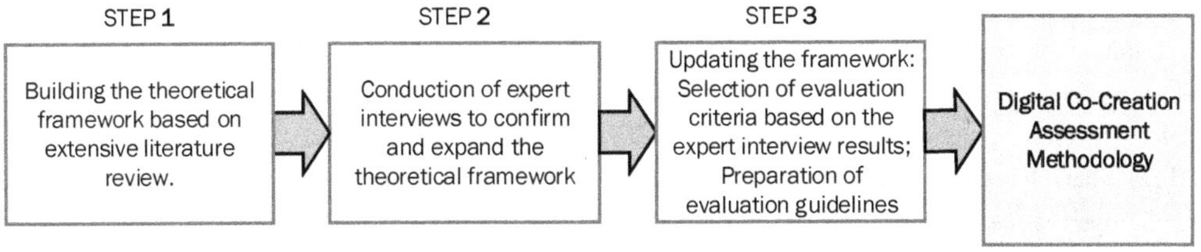

ure 1. Design Process of Digital Co-Creation Assessment Methodology

to increase the quality of public open spaces through ICT. The experts were selected based on their involvement in these four case studies.

In the context of this research, the validity and significance of the results are based more on to the richness of the data collected and the sample selected and the competencies of the researchers to analyze the data than on the size of the sample (Patton, 2002). Open-ended questions allow receiving more in-depth and open answers based on personal experiences and perspectives. Reflective dialogues enhanced the quality and amount of data collected due to subjective interpretation of wider context not limited to particular questions. The instrument used in this study is a questionnaire based on the theoretical framework and consisted of 4 question groups – general, place attractiveness, digital inclusiveness, and social responsiveness questions. The dimensions were integrated in the interview guide in order to ensure the inductive design of the assessment framework. The interviews were conducted in the period of December, 2017 - February, 2018. The average duration of each interview was 1,5 hours. All interviews, except one (E2), took place by Skype. Interviews were transcribed and analyzed using content analysis procedures (Krippendorff, 2003) in a deductive category application, bringing the empirical data in connection with the prior formulated theoretical aspects of analysis.

The final step towards the completion of the methodological framework was the preparation of assessment methodology – design of updated framework, selection of evaluation criteria and proposal of assessment guidelines. The qualitative data collected during the interviews were analysed in the context of respondents' ideas, arguments and opinions in order to deepen the researchers' understanding of the analysed issues. Qualitative research aimed at establishing similarities, differences and relations between the interview text segments. The following principles were guiding the selection of framework dimensions and criteria: clarity, logic and simplicity, applicability to different local/regional/national settings, relevance and data availability. The findings allowed us to explain the processes of digital co-creation in specific context i.e. design and improvement of public spaces. The selection of criteria was performed based on possibilities for implementation, feasibility and adaptability of the framework. It must be noted that the subjectivity in the choice of dimensions and criteria is inevitable given the diffuse nature of the concept of co-creation and the lack of more straightforward definitions. However, the goal was to offer a generalized approach to undertaking the evaluation of digital co-creation initiatives. The overall intention was to ensure that the key dimensions of concern are assessed in similar ways.

4. Results

4.1. Theoretical Framework for Conceptualizing Digital Co-Creation

The section provides an overview of the insights from the previous studies by proposing a theoretical framework summarizing the main preconditions for the digital co-creation of public spaces. The framework has three pillars, which are crucial in the co-creation of public open spaces design using the digital tools (see Figure 2). The Public Open Space (POS) Quality pillar refers to the factors enhancing social integration and generating pleasure to communities. Authors (Bobenberg, 2014; De Lange & De Waal, 2013; Nouri & Costa, 2017) suggest that functional, visual and physical qualities of space influence the social interactions, comfort and security settings and attract people to engage with the space. To this end, the Project for Public Spaces (2009) evaluated thousands of public spaces globally and identified four qualities determining its attractiveness: uses and activities; comfort and image; access and linkages; sociability.

The Digital Inclusiveness pillar explains the technological readiness of the place for enabling co-creation, measures preconditions for the inclusiveness of public open spaces. Griggs and Wild (2013) model, which helps the public organizations to weigh the benefits and risks associated with the use of ICT and social networking applications, forms the base for the technological evaluation layer. The inclusiveness of public open spaces has three dimensions: expansion-related technologies, risk-related technologies, and value-related social technologies. The expansion refers to the depth, breadth and speed of connection created by technological solution. A solution with a capability to develop a network rapidly would rank highly on expansion related metric. The related technologies refer to the degree of the risk mitigated in association with a particular application of ICT. The privacy and personal data protection helps to create a potentially active community and encourages a diversity of opinions. Therefore, it is essential to introduce technologies safeguarding user security and, in some cases, anonymity (Skaržauskienė et al., 2015). The value-related technologies refer to the quality of the content, values of the stakeholders and technological solutions to support the knowledge creating activities. The new generation applications focus on the users` needs and aim at technological innovation to improve the collective decision-making, teamwork and better mutual understanding. The users play the major role in deciding what data and information is necessary and useful. According to the research results, the highly value-related ICT tools have to contain the rich high quality content that remains relevant to the society over time. In addition, such technologies have to support the knowledge creation activities in a community: promote engagement and participation, facilitate more dynamic and "democratic" knowledge dissemination and integration, foster sustainability, etc. (Skaržauskienė et al., 2015).

In discussing the Social Responsiveness pillar, the research refers to the factors related to the capacity to involve people. The pillar is adapted from the Collective Intelligence Index (Skaržauskienė et al., 2015) and includes following dimensions: dynamism, openness, and flexibility; transparency; decentralization and self-organization; social maturity. Dynamism, openness and flexibility refers to the communities "with vague boundaries, allowing people the freedom to join or leave the community" (Luo, Xia, Yoshida, & Wang, 2009). Transparency refers to the information necessary to create trust between the community and the society (Prahalad & Ramaswamy, 2004). Theoretical and empirical study of Dabbish, Stuart, Tsay and Herbsleb (2012, p. 1278) suggest that "providing visibility of actions on shared artifacts supports cooperative work" and propose variety of ways that transparency can support innovation, knowledge sharing, and community building. Decentralization and self-organization describes the initiatives without central control. Following the Internet design, the networks adopted the decentralized structure, and contradicted the function of the traditional hierarchical mechanism. The structural units (nodes) being unable to interact with the center of network (which does not exist) have to interact with the whole network in the self-regulatory regime and develop one of the most productive forms of collaboration (Skaržauskienė et al., 2015). The social maturity dimension refers to the impact upon the society, social orientation and motivation, including the involvement and participation in social activities. The dimension describes the degree defining the sensitivity of group members to social cues and capacity to generate the public value. Meynhardt (2009, p. 212) explains

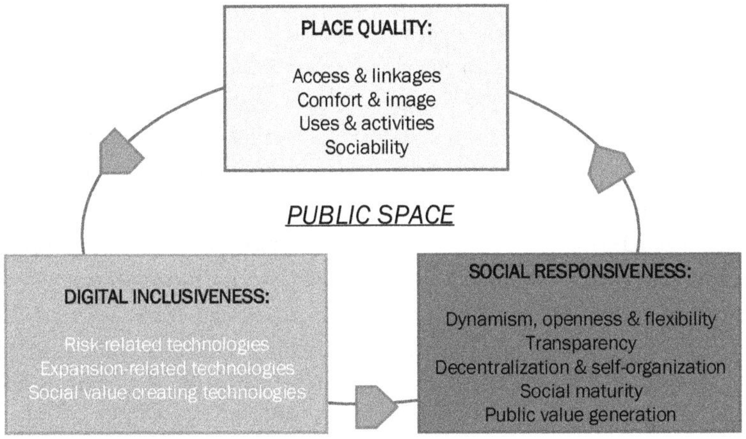

ure 2. Theoretical Framework
rce: Adapted from "What Makes a Successful Place?" by Project for Public Spaces (2009). Available at https://www.pps. /reference/grplacefeat; *"Social technologies and collective intelligence"* by Skaržauskienė, A., Ewart, J., Krzywosz-Rynkiewicz, alewska, A., Leichteris, E., Mačiulis, A., … Valys, T. (2015). In *Social technologies and collective intelligence.* Vilnius: Mykolas neris University; *"A Social Networking Adoption Model for Communication and Collaboration in e-Government"* (Vol. 1). by gs, K. Wild, R. (2013). In W. Castelnovo, E. Ferrari (Eds.), Proceedings of thr 13th European Conference on eGovernment 221-229). Como: Department of Theoretical and Applied Sciences. University of Insubria.

the public value as "any impact on shared experience about the quality of the relationship between the individual and society". According to Millard (2013), the public sector can create value for the public alone but its potential to do so increases by involving external actors and stakeholders. The quantitative criteria, however, cannot measure all aspects of public value, although some numeric data is extremely important. Collective intelligence of the community and "public value" for society considers new knowledge, ideas, problem solving methods and solutions, shaped up or structured opinions, innovations, prototypes, etc.

4.2. Digital Co-Creation Assessment Framework

The in-depth interviews of the research study reveal a wealth of insights into how to expand the theoretical framework. Through the analysis of the data, the insights were categorized based on the dimensions of the theoretical framework. The results of the expert interviews are summarized in Figure 3 and detailed with the illustrative quotes from the interviewed experts below.

The POS Quality pillar connects the factors enhancing the social integration and communities' satisfaction with the public place generated by digital co-creation initiative (4 dimensions and 13 evaluation criteria). The assessment of place quality provides the context of digital initiatives and offers operational canvas to describe and compare different case studies. The discussion on the evaluation of POS Quality divides into four areas based on the dimensions of the theoretical framework. Evaluating the access and linkages dimension, the experts stressed the importance of readability ('visible from outside' E1; 'ease with which visitors understand and remember the information' E2, E3), convenience for movement ('easily walk to the place' E2, E3; 'sidewalks lead to neighboring areas' E1) and accessibility ('transportation options' E1, E2; 'surrounding pedestrian paths' E3). When deliberating comfort and image dimension, the experts suggested to evaluate the criteria of captivation level ('good first impression' E3; 'people taking pictures' E2, E3), comfort and cleanness ('enough places to lounge' E1, E3; 'free of litter' E2; 'good maintenance' E1, E2, E3), safety level ('people feel safe' E2, E3; 'someone is responsible for safety' E2). Uses and activities dimension divides into level of equipment ('what equipment is present and who can use it' E1, E2, E3), level of vitality ('full or empty' E1; 'people standing in groups' E3) and variety of activities ('choices of things to do' E1, E2). In discussion on sociability of public open space, the experts mentioned welcoming ('would you meet your friend here' E2; 'locals use it with pride' E3; 'point to features of the place with pride' E3), level of publicness ('does the place include everyone' E2, 'inclusive to all social groups' E1, E7, E9), interactivity ('people talking with each other' E1, E2, E3; 'people smiling and making eye-contact' E2) and diversity ('mix of gender, nationalities, generations' E2, E3).

The expert discussions on the digital inclusiveness of co-creative initiatives allowed to detail the dimensions of theoretical model. In discussing risk-related technologies, the experts stressed the importance of security and privacy assurance technologies ('mechanisms for providing secure and legal online/offline activities' E5, E6; 'protection of personal data' E1; 'effective message control' E5). When talking about expansion-related technologies the interview participants elaborated on the availability of networking and collaboration technologies ('availability of various communication tools like chats, forums or social platforms' E5, E6; 'access by all devices' E5, E7). The dimension of social value of technologies divides into the following evaluation criteria based on the expert insights: existence of data collection and access technologies ('tools to collect data' E5; 'digital abilities to evaluate and analyze the performance of an initiative' E6; 'ability to share data with the public and re-use it for the public good' E5, E6); knowledge-creation technologies ('tools to add value to the content' E5, E6; 'how to generate feedback from the stakeholders E8, E9; 'ability to visualize and organize the knowledge with the help of IT' E5; 'technologies to involve crowds, groups of people into design processes' E7) and decision-making technologies ('how to involve people into brainstorming sessions in designing the spaces' E2; 'creating tools for voting and rating ideas suggestions' E5, E6; 'ways how to reach collective decision or conclusion' E7). The expert deliberations on the Digital Inclusiveness pillar, uncovered the need to expand the theoretical model by adding two dimensions important in evaluating digital co-creation initiatives. The experts (E5, E6, E7, E9) stressed the importance of pervasiveness of ICT tools referring to the ability of the digital tools to easily function when and where needed. In addition, the analysis of the qualitative data allowed to add the dimension of appropriateness referring to the ability of digital tools in addressing its group of users ('can the tool solve the problems of target groups' E5, E8; 'can everyone understand how to use it' E8, E9).

In reflecting on Social Responsiveness dimension, the interviews led to identification of eleven evaluation criteria. Dynamism, openness and flexibility dimension divides into criteria of interaction and engagement degree ('opportunities to disseminate knowledge generated by the involved community' E8; 'adoption of digital tools for different age groups' E7, E9; 'external relationships' E8, E9), supply of critical mass ('potential individuals/communities/target groups' E8, E9, 'unique, total and repeat visits' E7), and degree of diversity in the source of ideas ('different people providing ideas and participating' E8; 'number of diverse contributions' E8, E9; 'balanced representation of the community' E3, E7, E8). In discussing transparency issues in digital tools, two criteria were established development of transparent structure and culture ('clear rules of engagement' E7; 'clear roles and responsibilities' E9) and degree of independence ('need of a privacy policy' E8; 'equal rights for all participants involved in co-creative processes' E7, E8, E9). Decentralization and self-organization dimension evaluates by determining its' degree ('community has to have common norms' E9; 'shared mental models' E8; 'the community involved has to have a common vocabulary in discussing the issues' E7, E8). Interviewed experts in discussing the social maturity dimension elaborated on the social impact ('how to engage civic community' E8,

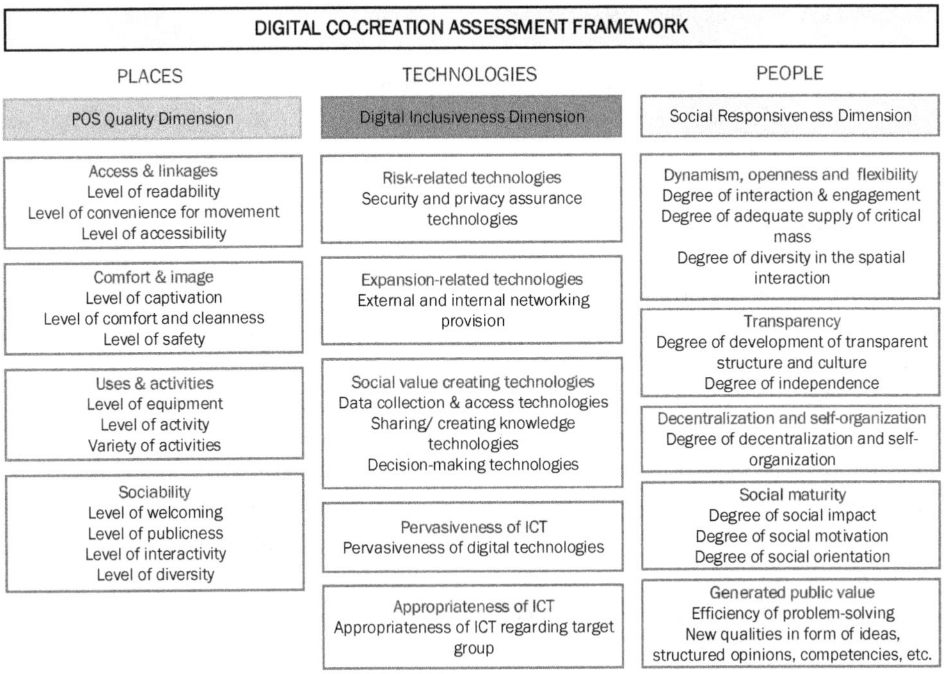

re 3. Digital Co-Creation Assessment Framework

E9; ‘what is the feedback from governmental entities’ E1, E8, E9; ‘interaction with community stakeholders’ E7, E8), social motivation (‘motivation of project initiators to deal with challenges in the society’ E7; ‘social sensitivity’ E8; ‘balancing individual and communities’ objectives’ E8) and social orientation (‘socio-cultural context of co-creative initiative’; ‘social responsibility’; ‘continuous learning’). In discussion on generated public value two criteria are important in evaluation of digital initiatives – efficiency of problem-solving (‘providing ideas and data to governmental and public institutions’ E7; ‘influence on public opinion’ E9; ‘awareness of the social issues’ E6, E7, E8) and new qualities in form of ideas, structured opinions, etc. (‘number of new ideas, projects’ E8; prototypes can come up from such co-creative initiatives’ E9; ‘ideas can be improved after comments’ E6).

5. Conclusions

Our proposed assessment approach focuses on facilitating a framework to evaluate digital co-creation initiatives aimed at improvement of public spaces and identify cases that can be potentially transformed into co-creative systems. The experts provided their knowledge on how to evaluate the digital co-creation initiatives aimed at creating social innovations in public spaces. Following the logic of theoretical framework, a hierarchical digital co-creation assessment framework (illustrated in Figure 3) consists of three building blocks: Public Open Space Quality, Digital Inclusiveness, and Social Responsiveness. Each dimension reflects from the grouping of different criteria presented in the theoretical framework and additional ones proposed by the experts.

The assessment criteria provide a context for measurable impacts and offer an operational tool to describe and to compare the different public open spaces. The proposed criteria are interdependent and not mutually exclusive. Their relative meaningfulness for a specific evaluation requires further assessment and trade-offs discussed in each case avoiding unnecessary effort and expense. This set of dimensions and criteria used in this paper is limited, but can easily be expanded. The list was not intended to be prescriptive but should offer an organizing framework which can be adapted to the needs of the user.

The assessment is a crucial aspect of the implementation of any initiative, as it provides the context for its impacts to be measurable and offers the operational tools to compare the different cases, as well as the same case before and after the strategy implementation. The proposed methodological framework is mainly concerned with assessing and monitoring the impacts and processes before, during, and after the implementation of cases where co-creation plays a vital role. The evaluation serves as a holistic monitoring and regulatory mechanisms allowing to establish whether the predefined goals have been achieved, to what extent and what areas need to be improved.

6. Limitations & Discussion

Digitally enhanced public open spaces are ideal environments for the social innovations to emerge due to the involvement of stakeholders and ICT in the knowledge creation. The proposed digital co-creation assessment framework focuses on facilitating framework to evaluate digital co-creation initiatives aimed at improvement of public spaces and identify cases that can be potentially transformed into co-creative systems. The framework provides a useful approach for the managers of co-creative initiatives, urban planners and public officials in allowing both quantitative or qualitative dimensions, the results remain explorative in nature. Context specific nature of the social aspects influencing success of co-creative initiatives remains one the main challenges for developing a universal methodology. While this study has certain limitations, they offer opportunities for future research. By testing the framework on real-life case studies and employing a more quantitative approach to evaluation of co-creative initiatives, the methodology will be developed into index-based assessment tool. The methodology provides a useful approach to develop explorative digital co-creation assessments as it allows identifying potential areas of improvement for co-creative initiatives and allows conducting comparable case study research.

References

Baldersheim, H., & Kersting, N. (2012). The wired city: A new face of power? A citizien perspective. In P. Peter, K. Mossberger, S. E. Clarke (Eds.), *The Oxford handbook of urban politics* (pp. 590-606). New York, NY: Oxford University Press.

Bason, C. (2015). *Leading public sector innovation: Co-creating for a better society*. Bristol, UK: Bristol University Press.

Bobenberg, W. (2014). A Method of Assessing Public Space Attractiveness with Use of Google Maps Case of Poznan MA. In J. Charytonowicz (Ed.), Advances in Human Factors and Sustainable Infrastructure 5th International Conference on Applied Human Factors and Ergonomics (pp. 119-127). Orlando, FL: Springer.

Brabham, D. C. (2009). Crowdsourcing the Public Participation Process for Planning Projects. Planning Theory, 8(3), 242-262. https://doi.org/10.1177/1473095209104824

Bulc, V. (2012). New organizational and social paradigm: From cooperation to co-creation and sustainable coexistence. Journal of Organisational Transformation & Social Change, 9(1), 29–39. doi 10.1386/jots.9.1.29_1.

Certomà, C., Dyer, M., Pocatilu, L., & Rizzi, F. (Eds.) (2017). Citizen Empowerment and Innovation in the Data-Rich City. New York, NY: Springer International Publishing.

Cheliotis, K. (2015). Capturing real-time public space activity using publicly available digital traces *(Technical Report No. 16-16).* The Workshops of the Tenth International AAAI Conference on Web and Social Media. Retrieved from https://pdfs.semanticscholar.org/c147/a4fcfeef9b5fb6e032bfd895b35e442bfe3e.pdf

Dabbish, L., Stuart, C., Tsay, J., & Herbsleb, J. (2012) Social coding in GitHub: transparency and collaboration in an open software repository. In CSCW '12 Proceedings of the ACM 2012 Conference on Computer Supported Cooperative Work (pp 1277–1286). New York, NY: ACM.

De Lange, M., & De Waal, M. (2013). Owning the city: New media and citizen engagement in urban design. First Monday, 18(11), 1–14. http://doi.org/10.5210%2Ffm.v18i11.4954

Franz, Y. (2015). Designing social living labs in urban research. Info, 17(4), 53-66. http://doi.org/10.1108/info-01-2015-0008

Griggs, K., & Wild, R. (2013). A Social Networking Adoption Model for Communication and Collaboration in e-Government (Vol. 1). In W. Castelnovo, E. Ferrari (Eds.), Proceedings of thr 13th European Conference on eGovernment (pp. 221-229). Como: Department of Theoretical and Applied Sciences. University of Insubria.

Hoelscher, M., Mildenberger, G., & Bund, E. (2015). A Methodological Framework for Measuring Social Innovation. Historical Social Research, 40(3), 49–78. http://doi.org/10.12759/hsr.40.2015.3.48-78

Jabareen, Y. (2009). Building a conceptual framework: philosophy, definitions, and procedure. International Journal of Qualitative Methods, 8(4), 49–62. https://doi.org/10.1177/160940690900800406

Krippendorff, K. (2003). Content Analysis: An Introduction to Its Methodology. Thousands Oaks, CA: SAGE Publications.

Lester, F. (2005). On the conceptual and philosophical foundations of research in mathematics education. ZDM, 37(6), 457–467. https://doi.org/10.1007/BF02655854

Luo, S., Xia, H., Yoshida, T., & Wang, Z. (2009). Toward Collective Intelligence of Online Communities: A Primitive Conceptual Model. Journal of Systems Science and Systems Engineering, 18(2), 203–221. https://doi.org/10.1007/s11518-009-5095-0

Mačiulienė, M. (2018). Mapping Digital Co-Creation for Urban Communities and Public Places. Systems, 6(14), 1–11. http://doi.org/10.3390/systems6020014

Martinus, K. (2014). Can Public Space be a Platform for Social Innovation? A Study of Sannomiya, Kobe, Japan. Japan Social Innovation Journal, 4(1), 44–54.

Meynhardt, T. (2009). Public value inside: What is public value creation? International Journal of Public Administration, 32(3–4), 192–219. https://doi.org/10.1080/01900690902732632

Millard, J. (2013). ICT-enabled public sector innovation: Trends and prospects. In *ICEGOV '13 Proceedings of the 7th International Conference on Theory and Practice of Electronic Governance* (pp. 77–86). New York, NY: ACM.

Mulder, I. (2012). Living Labbing the Rotterdam Way: Co-Creation as an Enabler for Urban Innovation. Technology Innovation Management Review, 2, 39–43.

Mulder, I., & Stappers, P. J. (2009). Co-creating in Practice : Results and Challenges. In Technology Management Conference (ICE), 2009 IEEE International (pp. 1–8). Leiden: IEEE.

Nouri, A. S., & Costa, J. P. (2017). Placemaking and climate change adaptation: New qualitative and quantitative considerations for the Place Diagram. Journal of Urbanism: International Research on Place Diagram, 10(3), 356–382. https://doi.org/10.1080/17549175.2017.1295096

Patton, M. Q. (2002). Qualitative Evaluation and Research Methods. Thousand Oaks, CA: Sage Publications.

Poplin, A. (2012). Playful public participation in urban planning: A case study for online serious games. Computers, Environment and Urban Systems, 36(3), 195-206. doi: 10.1016/j.compenvurbsys.2011.10.003

Prahalad, C. K., & Ramaswamy, V. (2004). Co-creating unique value with customers. Strategy & Leadership, 32(3), 4–9. http://doi.org/10.1108/10878570410699249

Project for Public Spaces. (2009). What Makes a Successful Place? Available at https://www.pps.org/reference/grplacefeat

Skaržauskienė, A., Ewart, J., Krzywosz-Rynkiewicz, B., Zalewska, A., Leichteris, E., Mačiulis, A., … Valys, T. (2015). Social technologies and collective intelligence. Vilnius: Mykolas Romeris University.

Stewart-Weeks, M. (2010). Social Innovation & The City: What is the Connection between Social Innovation and Urban Innovation … and Why Does it Matter ? What is the connection between Social Innovation & Urban Innovation … and Why Does it Matter? Social Spaces. Available at https://ink.library.smu.edu.sg/lien_research/49

6

Improving Value-at-Risk Estimation from the Normal EGARCH Model

Mahsa Gorji[1], Rasoul Sajjad[2]

ABSTRACT

Returns in financial assets display consistent excess kurtosis and skewness, implying the presence large fluctuations not forecasted by Gaussian models. This paper applies a resampling method bas on the bootstrap and a bias-correction step to improve Value-at-Risk (VaR) forecasting ability of n-EGARCH (normal EGARCH) model and correct the VaR for both long and short positions. Our aim to utilize the advantages of this model, but still use the bootstrap resampling method to accurate the tendency of the model tomiscalculate the VaR. Empirical results indicate that the bias-correcti method can improve the n-GARCH and n-EGARCH VaR forecasts so much that the acquired VaR p dictions are different from the proposed probability. Additionally, allowing asymmetry in the con tional variance using the EGARCH model with normal distribution instead of GARCH improves t performance of the bias-correction method in forecasting the VaR for almost all considered indic Moreover, the bias-corrected n-EGARCH model performs better than the simple t-EGARCH moc Thus, it seems that this model can take account of both the asymmetry in the conditional variar and leptokurtosis in returns distribution. However, we find that the superiority of the bias-correct n-EGARCH model over the t-EGARCH model is not completely confirmed for short positions based the censored likelihood scoring rule.

KEY WORDS: Bootstrap; EGARCH; GARCH; Value-at-Risk

---

[1] Faculty of Finance, University of Raja, Iran [2] Faculty of Finance, University of Essex, Colchester, United Kingdom

1. Introduction

Since the Basle Committee (1995; 1996) began allowing banks to implement internal VaR models for calculating capital requirements, various methods have been proposed to achieve this purpose. However, the theoretical and computational complexity of these methods has also been raised. Furthermore, various methods have been suggested for modeling conditional variance, and a large number of candidate distributions have been considered for modeling empirical features of the returns (Alexander, 2001; Bao, Lee, Saltoğlu, 2007). Although more complex shapes of t tails have the potential preference of increased abiliti to describe the VaR, they may lead to more uncertair in the parameters and hence in the VaR estimate its (Bams, Lehnert, & Wolff, 2005).

The simple method that can consider two chara teristics of financial asset returns, namely time-varyi volatility and excess kurtosis, is the GARCH model Engle (1982) and Bollerslev (1986). Researchers begi ning with Black (1976) have demonstrated that sto returns are negatively correlated with changes in r turn volatility. Nevertheless, symmetric models su

Correspondence concerning this article should be addressed to:
Mahsa Gorji E-mail: m.gorji@hotmail.com

as the GARCH model have difficulties in correctly modeling the tails of the returns distribution (Giot & Laurent, 2003) due to leverage effects. To overcome this shortcoming, various studies have proposed the inclusion different asymmetric terms in the conditional variance equation (Ding, Granger, & Engle, 1993; Engle & Ng, 1993; Glosten, Jagannathan, & Runkle, 1993). Nelson (1991) also proposed the exponential GARCH model, which was re-expressed by Bollerslev and Mikkelsen (1996).

Hartz, Mittnik and Paolella (2006) have developed a resampling method based on the bootstrap and bias-correction for improving the VaR forecasting ability of the n-GARCH (normal GARCH) model. Their proposed method has improved the VaR forecasts of the n-GARCH model. Our main objective is to extend their study by allowing asymmetry in conditional variance. To this end, we apply the n-EGARCH in addition to the n-GARCH model to consider certain theoretical advantages of this model over the n-GARCH. However, Fama (1965) has demonstrated that return distributions of financial instruments are more leptokurtic than normal distributions and tend to be exhibit "fat tails". In addition, empirical studies of high-frequency financial time series demonstrate that the tail behavior of GARCH models remains too short even with standardized Student's t innovations (Tsay, 2005). Therefore, we implement the bias-correction procedure based on the bootstrap method to remove the deficiencies of the n-GARCH and n-EGARCH models with respect to appropriate VaR forecasts. We try to conserve the simplicity of these methods, but still use the bootstrap resampling method to accurate for the tendency of these models to miscalculate the VaR. While Hartz et al. (2006), model the long VaR only, we try to extend their analysis by correcting the VaR for both long and short positions based on the aforementioned GARCH models (n-GARCH and n-EGARCH). Additionally, we evaluate models based on the censored likelihood (csl) scoring rule proposed by Diks, Panchenko, and Van Dijk (2011) in addition to the well-known Christoffersen's LR test. Empirical validation shows that considering asymmetry in conditional variance generally leads to improvements in accurately forecasting one-day-ahead VaR based on the bias-correction method for long and short positions, which is somewhat confirmed by the csl scoring rule.

The rest of the paper is organized as follows. Section 2 explains the methodology for estimating the distribution of the VaR point forecast and how it can be used to improve its accuracy. The empirical analysis and evaluation the performance of competing models in forecasting VaR are presented in Section 3. Finally, Section 4 concludes the paper.

2. Forecasting VaR

In general, for the set of equally spaced asset returns, r_t, $t = 1, \ldots, T$, the class of ARMA(p, q)–EGARCH (r, s) models is given by

$$r_t = a_0 + \sum_{i=1}^{p} a_i r_{t-i} + \varepsilon_t + \sum_{j=1}^{q} b_j \varepsilon_{t-j}, \qquad \varepsilon_t = z_t \sigma_t, \tag{1}$$

$$\ln \sigma_t^2 = c_0 + \sum_{i=1}^{r} c_i ln\sigma_{t-i}^2 + \sum_{j=1}^{s} d_j \left[|z_{t-j}| - E|z_{t-j}| \right] + \sum_{j=1}^{s} \theta_j z_{t-j} \tag{2}$$

where d_j represents the magnitude effect that indicates how much volatility increases autonomously of the direction of the shock. The θ_j is the sign effect. Both z_t and $|z_t| - E|z_t|$ are zero-mean iid sequences with continuous distributions. $E|z_t|$ depends on the assumption made on the unconditional density of z_t. For the standard Gaussian random variable t, $E|z_t| = \sqrt{2/\pi}$. The log of the conditional variance guarantees that forecasts of the conditional variance are non-negative (Nelson, 1991). Some additional properties of the EGARCH model can be found in Nelson (1991).

For a given return series and a chosen model from the n-ARMA-EGARCH class in (1) and (2), the usual conditional VaR forecast is acquired by estimating the unknown parameter vector $\theta = (a_0, \ldots, a_p, b_1, \ldots, b_q, c_0, \ldots, c_r, d_1, \ldots, d_s, \theta_1, \ldots, \theta_s)$ via conditional maximum likelihood.

We also define the set of estimated standardized residuals $\{\hat{z}_t\}$, as $\hat{z}_t = \hat{\varepsilon}_t / \hat{\sigma}_t$, with

$$\hat{\varepsilon}_t = r_t - \hat{a}_0 - (\sum_{i=1}^{p} \hat{a}_i r_{t-i}) - (\sum_{j=1}^{q} \hat{b}_j \hat{\varepsilon}_{t-j}), \tag{3}$$

$$\ln \hat{\sigma}_t^2 = \hat{c}_0 + \sum_{i=1}^{r} \hat{c}_i ln\hat{\sigma}_{t-i}^2 + \sum_{j=1}^{s} \hat{d}_j \left[|\hat{z}_{t-j}| - E|\hat{z}_{t-j}| \right] + \sum_{j=1}^{s} \hat{\theta}_j \hat{z}_{t-j} \tag{4}$$

then the h-step-ahead (time horizon, $h \in \mathbb{Z}$) VaR forecast is obtained by

$$\hat{v}_\lambda = \hat{v}_\lambda(h, T) = \Phi^{-1}(\lambda; \hat{\mu}_{T+h}, \hat{\sigma}_{T+h}^2), \tag{5}$$

where $\Phi^{-1}(\lambda;\mu,\sigma^2)$, indicates the inverse cdf of the standard normal distribution with mean μ variance σ^2 and λ, a given probability level, and

$$\hat{\mu}_{T+h} = \hat{a}_0 + \sum_{i=1}^{p}\hat{a}_i r_{T+h-i} + \sum_{j=1}^{q}\hat{b}_j\hat{\varepsilon}_{T+h-j}\,, \tag{6}$$

$$\ln\hat{\sigma}^2_{T+h} = \hat{c}_0 + \sum_{i=1}^{r}\hat{c}_i ln\hat{\sigma}^2_{T+h-i} + \sum_{j=1}^{s}\hat{d}_j\left[\left|\hat{z}_{T+h-j}\right| - E\left|z_{t-j}\right|\right] + \sum_{j=1}^{s}\hat{\theta}_j\hat{z}_{T+h-j} \tag{7}$$

The VaR for a short position is similarly computed where the same definition is used for the right tail of the distribution function, i.e., $1-\lambda$ substitutes for λ.

2.1. VaR forecast distribution

For implementing the bias-correction method we need to estimate VaR forecast distribution in addition to a VaR point estimator ($\hat{v}_\lambda$). Therefore, as Hartz et al. (2006) proposed, we apply the bootstrap method to this end. This method coincides with that described in Pascual, Romo and Ruiz (2006), Reeves (2005) and Trucíos and Hotta (2016). It is connected to the filtered historical simulation method proposed by Barone-Adesi, Giannopoulos and Vosper (1999; 2002) and the bootstrap methodology described by Dowd (2005).

Despite that the sampling distribution of the VaR point forecast is unknown and intangible, the bootstrap method provides the possibility for its approximation. Because, assuming the true data generating process is constant over time, the bias caused by the use of the inappropriate but simple n-GARCH model will display certain regularities and thus can be corrected based on a set of past VaR bootstrap distributions (Hartz et al., 2006). This is the assumption used in the bias-correction method described in Section 2.2.

For implementing B bootstrap iterations, the bth replication, b = 1, . . . , B, we should consider the following steps as Hartz et al. (2006) suggested:

Step 0: For a chosen set of values p, q, r, s (for which $p = r = s = 1$ and $q = 0$ is most common), obtain QML parameter vector estimate $\hat{\theta}$, estimated standardized residuals $\{\hat{z}_t\}$, then forecast VaR for a certain h (we consider h=1) by (5).

Step 1: Simulate the (b')th of B, n-ARMA(p, q)-EGARCH(r, s) time series, $\{r_t^{(b')}\}$, of length T, using the estimated parameter vector $\hat{\theta}$ and bootstrapped standardized residuals sequence $\{\hat{z}_t^{(b')}\}$. To eliminate the effect of initial values, we simulate $T+\ell$ series and then discard first ℓ observations ($\ell=T$).

Step 2: Obtain the QML parameter vector estimat $\hat{\theta}^{(b')}$ based on n-ARMA(p, q)-EGARCH(r, s) using th simulated time series $\{r_t^{(b')}\}$.

Step 3: Estimate a resampled VaR estimate, $\hat{v}_\lambda^{(b)}(h,T)$ using the *original series* $\{r_t\}$, and the bootstrap param eter vector estimate $\hat{\theta}^{(b')}$, via

$$\hat{\varepsilon}_t^{(b)} = r_t - \hat{a}_0^{(b)} - (\sum_{i=1}^{p}\hat{a}_i^{(b)}r_{t-i}) - (\sum_{j=1}^{q}\hat{b}_j^{(b)}\hat{\varepsilon}_{t-j}^{(b)}),\quad t = 1,\ldots,T,$$

$$\ln\hat{\sigma}_t^{2(b)} = \hat{c}_0^{(b)} + \sum_{i=1}^{r}\hat{c}_i^{(b)}ln\hat{\sigma}_{t-i}^{2(b)} + \sum_{j=1}^{s}\hat{d}_j^{(b)}\left[\left|\hat{z}_{t-j}^{(b)}\right| - E\left|z_{t-j}\right|\right] + $$

$$+\sum_{j=1}^{s}\hat{\theta}_j^{(b)}\hat{z}_{t-j}^{(b)}$$

and to calculate bootstrapped VaR forecast

$$\hat{v}_\lambda^{(b)}(h,T) = \Phi^{-1}\left(\lambda, \hat{\mu}_{T+h}^{(b)}, \hat{\sigma}_{T+h}^{2(b)}\right),$$

where

$$\hat{\mu}_{T+h}^{(b)} = \hat{a}_0^{(b)} + \sum_{i=1}^{p}\hat{a}_i^{(b)}r_{T+h-i} + \sum_{j=1}^{q}\hat{b}_j^{(b)}\hat{\varepsilon}_{T+h-j}^{(b)}\,,$$

$$\ln\hat{\sigma}_{T+h}^{2(b)} = \hat{c}_0^{(b)} + \sum_{i=1}^{r}\hat{c}_i^{(b)}ln\hat{\sigma}_{T+h-i}^{2(b)} + \sum_{j=1}^{s}\hat{d}_j^{(b)}\left[\left|\hat{z}_{T+h-j}^{(b)}\right| - E\left|z_{t-j}\right|\right] + $$

$$+\sum_{j=1}^{s}\hat{\theta}_j^{(b)}\hat{z}_{T+h-j}^{(b)},$$

are calculated using conditional expectations for unobserved values.

The primary VaR prediction, $\hat{v}_\lambda^{(0)}$, and the B bootstrapped VaR predictions, $\hat{v}_\lambda^{(b)}$, b=1,..., B, can be used to construct an empirical distribution function of VaR estimation. This function is given by

$$\hat{F}_{\hat{k}}(a;\lambda,h,T) = \frac{1}{B+1}\sum_{b=0}^{B}\psi_{(-\infty,a)}(\hat{v}_\lambda^{(b)}(h,T)), \tag{8}$$

where $\psi(.)$ is the indicator function. This function could be used to construct a bootstrap confidence interval for the VaR; for instance Christoffersen and Goncalves (2005) propose to use the bootstrap for constructing confidence intervals of a conditional VaR estimator. Nieto and Ruiz (2010) suggest a new bootstrap procedure to obtain prediction intervals of future VaR and Expected Shortfall (ES), as well. We use the bootstrap method as described in the previous section to obtain a more accurate VaR based on n-GARCH models (n-GARCH and n-EGARCH) as much as possible.

2.2. Bias-correcting VaR forecasts

The corrective method uses the VaR distributions (approximated based on the illustrated bootstrapped method) and an objective function, which is described by definition of the VaR. The VaR is defined to be the worst possible loss from an investment over a target horizon and for a given probability level (Crouhy, Galai, & Mark, 2001). Therefore, the evident criterion to construct this function is the observed frequency of exceptions, or past realized returns that are less (higher) than or equal to the predicted VaR for long (short) positions.

For a given probability level λ, the observed frequency of exceptions, denoted $\hat{f}$, for a set of successive VaR predictions for long positions obtained from the usual n-GARCH models between times, say, τ_1 and τ_2, and the equivalent realized returns is given by

$$\hat{f} = \frac{1}{\tau_2 - \tau_1 + 1}\sum_{t=\tau_1}^{\tau_2}\psi_{(-\infty,\hat{v}(t)]}\left(r_{t+h}\right), \qquad \hat{v}(t) = \hat{v}_\lambda(h,t) \tag{9}$$

The observed frequency of exceptions for a short position is similarly computed where the same definition is used for the right tail of the distribution function, i.e., $\psi_{[\hat{v}(t),+\infty)}$ substitutes for $\psi_{(-\infty,\hat{v}(t)]}$.

The observed frequency of exceptions is less (higher) than the real risk level λ, if the VaR forecasts calculated by the n-GARCH models tend to overestimate (underestimate) the risk. Therefore, the logic behind the bias-correction method is to find the quantile of past VaR distributions which causes observed frequency of exceptions conforms to (as close as possible) a given risk level.

Let $\{\hat{v}_\lambda^{[b]}(h,t)\}_{b=0}^{B}$ be the sorted VaR predictions, with length $(B+1)$ produced by the resampling algorithm with the original n-GARCH models forecast, $\hat{v}_\lambda^{(0)}(h,t)$, added, i.e., $\hat{v}_\lambda^{[b]}(h,t) \le \hat{v}_\lambda^{[b+1]}(h,t)$ for $b = 0, \ldots, B-1$. Calculating the correct quantile of the VaR distribution $\hat{F}_{\hat{k}}$ is equivalent to find the largest index b for the long VaR (the smallest for the short VaR), denoted b^*, such that for the conforming series $\{\hat{v}_\lambda^{[b^*]}(h,t)\}_{t=\tau_1}^{\tau_2}$, the observed frequency of exceptions is less than or equal to the given risk level. Therefore, we need a certain number of past VaR distribution predictions that precede the actual VaR prediction of interest. As Hartz et al. (2006) have described, we consider a moving window procedure for finding the proper quantile of the VaR distribution produced by the resampling algorithm. Common to all models is the construction of a moving window in which the model is recalculated for each window period, removing the first observations and adding new ones as the window advances. L is the fixed number of preceding VaR forecast distributions that we consider for finding the proper quantile for the h-step-ahead prediction for the downfall risk made at time T. Accordingly, the optimal quantile is described as

$$b^* = \max\{b : b \in \{0,1,\ldots,B\}\}\ s.t. \frac{1}{L}\sum_{t=T-L-h+1}^{T-h}\psi_{(-\infty,\hat{v}^{[b]}(h,t))}\left(r_{t+h}\right) \le \lambda. \tag{10}$$

where b^* denotes the greatest quantile of the last L feasible VaR distributions for which the conforming series of VaR predictions, $\left\{\hat{v}_\lambda^{[b^*]}(h,t)\right\}$, leads to an observed frequency of VaR exceptions that is equal to (or just smaller) than the given risk level. The b^* for a short position is similarly computed where it determines the smallest quantile of the VaR distributions and the $\psi_{(\hat{v}^{[b]}(h,t),\infty)}$ substitutes for $\psi_{(-\infty,\hat{v}^{[b]}(h,t))}$.

As the data generating process is not constant over time, calculating an optimal L would be reliable only for particular segment of a particular data set (Hartz et al., 2006). Thus, following the suggestion of Hartz et al. (2006) concerning the choice of L, we assume two sizes of the moving window (L) to examine whether this criterion could affect the results of our study.

We consider two values, L=250 and 500, (one and two years of trading data, respectively) to perform the bias-correction method.

3. Empirical analysis

We consider the daily percentage log-return series, defined by $r_t = (\ln p_t - \ln p_{t-1}) \times 100$, where p_t is the closing price index on day t. The data set analyzed in this paper comprises daily observations on three major stock market indices' returns; namely, the FTSE Composite, NIKKEI 225 and CAC (hereafter the FTSE, NIKKEI and CAC). The starting date for the series are August 27, 1999 for the FTSE; April 09, 1999 for the NIKKEI; and November 05, 1999 for the CAC.

The usual descriptive statistics of the data are given in Table 1. The moments of the stock index returns are shown along with the results of an aggregate autocorrelation (Ljung-Box) test for returns and their squares. As seen, for the FTSE and NIKKEI the skewness is significant and negative, indicating a possible leverage

Table 1. Moments of the FTSE, NIKKEI and CAC returns along with aggregate autocorrelation test results.

	FTSE	NIKKEI	CAC
Mean	0.0008	-0.004	-0.007
Minimum	-9.26	-12.11	-9.47
Maximum	9.38	13.23	10.59
Std. Dev.	1.276	1.565	1.550
Skewness	-0.126	-0.419	0.028
Kurtosis	8.715	9.361	7.540
	Ljung-Box test for returns		
Q-stat(12)	78.81	13.85	56.95
	{0}	{0.31}	{0}
Q-stat(24)	102.2	44.34	71.28
	{0}	{0.007}	{0}
Q-stat(36)	153.52	61.00	120.97
	{0}	{0.006}	{0}
	Ljung-Box test for squared returns		
Q-stat(12)	2797	3051	1988
	{0}	{0}	{0}
Q-stat(24)	4340	3860	3138
	{0}	{0}	{0}
Q-stat(36)	5351	4114	3907
	{0}	{0}	{0}

Note:
p-values in curly braces.
Q-stat (*q*) denotes a modified Ljung-Box type statistic.

effect in data, but for the CAC the skewness is positive, and the kurtosis is significantly higher than that of a Gaussian distribution (excess kurtosis), indicating fat-tailed returns for all series. This suggests the need for a fat-tailed distribution, for example Student's *t*, to describe the returns' conditional distribution. Furthermore, imposing an asymmetric parameter in the conditional variance equation enables us to capture possible leverage effects in the data. In addition, the large Q-statistics up to 12, 24 and 36 orders strongly reject the null hypothesis of no serial correlation in both returns and squared returns for the FTSE and CAC but only in returns for the NIKKEI index.

The estimation period is set to $T = 1000$, which corresponds to about four years of daily returns data for estimating the parameters of models. $B = 1000$ bootstrap replications are used for calculating the VaR forecast distributions.

For each series, we use $p = 2000$ out-of-sample values, and the last forecast is made for July 16, 2013 for ach series. The models are used to estimate one-day-ahead VaR (h=1) of both long and short trading positions (left and right tails of returns distribution) with different probabilities (at different tail quantiles): 0.5%, %, 5%, 95%, 99% and 99.5%.

For implementing the bias-correction method, we use the two values L = 250 and 500. So, an additional number of L=500 VaR forecast distributions resulting in a total of P +L=2500 VaR forecast distributions are considered.

In addition to the n-AR(1)-GARCH(1,1) and n-AR(1)-EGARCH(1,1) models, we consider the AR(1)-EGARCH(1,1) with the Generalized Error Distribution (GED) and t-AR(1)-EGARCH(1,1) (with Student's t innovations) to assess the performance of the bias-correction method.[1] The original form of this model is used for the comparison due to its ability to consider the asymmetry in the conditional variance and the excess kurtosis relative to the normal distribution. In this model, the conditional variance obtained is similar to the n-EGARCH model (i.e., Equation (2)), while the $E|z_t|$ for a Student's t distribution with $\upsilon > 2$ degrees of freedom is given by

$$E\left(|z_t|\right) = \frac{2\sqrt{\upsilon-2}\,\Gamma((\upsilon+1)/2)}{(\upsilon-1)\Gamma(\upsilon/2)\sqrt{\pi}}, \tag{11}$$

where $\Gamma(x)$ is the usual gamma function.

The corresponding VaR prediction for the t-AR(1)-EGARCH(1,1) model is given by

$$\hat{v}_\lambda = \hat{v}_\lambda\left(h,T\right) = \hat{\mu}_{T+h} + \hat{\sigma}_{T+h} F_t^{-1}\left(\lambda;\hat{\upsilon}\right), \tag{12}$$

where $F_t^{-1}(\lambda;\, \upsilon)$ is the inverse of the cumulative distribution function of the t-distribution with υ degrees of freedom and a standardized variance of one.

In the remainder of the paper, we first examine the VaR forecast distributions generated by the bootstrap algorithm. Then, we compare the VaR estimations of the competing models.

3.1. VaR forecast distribution

Figures 1–3 present the first VaR forecast distributions included in our analysis for the FTSE, NIKKEI and CAC for both long and short trading positions. The upper part of the figures refers to the VaR forecast distribution for the n-GARCH model, while the lower part of the figures refers to the VaR forecast distribution for the n-EGARCH model. Additionally, the vertical lines exhibit the usual n-GARCH and n-EGARCH VaR predictions, $\hat{v}^0$.

As seen from figures 1, 2 and 3, the risk in VaR forecasts for both long and short trading positions increases for smaller probability levels. The usual VaR predictions do not exactly coincide with the mode of the VaR forecast distributions. For instance, for the first VaR forecasts made for all series, the usual n-EGARCH VaR forecasts are smaller than the mode of the VaR forecast distributions for both long and short trading positions. On the other hand, the first VaR forecasts for all series from the usual n-GARCH model for short trading position are greater than the mode of the corresponding VaR forecast distributions.

3.2. Performance of Models in Forecasting VaR

For assessing the accuracy of competing methods, we define the Boolean sequence as

$$I_{t+1} = \psi_{(-\infty,\hat{v}_\lambda(1,t))}\left(r_{t+1}\right), \tag{13}$$

where $\hat{v}_\lambda(1,t)$ is one-step-ahead VaR predictions for λ, a given probability level, and r_{t+1} is the observed return. Christoffersen (1998) showed that evaluating interval forecasts can be reduced to examining whether the Boolean sequence, $\{I_t\}_{t=1}^{T}$, satisfies the unconditional coverage (UC) and independence (IND) properties.

Let $T_1 = \sum_{t=1}^{T} I_{t+1}$, the number of violations, and the failure rate be expressed as $\hat{f} = T^{-1}\sum_{t=1}^{T} I_{t+1} = T_1/T$. For testing the UC, the proper likelihood ratio statistic, also called the Kupiec (1995) LR unconditional test, (under the null hypothesis that, $\hat{f} = \lambda$) is

$$LR_{uc} = 2\ln\left[(1-\hat{f})^{T-T_1}(\hat{f})^{T_1}\right] - 2\ln\left[(1-\lambda)^{T-T_1}(\lambda)^{T_1}\right] \sim \chi_1^2,$$

$$P_{un} = 1 - F_{\chi_1^2}\left(LR_{un}\right), \tag{14}$$

For P_{un} below the desired significance level, the null hypothesis is rejected.

The LR_{cc} test adapted from Christoffersen (1998) is used to test the conditional coverage.

We compare models based on the p-values, and models with higher p-values are preferred.

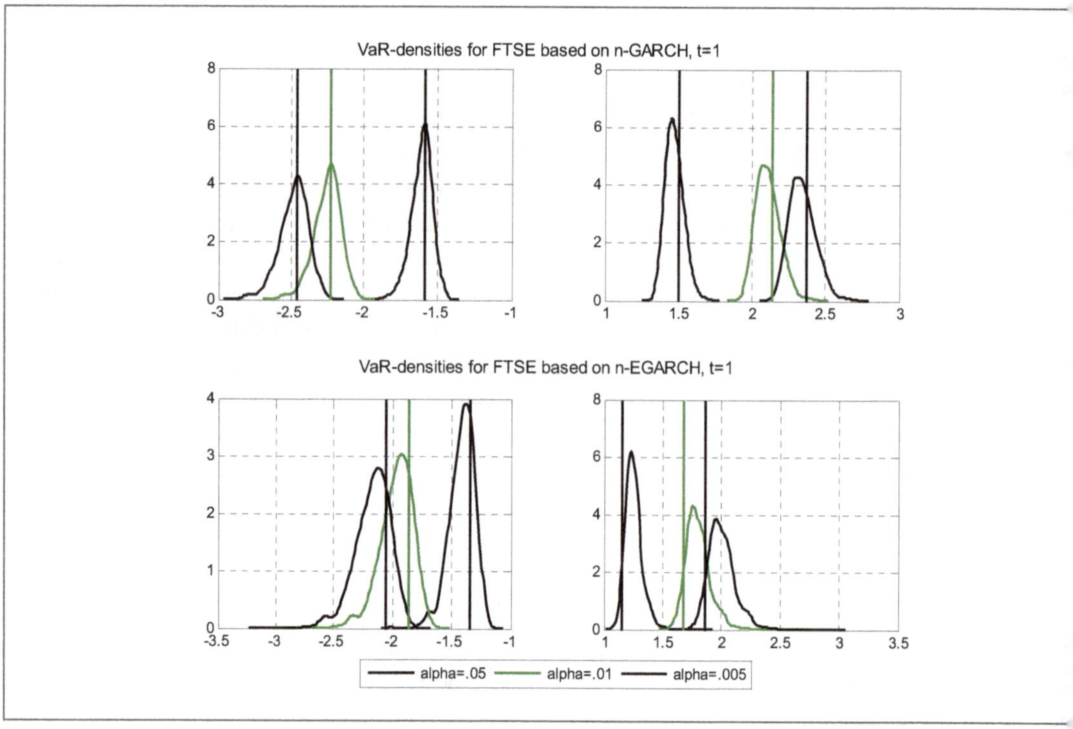

Figure 1. Vertical lines refer to the usual n-GARCH and n-EGARCH VaR predictions, $\hat{v}^0$. VaR forecast distributions for the first forecast - FTSE.

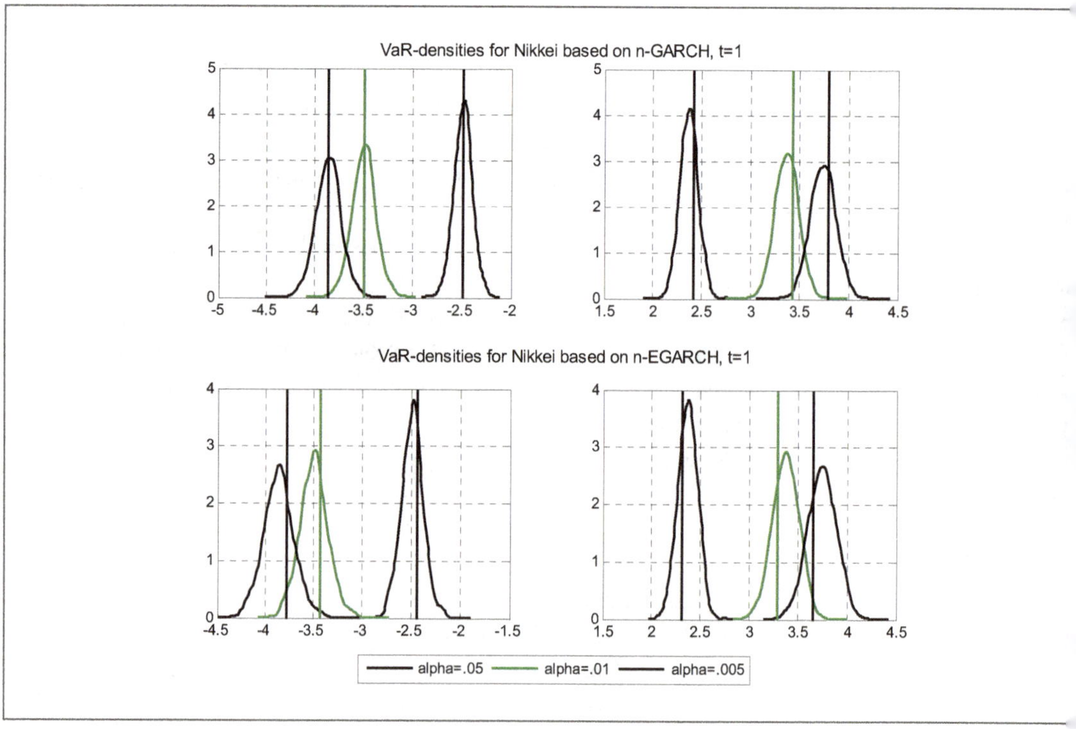

Figure 2. Vertical lines refer to the usual n-GARCH and n-EGARCH VaR predictions, $\hat{v}^0$. VaR forecast distributions for the first forecast - NIKKEI.

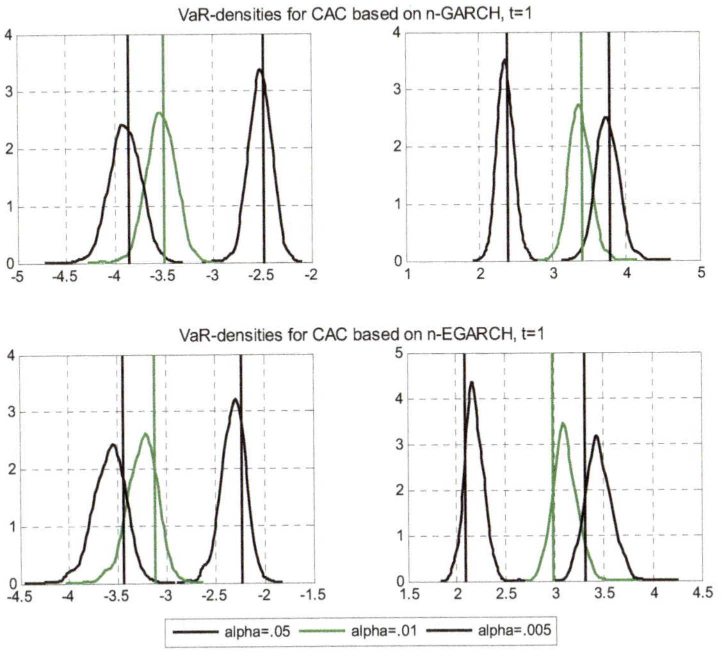

ure 3. Vertical lines refer to the usual n-GARCH and n-EGARCH VaR predictions, $\hat{v}^0$. VaR forecast distributions for the : forecast - CAC.

In addition to unconditional and conditional tests we consider a csl scoring rule suggested by Diks et al. (2011) to assess the performance of the bias-correction method. They have shown that this scoring rule is handy as the main interest lies in comparing the accuracy of density forecasts for a specific region, such as the left tail in financial risk management. While they have considered long VaR only, we also evaluate our models for both long and short positions. The censored likelihood (csl) score function is given by

$$S^{csl}(\hat{a}_t; r_{t+1}) = w_t(r_{t+1}) \log \hat{a}_t(r_{t+1}) + \\ +(1 - w_t(r_{t+1})) \log(1 - \int w_t(s)\hat{a}_t(s)ds), \quad (15)$$

$$d_{t+1}^{csl} = S^{csl}(\hat{a}_t; r_{t+1}) - S^{csl}(\hat{b}_t; r_{t+1}),$$

where $\hat{a}_t$ and $\hat{b}_t$ are two competing density forecasts and $w_t(r)$ is a threshold weight function $w_t(r) = I(r \le \hat{v}_t^{\alpha})$. Additionally, corresponding realizations of the variable r_{t+1} are accessible for $t = n, n+1, \ldots, T\text{-}1$. Then, $\hat{a}_t$ and $\hat{b}_t$ are comparable based on their average scores difference *d*, by testing if their difference is statistically significant[2].

In the following, we first concentrate on the measures LR_{cc}, LR_{ind} and LR_{uc}. The results for the seven competing models are given in Tables 2–4 for the FTSE, NIKKEI and CAC.

We first examine the capability of the bias-correction procedure to improve the VaR forecasts of the usual n-GARCH and n-EGARCH models. Comparing the forecasts from the usual models with the bias-corrected forecasts, we find that the P_{uc}-values for at least five out of the 6 specified probabilities for $L = 500$ are superior (larger) to those for the usual n-GARCH model, while for the n-EGARCH model the *p*-values for at least four out of the 6 cases for both window lengths are superior to those for the usual n-EGARCH model.

We found no P_{uc}-values below the 5% significance level for the bias-corrected VaR predictions of the n-EGARCH model with $L = 500$ for all series except the NIKKEI at 99%, while for the usual VaR forecasts, we

Table 2. Unconditional coverage, independence, conditional coverage—FTSE.

VaR models	$\hat{f}$	***p*-values**			$\hat{f}$	***p*-values**			
		P_{cc}	P_{ind}	P_{un}		P_{cc}	P_{ind}	P_{un}	***/**/*****
	VaR 5%				VaR 95%				
$\hat{f}_N$	0.0645	0.0133	0.4802	0.0043	0.0420	0.0600	0.0952	0.0918	5/3/3
$\hat{f}^*_{N-500}$	0.0545	0.4343	0.3598	0.3624	0.0495	0.0794	0.0245	0.9182	2/1/0
$\hat{f}_{EGARCH}$	0.0605	0.1052	0.7070	0.0367	0.0435	0.0803	0.0742	0.1730	4/4/2
$\hat{f}^*_{EGARCH-500}$	0.0505	0.6627	0.3674	0.9184	0.0520	0.1870	0.0742	0.6834	0/0/0
$\hat{f}_{t-EGARCH}$	0.0650	0.0120	0.6866	0.0032	0.0450	0.0951	0.0572	0.2970	5/5/4
	VaR 1%				VaR 99%				
$\hat{f}_N$	0.0210	<0.0001	0.2852	<0.0001	0.0070	0.3258	0.6456	0.1541	
$\hat{f}^*_{N-500}$	0.0145	0.0321	0.0699	0.0581	0.0130	0.3054	0.3990	0.1974	
$\hat{f}_{EGARCH}$	0.0205	0.0001	0.7898	<0.0001	0.0075	0.4440	0.6229	0.2397	
$\hat{f}^*_{EGARCH-500}$	0.0135	0.2235	0.3813	0.1353	0.0120	0.5049	0.4357	0.3835	
$\hat{f}_{t-EGARCH}$	0.0210	<0.0001	0.8094	<0.0001	0.0050	0.0429	0.7395	0.0129	
	VaR 0.5%				VaR 99.5%				
$\hat{f}_N$	0.0155	<0.0001	0.4905	<0.0001	0.0025	0.2111	0.8623	0.0792	
$\hat{f}^*_{N-500}$	0.0095	0.0331	0.5356	0.0112	0.0070	0.4403	0.6456	0.2319	
$\hat{f}_{EGARCH}$	0.0115	0.0015	0.4548	0.0004	0.0020	0.0950	0.8874	0.0304	
$\hat{f}^*_{EGARCH-500}$	0.0060	0.7654	0.6920	0.5388	0.0045	0.9074	0.7636	0.7471	
$\hat{f}_{t-EGARCH}$	0.0120	0.0006	0.4357	0.0001	0.0010	0.0082	0.9382	0.0020	

Note: $\hat{f}_N$: *observed downfall probability for n-AR(1)-GARCH(1,1) model;* $\hat{f}_{EGARCH}$: *observed downfall probability for n-AR EGARCH(1,1) model;* $\hat{f}_{t-EGARCH}$ *: observed downfall probability for t-AR(1)-EGARCH(1,1) model;* $\hat{f}^*_{N-500}$ ($\hat{f}^*_{EGARCH-500}$)*: observed dov fall probability for calibrated n-AR(1)-GARCH(1,1) (n-AR(1)-EGARCH(1,1)) model with L=500;* P_{un} (P_{ind}, P_{cc})*: probability of observ a sample with higher unconditional coverage test statistic (independence test statistic, conditional coverage test statistic). The res for both long and short positions are reported in the left and right panel of the table, respectively. */**/***: Number of p-values unconditional coverage are smaller than 0.10/0.05/0.01.*

have at least 2 *p*-values below the 1% level and one *p*-value below the 0.01%.

The results show that the usual VaR models based on normal innovations have difficulties with modeling large returns. In particular, the usual normal GARCH models consistently underestimate the return (risk) for all series for long positions. In other words, failure numbers are much greater than expected at a given quantile in the case of normal innovations.

Regarding independence of the VaR exceptions over time, for both the usual n-GARCH and n-EGARCH VaR forecast violations or those from the bias-correce 3. Unconditional coverage, independence, conditional coverage—NIKKEI.

els	$\hat{f}$	p-values			$\hat{f}$	p-values			
		P_{cc}	P_{ind}	P_{un}		P_{cc}	P_{ind}	P_{un}	*/**/***
	VaR 5%				VaR 95%				
	0.0605	0.1024	0.6599	0.0367	0.0430	0.2589	0.4619	0.1415	5/5/3
)0	0.0540	0.4759	0.3629	0.4175	0.0570	0.2923	0.4874	0.1596	0/0/0
RCH	0.0595	0.1415	0.5720	0.0581	0.0550	0.2789	0.2157	0.3123	4/2/2
RCH−500	0.0555	0.3158	0.3001	0.2671	0.0595	0.0537	0.1329	0.0581	2/1/0
ARCH	0.0620	0.0552	0.7064	0.0174	0.0555	0.1617	0.1204	0.2671	4/3/1
	VaR 1%				VaR 99%				
	0.0160	0.0123	0.1036	0.0131	0.0045	0.0205	0.7636	0.0056	
00	0.0125	0.3355	0.3138	0.2794	0.0130	0.3054	0.3990	0.1974	
RCH	0.0220	<0.0001	0.3342	<0.0001	0.0070	0.3258	0.6456	0.1541	
RCH−500	0.0130	0.2771	0.3413	0.1974	0.0150	0.0242	0.0801	0.0364	
ARCH	0.0180	0.0049	0.6493	0.0012	0.0055	0.0812	0.7156	0.0270	
	VaR 0.5%				VaR 99.5%				
	0.0100	0.0087	0.1918	0.0053	0.0010	0.0082	0.9382	0.0020	
00	0.0060	0.1392	0.0590	0.5388	0.0065	0.6037	0.6686	0.3634	
RCH	0.0110	0.0023	0.2373	0.0010	0.0025	0.2111	0.8623	0.0792	
RCH−500	0.0050	0.1172	0.0384	1.0000	0.0070	0.4403	0.6456	0.2319	
ARCH	0.0075	0.0866	0.0993	0.1401	0.0025	0.2111	0.8623	0.0792	

e: See the legend of Table 2 for explanations.

tion method, independence cannot be rejected; in other words, the occurrence of violations for VaR forecasts have no systematic pattern.

Considering the conditional coverage test statistic, we see that, for all series, the p-values for at least five out of the six specified probabilities for $L = 500$ are superior to those for the usual n-GARCH model, while for the n-EGARCH model the p-values for at least four out of the six cases for both window lengths are superior to those for the usual n-EGARCH model. Summarizing the results for the conditional coverage, the bias-correction method can improve the n-GARCH and n-EGARCH VaR forecasts so much that the VaR predictions acquired are different from the proposed probability.

Comparing the unconditional coverage results for the bias-correction method based on the n-EGARCH model with those based on the n-GARCH model, we

Table 4. Unconditional coverage, independence, conditional coverage—CAC.

VaR models	$\hat{f}$	*p*-values			$\hat{f}$	*p*-values			
		P_{cc}	P_{ind}	P_{un}		P_{cc}	P_{ind}	P_{un}	*/**/
	VaR 5%				VaR 95%				
$\hat{f}_N$	0.0760	<0.0001	0.5474	<0.0001	0.0400	0.0335	0.1306	0.0338	4/4/
$\hat{f}^*_{N-500}$	0.0575	0.2389	0.4389	0.1324	0.0520	0.0469	0.0147	0.6834	1/0/
$\hat{f}_{EGARCH}$	0.0715	0.0001	0.4849	<0.0001	0.0450	0.0951	0.0572	0.2970	3/3/
$\hat{f}^*_{EGARCH-500}$	0.0520	0.4741	0.2495	0.6834	0.0485	0.3093	0.1335	0.7571	0/0/
$\hat{f}_{t-EGARCH}$	0.0750	<0.0001	0.3454	<0.0001	0.0455	0.0981	0.0523	0.3487	3/3/
	VaR 1%				VaR 99%				
$\hat{f}_N$	0.0200	0.0001	0.1957	<0.0001	0.0095	0.8045	0.5356	0.8207	
$\hat{f}^*_{N-500}$	0.0095	0.8045	0.5356	0.8207	0.0145	0.1067	0.3474	0.0581	
$\hat{f}_{EGARCH}$	0.0215	<0.0001	0.1643	<0.0001	0.0115	0.4289	0.2617	0.5102	
$\hat{f}^*_{EGARCH-500}$	0.0135	0.2235	0.3813	0.1353	0.0120	0.3883	0.2873	0.3835	
$\hat{f}_{t-EGARCH}$	0.0185	0.0014	0.2313	0.0006	0.0080	0.1875	0.1153	0.3517	
	VaR 0.5%				VaR 99.5%				
$\hat{f}_N$	0.0100	0.0166	0.5148	0.0053	0.0060	0.7654	0.6920	0.5388	
$\hat{f}^*_{N-500}$	0.0055	0.8913	0.7156	0.7551	0.0060	0.7654	0.6920	0.5388	
$\hat{f}_{EGARCH}$	0.0145	<0.0001	0.3474	<0.0001	0.0055	0.8913	0.7156	0.7551	
$\hat{f}^*_{EGARCH-500}$	0.0065	0.6037	0.6686	0.3634	0.0050	0.9462	0.7395	1.0000	
$\hat{f}_{t-EGARCH}$	0.0110	0.0036	0.4744	0.0010	0.0050	0.9462	0.7395	1.0000	

Note: See the legend of Table 2 for explanations.

conclude that the n-EGARCH model outperforms the n-GARCH model as for all but the NIKKEI index: the *p*-values for at least four out of the six specified probabilities are superior to those for the n-GARCH model with $L = 500$. Similar results hold for the conditional coverage test statistic for all series. Additionally, the bias-correction method based on the n-EGARCH model is the only model never rejected by any of the three performance tests of Christoffersen (1998) for all the specified probabilities (even at 99.5% and 0.5% tails) and considered indices.

Consequently, the bias-correction method based on the n-EGARCH model leads to an acceptable performance for out-of-sample VaR prediction. In other words, it seems that allowing for an asymmetric response of the conditional variance to positive and negative shocks generally yields improvement in the VaR performance of the bias-correction method. Therefore, ble 5. Average score differences and tests of equal predictive accuracy for the censored likelihood (csl).

	FTSE	NIKKEI	CAC	FTSE	NIKKEI	CAC
	VaR 5%			VaR 95%		
$_{, 500}$	-0.0507	-0.0401	-0.0720	-0.1252	-0.2692	-0.1791
st stat.	-5.8568	-4.4134	-0.0001	-0.0023	-0.0004	-0.0018
$_{GARCH,500}$	-0.0569	-0.0181	-0.0793	-0.0179	-0.1373	-0.0395
st stat.	-6.4187	-4.6009	-0.0001	-4.2077	-0.0002	-0.0002
$_{,EGARCH-500}$	-0.0007	0.0204	-0.0059	-0.0539	-0.0976	-0.1273
st stat.	-8.2003	2.6194	-8.8945	-6.0130	-5.2386	-8.6942
$_{GARCH\_t,500}$	-0.0259	0.0283	-0.0540	0.0519	-0.1897	-0.0572
st stat.	-2.3995	1.8529	-6.6502	8.7729	-0.0001	-2.6532
	VaR 1%			VaR 99%		
$_{, 500}$	-0.0478	-0.0268	-0.0521	-0.4432	-0.6463	-0.3534
st stat.	-5.7177	-5.3513	-0.0001	-0.0010	-0.0005	-0.0004
$_{GARCH,500}$	-0.0572	-0.0057	-0.0392	-0.2748	-0.5455	-0.1229
st stat.	-3.9568	-3.9915	-0.0001	-0.0007	-0.0002	-0.0002
$_{,EGARCH-500}$	-0.0100	0.0031	0.0270	-0.0688	-0.2125	-0.2187
st stat.	-1.3473	1.5694	7.7423	-2.0162	-2.6433	-4.2149
$_{GARCH\_t,500}$	-0.0272	-0.0002	-0.0046	0.4595	-0.1076	0.3828
st stat.	-5.9952	-3.5245	-1.2083	2.7004	-2.0393	5.2561
	VaR 0.5%			VaR 99.5%		
$_{, 500}$	-0.0358	-0.0386	-0.0269	-0.5041	-0.7674	-0.1196
st stat.	-0.0002	-7.3189	-0.0002	-0.0005	-0.0004	-4.7315
$_{GARCH,500}$	-0.0446	-0.0066	-0.0457	-0.3150	-0.5415	0.4784
st stat.	-6.0635	-4.0795	-0.0001	-0.0004	-0.0003	0.0001
$_{,EGARCH-500}$	-0.0244	0.0019	0.0079	-0.0574	-0.1053	0.0808
st stat.	-3.4634	1.6062	5.2479	-1.3984	-2.5569	8.9946
$_{GARCH\_t,500}$	-0.0249	0.0062	-0.0116	0.7539	0.1648	1.2717
st stat.	-8.1588	1.0638	-2.7084	2.9685	1.3557	5.5332

ote: $d_{N,500}$ ($d_{EGARCH,500}$): average score difference based on n-AR(1)-GARCH(1,1) (n-AR(1)-EGARCH(1,1)) model relative to calibrated n-AR(1)-GARCH(1,1) (n-AR(1)-EGARCH(1,1)) model with L=500; $d_{N,EGARCH-500}$: average score difference for calibrated n-R(1)-GARCH(1,1) relative to calibrated n-AR(1)-EGARCH(1,1) model with L=500; $d_{EGARCH\_t,500}$: average score difference for t-R(1)-EGARCH(1,1) model relative to calibrated n-AR(1)-EGARCH(1,1) model with L=500. Additionally, the corresponding test atistics are shown. The results for both long and short positions are reported in the left and right panel of the table, respectively.

this probably tells us that considering asymmetry in conditional variance is crucial in determining a proper value of VaR.

The results slightly prefer the longer window of length $L = 500$, with a higher number of greater p-values and a smaller number of significant test statistics. Because the results hold for all series, we can say that the method is not openly sensitive to the choice of L. However, Hartz et al. (2006) found that the results slightly prefer the shorter window of length $L = 250$.

With respect to the results of the t-EGARCH model for the LR_{uc} test, we see that the t-EGARCH VaR forecasts for only one specified probability for the NIKKEI index are superior to the bias-corrected n-EGARCH VaR forecasts, while they are never better for the FTSE and CAC. Similar results hold for the conditional coverage test statistic for all series while the independence test statistics indicate no systematic problems. According to empirical results, the bias-correction method based on the n-EGARCH model performs better than the t-EGARCH model. Therefore, it seems that there is no need to consider a fat-tailed distribution to describe the returns' conditional distribution.

Table 5 presents the average score differences d with the accompanying tests of equal predictive accuracy for models relative to the bias-corrected n-GARCH and n-EGARCH models. The score difference d is computed by subtracting the score of the bias-corrected n-EGARCH from the score of n-EGARCH, bias-corrected n-GARCH, and t-EGARCH models, such that negative values of d indicate better predictive ability of the bias-corrected n-EGARCH model. Additionally, the score difference d for the n-GARCH and bias-corrected n-GARCH models is calculated and interpreted in a similar way. For all series, the csl scoring rule suggests superior or equal predictive ability of the bias-correction method in comparison with usual n-GARCH models. Comparing the results for the bias-correction method based on the n-EGARCH model with those based on the n-GARCH model, we conclude that the n-EGARCH model outperforms the n-GARCH model for both the FTSE and NIKKEI indexes (except the NIKKEI at 99%), but evidence is weaker when we consider the CAC index. On the other hand, the bias-correction method based on the n-EGARCH model performs better than the t-EGARCH model for the NIKKEI, while this is not true for short FTSE and CAC positions.

4. Conclusions

In this paper, we extend the study by Hartz et al. (2006) to take account of asymmetry in conditional variance and correct the VaR for both long and short positions. We focus on three extreme percentiles $\alpha = 0.5\%$, 1% and 5% in the empirical study. Our results are robust to the chosen bias-correction window length, with a slight preference for the longer window length of L=500 for the three real return series investigated.

Our findings support those found in the study by Hartz et al. (2006). They obtain similar results with the other data, finding that the bias-correction method based on the n-GARCH model performs better than the usual n-GARCH model. This is also confirmed by the csl scoring rule for both GARCH models which has not been considered by Hartz et al. (2006). Our empirical study shows that the bias-correction method based on the n-EGARCH model instead of n-GARCH leads to improvements in correctly forecasting one-day-ahead VaR for long and short positions of almost all real return series investigated based on the three performance tests of Christoffersen (1998), while the independence of the VaR violations is unaffected by this method. We found that the bias-corrected n-EGARCH model is the only model never rejected by any of the three performance tests for all the specified probabilities and real return series investigated. Overall, it seems that allowing for an asymmetric response of the conditional variance to positive and negative shocks yields an improvement in the VaR performance based on the bias-correction method in terms of the three performance tests, but the improvement is not highly confirmed based on the csl scoring rule.

Moreover, the bias-correction method based on the n-EGARCH model performs better than the t-EGARCH model based on three performance tests. This is also true even for the NIKKEI with the most skewness and kurtosis in our data investigated. Thus, it seems that the bias-corrected n-EGARCH model can take account of both the asymmetry in the conditional variance and leptokurtosis in return distribution. However, we observe that the superiority of this model is not maintained in terms of predictive power according to the csl scoring rule for short positions. Thus, further research is advisable to adjust the standard VaR predictions of the n-GARCH models based on csl scoring rule rather than the observed frequency of violations. Additionally, future work could extend the methodology to other types of GARCH models such as the power (G)ARCH models of Brooks, Faff, McKenzie and Mitchell (2000) or several GARCH models considered by Loudon, Watt and Yadav (2000).

References

Alexander, C. (2001). *Market models: A guide to financial data analysis.* Chichester, UK: Wiley.

Bams, D., Lehnert, T., & Wolff, C.C.P. (2005). An evaluation framework for alternative VaR-models. *Journal of International Money and Finance, 24*(6), 944–958.Bao, Y., Lee, T.H., & Saltoğlu, B. (2007). Comparing density forecast models. *Journal of Forecasting, 26*(3), 203–225.

Barone-Adesi, G., Giannopoulos, K., & Vosper, L. (1999). VaR without correlations for portfolios of derivative securities. *Journal of Futures Markets, 19*(5), 583–602.

Barone-Adesi, G., Giannopoulos, K., & Vosper, L. (2002). Backtesting derivative portfolios with filtered historical simulation (fhs). *European Financial Management, 8*(1), 31–58.

Basle Committee on Banking Supervision. (1995). *An internal model-based approach to market risk capital requirements.* Retrieved from https://www.bis.org/publ/bcbsc224.pdf

Basle Committee on Banking Supervision. (1996). *Overview of the amendment to the capital accord to incorporate market risks.* Retrieved from http://www.bis.org/publ/bcbs23.pdf

Black, F. (1976). Studies in Stock Price Volatility Changes. In *Proceedings of the 1976 Business Meeting of the Business and Economic Statistics Section* (pp. 177-181). Washington, DC: American Statistical Association.

Bollerslev, T. (1986). Generalized autoregressive conditional heteroskedasticity. *Journal of Econometrics, 31*, 307–327.

Bollerslev, T., & Mikkelsen, H. O. (1996). Modeling and pricing long memory in stock market volatility. *Journal of Econometrics, 73*, 151-184.

Brooks, R.D., Faff, R.W., McKenzie, M.D. & Mitchell, H. (2000). A multi-country study of power ARCH models and national stock market returns. *Journal of International Money and Finance, 19*(3), 377-397.

Christoffersen, P.F. (1998). Evaluating intervals forecasts. *International Economic Review 39*(4), 841–862.

Christoffersen, P., & Gonçalves, S. (2005). Estimation risk in financial risk management. *Journal of Risk, 7*, 1-28.

Crouhy, M., Galai, D., & Mark, R. (2001). Risk management. New York, NY: McGraw-Hill.

Diks, C., Panchenko, V., & van Dijk, D. (2011). Likelihood-based scoring rules for comparing density forecasts in tails. *Journal of Econometrics, 163*(2), 215–230.

Ding, Z., Granger, C.W.J., & Engle, R.F. (1993). A long memory property of stock market returns and a new model. *Journal of Empirical Finance, 1*(1), 83-106.

Dowd, K. (2005). *Measuring market risk* (2nd ed.). Chichester, UK: John Wiley & sons, Ltd.

Engle, R.F. (1982). Autoregressive conditional heteroscedasticity with estimates of the variance of United Kingdom inflation. *Econometrica, 50*(4), 987–1008.

Engle, R.F., & Ng, V. (1993). Measuring and testing the impact of news on volatility. *The Journal of Finance, 48*(5), 1749-1778.

Fama, E.F. (1965). The behavior of stock market price. *Journal of Business, 38*(1), 34–105.

Giot, P., & Laurent, S. (2003). Value-at-risk for long and short trading positions. *Journal of Applied Econometrics, 18*(6), 641-663.

Glosten, L.R., Jagannathan, R., & Runkle, D.E. (1993). On the relation between the expected value and the volatility of the nominal excess return on stocks. *The Journal of Finance, 5*(48), 1779-1801.

Hartz, C., Mittnik, S., & Paolella, M. (2006). Accurate value-at-risk forecasting based on the normal-GARCH model. *Computational Statistics & Data Analysis, 51*(4), 2295-2312.

Kupiec, P.H. (1995). Techniques for verifying the accuracy of risk measurement models. *The Journal of Derivatives, 3*(2), 73–84.

Loudon, G.F., Watt, W.H., & Yadav, P.K. (2000). An empirical analysis of alternative parametric ARCH model. *Journal of Applied Econometrics, 15*(2), 117-136.

Nelson, D.B. (1991). Conditional heteroskedasticity in asset returns: A new approach. *Econometrica, 59*(2), 347–370.

Nieto, M.R., & Ruiz, E. (2010). Bootstrap prediction intervals for VaR and ES in the context of GARCH models (Working Paper No. 10-28). Departamento de Estadística, Universidad Carlos III de Madrid. Retrieved from http://earchivo.uc3m.es/bitstream/handle/10016/8524/ws102814.pdf?sequence=1

Pascual, L., Romo, J., & Ruiz, E. (2006). Bootstrap prediction for returns and volatilities in GARCH models. *Computational Statistics & Data Analysis, 50*(9), 2293–2312.

Reeves, J. (2005). Bootstrap prediction intervals for ARCH models. *International Journal of Forecasting, 21*(2), 237-248.

Trucíos, C., & Hotta, L. (2016). Bootstrap prediction in univariate volatility models with leverage effect. *Mathematics and Computers in Simulation, 120*, 91-103.

Tsay, R.S. (2005). Analysis of financial time series. New Jersey, NJ: A John Wiley & Sons Inc.

Endnotes

1 *For the sake of brevity, only the results for Student's t distribution are presented in this paper. The results for the GED, which are very similar to those for the Student's t distribution, are available from the authors upon request.*

2 *For a more technical definition of the method, please refer to Diks et al. (2011).*

7

ynamics of Decision Making in Cross-unctional Teams

unde Anibaba[1], Godbless Akaighe[1]

STRACT

Group decision making is often associated with better qualitative decisions and outcomes than decisions made by individuals alone. The dynamics of the group decision-making process, as opposed to the consequences of such decisions, have received limited research attention. While there is considerable evidence to support that cross-functional team decision making facilitates easy implementation of decisions, and higher participation in decision making, the intricacies involved in the decision-making process remain underexplored. The paper aims to understand how different factors drive the behavior of the team members in the decision-making process in cross-functional teams and how decisions are reached in such teams. Under simulation conditions, we observed decision-making sessions involving six groups of six managers each, representing six different functions in a hypothetical organization. We find that the behavior of team leaders, the presence of `dominant' team members and the self-interest of team members, drove the process and defined the final output.

Y WORDS: group decision making, cross-functional teams, consensus, leadership

gos Business School, Nigeria

1. Introduction

Extant literature suggests that the use of teams generally, and cross-functional teams, in particular, is an increasingly popular phenomenon in today's organizations (Lacerenza, Marlow, Tannenbaum & Salas, 2018). Cross-functional teams (CFTs) are becoming commonplace in areas such as research and development, manufacturing, marketing, new product development, launching a new technology, and other strategic areas of the business (Daspit, Justice Tillman, Boyd, & Mckee, 2013; Griffin, 1997; Kotlarsky, van den Hooff, & Houtman, 2015; Lovelace, Shapiro, & Weingart, 2001; Mathieu, Tannenbaum, Donsbach, & Alliger, 2014; Sangeetha, & Kumaran, 2018). The logic is that team members bring a diversity of knowledge, experience, and expertise to organizational activities and processes, which could potentially improve team effectiveness and lead to more desirable outcomes for the organization. CFTs are also thought to ease the burden of decision making on individual managers in an increasingly complex and dynamic world, speed up decision making and product development, increase creative and innovative capacity of teams, facilitate team member interactions, and ultimately aid successful execution of decisions and of projects (Alper, Tjosvold, & Law, 1998; Cui, 2016; Daspit *et al.*, 2013; Katzenbach & Smith, 1992; Lin, Wang, & Kung, 2015; Parker, 2003; Sangeetha & Kumaran, 2018).

rrespondence concerning this article should be addressed to: **tunde Anibaba**, Lagos Business School, Nigeria. E-mail: yanioa@lbs.edu.ng

However, the increasingly popular 'dark-side' metaphor finds expression in this body of literature, as team-based decision making is also thought to be associated with suboptimal outcomes. The latter are thought to stem from the diverse views and functional expertise of team members, information asymmetry, their personal interests and preferences, as well as a general lack of team competencies (Cui, 2016; Lacerenza, et al., 2018). In essence, it is important to understand the mechanisms that mediate the relationship between team-based decision making and the desired performance outcomes. Consistent with McGrath's (1984) input-process-output heuristic that has dominated much of team effectiveness research, it is evident that team processes are fundamental to team outcomes. As such, the decision-making process has been argued to affect not just the eventual outcome of the team, but also its overall functioning, including members' satisfaction, group interactions, participation level and socio-emotional behavior of group members (Nel, Pitt, Berthon, & Prendergast, 1996). As a result, extant research has focused extensively on understanding how team processes drive team effectiveness and outcomes. However, recent research suggests that our insight into the workings of cross-functional teams is still deficient.

In their study of the impact of team training on team performance in the aviation sector, Littlepage, Hein, Moffett, Craig, and Georgiou (2016) observe that adequate research into team coordination in cross-functional teams is still lacking. Cui (2016) suggests from their field study of micro-decision processes in BMW and Nokia that the intricacies of the micro-processes of decision making in cross-functional teams are still poorly understood, more so in light of the fact that research into interventions to facilitate team effectiveness are often carried out in isolation of one another. As a result, it is not clear how those interventions jointly affect team effectiveness and team outcomes, especially as data for different variables are typically collected at different points in time, often after the team event has taken place. A related issue is the need for researchers to move from the retrospective nature by which team processes are captured, in order to adequately account for the genuinely complex and dynamic nature of teamwork and team membership in today's organizations (Matheiu, Maynard, Rapp & Gilson, 2008; Cristofaro, 2017).

We take our cue from the preceding, and with the aid of a simulated decision-making exercise, we explore the micro-processes of decision making in six hypothetical cross-functional teams. We aim to explore how different social interaction processes that have been identified in the literature interact to define CFT decision-making outcomes. By this, we hope to contribute to providing a more holistic understanding of the dynamics that facilitate or hinder decision making effectiveness in cross-functional teams.

Thus, the objective of the study is to explore the dynamics of cross-functional team decision making. In precise terms, the study seeks to provide deeper insights into how members of cross-functional teams interact during the decision-making process. This paper brings together the teamwork and group decision-making literature to offer a nuanced explanation of the dynamics of decision-making in multi-functional teams. We hope to shed some light, for example, on how teams may reach mutually acceptable decisions/consensus in spite of functional and personal interests, and how the nature of leadership may influence group interactions to achieve the desired outcome.

This paper is organized as follows. In the following section, we pool together some of the literature on group decision making, cross-functional teams and team effectiveness to form a conceptual framework for the study. Next, we describe the research method, including an overview of the simulation exercise, a description of the participants and the context of the simulation. We present a summary of the results and conclude with a discussion of those results, its limitations and fruitful areas for future research.

2. Conceptual Overview

2.1. Group Decision Making

Group decision-making (GDM) involves two or more individuals in a group arrangement evaluating alternative courses of action on a problem and selecting the best option for the benefit of the group, on behalf of the organization (Chen, Xu, & Xia, 2013; Lunenburg, 2011). Due to the complexities of organizational problems and the dynamic business environment, group decision making has become popular to assess all possible sides to an identified organizational problem towards ensuring that the best decision is taken or the organization (Haslam et al., 2014; RodríGuez, MartıNez, & Herrera, 2013; Yates, & de Oliveira, 2016). GDM in modern organizations also considers the need to harness the skills, knowledge, and experience of the group members (Gillet, Schram, & Sonnemans, 2009; Kocher & Sutter, 2005), and is thought to strengthen innovation in the organization, qualitative debate, interpersonal relationship and problem-solving skills of individuals across functional areas of the organization (Amabile, Conti, Coon, Lazenby, & Herron, 1996; Choi, Raghu, Vinzé, & Dooley, 2017; Liao, Xu, Zeng, & Xu, 2016).

Extant literature suggests that group decisions are more reliable and tend to have more weight than individual decisions in organizations (Saaty, & Peniwati, 2013). An effective GDM process has the potential to ensure high participatory rate and ultimately achieve consensus decision (Chiclana, García, del Moral, & Herrera-Viedma, 2013). It facilitates the buy-in and engagement that required at the implementation stage.

2.2. *Cross-Functional Teams*

Cross-functional teams are made up of a "group of people representing a variety of departments, disciplines, or functions; whose combined effort is required to achieve the team's purpose" (Wang & He, 2008, p. 753). The members of the team could also be experts in various fields, who can bring their knowledge and experience to bear on the team's goals (Cohen & Levinthal, 1990; Dahlin & Weingart, 1996; Lovelace *et al.*, 2001). They are often established with the objective of achieving a set goal or taking a decision, such as closing a product line, improving product/service quality and productivity of an organization or launching a new product (Alexander et al., 2005; Athanasaw, 2003; Pakarinen, & Virtanen, 2017), usually in a temporary arrangement (Edmondson, & Harvey, 2017). While they typically involve different personalities and interests, thus potentially causing friction and reducing the effectiveness of the team (Kaufmann, & Wagner, 2017), extant literature suggests that cross-functional teams have become accepted across organizations for business analyses, information integration, knowledge sharing and decision making in both public and private sector organizations (Choi, & Lee, 2016; Littlepage et al., 2016; Piercy, Phillips, & Lewis, 2013).

The benefits of employing cross-functional teams for decision making include (1) the likelihood that they will make better decisions drawing from their varied backgrounds and experience (2) they promote decentralized decision making in the organization (3) the reduction of overload of decision making at the top echelon of an organization (4) the decision-making cuts across departments and vertical organizational structures (Henke, Krachenberg, & Lyons, 1993).

We noted above that a typical characteristic of cross-functional teams is that members of the team come from different management / departmental functions so that each departmental function is represented in the team. In this case, the mandate of team members is to protect the interest of their functional departments, by ensuring due consideration is given to their viewpoints in the decision to be taken (Bitter, van Veen-Berkx, Gooszen, & van Amelsvoort, 2013; Pakarinen, & Virtanen, 2017). Herein also lies one of the problems with decision-making in cross-functional teams – the potential that one team's interest will be maximized at the expense of another. For example, while the manufacturing team's interest may be cost minimization, marketing may typically be focused on revenue maximization (Cui, 2016). These issues are amplified by the fact that such teams are often temporary/ad-hoc in nature, so that they do not have as much of an opportunity to 'develop a team identity, shared mental models and trust' (White, Eklund, McNeal, Hochhalter, & Arroliga, 2018) required to facilitate better interaction within the team. An important challenge CFT's face, therefore, is how to coordinate the team to ensure that micro-objectives of team members align with the broader organizational objectives. In the following section, we briefly review the literature around some critical characteristics that the research suggests are essential in this regard.

The leadership style/behavior of the leader

In cross-functional teams, there is usually a leader who wields significant influence on the activities and outcomes of the team (Ehrhardt, Miller, Freeman, & Hom, 2014; Kozlowski & Bell, 2003). The leadership style/ behavior of the team leader either facilitates or hinders the decision-making process, encourages members to participate in the process or hold back their opinions. In essence, the contribution of team members to the decision-making process can be significantly influenced by the leaders' style (Ehrhardt *et al.*, 2014; Gurerk, Irlenbusch, & Rockenbach, 2009). A cross-functional team leader that adopts an autocratic leadership style, for instance, controls the group and dictates the process, limits communication and dominates the decision-making process. This somewhat forces the group members to a narrow view of issues based on the subjective idea of the leader, because the autocratic leadership behavior places less emphasis on people (De Hoogh, Greer, & Den Hartog, 2015; Puni, Ofei, & Okoe, 2014). Typically, an autocratic leadership style is thought to hinder the free flow of communication, innovation and creativity in a team while a participatory/democratic leadership behavior in a team promotes a shared level of involvement in the decision-making process (Odoardi, Montani, Boudrias, & Battistelli, 2015; Rossberger, & Krause, 2015).

Influence of dominant members

Dominant members of a cross-functional team are great influencers of decision making due to their strong emotions, in-depth-knowledge and assertive personality, which wields some influence on the team (Lerner, Li, Valdesolo, & Kassam, 2015; Kirchhoff, Lemos & Dessai, 2013; Moon, Baxter, & Klein, 2015). The role of individual personality in a cross-functional team is a factor that can swing decisions in the direction of the dominant person's preference regardless of the validity of that preference. Individuals with strong personalities and authoritative postures tend to influence the debate more than team members who are quiet and not as opinionated (boldness and activity) (Brown & Irving, 2013; Planas-Sitja, Deneubourg, Gibon, & Sempo, 2015). The knowledge and expertise of team members could also position them to dominate the deliberations and influence the eventual outcome positively or otherwise (Hauer et al., 2016; Oliveira, Rozenfeld, Phaal, & Probert, 2015; Pérez, Cabrerizo, Alonso, & Herrera-Viedma, 2014; Schickramm, Saenz-Segura, Schipper, & Handgraaf, 2015).

The interest of team members

Ideally, the overall benefit of the organization should be the motivating factor in cross-functional team decision making, but this is not always the reality. The literature suggests that individual team members tend to protect their interest such their jobs, their reputation and also defend the position of their departmental units (Binderkrantz, Christiansen, & Pedersen, 2015). Such vested interests cause team members to hoard useful information, tend to heighten the debate, generate conflict and elongate the decision-making process unduly (Brown, & Irving, 2013; Evans, Hendron, & Oldroyd, 2014; Kish-Gephart, Detert, Treviño, Baker, & Martin, 2014; Mihalache, Jansen, Van den Bosch, & Volberda, 2014). The literature suggests that the leader has a responsibility to manage such situations, through transformational leadership, which will encourage the members to rise above their interest to the overall benefit of the group and the organization (Bouwmans, Runhaar, Wesselink, & Mulder, 2017).

Team cooperation

The level of collaboration of a cross-functional team is an essential factor in the decision-making process. The literature suggests that a lack of cooperation amongst the team members aided by self-interest and diverse orientation will create difficulty in arriving at early decisions, and subsequently impede the implementation of any decision(s) reached (Anthony, Green, & McComb, 2014; Carson, Tesluk, & Marrone, 2007; Pinto, Pinto, & Prescott, 1993). Team cooperation can be a function of the understanding of the overall objective, the common good of the decision to the organization and the team members' willingness to let go ego and self-interest as a result of their individual functional expertise (Bagozzi, Belschak, Verbeke, & Gavino, 2016; Kim & Johnson, 2014; Ridge & Ingram, 2017). With respect to functional background and the tendency to operate at cross purposes, a number of authors suggest the need for behavioral integration (Hambrick, 1994; Simsek, Veiga, Lubatkin, & Dino, 2005; Soldan & Bowye, 2009) which is defined as "the degree to which mutual and collective interaction exists within the group" (Hambrick, 1994, p. 188) for the harmonization of the team. The argument is that, for people from various fields of expertise, there is bound to be divergent opinion, ideas, orientations, and positions, albeit insightful that will create a slow and torrid decision-making process without team cooperation, orientation and behavioral integration (Tekleab, Karaca, Quigley, & Tsang, 2016).

3. Method

3.1. *Research design*

This paper is an exploratory study aimed at capturing the dynamics of decision making in cross-functional teams via direct observation of the behavior of the participants during the decision-making process (Gummerson, 2000; Shukla, 2008). We use this method in an attempt to observe and document real-time interaction among team members in the simulated decision-making exercise, and circumvent one of the weaknesses Matheiu et al. (2008) identified in extant research on team effectiveness, that is the retrospective collection of data.

3.2. *The exercise*

The fictional case authored by Edmondson and Feldman (2003) forms the basis for this CFT decision-making exercise.

'The case, inspired by a real decision facing a major telecommunications company, describes a cross-functional management team convened by the CEO for the purpose of developing a recommendation about whether to conduct a full-scale launch of a new high-speed Internet access service. In the class session, groups of six participants are asked to conduct team meetings to arrive at a consensus about the launch decision--drawing from the information contained in the shared case and from privately held information contained in individual role sheets provided separately to each member. Although different team members hold very different perspectives about the launch, teams can arrive at thoughtful recommendations by working together to share their knowledge.' – *Harvard Business School Press*

3.3. *The participants*

To study the dynamics of cross-functional team decision making, we engage a total of thirty-six (36) subjects split into six (6) groups of six (6) members each. The overall study sample comprised of 55% male and 45% female, all working professionals and executives with average professional working experience of 10 years, from public and private sector organizations. In addition to the base case, each team member received a separate role sheet describing the role they were to play in their respective teams. To facilitate an in-depth understanding of their roles participants with the same characters were asked to discuss the role among themselves to help them get into the parts. When they were ready, each team of 6 was led into separate syndicate rooms where the meeting was to be held. Each participant was also required to put a name/role tag in front of them for easy identification by their team members and the observer that was assigned to each team.

Five of the six groups had the same task, while the last group served as a control group. There were no roles assigned to the sixth group; they were merely given the base case and asked to make a recommendation to the CEO of the organization as best they could. They were asked to return to the classroom within 45 minutes.

3.4. *Data collection procedures*

Each team of six executives was assigned an observer who took notes on their team's interactions to the point when they made a decision or the time allotted for the meeting was up. The observers were briefed on the purpose of the simulation and were instructed not to make any comments throughout the process. Specifically, the observers were expected to make notes on 1. Whether their team was clear on the task at hand; 2. What (if any) specific procedures they use to address the problem; 3. Group behavior and participation pattern; 4. The energy/enthusiasm level of the group; 5. The participation level and dynamics of the team. 6. Whether the team reached a decision and how (consensus, bulldozing, voting, bargaining, or other).

4. Results

In the following section, we report the findings from the decision sessions across the groups below, first in a summary table and in more detail after that:

The table above shows a summary of the findings of the cross-functional teams' decision-making sessions involving six groups on the designated task of whether to launch a product or not. We discuss the findings in detail according to their groups:

Group 1:

The group leader began the deliberations by explaining the task at hand, so the task appeared clear to the group. In the beginning, the group leader directed the conversation by asking for the opinions of each team

Table 1.

Decision-making processes	Group 1	Group 2	Group 3	Group 4	Group 5	Group 6 (control)
Clarity of group task	Yes	Yes	Yes	Yes	No	Yes (eventually)
Group behavior and participation pattern	Free participation, various perspectives were aired	Open minded and strong voices	High participation, differing views, constant interruption, dominant members	Low cohesiveness, dissenting voices, dominant member control	Poor group coordination, robust discussions, dominant member imposition	Open participation, mutual trust, knowledge sharing, leadership discovery
Leadership in the group	Weak leadership	Strong leadership	Laissez-faire leadership	Weak leadership	Democratic leadership	Leader Emergence
How decision was reached	Voting	Consensus	Bullying	Voting	Voting	Consensus
Satisfaction about the decision	Low satisfaction	High satisfaction	Low satisfaction	Low satisfaction	Low satisfaction	High satisfaction

member and coordinated the deliberations. While the group demonstrated considerable enthusiasm and energy during the deliberations, there was cautious optimism in the group about the decision to launch the product immediately. Initially, team members didn't quite disagree with the team leader. They responded to his 'body language' with low participation. However, at a point, the members began to participate freely almost tending towards 'analysis paralysis.' They expressed many different perspectives on the pros and cons of each decision alternative, ostensibly because of their various areas of functional expertise. In the end, the leader could not quite channel the discussions towards a consensus decision, and the session ended with a call for a vote. , and it appeared that those who were the minority were not satisfied with the final decision at the end, which was to launch the product.

Group 2:

The group took the time to understand the task. A detailed analysis was carried out by group members. The members were open-minded albeit with some dissenting voices. There was trust in the group leader who displayed a courageous persona in leading the task. There appeared to be a high level of consensus in the decision-making process, with a good level of interest and a pretty much smooth decision-making process. However, there was a flash of dominance by a particular group member who wanted to be in control and be always heard, but the leader managed to direct the proceedings. In the end, the decision was taken to launch the product in a consensus manner, and the members appeared satisfied with the decision.

Group 3:

The group task was clear. At the initial stage, there was a mutual understanding in the group and adequate consistency in the participation level, as members seemed to defer in opinion from the team leader. However, after each member expressed their preference, the conversation heated up, members constantly interrupted one another, and they stopped listening to each other. The leader 'withdrew' in the face of the heated discussions, and an informal leader emerged as some members became adamant about their positions; this went overboard at some point and affected the team spirit. The leader was not assertive, and a few dominant members of the team decided to delay the product launch, by bullying the other members, leading to low satisfaction with the decision by other group members.

Group 4:
The task was unclear in the beginning as the leader did not sufficiently articulate it to group members. It became clear much later as some members of the group began to explain. The team leadership appeared weak, and a dominant member capitalized on the lack of direction and guidance in the team to influence the discussion. In the process, there were dissenting voices, and the cohesiveness of the group was low. The decision was put to the vote. Based on the voting, a decision was taken to launch the service, but the satisfaction level was low amongst other team members as the decision makers ignored their concerns.

Group 5:
The group found it difficult to establish the task initially, lead to confusion and lack of coordination in addressing the problem. The group leader demonstrated a democratic leadership style. The discussion in the group become robust, but the 'body language' of the group leader hindered decision making. Put in another way, the team leader was not decisive, appearing over democratic, and providing no clear direction on many occasions. During the decision-making process, a group member took advantage of the democratic nature of the group leader to impose his views on the group. In the end, there was no consensus, and members had to vote, deciding to launch the product. As may be expected, those not in favor of the decision were not satisfied as they resigned to the decision of the majority.

Group 6:
This group was a control group for leadership emergence. In this group, there were no defined roles and no leader assigned. The group members began by trying to understand the task. During the deliberations, a leader emerged because of the need to guide the discussions and provide direction for other members. There was mutual trust between members and high interest in solving the problem. The team members did not hold back their participation. As deliberations became more intense, another group leader emerged, apparently as a result of his superior knowledge and information on the technical issues around the industry. The second leader proved his mettle in establishing industry trends and galvanizing opinions towards a well-informed decision. Other members trusted the experience and knowledge of the new leader. The group came to a consensus on the strength of the information and analyses provided by the new leader. Members were happy with the decision to delay the launch of the product until there was more information available.

5. Discussions

One of the findings that stood out in this simulation is the role of leaders in facilitating the decision-making process. We saw that leadership effectiveness was not a function of the position, as much as style and competence of the leader. It was also evident that a leader will often *emerge* when there was a task to be accomplished not so much to control as to guide the decision-making process. Hence where leaders with formal authority do not step up to their role, others with influence (or informal authority) will, otherwise as we observed in the study, other team members will capitalize on the leader's weakness to dominate the discussions, leading to a slower decision-making process and possible bullying. It is possible that those teams without effective leadership eventually decided because the researcher timed simulation and told the teams they had to reach a decision within the stipulated time. Research supports our position that individuals who are willing to take up responsibility in decision-making processes often emerge as leaders (see Ertac & Gurdal, 2012). The finding of our study on leaders' role in facilitating group decision making aligns with the literature on leaders' authority in group decision making. Verbeek (2017) research supports the position of having a persistent leader, such that the leadership style in decision making can be responsible for the poor performance of a group, especially in crisis situations. Previous research also established that the steadfastness and consistency of leaders' behavior, and their ability to channel group members to make informed choices on novel strategies to solving organizational problems in the face of pressures, is important for business success and sustainability (Smith, 2014; Smith, Binns, & Tushman, 2010). In leadership emergence, dominant personalities as group members have also emerged as leaders where the team leader shows laissez-faire or passive leadership. From our study, members with dominant personalities capitalized on the leaders' passiveness or lack of decisiveness to 'control' the decision-making process. Peng, Xiao, Yang, Wu and Miao (2014) research supports out finding that dominant personalities in groups eventually control decision debates and sway the decisions in some ways through their strong opinions, information use, and vocal dispositions.

From our findings, one of the factors that contributed to conflict in the teams was the fact that the role sheets given to each team member contained information about the personal and departmental interests of that team member, which was supposed to influence their contribution to the discussions. For example, the VP, Finance had his bonus tied to the launch of the service, so he was naturally predisposed to it. The HR Director, on the other hand, was worried that he would not be able to hire and train staff for it in good time and was expected to be against the launch. However, where the leader encouraged open communication and was able to extract the relevant information from the team members through structured questioning, other team members conceded some of their preferences to arrive at a consensus decision that worked for everyone. However, when the interests of the members are mostly undisclosed, it hinders the decision-making process. The literature supports our findings that the personal interest of team members tend to interfere with the overall interest of the group in decision making. Liu and Wei (2000) found that personal interest and emotional factors becloud the judgment of decision makers especially in complex decisions, hence the need for the analytical hierarchical process (AHP) to quantify and rank decisions in areas such as project evaluation, risk assessment, and performance evaluation, to reduce the self-serving interest of decision makers. Yan, Liu, and Skitmore (2018) research also supports our findings on how personal interest impair sound judgment in group decision making by positing that organizations must be aware of the conflict between company interest and personal interest of members in factors affecting group bidding decision for construction projects and take steps to mitigate such conflict of interest through collaboration and learning orientation.

Team cooperation is a fundamental ingredient in cross-functional decision making. From our findings, we observe that a team with a high level of collaboration for the decision-making task had quality debates, free flow of information, coordination and faster decision making. This finding implies that team cooperation promotes considerable team consensus, focus on the core of the decision tasks and effective decision making. This finding is consistent with previous research by De Jong, Dirks, and Gillespie (2016) that team cooperation and teamwork interaction play a vital role in the accomplishment of teams, pointing that intra-team trust and team coherence facilitate team interaction, effective communication, and decision making. Pinto et al. (1993) also established that interpersonal relationship and personalities of group members are antecedents of cross-functional team cooperation. Similarly, Alper et al. (1998) research are consistent with our findings on team cooperation for quality debates and faster decision making that controversy in group decision making is curbed by team cooperation, and well-coordinated team management leading to faster decisions regarding their internet affairs and set tasks. Thus, we suggest that the leader of cross-functional teams should continuously ensure that the integration mechanism of the team is active to harmonize the divergent orientations and opinions of team members to achieve cohesion of ideas and thoughts, towards smooth decision-making process and optimal decision for the group.

6. Limitation of the study and conclusion

The findings of this study are observations from a decision-making simulation conducted under classroom conditions during an executive education programme at the Lagos Business School and should be interpreted in that light. The use of proxy team members for executive positions in the simulation is a limitation to the extent of generalization of the dynamics of decision making in cross-functional teams. As research on decision making in cross-functional teams continue, our understanding of how leadership defines the willingness of team members to let go of self-interest in favor of the organization's interest will be illuminated.

In conclusion, we believe that perhaps the single most crucial factor to the effectiveness of the decision-making process in cross-functional teams is leadership, and our study offers essential insight into the role of the leader in that respect.

References

Alexander, J. A., Lichtenstein, R., Jinnett, K., Wells, R., Zazzali, J. & Liu, D. (2005). Cross - Functional team processes and patient functional improvement. *Health Services Research, 40*(5), 1335–1355.

Alper, S., Tjosvold, D., & Law, K. S. (1998). Interdependence and controversy in group decision making: Antecedents to effective self-managing teams. *Organizational Behavior and Human Decision Processes, 74*(1), 33-52.

Amabile, T. M., Conti, R., Coon, H., Lazenby, J., & Herron, M. (1996). Assessing the work environment for creativity. *Academy of Management Journal,* 39, 1154-1184

Anthony, E. L., Green, S. G., & McComb, S. A. (2014). Crossing functions above the cross - Functional project team: The value of lateral coordination among functional department heads. *Journal of Engineering and Technology Management, 31*, 141-158.

Athanasaw, Y.A. (2003). Team characteristics and team member knowledge, skills, and ability relationships to the effectiveness of cross-functional teams in the public sector, *International Journal of Public Administration, 26*(10–11), 1165–1203.

Bagozzi, R. P., Belschak, F., Verbeke, W., & Gavino, J. C. (2016). Salesperson Self - Regulation of pride: Effects on adaptability, effort, and citizenship behaviors between independent-based and interdependent-based cultures. *Spanish Journal of Marketing-ESIC, 20*(1), 1-17.

Binderkrantz, A. S., Christiansen, P. M., & Pedersen, H. H. (2015). Interest group access to the bureaucracy, parliament, and the media. *Governance, 28*(1), 95-112.

Bitter, J., van Veen-Berkx, E., Gooszen, H.G., & van Amelsvoort, P. (2013). Multidisciplinary teamwork is an important issue for healthcare professionals, *Team Performance Management, 19*(5), 263–278.

Bouwmans, M., Runhaar, P., Wesselink, R., & Mulder, M. (2017). Fostering teachers' team
learning: An interplay between transformational leadership and participative decision-making? *Teaching and Teacher Education, 65*, 71-80.

Brown, C., & Irving, E. (2013). Individual personality traits influence group exploration in a feral guppy population. *Behavioral Ecology, 25*(1), 95-101.

Carson, J. B., Tesluk, P. E., & Marrone, J. A. (2007). Shared leadership in teams: An investigation of antecedent conditions and performance. *Academy of Management Journal, 50*(5), 1217-1234.

Chen, N., Xu, Z., & Xia, M. (2013). Interval-valued hesitant preference relations and teir applications to group decision making. *Knowledge-Based Systems, 37*, 528-540.

Chiclana, F., García, J. T., del Moral, M. J., & Herrera-Viedma, E. (2013). A statistical comparative study of different similarity measures of consensus in group decision making. *Information Sciences, 221*, 110-123.

Choi, E., & Lee, K. C. (2016). The relationship between social network structure dynamics and innovation: Micro-level analyses of virtual cross-functional teams in a multinational B2B firm. *Computers in Human Behavior, 65*, 151-162.

Choi, B., Raghu, T. S., Vinzé, A., & Dooley, K. J. (2017). The effectiveness of standards consortia: Social network perspectives. *Information Systems Frontiers,* 1-12. https://doi.org/10.1007/s10796-017-9759-x. Cohen, W. M., & Levinthal, D. A. (1990). Absorptive capacity: A new perspective on learning and innovation. *Administrative Science Quarterly,* 35, 128- 152.

Cristofaro, M. (2017). Reducing biases of decision-making processes in complex organizations. *Management Research Review, 40*(3), 270-291.

Cui, Z. (2016). Decision making in cross-functional teams: The role of decision power. *Decision Sciences, 47*(3), 492-523.

Dahlin, K., & Weingart, L. R. (1996). Absorptive capacity-A link between group diversity and group performance. Paper presented at the annual meeting of the Academy of Management, Cincinnati

Daspit, J., Justice Tillman, C., Boyd, N. G., & Mckee, V. (2013). Cross-functional team effectiveness: An examination of an internal team environment, shared leadership, and cohesion influences. *Team*

Performance Management: An International Journal, 19(1-2), 34-56.

De Hoogh, A. H., Greer, L. L., & Den Hartog, D. N. (2015). Diabolical dictators or capable

commanders? An investigation of the differential effects of autocratic leadership on team performance. *The Leadership Quarterly, 26*(5), 687-701.

De Jong, B. A., Dirks, K. T., & Gillespie, N. (2016). Trust and team performance: A meta-analysis of main effects, moderators, and covariates. *Journal of Applied Psychology, 101*(8), 1134.

Edmonson, A. C., & Feldman, L. (2003). The BCPC Internet Strategy Team: An Exercise.

HBS 604-035. Boston: MA: Harvard Business School Publishing. Edmondson, A.C., & Harvey, J. F. (2017). Cross-boundary teaming for innovation:

Integrating research on teams and knowledge in organizations, *Human Resource Management Review, 28*(4), 347-360.

Ehrhardt, K., Miller, J. S., Freeman, S. J., & Hom, P. W. (2014). Examining project commitment in cross-functional teams: Antecedents and relationship with team performance. *Journal of Business and Psychology, 29*(3), 443-461.

Ertac, S., & Gurdal, M. Y. (2012). Deciding to decide: Gender, leadership, and risk-taking in groups. *Journal of Economic Behavior & Organization, 83*(1), 24-30.

Evans, J. M., Hendron, M. G., & Oldroyd, J. B. (2014). Withholding the ace: The individual -and unit-level performance effects of self-reported and perceived knowledge hoarding. *Organization Science, 26*(2), 494-510.

Gillet, J., Schram, A., & Sonnemans, J. (2009). The tragedy of the commons revisited: The importance of group decision-making. *Journal of Public Economics, 93*(5), 785-797.

Griffin, A. (1997). The effect of project and process characteristics on product development cycle time. *Journal of Marketing Research*, 34, 24-35.

Gummesson, E. (2000). *Qualitative methods in management research.* Thousand Oaks, CA: Sage Publications.

Gurerk, O., Irlenbusch, B., & Rockenbach, B. (2009). Motivating teammates: The leader's choice between positive and negative incentives. *Journal of Economic Psychology,* 30, 591–607.

Hambrick, D.C. (1994). Top management groups: A conceptual integration and reconsideration of the team label. In B.M. Staw, & L.L. Cummings (Eds.), Research in organizational behavior (pp. 171–214). Greenwich, CT: JAI Press

Haslam, C., Haslam, A. S., Knight, C., Gleibs, I., Ysseldyk, R., & McCloskey, L. G. (2014). We can work it out: Group decision-making builds social identity and enhances the cognitive performance of care residents. *British Journal of Psychology, 105*(1), 17-34.

Hauer, K. E., Cate, O. T., Boscardin, C. K., Iobst, W., Holmboe, E. S., Chesluk, B.,... O'Sullivan, P. S. (2016). Ensuring resident competence: A narrative review of the literature on group decision making to inform the work of clinical competency committees. *Journal of Graduate Medical Education, 8*(2), 156-164.

Henke, J. W., Krachenberg, A. R., & Lyons, T. F. (1993). Perspective: Cross-functional Teams: Good concept, poor implementation! *Journal of Product Innovation Management, 10*(3), 216-229.

Katzenbach, J. R. & Smith, D. K. (1992). *The wisdom of teams.* Cambridge, MA: Harvard Business School Press.

Kaufmann, L., & Wagner, C. M. (2017). Affective diversity and emotional intelligence in cross-functional sourcing teams. *Journal of Purchasing and Supply Management, 23*(1), 5-16.

Kim, J. E., & KP Johnson, K. (2014). Shame or pride? The moderating role of self-construal on moral judgments concerning fashion counterfeits. *European Journal of Marketing, 48*(7-8), 1431-1450.

Kirchhoff, C. J., Lemos, M. C., & Dessai, S. (2013). Actionable knowledge for environmental decision making: broadening the usability of climate science. *Annual Review of Environment and Resources*, 38, 393-414

Kish-Gephart, J., Detert, J., Treviño, L. K., Baker, V., & Martin, S. (2014). Situational moral disengagement: Can the effects of self-interest be mitigated? *Journal of Business Ethics, 125*(2), 267-285.

Kocher, M., & Sutter, M. (2007). Individual versus group behavior and the role of the decision making procedure in gift-exchange experiments. *Empirical, 34,* 63–88.

Kotlarsky, J., van den Hooff, B., & Houtman, L. (2015). Are we on the same page? Knowledge boundaries and transactive memory system development in cross-functional teams. *Communication Research, 42*(3), 319-344.

Kozlowski, S., & Bell, B. S. (2003). Workgroups and teams in organizations. In W. C. Borman, D. R. Ilgen, & R. J. Klimoski (Eds.), Handbook of psychology: Industrial and organizational psychology (Vol. 12, pp. 333–375). London, UK: Wiley

Lacerenza, C. N., Marlow, S. L., Tannenbaum, S. I., & Salas, E. (2018). Team development interventions: Evidence-based approaches for improving teamwork. *American Psychologist, 73*(4), 517.

Lerner, J. S., Li, Y., Valdesolo, P., & Kassam, K. S. (2015). Emotion and decision making. *Annual Review of Psychology, 66*, 1-25

Liao, H., Xu, Z., Zeng, X. J., & Xu, D. L. (2016). An enhanced consensus reaching process in group decision making with intuitionistic fuzzy preference relations. *Information Sciences, 329*, 274-286

Lin, Y., Wang, Y., & Kung, L. (2015). Influences of cross-functional collaboration and knowledge creation on technology commercialization: Evidence from high-tech industries. *Industrial Marketing Management, 49*, 128-138.

Littlepage, G. E., Hein, M. B., Moffett III, R. G., Craig, P. A., & Georgiou, A. M. (2016). Team training for dynamic cross-functional teams in Aviation: Behavioral, cognitive, and performance outcomes. *Human Factors, 58*(8), 1275-1288.

Liu, P. H., & Wei, C. C. (2000). A group decision-making technique for appraising the performance of organizations. *International Journal of the Computer, the Internet and Management, 8*(2), 39-49.

Lovelace, K., Shapiro, D. L., & Weingart, L. R. (2001). Maximizing cross-functional new product teams' innovativeness and constraint adherence: A conflict communications perspective. *Academy of Management Journal, 44*(4), 779-793.

Lunenburg, F. C. (2011). Decision making in organizations. *International Journal of Management, Business, and Administration, 15*(1), 1-9.

Mathieu, J., Maynard, M. T., Rapp, T., & Gilson, L. (2008). Team effectiveness 1997-2007: A review of recent advancements and a glimpse into the future. *Journal of Management, 34*(3), 410-476.

Mathieu, J. E., Tannenbaum, S. I., Donsbach, J. S., & Alliger, G. M. (2014). A review and integration of team composition models: Moving toward a dynamic and temporal framework. *Journal of Management, 40*(1), 130-160.

McGrath, J. E. (1984). *Groups: Interaction and performance,* England Cliff, NJ: Prentice-Hall Inc.

Mihalache, O. R., Jansen, J. J., Van den Bosch, F. A., & Volberda, H. W. (2014). Top management team shared leadership and organizational ambidexterity: A moderated mediation framework. *Strategic Entrepreneurship Journal, 8*(2), 128-148.

Moon, B. M., Baxter, H. C., & Klein, G. (2015). Expertise management: challenges for adopting naturalistic decision making as a knowledge management paradigm. International conference on Naturalistic decision making 2015. Retrieved from http://www2.mitre.org/public/ndm/papers/MoonBaxterGAKlein.pdf

Nel, D., Pitt, L. F., Berthon, P., & Prendergast, G. (1996). Social decision schemes and group processes: Some impacts on decision making. *Journal of Managerial Psychology, 11*(6), 4-17.

Odoardi, C., Montani, F., Boudrias, J. S., & Battistelli, A. (2015). Linking managerial practices and leadership style to innovative work behavior: The role of group and psychological processes. *Leadership & Organization Development Journal, 36*(5), 545-569.

Oliveira, M. G., Rozenfeld, H., Phaal, R., & Probert, D. (2015). Decision making at the front end of innovation: The hidden influence of knowledge and decision criteria. *R&D Management, 45*(2), 161-180.

Pakarinen, M., & Virtanen, P. J. (2017). Matrix organizations and cross-functional teams in the public sector: a systematic review. *International Journal of Public Sector Management, 30*(3), 210-226.

Parker, G. M. (2003). *Cross-functional teams: Working with allies, enemies, and other strangers.* San Francisco, CA: Jossey-Bass.

Peng, J., Xiao, W., Yang, Y., Wu, S., & Miao, D. (2014). The impact of trait anxiety on self-frame and decision making. *Journal of Behavioral Decision Making, 27*(1), 11-19.

Pérez, I. J., Cabrerizo, F. J., Alonso, S., & Herrera-Viedma, E. (2014). A new consensus model for group decision-making problems with non-homogeneous experts. *IEEE Transactions on Systems, Man, and Cybernetics: Systems, 44*(4), 494-498.

Piercy, N., Phillips, W., & Lewis, M. (2013). Change management in the public sector: The use of cross-functional teams. *Production Planning & Control, 24*(10-11), 976-987.

Pinto, M. B., Pinto, J. K., & Prescott, J. E. (1993). Antecedents and consequences of project team cross-functional cooperation. *Management Science, 39*(10), 1281-1297.

Planas-Sitja, I., Deneubourg, J. L., Gibon, C., & Sempo, G. (2015). Group personality during collective decision-making: a multi-level approach. *Proceedings of the Royal Society of London B: Biological Sciences, 282*(1802), 1-9.

Puni, A., Ofei, S. B., & Okoe, A. (2014). The effect of leadership styles on firm performance in Ghana. *International Journal of Marketing Studies, 6*(1), 177.

Ridge, J. W., & Ingram, A. (2017). Modesty in the top management team: Investor reaction and performance implications. *Journal of Management, 43*(4), 1283-1306.

RodríGuez, R. M., MartıNez, L., & Herrera, F. (2013). A group decision-making model dealing with comparative linguistic expressions based on hesitant fuzzy linguistic term sets. *Information Sciences, 241*, 28-42.

Rossberger, R. J., & Krause, D. E. (2015). Participative and team-oriented leadership styles, countries' education level, and national innovation: the mediating role of economic factors and national cultural practices. *Cross-Cultural Research, 49*(1), 20-56.

Saaty, T. L., & Peniwati, K. (2013). *Group decision making: drawing out and reconciling differences.* Pittsburgh, PA: RWS Publications.

Sangeetha, P., & Kumaran, S. (2018). Impact of shared leadership on cross-functional team effectiveness and performance with respect to manufacturing companies. *Journal of Management Research, 18*(1), 44-55.

Schickramm, L., Saenz-Segura, F., Schipper, R. A., & Handgraaf, M. (2015, April). The influence of group identity on farmer's decision making: an experimental economics approach on a family farming case in Costa Rica. Paper prepared for presentation at the 89th Annual Conference of the Agricultural Economics Society, University of Warwick, England, UK.

Shukla, P. (2008). *Essentials of marketing research.* London, UK: Bookboon.

Simsek, Z., Veiga, J.F., Lubatkin, M.H., & Dino, R.N (2005). Modeling the multilevel determinants o top management team behavioral integration *Academy of Management Journal, 48*(1), 69–84.

Smith, W. K. (2014). Dynamic decision making: A model of senior leaders managing strategic paradoxes. *Academy of Management Journal, 57*(6) 1592-1623.

Smith, W. K., Binns, A., & Tushman, M. L. (2010) Complex business models: Managing strategic paradox simultaneously. *Long Range Planning, 43* 448 – 461.

Soldan, Z., & Bowyer, K. (2009). Behavioral integration and performance: The moderating effect o diversity. *European Journal of Management, 9*(1) 62–72

Tekleab, A. G., Karaca, A., Quigley, N. R., & Tsang E. W. (2016). Re-examining the functional diversity–performance relationship: The roles o behavioral integration, team cohesion, and team learning. *Journal of Business Research, 69*(9), 3500-3507.

Verbeek, B. (2017). *Decision-making in Great Britain During the Suez Crisis: Small groups and a persistent leader.* Oxford, UK: Routledge.

Wang, S., & He, Y. (2008). Compensating non-dedicated cross-functional teams. *Organization Science* 19, 753–765.

White, B. A. A., Eklund, A., McNeal, T., Hochhalter A., & Arroliga, A. C. (2018). Facilitators and barriers to ad hoc team performance. *Baylor University Medical Center Proceedings, 31*(3), 380-384.

Yan, P., Liu, J., & Skitmore, M. (2018). Individual group, and organizational factors affecting group bidding decisions for construction projects. *Advances in Civil Engineering, 1, 1-10.*

Yates, J. F., & de Oliveira, S. (2016). Culture and decision making. *Organizational Behavior and Human Decision Processes, 136*, 106-118.

8

esign Mentoring Approach in Companies n Poland

gorzata Baran[1]

STRACT

In the contemporary world of business, mentoring has become common practice. Its objectives include the personal and professional development of employees, training new employees, nurturing talents, planning for successions and developing leaders. A literature review has enabled the author to conclude that a structured, systematic, coordinated and evaluated mentoring program helps businesses achieve the expected results, i.e., the construction of lasting mentoring relationships leading to the realization of intended goals and benefits. The question therefore arises, how do companies build effective mentoring programs? The aim of the article is to determine the conditions for building effective mentoring programs. The research was conducted on a non-probable sample of 30 companies operating in Poland that have implemented mentoring programs within the last 3-5 years. Triangulation of research methods was applied. PAPI and IDI methods were used to survey representatives of chosen companies who manage mentoring programs.

The effective mentoring program is achieved by defining the roles of participants in the mentoring process precisely and by defining their competencies, responsibilities and objectives. Furthermore, it is important to establish transparent rules for participation in the mentoring program, i.e., participation criteria for mentors, selection criteria for mentees and placement criteria for bringing participants together into suitable pairs or groups. It is crucial to provide mentoring participants with support in the form of advice, consultation before and between mentoring sessions, and monitoring their expectations of and satisfaction from participating in the program.

WORDS: formal mentoring, mentorship, effectiveness, mentoring programs

llegium Civitas, Poland

1. Introduction

In the contemporary world of business, companies increasingly focus on ways to manage the organization's most valuable asset, namely, employees with unique knowledge and many years of experience. Thus, mentoring has become common practice. Mentoring objectives include the personal and professional development of employees, training new employees, nurturing talents, planning for successions and developing leaders (Clutterbuck, 2002; Gravells, 2008; Hansford & Ehrich, 2006; Meginson & Stokes, 2004). These objectives clearly contribute to the development of the whole organization by enabling the employees to realize their potential by motivating them to action, by increasing their productivity and by raising their chances of success (Allen, 2007; Friday & Friday, 2002; Higgins, 2000; Irving, Moore, & Hamilton, 2003; Willson & Elman, 1990). Mentoring can be effective at every stage of an

respondence concerning this article should be addressed to: **gorzata Baran**, Collegium Civitas, Pl. Defilad 1 PKiN XIIp., szawa 00-901, Poland. E-mail: malgorzata.baran@civitas.edu.pl employee's career (Chao, 1997; Dreher & Ash, 1990; Fagenson, 1989; Fajana & Gbajumo-Sheriff, 2011); however, the biggest challenge that the company faces in its mentoring program is the achievement of objectives not only of individual employees or groups of employees but also of the entire organization (Hansford, Ehrich, & Tennent, 2004; Irving et al., 2003; Klasen & Clutterbuck 2002; Parsloe, 2000).

A literature review has enabled the author to conclude that a structured and properly coordinated mentoring program allows businesses to achieve expected results, i.e., the construction of lasting mentoring relationships that lead to the realization of intended goals and benefits (Bedwell et al., 2011; Eby & Lockwood, 2005; Friday & Friday, 2002; Garvey & Alred, 2011; Ragins & Cotton, 1999). The question, therefore, arises of how companies build successful mentoring programs. This question became the subject of research conducted by the author in the fourth quarter of 2015 and the beginning of 2016 with funding from research project no. PN/1/2015/CC. The aim of this research was to assess the degree of organizational preparation for operating mentoring programs in companies in Poland. In particular, the selection process and the selection of mentoring participants were examined. Research was conducted on a special, selected sample of 30 companies operating in Poland that had successfully implemented mentoring programs at least 3-5 years (in some cases over the past decade or more) prior to the survey. The aim of the article is to present the author's own research findings on the building of effective mentoring programs in enterprises in Poland and on the tools used to assess the degree of organization preparation for implementing effective mentoring programs.

2. The essence of mentoring

There are numerous definitions of mentoring in the scholarly literature. Mentoring, as it is widely understood in business, is a way to help individuals and organizations achieve business objectives based on the potential of the participant to make use of the knowledge and experience of the mentor (Coaching Center, 2016). Mentoring is a way of developing the personal potential of employees by working with an experienced person who boasts a great deal of professional business knowledge. As a result, mentoring includes the mentor's direct assistance in the mentee's development, professional advice and the informal exchange of information (Listwan, 2005).

In numerous research studies, both mentors and mentees suggest that mentoring not only constitutes the dissemination of knowledge, the mastering of skills, and the personal and professional development of the employee but also the accrual of both a high level of satisfaction from just participating in the mentoring process and the benefits from building relationships (Baran, 2014; Clutterbuck, 2002; Henriques & Curado, 2009; Kram, 1985; Parsloe, 2000).

Apart from benefiting the mentor and mentee, mentoring can also be beneficial to the whole organization as shown by Wilson and Elman (1990) and Megginson et al. (2008). To clarify the concept of the "mentoring process," it is worth noting the definition by Garvey, Stokes and Megginson, who defined it as a process launched intentionally within the organizational environment (Garvey et al., 2009). Mentoring is characterized by a mode of implementation comprising a formalized process that deliberately enables the mentor's experience to support the mentee in line with the aims of the organization. The concomitance of development objectives of the mentee and organization is known as "organised mentoring" (Garvey & Alred, 2011).

The informal method of the mentoring process in an organization can be identified as a process that has not been formalized, existing without documented rules, organizational regulations and appropriate structures within the organization. It develops spontaneously and occurs as a result of the mentor-mentee relationship, which involves a willingness of both parties to cooperate, invest time and exhibit mutual trust (Baran, 2016). It is often seen as a process to achieve specific demands, very often to produce career-related support (Chao, Walz, & Gardner, 1992). Usually, it is based on unwritten rules of the traditional master-student relationship. On the other hand, formal mentoring is a formalized process, located in the organizational structure, based on contracts, procedures, and regulations (Baran, 2016). This type of mentoring is formed through an organized and planned matching of mentor and mentee by the organization (Ragin & Cotton, 1999). The mentoring sessions are based on a schedule of meetings and evaluations that impact the mentee's work. The whole process is structured and the rela-ion between mentor and mentee is coordinated using tandard norms, action plans and particular objectives Bahniuk & Hill, 1998; Bednell et al., 2012; Hansford & :hrich, 2006, Noe, 1988).

Regardless of the kind of mentoring used and re- ;ardless of the size and specialization of the organiza- ion, the basic mentoring scheme remains unchanged Allen, 2007; Holiday, 2006; Klasen & Clutterbuck, :002; Kram, 1985; Megginson & Clutterbuck, 1995; 'arsloe, 1992); its objectives are related to the organi- ational culture, organizational structure and strategy. n the literature review of the best practices of mentor- ng schemes conducted by the author, there are some :ey steps of effective mentoring schemes in all types of ›rganization (Allen, Finkelstein & Poteet, 2011; Cran- vell-Ward, Bossons, & Gover, 2004; Klasen & Clut- erbuck, 2002; Megginson et al., 2008; Merrick, 2009; Ramaswami & Dreher, 2007; Schein, 2010; Sontag, /appie, & Wanberg, 2007), these are as follows:

- estimating the expected benefits for the organization, the mentors and the mentees,
- determining the timeframe in which the benefits should become apparent,
- engagement and support of senior and middle management and the HR department in the mentoring process,
- coordination and supervision,
- monitoring of the process and the procedures used, evaluating, informational and promotional activities,
- recruitment and selection of mentors, mentees, pairing mentors and mentees,
- estimating the mentoring process plan – duration, number of sessions, training, advice, evaluation,
- and evaluating the mentoring process in the organization.

3. Characteristics of mentoring programs

Many authors contend that appropriately planned, ›rganized and managed mentoring programs can ef- ectively help employees meet their own goals and the goals and strategies of the organization (Clutterbuck, 2002; Friday & Friday, 2002; Hansford & Ehrich, 2006; Kram, 1983; Ragins & Cotton, 1999).

Mentoring relationships produced in the framework of formal and coordinated mentoring programs differ fundamentally from relationships produced in the context of informal mentoring (Allen, Eby, & Lentz, 2006). This difference exists regardless of what type of mentoring the organization uses, from community-based relationships to e-mentoring relationships, including peer mentoring, group mentoring, mutual mentoring, reverse mentoring, team mentoring and virtual mentoring (Baran, 2016; Garvey & Alred, 2011; Higgins, 2000; Klasen & Clutterbuck, 2002; Ragins & Kram, 2007; Stokes & Merrick, 2013). The key difference between the two systems is the way in which relationships are built, while informal mentoring relationships are produced in conditions of mutual understanding and need from both sides, mentoring pairs in formal programs are formed as a result of specific HR processes (Ragins, 2002). Formal and informal mentoring relationships also differ in the structure of the relationship (Ragins & Cotton, 1999). Informal relationships are not bound by schedules, predetermined durations and imposed rules. In contrast, formalized mentoring is characterized by a more structured mentoring process, comprising the selection of mentors and mentees, placing them in pairs, interim feedback and evaluation. Implementation of mentoring sessions takes place with the use of standards, constant action plans and time frames (Baugh & Fagenson-Eland, 2007; Eby, 1997; Higgins & Kram, 2001; Ragins & Cotton, 1999).

In the literature, on the subject, some authors suggest that informal mentoring can be more valuable than a formal system on average (Chao et al., 1992). Nevertheless, the study by Ragins (2002) showed that formal mentoring programs have the potential to produce as many benefits as informal ones. Furthermore, formal mentoring is an important tool for the organization in the process of employee development, increasing both the productivity and efficiency of the employees (Ragins, 2002). If a mentoring program is formal, it allows employers to manage the program and its participants effectively (Wilson & Elman, 1990). By devoting time to the careful preparation of rules, procedures, criteria, schedules and participating employees, employers are able to ensure the effectiveness of the program, i.e., they are able to ensure its timely implementation and the achievement of its designated objectives (Friday & Friday, 2002; Irving et al., 2003).

4. Methodology

This study was conducted at the turn of 2015 and 2016 within the research project (PN/1/2015/CC). Mentoring research in selected Polish companies was based on the triangulation of research methods, which was supposed to increase the credibility of the obtained materials and their interpretation (Hensel & Glinka, 2001). Three research methods were used in the study:

- A quantitative study based on PAPI (direct questionnaire, paper-and-pencil interview)
- A qualitative study based on the IDI (individual, in-depth interview)
- Analysis of existing data (documents from companies).

The study was conducted on a non-probable (purposeful as described by Babbie, 2003; Frankfort-Nachmias & Nachmias, 2001) sample of 30 companies operating in Poland that use mentoring. The term "companies in Poland" used in this work refers to companies that are both registered in the Polish National Court Register and who conduct their business activities in Poland. The first criterion of a company's participation in the study was using a mentoring process for a minimum of 3-5 years and organizing mentoring programs. The second criterion taken into account was the size of the organization that used mentoring (in order to diversify the sample with small, medium and large companies). The purpose of such selection criteria was to obtain a variety of organizations with extensive experience in the implementation of mentoring and the use of mentoring programs.

The task of producing a representative sample of companies that use mentoring programs proved to be difficult to achieve, mainly due to the lack of registers available, i.e., databases containing such entities. Therefore, the selection of companies took place through cooperation with mentor associations and organizations associating mentoring organizations in Poland. The main research method used in the study was the direct questionnaire interview PAPI. The choice of such a research technique was dictated by the complexity of the research problem, which influenced the very large questionnaire survey (consisting of 37 questions and response cards for the responders). PAPI was used to survey representatives of companies managing mentoring processes, who were coordinators of mentoring programs (often in HR departments). The PAPI method allowed the author to obtain aggregate data b using standardized questions (Babbie, 2003).

In the qualitative study, the method of data collec tion was based on individual in-depth interviews (IDI) which were also carried out with the coordinators o mentoring processes. In-depth interviews were carrie out using a scenario that included questions and a lis of issues to be discussed. The qualitative method per mitted an in-depth analysis of the mentoring issues i the surveyed companies and an answering of question that could not be asked under standardized condition using the questionnaire survey.

A group of 30 companies took part in the research which includes 4 (13%) small companies (with 10-4 employees), 6 (20%) medium companies (with 50-24 employees), and 20 (67%) large companies (with a least 250 employees). For the respondents' industria sector, the sample consists of 15 (50%) service compa nies, 7 (23%) manufacturing companies, and 8 (28% trading companies. All the companies operate wit Polish capital.

The aim of the study was to determine how com panies were building effective mentoring programs Based on a literature review, elements of the proces initiating mentoring in the organization—directl concerning program participants and their prepara tion to participate in the process—were identified. On of the elements that characterized the system was th formal program coordinators' selection of candidate as mentors and potential mentees to participate in th program and the way in which they were put into pair or mentoring groups. Further, selected elements of th mentoring process in the organization concerned th competence of the program participants, their roles i the process, expectations of and benefits from partici pation in the process and the roles of superiors.

At the same time, based on the evaluated practice of the surveyed companies, an attempt was made t create a tool for measuring the level of preparation o organizations to build effective mentoring programs.

5. Participant selection process in business mentoring programs in companies in Poland—presentation of research results

The vast majority of companies surveyed (86.6%) in dicated that a system had been created where mentor

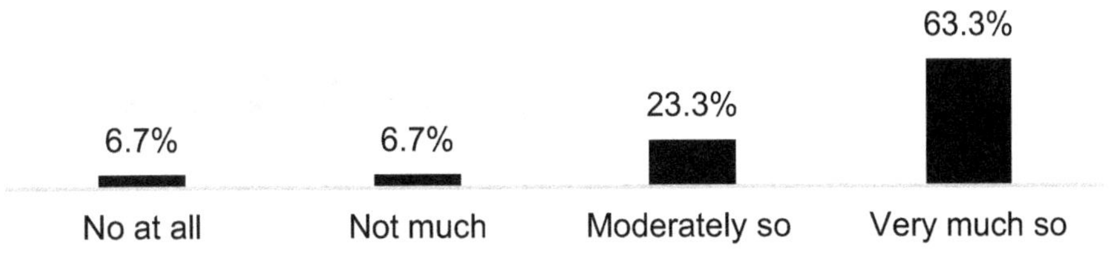

ure 1. Degree of agreement with the statement "Before the mentoring process started, a system was created whereby tors and mentees were selected and placed into pairs" N = 30

and mentees were selected and placed into pairs or groups. Only 13% of companies stated that no selection system at the stage of implementing mentoring programs had been established in the company—cf. Figure 1.

An analysis of the methods used for selecting mentors to participate in the implementation of mentoring programs in the surveyed companies showed that the main criteria comprised following:

- substantive knowledge of the sector (96.7%),
- the amount of experience in the organization (90%),
- knowledge about management and managerial skills (90%),
- ability and willingness to share knowledge (90%),
- availability (86.7%),
- opinion of the mentor's milieu on their knowledge and experience (80%),
- position/standing in the company (70%),
- whether or not the mentor volunteered (63.3%).

It is worth noting that none of the surveyed organizations considered gender or age of the candidate as a criterion for selecting mentors.

In contrast, the analysis of the methods used for selecting mentees to participate in mentoring programs showed that more than half of the companies turned to nominations by superiors (53.3%), while simultaneously taking into account survey findings on employee training and developmental needs. One in three companies taking part in this study indicated that the selection of mentees took place differently than indicated above, i.e., in those companies a crucial factor was the candidates' earlier roles as mentees in talent programs (30%). In addition, the opinion of the HR department played a significant role in the respondents' opinion of the analyzed process (15%).

In more than half of the surveyed companies, an individual or a coordinating team for mentoring in the company was responsible for the selection of participants in the mentoring process and their suitable placement into pairs or groups. The results of the study indicate that it is most common for the process manager to collect applications from people who — meeting set criteria — are willing to mentor and to match them to mentees in response to the identified developmental needs of the mentees (56.7%). The second most used method, albeit decidedly less common, is the recommendation of mentoring pairs by a specialist or the HR manager (36.7%). It is worth noting that none of the organizations employed a selection system in which mentoring pairs were chosen at a draw (see Figure 2).

Another important aspect of this study was to see if companies were mindful of avoiding codependency between mentor and mentee during the selection of mentoring pairs or groups (Figure 3). For most companies surveyed (86%), the lack of codependency between mentor and mentee constitutes one of the main principles of the mentoring process.

As seen in Table 1, the problem of codependency affects small businesses most acutely.

Figure 2. Ways of selecting participants for business mentoring relationships [3]

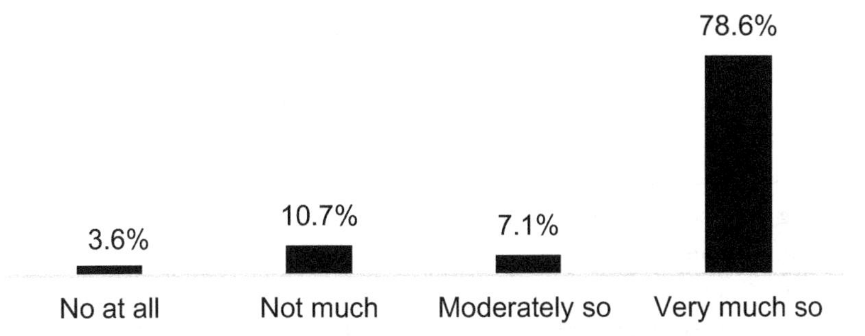

re 3. On a scale of 1 (not at all) to 4 (very much so), degree of agreement with the statement "When matching men- with mentees, care is taken to avoid any codependency between the two" N = 30

le 1. Average degree of agreement with the statement "When matching mentors with mentees, care is taken to avoid codependency between the two" according to the size of the companies.

Small companies	Medium companies	Large companies
2.0	3.95	4.0

At this point it is worth noting that the evaluation ɋuestion concerning which businesses take care to ıvoid codependency between the mentor and mentee s positively correlated with the size of the organization — the result of Spearman's correlation turned out to be very high, at 0.751 with a significance level of < 0.01. This means that the bigger the company, the more care taken to avoid codependency between the mentor and mentee in the mentoring process.

6. Company preparation for building effective mentoring program—results of research on companies

In the context of examining companies that have experience implementing mentoring programs over many years, program coordinators were asked a set of questions concerning the degree of preparation of the company's employees to participate in mentoring processes. A suitable set of questions—developed on the basis of a literature review—has enabled not only an exposition of how a mentoring process was prepared in the surveyed organizations but also the creation of tools measuring the degree of organizational preparation for building effective mentoring programs (which will be discussed in more detail later in the article).

To assess how the surveyed companies a) prepared employees to participate in the mentoring process and b) were able to build effective mentoring program, a set of questions was posed to them to determine how much they agreed with the following statements:

1. Before launching the mentoring program in the company, a system was created to select and appropriately pair mentors and mentees.
2. Before launching the mentoring program, the core competencies of a potential mentor were defined.
3. Before launching the mentoring program, the core competencies of a potential mentee were defined.

4. Before launching the mentoring program, the developmental/competence needs of the mentor/mentee participants in the program were identified.
5. The roles of mentor and mentee were clearly defined and understood from the very start of implementation of mentoring in the company.
6. When matching mentors with mentees, care is taken to avoid any codependency between the two.
7. Before launching the mentoring program, the expectations of future mentors were assessed.
8. Before launching the mentoring program, the expectations of future mentees were assessed.
9. Before launching the mentoring program, specific benefits resulting from participation in the program were outlined to future mentors.
10. Before launching the mentoring program, specific benefits resulting from participation in the program were outlined to future mentees. Table 2 shows the percentage distributions for all answers to the above 10 questions.

It is worth noting that for all the analyzed questions, the percentage of positive statements ("Very much so" and "Moderately so") was dominant, which means that most of the preparatory elements of the analyzed process were carried out by the surveyed companies. Calculations were made to verify if the size of the company significantly influenced the answers to the above mentoring preparation questions. Each answer (on a scale of 1 to 4) was compared by calculating the Kruskal-Wallis non-parametric significance test (this test was chosen because more than two groups were being compared).

The answers to four statements turned out to be significantly different depending on the size of the company. They include the following:

1. Before launching the mentoring program in the company, a system was created to select and appropriately pair mentors and mentees.
2. Before launching the mentoring program, specific benefits resulting from participation in the program were outlined to future mentors.
3. Before launching the mentoring program, the expectations of future mentees were assessed.
4. The roles of mentor and mentee were clearly defined and understood from the very start of implementation of mentoring in the company.

In each of these statements, answers from small companies differed significantly from those of medium and large companies. Small companies rarely define the specific benefits of mentoring before implementation of the mentoring process. They also fail to attach sufficient importance to the definition of the roles of mentor and mentee, hence limiting the participants' understanding of their roles in the process from the outset. In contrast, according to the response from medium and large companies, it was more common to offer training, advisory and consultative support, especially for mentors, as well as for mentees. In addition, participants in mentoring programs usually sign a mentoring contract defining the objectives of mentoring, as well as the roles, tasks and responsibilities of participants. Similar differences between small, medium and large companies were observed in the evaluation of the expectations of people who participate in the program as mentees. In this particular case, there is a linear correlation: the larger the company, the more frequently the expectations of mentors are evaluated.

Using the list of variables based on the questions listed earlier, a scale was developed to show the extent of the organization's preparation to build successful mentoring programs. The scale was created to ensure good preparation of the company employees to perform their assigned roles in the mentoring process. Suitable preparation enables the development of effective mentoring, i.e., relationships that lead to the achievement of mentoring objectives while contributing to high levels of satisfaction of the mentoring participants by just participating in the program. The scale includes questions about the process of preparation by the organization to run mentoring programs. All the selected questions shared a common way of measuring the degree of agreement: respondents had to answer each question on a scale of 1 to 4 (where 1 means "Not at all" and 4 means "Very much so"). By summing up the answers of the questions included in the scale and dividing the sum by the number of questions, a measure was obtained which, like a single question, produced a value between 1 and 4.

The proposed scale of organizational preparation for building effective mentoring programs yielded the following values:

- "1" means that the company is completely unprepared to build successful mentoring programs,
- "2" means that the degree of organizational preparation to build effective mentoring programs is low

le 2. Comparison of answers to questions on the organization's preparation to build effective mentoring programs

tement	Degree of agreement with the statement			
	Very much so	Moderately so	Not much	Not at all
efore launching the mentoring gram in the company, a system was ted to select and appropriately pair ntors and mentees.	63.3%	23.3%	6.7%	6.7%
efore launching the mentoring gram, the core competencies of a ential mentor were defined.	70%	13.3%	16.7%	0%
efore launching the mentoring gram, the core competencies of a ential mentee were defined.	43.3%	30%	20%	6.7%
efore launching the mentoring gram, the developmental/ npetence needs of the mentor/ ntee participants in the program were ntified.	63.3%	26.7%	3.3%	6.7%
he roles of mentor and mentee were rly defined and understood from very start of implementation of ntoring in the company.	60%	23.3%	16.7%	0%
hen matching mentors with mentees, is taken to avoid any codependency ween the two.	78.6%	7.1%	10.7%	3.6%
efore launching the mentoring gram, the expectations of future ntors were assessed.	53.3%	16.7%	16.7%	13.3%
efore launching the mentoring gram, the expectations of future ntees were assessed.	50%	26.7%	13.3%	10%
efore launching the mentoring gram, specific benefits resulting n participation in the program were ined to future mentors.	56.7%	26.7%	16.7%	0%
Before launching the mentoring gram, specific benefits resulting n participation in the program were lined to future mentees.	50%	33.3%	10%	6.7%

Table 3. Comparison of answers to questions on the organization's preparation to build effective mentoring programs according to company size.

Variables	Small company – average response	Medium company – average response	Large company – average response	The Kruskal-Wa significance te for independe samples (p-val
1. Before launching the mentoring program in the company, a system was created to select and appropriately pair mentors and mentees.	2.5	3.0	3.8	0.007
2. Before launching the mentoring program, the core competencies of a potential mentor were defined.	3.33	3.5	3.6	0.624
3. Before launching the mentoring program, the core competencies of a potential mentee were defined.	2.8	2.5	3.3	0.335
4. Before launching the mentoring program, the developmental/competence needs of the mentor/mentee participants in the program were identified.	2.8	3	3.76	0.079
5. The roles of mentor and mentee were clearly defined and understood from the very start of implementation of mentoring in the company.	2.67	3.75	3.6	0.030
6. When matching mentors with mentees, care is taken to avoid any codependency between the two.	2	3.95	4	0,0001
7. Before launching the mentoring program, the expectations of future mentors were assessed.	2.17	3	3.5	0.18
8. Before launching the mentoring program, the expectations of future mentees were assessed.	2	3	3.5	0.014
9. Before launching the mentoring program, specific benefits resulting from participation in the program were outlined to future mentors.	2.5	3.75	3.6	0.005
10. Before launching the mentoring program, specific benefits resulting from participation in the program were outlined to future mentees.	3.17	3.5	3.6	0.663

e 4. Consistency of scale regarding the organization's preparation to build effective mentoring program.

stions included in the scale *preparation of participants* for toring	Cronbach's coefficient alpha after exclusion from the scale	Cronbach's coefficient alpha for the *entire* scale
fore launching the mentoring program in the company, a system was ed to select and appropriately pair mentors and mentees.	0.878	
ore launching the mentoring program, the core competencies of a ntial mentor were defined.	0.887	
fore launching the mentoring program, the core competencies of a ntial mentee were defined.	0.890	
fore launching the mentoring program, the developmental/ petence needs of the mentor/mentee participants in the program identified.	0.883	
e roles of mentor and mentee were clearly defined and understood the very start of implementation of mentoring in the company.	0.867	0.887
ıen matching mentors with mentees, care is taken to avoid any pendency between the two.	0.878	
fore launching the mentoring program, the expectations of future tors were assessed.	0.863	
fore launching the mentoring program, the expectations of future tees were assessed.	0.868	
fore launching the mentoring program, specific benefits resulting from cipation in the program were outlined to future mentors.	0.871	
efore launching the mentoring program, specific benefits resulting participation in the program were outlined to future mentees.	0.875	

- "3" means that the degree of organizational preparation to build effective mentoring programs is high,
- "4" means that the company is completely prepared to build successful mentoring programs.

Ihe creation of the scale allowed the author to develop ı tool that companies could use for their own purposes ınd needs to evaluate the process of organizational preparation to implement mentoring in the company. Ihe resulting knowledge can encourage the company o initiate improvement actions or corrective measures, if necessary, and will produce better/more effective mentoring processes in the organization.

To assess the reliability of the newly created scale, Cronbach's coefficient alpha was calculated[1] for the whole scale, and for each of the items included in its composition after its exclusion in order to see if the reliability of the scale would be higher or lower after exclusion of individual questions.

Table 4 shows the results of the calculated coefficients. Cronbach's coefficient alpha for the entire scale turned out to be very high, at 0.887[2]. One of the ele-

Table 5. Average of scale regarding the organization's preparation to build effective mentoring programs according t company size.

Scale	Small company – average	Medium company – average	Large company – average	The Kruskal-Wal significance tes for independer samples (p-valu
The scale of preparation of participants in mentoring	2.83	3.56	3.58	0.029

ments (no. 3) after exclusion from the scale would have only raised the scales consistency slightly, but the decision was made not to exclude this position, given the high level of consistency of the whole scale.

To verify whether there were differences in the scale due to the size of the company implementing mentoring processes, a comparison of averages was made. The result confirmed that the average of the scale showing the degree of preparation of participants in mentoring increases with company size (cf. Table 5).

Both the size of the company and the scale of the preparation of mentoring participants were high and significantly statistically correlated to one another—the Spearman's correlation coefficient between these two variables was 0.435 ($p < 0.05$). Therefore, it can be concluded that the larger the company (among those surveyed), the better prepared it is to build lasting and effective mentoring programs based on matching mentoring participants, understanding their individual roles, and knowing the principles of mentoring. This leads to the implementation of the designated objectives and the acquisition of benefits expected by the participants and the organization in the mentoring process.

7. Conclusions

The essence of effectively implementing a formal mentoring program is, in the opinion of the author, the decision-making process by the employer (e.g., the mentoring coordinator) that aims to build lasting relationships between mentor and mentee. This allows participants of the mentoring process to fulfill their needs, meet their expectations, and achieve predefined benefits, all of which directly contribute to the effectiveness of the whole mentoring process in the organization This effectiveness is achieved by defining the roles o participants in the mentoring process precisely and b defining their competencies, tasks, responsibilities an mentoring objectives. Furthermore, it is important t establish transparent rules for participation in the men toring program, i.e., participation criteria for mentors selection criteria for mentees and placement criteri for bringing participants together into suitable pair or groups. At the same time, it is very helpful to pro vide mentoring participants with support in the forn of advice, consultation before and between mentorin sessions, and monitoring their expectations of and sat isfaction from participating in the program. Implemen tation of all these elements increases the effectivenes of mentoring programs. This research indicates tha the larger the company, the more attention it pays t include all of the aforementioned elements in the men toring process, thereby being better prepared to buil mentoring programs. Consequently, the company ca successfully implement its mentoring program.

The results of the study – despite the proven statisti cally significant correlations – have not been general ized, since only a group of 30 companies was exam ined. Furthermore, the results described in this articl incorporate only selected elements of the busines mentoring process, resulting in an analysis that ma appear to the reader somewhat terse and incomplete So far, only a few mentoring studies have been con ducted in Poland, focusing on identifying mentorin needs and expected benefits. The mentoring proces has not been examined in terms of its effectiveness, a presented in this article. The study has obvious limita tions, mainly due to a small and non-probable sample

Therefore, it is recommended that further research makes use of a larger sample in order to generalize the conclusions. Despite perceptible limitations, the study is important for HR practitioners and managers because it enhances managerial knowledge of mentoring effectiveness and allows companies to better prepare themselves for mentoring processes through the proposed tool to assess organizational readiness for mentoring. At the same time, the article does not exhaust the research problem, it merely contributes to further research into the determinants of mentoring process in enterprises.

References

Allen, T. D. (2007). Mentoring Relationships From the Perspective of the Mentor. In B. R. Ragins, K. E. Kram (Eds.), *The Handbook of Mentoring at Work: Theory, Research, and Practice* (pp. 123-147). Thousand Oaks, CA: Sage.

Allen, T. D., Eby, L. T., & Lentz, E. (2006). Mentorship behaviors and mentorship quality associated with formal mentoring programs: Closing the gap between research and practice. *Journal of Applied Psychology,* 91(3), 567-578. http://dx.doi.org/10.1037/0021-9010.91.3.567

Allen, T. D., Finkelstein, L. M. & Poteet, M. L. (2011). *Designing workplace mentoring programs: An evidence-based approach.* United Kingdom: Chichester, UK: John Wiley & Sons.

Babbie, E. (2003). *Badania społeczne w praktyce* [The Practice of Social Research]. Warszawa: PWN.

Bahniuk, M. H., Hill, S. K. (1998). Promoting career success through mentoring. *Review of Business,* 19 (3), 4-7.

Baugh, S. G. & Fagenson-Eland, E. A. (2007). Formal mentoring programs: a poor cousin to informal relationships? In B. R. Ragins, K. E. Kram (Eds.), *The Handbook of Mentoring at Work: Theory, Research, and Practice* (pp. 249-272). Thousand Oaks, CA: Sage.

Baran, M. (2014). Mutual mentoring as a tool for managing employees of different generations in the enterprise. *Journal of Positive Management*, 5(2), 20-29. http://dx.doi.org/10.12775/JPM.2014.010

Baran, M. (2016). The Mentor's Role Within the Company. *Studia i Materiały/Wydział Zarządzania. Uniwersytet Warszawski,* 2(21), 133 – 143.

Bedwell W.L., Weaver S.J., Salas E., Tindall M. (2011). *Emerging conceptualizations as adult training and learning.* The Oxford Handbook of Lifelong Learning, Oxford, UK: University Press.

Chao, G.T. (1997). Mentoring phases and outcomes. *Journal of Vocational Behavior*, 51, 15-28.

Chao, G. T., Walz, P. M., & Gardner, P. D. (1992). Formal and informal mentorships: A comparison on mentoring functions and contrast with non-mentored counterparts. *Personnel Psychology*, 45, 619-636.

Clutterbuck, D. (2002). *Każdy potrzebuje mentora: Jak kierować talentami* [Everyone Needs a Mentor: Fostering Talent in Your Organisation]. Warszawa: Petit.

Coaching Center. (2011). *Mentoring - podstawowe informacje* [Mentoring – basic information]. Retrieved from: http://www.coachingcenter.pl.

Cranwell-Ward, J., Bossons, P. & Gover, S. (2004). *Mentoring: A Henley Review of Best Practice.* London, UK: Palgrave Macmillan.

Dreher, G. F., & Ash, R. A. (1990). A comparative study of mentoring among men and women in managerial, professional, and technical positions. *Journal of Applied Psychology*, 75, 525-35.

Eby, L. T. (1997). Alternative forms of mentoring in changing organizational environments: A conceptual extension of the mentoring literature. *Journal of Vocational Behaviour, 51*(1), 125-144. https://doi.org/10.1006/jvbe.1997.1594

Eby, L. T., & Lockwood, A. (2005). Proteges' and mentors' reactions to participating in formal mentoring programmes: A qualitative investigation. *Journal of Vocational Behaviour,* 67(3), 441-458. http://dx.doi.org/10.1016/j.jvb.2004.08.002

Fagenson, E.A. (1989). The mentor advantage: Perceived career/job experiences of proteges vs. non-proteges. *Journal of Organizational Behavior, 10*(4), 309-20. https://doi.org/10.1002/job.4030100403

Fajana, S., & Gbajumo-Sheriff, M. (2011). Mentoring: An Human Resource Tool for Achieving Organisational Effectiveness. In A. A. Olowu (Ed.), *Mentoring: A Key Issue in Human Resource Management* (pp. 420-432). Ife, Nigeria: The Ife Centre for Psychological Studies.

Frankfort-Nachmias Ch., & Nachmias D. (2001). *Metody badawcze w naukach społecznych* [Research Methods in Social Sciences]. Poznań: Wyd. Zysk i S-ka.

Friday, E. & Friday, S. S. (2002). Formal Mentoring: Is there a strategic fit? *Management Decision*, 40(2), 152-157. https://doi.org/10.1108/00251740210422820

Garvey, B. & Alred, G. (2011). Mentoring and the tolerance of complexity. *Futures*, 33, 519-530.

Garvey, B., Stokes, P., and Megginson, D. (2009). *Coaching and Mentoring Theory and Practice*. London, UK: Sage.

Gravells, J. (2008). Case study 13: Mentoring dla właścicieli małych firm w Nottingham [Case study 13: Mentoring owners of micro businesses in Nottingham]. In D. Megginson, D. Clutterbuck, B. Garvey, P. Stokes, and R. Garrett-Harris (Ed.), *Mentoring w działaniu* [Mentoring in Action] (pp. 177-187). Poznań: Dom Wydawniczy REBIS.

Hansford, B. & Ehrich, L. C. (2006). The principalship: How significant is mentoring? *Journal of Educational Administration*, *44*(1), 36-52. https://doi.org/10.1108/09578230610642647

Hansford, B., Ehrich, L. C. & Tennent, L. (2004). Formal mentoring programs in education and other professions: A review of the literature. *Educational Administration Quarterly*, *40* (4), 518-540. https://doi.org/10.1177/0013161X04267118

Henriques, P. L., & Curado, C. (2009). Publishing the boundaries on mentoring: Can mentoring be a knowledge tool? *Journal of Business Economics and Management*, 10(1), 85-97. https://doi.org/10.3846/1611-1699.2009.10.85-97

Hensel P., Glinka B. (2012). Teoria ugruntowana [Well-established theory]. In D. Jemielniak (Ed.), *Badania jakościowe. Metody i narzędzia* [Qualitative research. Methods and tools] (Vol. 1, pp. 89-113). Warszawa: Wydawnictwo Naukowe PWN.

Higgins, M. C. (2000). The more, the merrier? Multiple developmental relationships and work satisfaction. *Journal of Management Development*, *19*(4), 277-296. https://doi.org/10.1108/02621710010322634

Higgins, M. C., & Kram, K. E. (2001). Reconceptualizing mentoring at work: A developmental network perspective. *Academy of Management Review*, 26(2), 264-288. https://doi.org/10.1177/1534484306290227

Holiday, M. (2006). *Coaching, mentoring i zarządzanie: Jak rozwiązywać problemy i budować zespół* [Coaching, Mentoring and Managing: Breakthrough Strategies to Solve Performance Problems and Build Winning Teams]. Gliwice: Wydawnictwo HELION.

Irving, E. S., Moore, W. D., & Hamilton, R. J. (2003). Mentoring for high ability school students. *Education and Training*, 45(2), 100-109. https://doi.org/10.1108/00400910310464071

Klasen, N. & Clutterbuck, D. (2002). *Implementing Mentoring Schemes. A practical guide to successful programs*. Routledge Taylor & Francis Group: London & New York.

Kram, K. E. (1983). Phases on the mentor relationship. *Academy of Management Journal*, *26*(4), 608-625. https://doi.org/10.5465/255910

Kram, K. E. (1985). *Mentoring network: Developmental relationships in organizational life*. Glen View, IL: Scott Foreman.

Listwan, T. (2005). *Słownik zarządzania kadrami* [Dictionary of human resources management]. Warszawa: C.H. Beck.

Megginson, D., & Clutterbuck, D. (1995). *Mentoring in Action*. London, UK: Kogan Page.

Megginson, D., Clutterbuck, D., Garvey, B., Stokes, P., & Garrett-Harris, R. (2008). *Mentoring w działaniu: Przewodnik praktyczny* [Mentoring in Action: A Practical Guide for Managers]. Poznań: Dom Wydawniczy REBIS.

Megginson, D., Stokes, P. (2004). Mentoring for export success. In J. Stewart, G. Beaver (Eds.), *HRM in Small Organizations: Research and Practice* (pp. 265-285). Abingdon, UK: Routledge.

Merrick, L. (2009). How to set up a mentoring program. *Coaching at Work*, 3(4), 52–54.

Noe, R. A. (1998). An investigation of the determinants of successful assigned mentoring relationships. *Personnel Psychology*, *41*(3), 457-479. https://doi.org/10.1111/j.1744-6570.1988.tb00638.x

Parsloe, E. (1992). *Coaching. Mentoring and Assessing: A Practical Guide to Developing Competence*. London, UK: Kogan Page.

Parsloe, E. (2000). *Coaching i mentoring* [Coaching and Mentoring]. Warszawa: Petit.

Ragins, B. R. (2002). Understanding diversified mentoring relationships: definitions, challenges, and strategies. In D. Clutterbuck, B. R. Ragins (Eds.), *Mentoring and Diversity: An International Perspective* (pp. 23-53). Oxford, UK: Butterworth Heinemann.

Ragins, B. R., & Cotton, J. L. (1999). Mentor functions and outcomes: A comparison of men and women in formal and informal mentoring relationships. *Journal of Applied Psychology, 84*(4), 529-550.

Ragins, B. R., & Kram, K. E. (2007). The roots and meaning of mentoring. In B. R. Ragins, K. E. Kram (Eds.), *The Handbook of Mentoring at Work: Theory, Research, and Practice* (pp. 3-15). Thousand Oaks, CA: Sage.

Ramaswami, A., & Dreher, G. F. (2007). The benefits associated with workplace mentoring relationships. In T. D. Allen, L. T. Eby (Eds.), *The Blackwell Handbook of Mentoring: A Multiple Perspectives Approach* (pp. 211-231). Malden, MA: Blackwell Publishing.

Schein, E. H. (2010). *Organizational Culture and Leadership*. San Francisco, CA: Jossey-Bass.

Sontag, L.P., Vappie, K., & Wanberg, C. R. (2007). The practice of mentoring: MENTTIUM corporation. In B. R. Ragins, K. E. Kram (Eds.), *The Handbook of Mentoring at Work: Theory, Research and Practice* (pp. 593–616). Thousand Oaks, CA: Sage.

Stokes, P., & Merrick, L. (2013). Designing Mentoring Schemes for Organizations In J. Passmore, D. B. Peterson, & T. Freire (Eds.), *The Wiley-Blackwell Handbook of The Psychology of Coaching and Mentoring* (pp. 197- 216). Chichester, UK: John Wiley & Sons Ltd.

Wilson, J. A., & Elman, N. S. (1990). Organizational Benefits of Mentoring. *Academy of Management Executive*, 4(4), 88-94.

Endnotes

1 *Cronbach's coefficient alpha measures the internal consistency of all elements in a given scale and thus determines whether the latter are studying the same phenomenon.*

2 *It is generally assumed that if the value of Cronbach's coefficient alpha is over 0.7, it signifies a high consistency of the scale.*

3 *Answers do not add up to 100% because respondents could choose more than one answer.*

The Business Model and its Core Elements: Proposal of Definition and Table of Core Elements

Arturo Orea Rocha[1], Carmelo García Pérez[1], Fernando Crecente Romero[1], Maria Teresa del Val Núñez[1]

ABSTRACT

The concept of the business model has garnered the attention of business administration resea ers and professionals for over 50 years, and especially since the last decade of the 20th centur a result of the appearance and widespread use of the internet in business.

Despite the large number of doctrinal contributions, studies and analyses carried out, th years of research have not resulted in consensus among authors and professionals regarding ei a definition or the core elements of a business model.

This article provides a proposal for the definition of business model, as well as a proposa a table of elements which includes those that we believe will be of great importance in the fut of organisations, such as their approach to security, the code of ethics and their own capacity transformation. To create the definition and table of elements, numerous publications regarc the concept of the business model were analysed, mainly from between 1996 and 2017, when concept was most highly developed in the academic literature.

The article suggests future lines of research to study the evolution of the concept of the mo the greater or lesser importance of certain elements, as well as the impact on the bottom line of transformation of and innovation in the model itself.

KEY WORDS: Business model, value proposition, market segmentation, transformation, code of ethics, security

[1] University of Alcalá, Spain

1. Introduction

According to García-Echevarría (2002, p. 55) "of every 10 strategic designs, nine are not successfully implemented. The inability to achieve their goals proposed, with the new dimensions of companies and their growth, is directly related to the suitable selection and implem tation of the business management models used".

Does the concept of the business model for manag organisations in general, and businesses in particu have an influence on the reality described above? C by conceptualising the business model and establi ing the keys for its implementation, will it be poss to determine if it can effectively meet businesses' n to fulfil their strategic objectives for growth. Despit widespread use, the concept is still confusing and it e "seems that the executives, reporters, and analysts w

Correspondence concerning this article should be addressed to: **Carmelo García Pérez**, Economics Department, University of Alcalá, Plaza Victoria 2, 28802, Alcalá de Henares, Madrid, Spain. E-mail: carmelo.garcia@uah.es use the term 'business model' don't have a clear idea of what it means" (Linder & Cantrell, 2000, p.2). Thus, there is still no consensus regarding its definition; as such, Porter's (Porter, 2001, p.71) statement remains true: "the definition of a business model is murky at best".

The objective of this paper is to provide a complete definition of business model that is easy to understand and put into practice, and to include in said definition a system of core elements which are interrelated in order to guarantee their implementation. To do so, based on the bibliographic analysis methodology, a review of 200 contributions published in the academic literature between 1996 and 2017 is carried out, with the aim of determining the concept of business model and its key characteristics. Certainly, the conceptualisation of the business model and of its implementation is complex, as it is of vital importance for the management of any organisation in general, and companies in particular, in order to achieve their strategic and growth objectives, and, therefore, to ensure their long-term sustainability. Whether intuitively or in a perfectly defined and structured manner, every organisation sets out to fulfil its mission, its vision and its objectives, following the road map established by its business model and the elements that comprise it.

The concept became a part of doctrinal analysis, academic research and business practice in the 1990s, as a result of the internet´s boom and the possibilities that new technologies offered to create disruptive ways of doing business, establishing innovative value propositions and new ways of establishing relationships with key customers and partners. The technological development of the last 25 years in the digital field has been exponential, unimaginable and of such a magnitude that it has highlighted the value of the concept of business model and of its constitutive elements, reinforcing the need to master its definition and description and making the concept useful and relevant. With the advance of new Information and Communications Technologies (ICT), and of the development of digitalisation in companies, innovation in the model and its elements, the own model's capacity for transformation, led by the management, and their ability to innovate, create new value propositions, adapt the model's elements to the new demands, made possible by the technology, and, finally, to cooperate and co-create with their strategic partners will be increasingly important.

This article is organised as follows: the next section, section two, provides a review of how the concept of business model has evolved in the academic literature and the main definitions that have particularly enriched the concept through their contribution. Section three identifies the different elements of the business model set forth by the different authors in the bibliographic review. Section four proposes both a definition and a table of elements of the business model, which are complete, yet simple. Finally, the main conclusions of the study are presented and future lines of research are suggested.

2. Evolution of the Concept of Business Model

According to Osterwalder, Pigneur and Tucci (2005), the term "Business Model" appears in the literature for the first time in an article by Bellman, Clark, Malcolm, Craft and Ricciardi (1957). It appeared again in the title and abstract of another academic article by Jones in 1960, (as cited in Osterwalder et al., 2005, p. 4) but it wasn't until the end of the 1990s that its use became widespread as a concept, connected to the emergence of the internet in the economy and in business. It was debated widely in a variety of academic fields and practical applications, and especially with regard to Information and Communications Technologies (ICT), online electronic commerce and business administration (Pateli & Giaglis, 2003). Since the appearance of the term in 1957, many Business Management and Administration authors and academics have delved into the concept to try to give it a definition, as such a definition is not evident.

There have even been scholars of the doctrine, such as Michael Lewis (Lewis, 1999), who have referred to the business model as an art; and, as an art, it is the type of thing that people may recognise as good or bad, but it is difficult to define (Ovans, 2015). Lewis (1999, p. 391), on the other hand, defines "Business Model" very simply: "all it (business model) really meant was how you planned to make money".

Lewis' definition, like that of many other Business Management and Administration scholars, is based on the concept in "The Theory of the Business" by Drucker (1994). Drucker, who never used the term "business model", based his definition on the assumptions upon which the given business or organisation was built, and which shape the culture of the organisation, condition its decisions with regard to what to do or what not to do, and define what the company or organisation sees as an acceptable result, all in terms of the market in which it operates, its customers and competitors, its competitive advantage, its culture, values, technology, and its strengths and weaknesses. The author emphasises the assumptions, to explain that what underlies the poor financial situations of many successful companies is the fact that their "business theories", that is, their "assumptions about how a company obtains its income", are no longer valid. His "The Theory of the Business", built around the aforementioned assumptions, is closer to Michael Porter's definition of strategy (Porter, 1996).

On the foundations of Drucker's contributions, Magretta (2002, p. 86) provided her definition in the following manner: "business models are, at heart, stories – stories that explain how enterprises work. A good business model answers Peter Drucker's age-old questions: Who is the customer? And what does the customer value? It also answers the fundamental questions every manager must ask: How do we make money in this business? What is the underlying economic logic that explains how we can deliver value to customers at an appropriate cost?" Magretta approaches her definition from a return to the basic principles of business management. According to Magretta, the concept expanded in doctrine and in the practice of Business Administration as a result of the introduction of the personal computer and spreadsheets as essential elements of business management, as they resulted in a true revolution in terms of being able to test a great number of management variables. They enabled professionals to carry out all kinds of sensitivity analyses and to delve deeper into the study of the behaviour of specific variables and their impact on the bottom line. Thus, they could model businesses and anticipate the results before launching a business, instead of analysing them after the fact, once they had implemented an action plan expecting a specific result. This allowed for a shift from management based on applying theory and trial and error analysis to management based on laboratory analysis, or, more accurately, spreadsheet analysis, which enabled potential entrepreneurs to "model" the business based on an analysis of the behaviour of its elements and by varying hypotheses and scenarios. This dynamic contributed decisively both to the advent of the concept "business model" and to its expansion in doctrine and business practice.

The rapid, intense development of Information and Communications Technologies (ICT), the expansion of the internet and an increasingly changing environment were also important factors for its popularisation (Jansen, Steenbakkers, & Jägers, 2007). This means that most of the bibliography and research on business models has dealt with internet and electronic businesses (Hedman & Kalling, 2003). In 2005, Osterwalder, Pigneur and Tucci published an interesting study in which they demonstrated the close relationship between the concept "business model" and the development of Information and Communications Technologies, relating the number of times the term appeared in academic and specialised journals and the evolution of the NASDAQ index between 1996 and 2003. It is of enormous interest, and certainly very illustrative, that the two curves run parallel, as can be seen in Figure 1. According to the authors, "it is not quite clear what to conclude from this observation besides the fact that the topic of business models probably has a relationship with technology" (Osterwalder et al., 2005, p.4).

Naturally, technology, information systems and bandwidth have made all types of communication possible around the world, making information accessible to a number of people that was unthinkable before this technological leap. Above all, said advances have decreased transaction costs (Amit & Zott, 2001; Tapscott, Ticoll, & Lowy, 2000), such that the opportunities and possibilities for designing businesses increased at a faster pace than the increase in the availability and cost of information and communication technologies. This same availability at reasonable costs made possible the advent of business models based on interrelated offers of captive products, designed specifically to reinforce and support one another. Think, for example, of Apple and its business model based on iTunes: the music access and download service using software through its website is closely linked to the sale of the iPod, its digital music player. "In terms of business models, this website (Apple's website) forms a whole set of business design choices that reinforce one another" (Osterwalder et al., 2005, p. 4). In that same study, the authors underline that the review of the literature clearly shows two focuses. On the one hand, there are

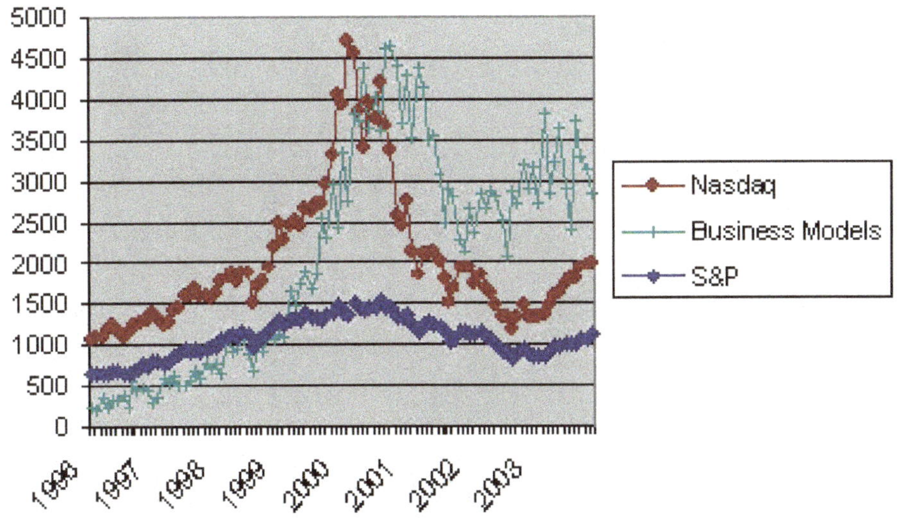

ıre 1. Occurrences of the Term "Business Model" Compared to NASDAQ Fluctuations
pted from Clarifying business models: Origins, present, and future of the concept by Osterwalder, A., Pigneur, Y., & Tucci, (2005). In Communications of the association for Information Systems, 16(1), 1, p. 4.

ıuthors who emphasise the way in which a company does business (Galper, 2001; Gebauer & Ginsburg, 2003), and, on the other, those who focus on modelling the logical story that describes a company's business, in an attempt to simplify it and make it explainable by listing its elements and describing the relationships between them (Gordijn, 2002; Osterwalder, 2004).

In any event, the concept of business model is a complex phenomenon with multiple facets that "integrates a variety of academic and functional disciplines, gaining prominence in none" (Chesbrough & Rosenbloom, 2002, p. 533).

The conceptualisation of the business model has not been without its critics. Along the lines of Schneider and Spieth (Schneider & Spieth, 2013), business model researchers have been accused of lagging behind the reality of businesses and of lacking formal structure (Casadesus-Masanell & Ricart, 2010; Plé, Lecocq & Angot, 2010; Zott, Amit, & Massa, 2011). Other authors claim that the concept lacks sufficient theoretical foundations (George & Bock, 2011; Morris, Schindehutte, & Allen, 2005; Nenonen & Storbacka, 2010; Teece, 2010). Additionally, there are authors who argue that the concept is based on different theoretical approaches that are inconsistent with one another (Camisón & Villar-López, 2010; Casadesus-Masanell & Ricart, 2010; Zott et al., 2011). Finally, in recent years, some authors have questioned whether efforts dedicated to debating the definition of business model should have been spent on more practical purposes (Baden-Fuller & Haefliger, 2013).

Some authors state that the business model needs to adapt its spatial dimensions, organisational limits and structure. An organisation's strategic choices "can make the difference in terms of the company's ability to access resources, develop competences, create a network, benefit from knowledge spill-overs and therefore excel, innovate and implement its strategy" (Onetti, Zucchella, Jones, & McDougall-Covin, 2012, p. 358).

Table 1. Distribution of the number of elements in the concept of business model in the studies analysed

Number of elements	Number of studies	%
3	5	11%
4	11	24%
5	4	9%
6	12	27%
7	5	11%
8	3	7%
9	1	2%
10	2	4%
12	1	2%
15	1	2%

Others, like Kraussl-Derzsi (2011) emphasise technology, and argue that in order to be viable, a business model must be technologically viable, and it will be when a technologically acceptable solution makes it possible to provide the service as expected; therefore, a business model is viable if it is viable in terms of value and technology (D'Souza, Wortmann, Huitema, & Velthuijsen, 2015).

In this study, the period from 1996 to 2016 has been identified as having the greatest number of publications on the concept of business model, and as also offering the most exhaustive definitions of said concept. During this period, 28 definitions were published that offered additional contributions to the concept. Said definitions are presented in Table A.1 of the Appendix. Three currents of thinking can be identified here. First, there are the authors who define business model by focusing on the value management the organisation provides (13 authors). Others define the concept in relation to the organisation's structure (10 authors). Finally, a series of authors agrees in focusing the definition on those activities that the organisation must perform to achieve its objectives (five authors). Thus, it can be observed that in recent years the focus has been more on organisational structures and the activities required to meet the organisation's objectives, instead of the main focus of earlier years, which was value creation.

This in no way means that each of these "schools" ignores or disregards the other approaches. Indeed, every organisation must consider all three aspects: value, organisation, and activities to fulfil objectives.

3. The Elements that Constitute the Business Model as Proposed in the Academic Literature

It is also of great interest to analyse the concept of business model itself, which is characterised not just by its definition, but also by the elements that comprise it. To that end, 45 studies with their different lists have been analysed; these studies are considered to be sufficiently representative both due to their relevance, as well as the novelty of each of their contributions. Table A.2 of Appendix offers a complete list of these studies with the authors and the elements defined as integral to the business model by each of them. This table identifies 30 different elements from the theories of the 45 studies cited. Over 70% of the authors add at least one additional element to the panel.

Most offer a definition with few elements. Table 1 shows the 30 elements identified, as well as their frequency. Here, it can be seen that the most popular le 2. Most relevant core elements and number of studies that identify them

nents	Number of times	%
e Proposition	31	69%
enue Stream	23	51%
tomers	18	40%
et Market / Segmentation	16	36%
Resources	14	31%
e Chain	14	31%
Partners	14	31%
npetitive Strategy	13	29%
erentiating Competences	12	27%
duct	12	27%
anization and Organizational culture	11	24%
t Structure	9	20%
Processes	8	18%
itability and Stakeholders	8	18%
ribution Channel	8	18%
iness Logic	7	16%
nnology	7	16%
ncing	6	13%
porate Governance and tainability	6	13%
astructure	4	9%
s Process	4	9%
erations	4	9%
tioning	3	7%
Information	3	7%
nd	3	7%
sion	2	4%
al Framework	2	4%
npetitive Situation	2	4%
Executives	1	2%
croeconomics	1	2%

Table 3. Sub-elements and the core elements that contain them

Elements	Sub-elements
Revenue Stream	price decisions and discounts that affect price
Customers	customer relationship management (CRM)
Key Resources	installed production capacities
Value Chain	company's position in the value chain
Key Partners	suppliers of raw materials or parts of the process that are fundamental to providing t service (in the case of service companies)
Profitability and Stakeholders	everything involving the company's profits and compensation of owners and shareholders
Business Logic	its long-term sustainability
Distribution Channel	logistic flow to bring the product/service to the end customer through the value cha
Technology	state of the art for producing the product or providing the service
Digitalisation	Information and Communications Technologies (ICT)
Corporate Governance and Sustainability	all environmental aspects involved in managing the business
Key Information	content and quality of the management information
Mission	Vision

number of elements is six; said number of elements is proposed by 12 out of the 45 studies (27%). Thirty-two of 42 studies (71%) propose a definition of six or fewer elements. Table 3 shows the number of times the 30 elements are proposed in the 45 studies. It becomes clear that there are several elements that are dominant in this study. The most commonly cited element is the value proposition, mentioned by 69% of the authors studied as one of the elements comprising the business model, followed by revenue stream (51%), customer relationships (40%), customer segmentation and the target market (36%), key resources, the position in the value chain and the network of key partners (31%), competitive strategy (29%), differentiating competences and the product (27%) and organization and organizational culture, which was named by 24% of the studies.

In order to compile Table 2, we have unified terminology, interpreting the meaning indicated by the corresponding author and identifying each element according to that meaning, in a way that some of the elements include sub-elements that fully identify them.

Table 3 presents the sub-elements found in the bibliography which are identified as part of a larger element.

From this analysis, it can also be concluded that greater dissemination of the concept, through an increase in research interest and its more widespread use in business practice, does not have a direct impact on the identification of more or new elements, or on a greater consensus with regard to said elements.

4. Towards a Proposal for a Business Model Definition and its Core Elements

Twenty-eight main definitions have been identified in this article. Each contributes to completing the concept, but they do so in a complex manner; therefore, none has evoked the consensus of Business Administration and Management theoretical and practical professionals.

A review of the literature is rounded out with the contribution of a definition of business model. The originality of this definition is based on the fact that it is both complete and easy to understand and communicate, following the principle that only what is understood can be communicated, and one can only implement something that they understand.

Thus, the following definition is proposed:

> *"A business model is the story about an organisation's value proposition, defined through a panel of key elements that comprise its way of operating, and based on three fundamental characteristics:*
>
> - *It must be unique, to guarantee the generation of competitive advantages and that it will be chosen by customers in the short term*
> - *It must be adaptable, to guarantee its long-term viability*
> - *It must be scalable, to ensure that revenue grows above investment in resources"*

In this definition, we have tried to integrate different points of view to propose a concept that will be useful, following Jensen (2013), who insists that the effectiveness of any definition of business model is directly related to its ability to describe the reality of the business or organisation.

To round out the proposed definition, this study also offers a proposed table of elements, which includes those that are considered to be key to conceptualise the business model. Said elements are considered from a dynamic point of view, such that the company's ability to transform the model to adapt it to the changes in its environment will guarantee its long-term survival. This proposal, set out in Table 4, consists of a system of 11 elements that constitute the business model. As can be deduced from the frequency data from Table 1, the proposed table does not follow the majority opinions of the authors analysed, who mainly choose panels of fewer than six elements.

According to most of the authors selected (69%, as noted in Table 2), the central foundation of the business model is the value proposition, which must lay out the customer needs that the model meets, the problems it solves for them, the value it provides to them, and must describe the customer experience and the aspects that differentiate the company from its competition.

Additionally, the first pillar of the model is the customers to whom the proposition is directed. The model must set parameters for their segmentation, the identification of key customers, and the management of a differentiating relationship with each segment. It must also establish the communication channels and commercial and logistical relations with said customers.

A second pillar is talent and its management in the organisation. This includes all aspects related to recruiting and retaining talent, access to human capital, developing corporate DNA, employees' focus on the customer and their identification with the organisation's business model. Thirty-one percent of the authors analysed include talent management as a key element of the business model.

Financial aspects are included in the foundation of the model: revenue stream and its sustainability, and the organisation's cost structure, which includes aspects of risk, such as critical items, fixed and variable cost structures, degree of automation and economies of scale.

Surrounding all of this is the necessary infrastructure. This includes, on the one hand, key partners and the degree of reliance on them, technology or the production of the good or service provided and corporate social responsibility; on the other, the model must describe all key aspects of the infrastructure depending on the business, such as those related to environmental protection, or collaboration with development and education in the community.

This proposal includes three new elements, which are considered to be essential in describing all current and future business models, and which will continue to be increasingly important. These three elements are the approach to security aspects, complying with regulations and the ethical code and the ability to transform the model itself.

The first two will be increasingly demanded by society, and, therefore, by customers, shareholders and

Table 4. Proposal for a table of core elements that comprise the business model

STRUCTURAL AXIS	CENTRAL AXIS VALUE PROPOSAL AND ITS TRANSFORMATION	TRANSPARENCY AXIS
Structure	**Which of my customers' needs do I satisfy?**	**Compliance management**
Structure	Which of my customers' needs do I satisfy?	Compliance management
Key partners	How do I help my customers to be successful?	
Suppliers	What problems do I solve?	
Level of reliance	What differentiates me from my competition?	
Production	What is the customer's experience?	
Technology		
Corporate Social Responsibility	**Transformation Ability**	**Approach to Security**
Environmental protection	Leadership	Policy
Sustainability	Adaptation experiences	Organisation
Community Development	Disruptive models	Resources
	Co-creation	
	Digital transformation	
	Impact to bottom line	
	Barriers to change and their management	
TALENT PILLAR	**CUSTOMER PILLAR**	**FINANCIAL PILLAR**
Talent Management	**Customer Segmentation**	**Revenue Stream**
What talent do I need?	How many customer segments do I identify?	Volatility
Do I have access to the human capital I need?	What is my model to each segment (CRM)?	
What is my corporate DNA like?	What is the model for relations with key customers?	
Is my organization focused on the customer?		
Does the team identify with the model?	**Channels**	**Cost Structure**
What are my recruitment and retention tools?	How do we make ourselves known?	Criticality
How do I manage motivation?	How do we help customers choose us?	Fixed/variable structure
Compensation and performance evaluation systems	What is the purchase process like?	Economies of scale
Do I offer company training? Do I measure its impact?	How do we ensure delivery to the customer?	Cooperation
Tools for managing diversity	What is after sales service like?	Degree of automation

stakeholders; organisations will no longer be able to exist without offering sufficient guarantees of transparency with regard to their commitments and procedures related to said aspects.

The third refers to innovation in the model itself so as to guarantee long-term sustainability. Innovation has been incorporated into the debate surrounding the business model over the last 15 years, both by researchers and in the practice of managing companies; however, it is notable that in the review of the literature, research on innovation in business models has mainly focused on processes of organizational change, the results of said change or its implications and consequences (Foss & Saebi, 2017).

Innovation in the business model is described as the model's own ability for transformation, with innovation being included as an element that characterises the business model itself. Innovation within the model allows it to evolve, driven by the digital transformation and the elimination of barriers, towards a future of greater cooperation with customers and key partners, of successful shared projects and of co-creation as the basis of new value propositions that adapt to the organization to guarantee its viability constantly.

5. Conclusions

The aim of this work was to offer a proposal for a business model definition and a table of 11 core elements: the value proposition, customer segmentation, channels for accessing customers, talent management, revenue stream, cost structure, required infrastructure, corporate social responsibility, the approach to security, the code of ethics and regulatory compliance and the ability for transformation.

These last three are new additions to the elements of a business model, and open up future possibilities for research to investigate the evolution of the model towards a greater focus on those elements, and to analyse the impact on the bottom line of transforming the model itself. The model must undergo constant adaptations to guarantee the organization's future sustainability, which is of great interest to business administration.

References

Afuah, A. & Tucci, C. L. (2001). *Internet business models and strategies: Text and cases.* New York, NY: McGraw-Hill / Irwin.

Ahokangas, P., Juntunen, M., & Myllykoski, J. (2014). Cloud computing and transformation of international e-business models. In R. Sanchez, A. Heene (Eds.), *A Focused Issue on Building New Competences in Dynamic Environments* (pp. 3-28). Bingley, UK: Emerald Group Publishing Limited.

Al-Debei, M. M., El-Haddadeh, R., & Avison, D. (2008, August). Defining the business model in the new world of digital business. Paper presented at Fourteenth Americas Conference on Information Systems, Toronto, ON.

Alt, R., & Zimmermann, H. D. (2001). Preface: introduction to special section–business models. *Electronic Markets, 11*(1), 3-9.

Amit, R., & Zott, C. (2001). Value creation in e-business. *Strategic Management Journal, 22*(6-7), 493-520.

Amit, R., & Zott, C. (2015). Crafting business architecture: The antecedents of business model design. *Strategic Entrepreneurship Journal, 9*(4), 331-350.

Andersson, B., Bergholtz, M., Edirisuriya, A., Ilayperuma, T., Johannesson, P., Gordijn, J. & Hahn, A. (2006). Towards a reference ontology for business models. In *International Conference on Conceptual Modelling* (pp. 482-496). Heidelberg: Springer.

Applegate, L. M. (2001). *E-business Models: Making sense of the Internet business landscape in Information technology and the future enterprise: New models for managers.* Upper Saddle River, NJ: Prentice Hall.

Baden-Fuller, C., MacMillan, I. C., Demil, B., & Lecocq, X. (2008). Call for papers for Long Range Planning Special Issue on business models.

Baden-Fuller, C., & Morgan, M. S. (2010). Business models as models. *Long Range Planning, 43*(2-3), 156-171.

Baden-Fuller, C., & Haefliger, S. (2013). Business models and technological innovation. *Long Range Planning, 46*(6), 419-426.

Bellman, R., Clark, C. E., Malcolm, D. G., Craft, C. J., & Ricciardi, F. M. (1957). On the construction of a multi-stage, multi-person business game. *Operations Research, 5*(4), 469-503.

Betz, F. (2002). Strategic business models. *Engineering Management Journal, 14*(1), 21-28.

Brandenburger, A. M., & Stuart Jr, H. W. (1996). Value-based business strategy. *Journal of Economics & Management Strategy, 5*(1), 5-24.

Camisón, C., & Villar-López, A. (2010). Business models in Spanish industry: a taxonomy-based efficacy analysis. *M@n@gement, 13*(4), 298-317.

Casadesus-Masanell, R., & Ricart, J. E. (2010). From strategy to business models and onto tactics. *Long Range Planning, 43*(2-3), 195-215.

Casadesus-Masanell, R., & Ricart, J. E. (2011). How to design a winning business model. *Harvard Business Review, 89*(1-2), 100-107.

Chesbrough, H., & Rosenbloom, R. S. (2002). The role of the business model in capturing value from innovation: evidence from Xerox Corporation's technology spin-off companies. *Industrial and corporate change, 11*(3), 529-555.

Chesbrough, H. (2003). *Open innovation.* Boston, MA: Harvard Business School Press.

Demil, B., & Lecocq, X. (2010). Business model evolution: in search of dynamic consistency. *Long Range Planning, 43*(2-3), 227-246.

Donath, R., Kalakota, R., & Cerf, B. S. (1999). Taming e-business models. *ISBM Business Marketing Web Consortium, 3*(1), 1-24.

Drucker, P. F. (1994). The theory of the business. *Harvard Business Review, 72*(5), 95-104.

D'Souza, A., Wortmann, H., Huitema, G., & Velthuijsen, H. (2015). A business model design framework for viability; a business ecosystem approach. *Journal of Business Models, 3*(2), 1-29.

Dubosson-Torbay, M., Osterwalder, A., & Pigneur, Y. (2002). E-business model design, classification, and measurements. *Thunderbird International Business Review, 44*(1), 5-23.

Eyring, M. J., Johnson, M. W., & Nair, H. (2011). New business models in emerging markets. *Harvard Business Review, 89*(1-2), 88-95.

Foss, N. J., & Saebi, T. (2017). Fifteen years of research on business model innovation: How far have we come, and where should we go? *Journal of Management, 43*(1), 200-227.

Galper, J. (2001). Three business models for the stock exchange industry. *The Journal of Investing, 10*(1), 70-78.

García-Echevarría, S. (2002). Modelos de gestión de la empresa multinacional [Management models in multinational companies]. *Información Comercial Española*, 799, 55-70

Gebauer, J., & Ginsburg, M. (2003). The US wine industry and the internet: an analysis of success factors for online business models. *Electronic Markets, 13*(1), 59-66.

George, G., & Bock, A. J. (2011). The business model in practice and its implications for entrepreneurship research. *Entrepreneurship Theory and Practice, 35*(1), 83-111.

Giesen, E., Riddleberger, E., Christner, R., & Bell, R. (2010). When and how to innovate your business model. *Strategy & Leadership, 38*(4), 17-26.

Gordijn, J. (2002). *Value-based requirements engineering - exploring innovative e-commerce ideas* (Unpublished doctoral dissertation). Vrije Universiteit; Amsterdam.

Halme, M., Anttonen, M., Kuisma, M., Kontoniemi, N., & Heino, E. (2007). Business models for material efficiency services: Conceptualization and application. *Ecological Economics, 63*(1), 126-137.

Hamel, G., & Ruben, P. (2000). *Leading the revolution.* Boston, MA: Harvard Business School Press.

Hedman, J., & Kalling, T. (2003). The business model concept: theoretical underpinnings and empirical illustrations. *European Journal of Information Systems, 12*(1), 49-59.

Hoque, F. (2002). *The alignment effect: How to get real business value out of technology.* Upper Saddle River, NJ: Ft Press.

Jansen, W., Steenbakkers, W., & Jägers, H. (2007). *New business models for the knowledge economy.* Hampshire, UK: Gower Publishing Ltd.

Jensen, A. B. (2013). Do we need one business model definition?. *Journal of Business Models, 1*(1), 61-84

Jones, G. M. (1960). Educators, electrons, and business models: A problem in synthesis. *The Accounting Review, 35*(4), 619-626.

Kindström, D. (2010). Towards a service-based business model–Key aspects for future competitive advantage. *European Management Journal, 28*(6), 479-490.

Kordnaeij, A., Mohtadi, M., Abdi, R., & Danaeefard, H. (2011). One man international company business model. *European Journal of Scientific Research, 50*(3), 300-316.

Kraussl-Derzsi, Z. (2011). *Operationalized Alignment: Assessing feasibility of value constellations exploiting innovative services* (Unpublished doctoral dissertation). Vrije Universiteit, Amsterdam.

Kujala, S., Artto, K., Aaltonen, P., & Turkulainen, V. (2010). Business models in project-based firms–Towards a typology of solution-specific business models. *International Journal of Project Management, 28*(2), 96-106.

Lewis, M. (1999). *The new new thing: A Silicon Valley story*. New York, NY: WW Norton & Company.

Linder, J. C., & Cantrell, S. (2000). *Changing Business Models: Surveying the Landscape*. Cambridge, UK: Accenture Institute for Strategic Change.

Llorens-Bueno, G.A. (2010). *Una perspectiva al concepto de modelo de negocios [A perspective to the business model concept]* (Unpublished doctoral dissertation). Universitê Libre des Sciences de l'Entreprise et des Technologies de Bruxelles, Santiago de Chile.

Magretta, J. (2002). Why business models matter. *Harvard Business Review*, 80(5), 86-92.

Mahadevan, B. (2000). Business models for Internet-based e-commerce: An anatomy. *California Management Review, 42*(4), 55-69.

Markides, C. C. (1999). A dynamic view of strategy. *Sloan Management Review, 40*(3), 55-63.

Mason, K. J. & Spring, M. (2010, September). The practice of business models. Paper presented at Twenty-sixth IMP (Industrial Marketing & Purchasing Group) Conference, Budapest.

Morales, I. (2011). Las pymes en México, entre la creación fallida y la destrucción creadora. *Economía Informa, 366*, 39-48.

Morris, M., Schindehutte, M. & Allen, J. (2005), The entrepreneur's business model: toward a unified perspective, *Journal of Business Research*, 58, 726-735

Nenonen, S. & Storbacka, K. (2010). Business model design: conceptualizing networked value co-creation. *International Journal of Quality and Service Sciences, 2*(1), 43-59.

Okkonen, L., & Suhonen, N. (2010). Business models of heat entrepreneurship in Finland. *Energy Policy, 38*(7), 3443-3452.

Onetti, A., Zucchella, A., Jones, M. V., & McDougall-Covin, P. P. (2012). Internationalization, innovation and entrepreneurship: business models for new technology-based firms. *Journal of Management & Governance, 16*(3), 337-368.

Osterwalder, A. (2004). The business model ontology: A proposition in a design science approach (Unpublished doctoral dissertation). University of Lausanne.

Osterwalder, A., Pigneur, Y., & Tucci, C. L. (2005). Clarifying business models: Origins, present, and future of the concept. *Communications of the association for Information Systems*, 16(1), 1-25

Osterwalder, A., & Pigneur, Y. (2010). *Business model generation: A handbook for visionaries, game changers, and challengers*. Hoboken, NJ: John Wiley & Sons, Inc.

Ovans, A. (2015). What is a business model?. Harvard Business Review, 23, 1-7.

Pateli, A. & Giaglis, G. (2003, June). A framework for understanding and analysing e-business models. Paper presented at Sixteenth Bled e-Commerce Conference, Bled, Slovenia.

Petrovic, O., Kittl, C., & Teksten, R. (2001, June). Developing business models for e-business. Paper presented at Fourteenth Bled Electronic Commerce Conference, Bled, Slovenia.

Plé, L., Lecocq, X., & Angot, J. (2010). Customer-integrated business models: a theoretical framework. *M@n@gement, 13*(4), 226-265.

Porter, M. E. (1996). What is strategy? *Harvard Business Review, 74*(6), 61-78.

Porter, M. E. (2001). Strategy and the Internet. *Harvard Business Review, 79*(3), 62-78.

Rajala, R., & Westerlund, M. (2005, June). Business Models: A new perspective on knowledge-intensive services in the software industry. Paper presented at Eighteenth Bled e-Conference, Bled, Slovenia.

Rayport, J. F., & Jaworski, B. J. (2002). *Introduction to e-commerce*. New York, NY: McGraw-Hill.

Ricart, J. E. (2009). Modelo de Negocio: El eslabón perdido en la dirección estratégica [Business Model: the missing link to strategic management]. *Universia Business Review*, (23), 12-25.

Salas-Fumás, V. (2009). Modelos de negocio y nueva economía industrial [Business Models and the new industrial economy]. *Universia Business Review*, (23), 122-143.

Schneider, S., & Spieth, P. (2013). Business model innovation: Towards an integrated future research agenda. *International Journal of Innovation Management, 17*(01), 1-34.

Shafer, S. M., Smith, H. J., & Linder, J. C. (2005). The power of business models. *Business Horizons, 48*(3), 199-207.

Svejenova, S., Planellas, M., & Vives, L. (2010). An individual business model in the making: A chef's quest for creative freedom. *Long Range Planning, 43*(2-3), 408-430.

Tapscott, D., Ticoll, D.L. & Lowy, A. (2000). *Digital capital: Harnessing the power of business webs.* Boston, MA: Harvard Business School Press.

Teece, D. J. (2010). Business models, business strategy and innovation. *Long range planning,* 43(2-3), 172-194.

Timmers, P. (1998). Business models for electronic markets. *Electronic Markets, 8*(2), 3-8.

Van der Vorst, J. G., Van Dongen, S., Nouguier, S., & Hilhorst, R. (2002). E-business initiatives in food supply chains; definition and typology of electronic business models. *International Journal of Logistics, 5*(2), 119-138.

Vives, L., & Svejenova, S. (2009). Innovando en el modelo de negocio: la creación de la banca cívica [Innovating in the business model: The creation of civic banking]. *Universia Business Review, 3*(23), 70-85.

Weill, P., & Vitale, M. (2001). *Place to space: Migrating to e-Business Models.* Boston, MA: Harvard Business School Press.

Wikström, K., Artto, K., Kujala, J., & Söderlund, J. (2010). Business models in project business. *International Journal of Project Management, 28*(8), 832-841.

Winter, S. G., & Szulanski, G. (2001). Replication as strategy. *Organization Science, 12*(6), 730-743.

Yip, G. S. (2004). Using Strategy to Change Your Business Model. *Business Strategy Review, 15*(2), 17-24.

Yunus, M., Moingeon, B., & Lehmann-Ortega, L. (2010). Building social business models: Lessons from the Grameen experience. *Long Range Planning,* 43(2-3), 308-325.

Zott, C., Amit, R., & Massa, L. (2011). The business model: recent developments and future research. *Journal of Management,* 37(4), 1019-1042.

Appendix

le A.1 Most notable definitions in the literature

hor(s)	Year	Focus	Definitions
ah & Tucci	2001	set of activities	Business model is the method by which a firm builds and uses its resources to offer its customers better value than its competitors and to make money doing so. It details how a firm makes money now and how it plans to do so in the long term. A business model can be conceptualized as a system that is made up of components, linkages between the components, and dynamics
kangas; tunen & ykoski	2014	organizational structure	Business models, built around the business opportunity, answer the questions of what companies are offering to their customers in terms of products/services and value proposition, how and where they are planning to do that in practice, and why they think they can do it profitably
)ebei, El- dadeh & Avison	2008	organizational structure	The business model is an abstract representation of an organization, be it conceptual, textual, and/or graphical, of all core interrelated architectural, co-operational, and financial arrangements designed and developed by an organization presently and in the future, as well as all core products and/ or services the organization offers, or will offer, based on these arrangements that are needed to achieve its strategic goals and objectives
t & Zott	2015	set of activities	The business model describes the system of interdependent activities performed by a focal firm and its partners and the mechanisms that link these activities to each other, to serve a specific purpose toward the fulfillment of the overall objectives. This activity system, in addition to designing the internal organization, needs to consider goals, templates, stakeholders' activities and environmental constraints
ersson et al.	2006	organizational structure	Business models are created in order to make clear who the business actors are in a business case and to make their relations explicit. Relations in a business model are formulated in terms of values exchanged between the actors.
en-Fuller, :Millan, Demil & ɔcq	2008	organizational structure	Business model is the logic of the firm, the way it operates and how it creates and captures value for its stakeholders
ıdenburger & art	1996	value management	A Business Model is oriented to the total added value created among the different players in the chain. It sets the basis for capturing value by the firm in question, by co-defining the overall value created among the whole chain of transactions, which can be considered the upper limit for the value capture of the given firm

Table A.1 Most notable definitions in the literature (Continued)

Author(s)	Year	Focus	Definitions
Casadesus-Masanell & Ricart	2010	organizational structure	Business models are composed of two different sets of elements: (a) the concrete choices made by management about how the organization must operate, and (b) the consequences of these choic
Chesbrough & Rosenbloom	2002	value management	The functions of a business model are to articulate the value proposition, identify a market segment, define the structure of the value chain; estimate the cost structure and profit potential of producing the offering, describe the position of the firm with the value network and formulate the competitive strategy
Demil & Lecocq	2010	organizational structure	Business Model can be described with three core components: its resources and competences, its organizational structure and its propositions for value delivery. The interactions between and with them constitute its dynamics. The capability that allows a firm to change them while at the same time building and maintaining sustainable performance is labelled as its "dynamic consistency"
George & Bock	2011	organizational structure	A business model is the design of organizational structures to enact a commercial opportunity
Lewis	1999	value management	All what business model really meant was how you planned to make money
Linder & Cantrell	2000	value management	Business model is the organization's core logic for creating value The business model of a profit oriented enterprise explains how makes money
Llorens-Bueno	2010	set of activities	Theoretical scheme of a system, made to facilitate its understanding and set of organized activities, that comprises commercial, financial and industrial aspects, interrelated to deliv products and services to the customers
Magretta	2002	value management	Business models are stories that explain how enterprises work, and answer the questions: Who is the customer? What does the customer value? How do we make money in this business? Wha is the underlying economic logic that explains how we can deliv value to customers at an appropriate cost?
Morales	2011	organizational structure	Through the Business Model you describe how you imagine you organization or Company by defining your firm´s "core business including: why it was founded, the main activities made, how value is captured and how cash flows arise
Osterwalder et al.	2005	value management	A business model is a conceptual tool containing a set of object concepts and their relationships with the objective to express the business logic of a specific firm. Therefore we must consider which concepts and relationships allow a simplified description and representation of what value is provided to customers, how this is done and with which financial consequences.

le A.1 Most notable definitions in the literature (Continued)

hor(s)	Year	Focus	Definitions
rwalder & eur	2009	value management	A business model describes the rationale of how an organization creates, delivers, and captures value
ovic, Kittl & ten	2001	value management	A business model describes the logic of a 'business system' for creating value, that lies behind the actual processes
la & Westerlund	2005	value management	The concept of the business model refers to the ways of creating value for customers and to the ways a business turns market opportunities into profit through sets of actors, activities and collaboration
rt	2009	set of activities	A business model consists of a firm´s set of choices and the consequences of those decisions
s-Fumás	2009	value management	Analysis unit to study the firm´s path-dependence decisions, that finally describe the value proposition able to explain the commercial success of a certain way of doing business
er, Smith & er	2005	value management	Business model as a representation of a firm's underlying core logic and strategic choices for creating and capturing value within a value network
enova, Planellas ves	2010	organizational structure	Business models are depicted as organizational devices that reveal a company's logic for creating and capturing value, and also its approach to constant renewal.
mers	1998	value management	Definition of a business model: an architecture for the product, service and information flows, including a description of the various business actors and their roles, a description of the potential benefits for the various business actors and a description of the sources of revenues.
l & Vitale	2001	organizational structure	The business model describes the roles and relationships among a firm´s customers, allies and suppliers, the major flows of product, information and money, and the major benefits to the participants
ter & Sulanzki	2001	set of activities	The business model is a complex set of interdependent routines that is discovered, adjusted, and fine-tuned by "doing"
ström, Artto, la & Söderlund	2010	value management	The business models are used for describing or designing the activities needed or wanted from the involved organization(s) to create value for customers and other stakeholders in the surrounding environment

Table A.2a List of authors and elements

Elements	Author(s)										
	Afuah & Tucci 2001	Al-Debei et al. 2008	Alt & Zimmerman 2001	Amit & Zott 2015	Applegate 2001	Baden-Fuller & Morgan 2010	Betz 2002	Casadesus-Masanell & Ricart 2011	Chesbrough & Rosenbloom 2002	Chesbrough 2003	De & Le 2C
Value Proposition	X	X		X	X				X	X	X
Revenue Stream	X	X	X			X				X	X
Customers						X					
Target Market / Segmentation	X					X			X	X	
Key Resources							X				X
Value Chain	X										
Key Partners						X			X	X	
Competitive Strategy		X		X	X				X		
Differentiating Competences		X		X				X	X	X	
Product					X						
Organization and Organizational culture		X	X		X						X
Cost Structure	X		X								
Key Processes	X								X	X	X
Profitability and Stakeholders					X		X				X
Distribution Channel		X						X			
Business Logic											
Technology			X								
Financing							X				
Corporate Governance and Sustainability	X			X				X			
Infrastructure											
Sales Process					X		X				
Operations					X						
Positioning											
Key Information											
Brand					X						
Mission			X								
Legal Framework			X								
Competitive Situation											
Key Executives											
Macroeconomics											
Number of elements	7	6	6	4	8	4	4	3	6	6	6

ble A.2b List of authors and elements

Elements	Author(s)							
	Donath, Kalakota & Cerf 1999	D´Souza et al. 2015	Dubosson-Torbay, Osterwalder & Pigneur 2002	Eyring, Johnson & Nair 2011	George & Bock 2011	Giesen, Riddleberger, Christner & Bell 2010	Gordijn 2002	Halme, Anttonen, Kuisma, Kontoniemi & Heino 2007
ue Proposition		X	X	X		X	X	
enue Stream		X	X	X		X		
tomers	X	X	X					
get Market / Segmentation			X				X	
Resources		X	X	X	X			
ue Chain	X		X		X			
Partners		X	X				X	
npetitive Strategy		X					X	
erentiating Competences								X
duct		X			X			
anization and Organizational culture					X			
t Structure			X	X				
Processes		X	X					
fitability and Stakeholders			X					
ribution Channel					X			X
iness Logic		X				X		
nology		X	X		X			
ancing			X					X
porate Governance and Sustainability	X							
astructure			X					
es Process								
erations								
itioning	X					X		
Information	X		X					
nd			X					
sion								
al Framework								
npetitive Situation								X
Executives								
croeconomics								
nber of elements	5	10	15	4	6	4	4	4

Table A.2c List of authors and elements

Elements	Author(s)									
	Hamel & Ruben	Hedman & Kalling	Hoque	Kindström	Kordnaeij, Mohtadi, Abdi & Danaeefard	Kujala, Artto, Aaltonen & Turkulainen	Linder & Cantrell	Magretta	Mahadevan	Markides
	2000	2003	2002	2010	2011	2010	2000	2002	2000	1999
Value Proposition			X	X		X	X	X	X	
Revenue Stream				X		X	X		X	
Customers	X				X	X	X	X		X
Target Market / Segmentation	X		X	X						
Key Resources	X	X	X							
Value Chain		X	X			X				
Key Partners		X		X		X				
Competitive Strategy	X		X	X						
Differentiating Competences			X	X		X				
Product	X	X			X					X
Organization and Organizational culture			X			X		X		
Cost Structure	X	X								
Key Processes		X								
Profitability and Stakeholders										
Distribution Channel										
Business Logic	X						X			
Technology										
Financing					X					X
Corporate Governance and Sustainability			X							
Infrastructure					X					X
Sales Process							X			
Operations									X	
Positioning										
Key Information										
Brand			X							
Mission			X							
Legal Framework			X							
Competitive Situation			X							
Key Executives		X								
Macroeconomics										
Number of elements	8	7	12	6	4	7	5	3	3	4

e A.2d List of authors and elements

Elements	Author(s)									
	Mason & Spring 2010	Morris et al. 2005	Okkonen & Suhonen 2010	Osterwalder & Pigneur 2010	Petrovic et al. 2001	Rayport & Jaworski 2002	Ricart 2009	Shafer et al. 2005	Teece 2010	Timmers 1998
Proposition	X			X	X	X	X	X	X	
ue Stream			X	X	X		X		X	X
ners	X			X	X	X	X			
Market / Segmentation	X	X		X					X	
sources				X	X	X				
Chain		X				X	X			
rtners						X	X		X	X
etitive Strategy				X			X	X		
ntiating Competences		X					X	X		
ct		X	X			X				
zation and Organizational culture										
tructure				X						
ocesses				X			X			
bility and Stakeholders	X		X							
ution Channel		X	X				X			
ss Logic				X			X			X
ology	X								X	
ing						X				
ate Governance and Sustainability										
ructure										
Process										
tions					X					
ning	X									
formation										X
n										
Framework										
etitive Situation										
ecutives										
economics		X								
er of elements	6	6	4	9	5	7	10	3	5	4

Table A.2e List of authors and elements

Elements	Author(s)					
	Van der Vorst, Van Dongen, Nouguier & Hilhorst 2002	Vives & Svejenova 2009	Weill & Vitale 2001	Wikström et al. 2010	Yip 2004	Yunus, Moing & Lehmann-O 2010
Value Proposition	X	X	X	X	X	X
Revenue Stream		X	X	X		
Customers		X		X	X	
Target Market / Segmentation		X	X		X	
Key Resources	X				X	
Value Chain	X		X			
Key Partners	X					
Competitive Strategy				X		X
Differentiating Competences				X		
Product		X			X	
Organization and Organizational culture		X		X	X	
Cost Structure	X					
Key Processes						
Profitability and Stakeholders		X				X
Distribution Channel						
Business Logic			X			
Technology			X			
Financing						
Corporate Governance and Sustainability		X				
Infrastructure	X					
Sales Process						
Operations					X	
Positioning						
Key Information						
Brand						
Mission						
Legal Framework						
Competitive Situation						
Key Executives						
Macroeconomics						
Number of elements	6	8	6	6	7	3

10

he Implementation of Fuzzy Logic
ı Forecasting Financial Ratios

ıasz Korol[1]

STRACT This paper is devoted to the issue of forecasting financial ratios. The objective of the conducted research is to develop a predictive model with the use of an innovative methodology, i.e., fuzzy logic theory, and to evaluate its effectiveness. Fuzzy logic has been widely used in machinery, robotics and industrial engineering. This paper introduces the use of fuzzy logic for the financial analysis of enterprises. While many current phenomena in finance and economics are fuzzy, they are treated as if they are crisp. Fuzzy logic provides an appropriate tool for modeling imprecise, uncertain and ambiguous phenomena. Because the financial situation of a company is affected by many factors (economic, political, psychological, etc.) that cannot be precisely and unambiguously defined, the approach used in this paper greatly enhances the predictive power of financial analysis and makes it an economically useful tool for the management of enterprises. Empirically, this paper employs three testing samples: Central European enterprises, Latin American companies and global firms. From the verification of these models, it is evident that the refined processes are effective in improving the forecasting of financial situations of all three types of enterprises. The models created by the author are characterized by high efficiency. This study is one of the world's first attempts to combine ratio analysis with fuzzy logic to predict the financial situations of companies.

WORDS: decision support systems, financial ratios, fuzzy logic, forecasting, financial crisis

ıitechnika Gdanska - Faculty of Management and Economics, Poland

1. Introduction

Many economists specializing in issues of financial analysis entered the twenty-first century with illusory euphoria, hoping for an increased integration of financial markets, faster and more effective use of information and effective forecasting of economic phenomena using sophisticated statistical and econometric models and artificial intelligence. The global financial crisis that began in mid-2008 refuted the myth of safe economic regions of the world, as well as countries and enterprises. We are currently witnessing unprecedented events, such as the reduction of the U.S. credit rating from AAA to AA+ for the first time in history and the collapse of various global enterprises, including many that previously had impeccable economic reputations. Questions arise about the causes of the crisis and the possibility of its earlier forecasting. Within this context, it is worth assessing the usefulness of early warning models, which aim to capture the early symptoms of the deteriorating economic situation of a country, enterprise or household.

ʳespondence concerning this article should be addressed to: **ıasz Korol**, Politechnika Gdanska - Faculty of Management Economics, Narutowicza 11/12, Gdansk 80-233, Poland. ail: tomasz.korol@zie.pg.gda.pl

In this paper, the author refers to the issue of effectiveness of the methods of the economic analysis of enterprises to assess these companies' financial standing in the era of globalization, general uncertainty and risk as well as extremely rapid changes in these companies' environments. The author attempts to answer the question of whether the methods dating back to the second half of the nineteenth century are congruent with the present time.

The aim of the studies undertaken in this paper is to implement the fuzzy logic methodology in the ratio analysis used in enterprises and to verify the effectiveness of fuzzy logic models developed for the purposes of financial analysis. This verification was carried out with two types of enterprises: those in a bad financial situation and those in a good financial situation. A novel analytical approach proposed by the author is to adapt the ratio analysis to the conditions under which companies must currently operate. The traditional zero-one (good/bad) evaluation criteria for ratios have lost their relevance. The inadequacy of the traditional ratio analysis is expressed with the use of bivalent logic to describe and evaluate the phenomena that are fuzzy, vague and ambiguous. After more than one hundred years since the development of the first financial ratios, it is now worthwhile to consider the implementation of a different approach to the evaluation of these ratios, to which the criteria referring to the fuzzy set theory are applied. The financial situations of enterprises are affected by many internal (Asgharian, 2003; Kash & Darling, 1998; Stokes & Blackburn, 2002) and external (Bhattacharjee, Highson, & Holly, 2003; Dyrberg Rommer, 2005; Everett & Watson, 1998; Hunter & Isachenkova, 2006; Robson, 1996) factors, which cannot be defined precisely and unambiguously. In addition, these factors at different stages of the life cycle of a company may affect the company's economic situation or cause chain reactions (du Jardin & Severin, 2012). In addition, the finding that a company is in a "good" or "bad" financial situation is imprecise because in the current economic reality, analysts rarely analyze wholly "good" or "bad" companies. On the other hand, using the traditional financial ratios based on the classic set theory makes it difficult to determine the precise degree of risk or the advancement of a positive situation, whether it is a somewhat positive or highly positive situation. Additionally, the manner of interpretation of the calculated values of the indicators is still controversial. First, it is difficult to determine the optimal ranges of values of financial indicators in a rapidly changing environment. For example, does the minimum value of 1.3 appointed by an analyst eight years ago during the global financial crisis remain valid as the limit for the current liquidity of a company? Even if an analyst designates the current limit for the investigated company, there is another controversial aspect related to ratio analysis; namely, when using the classic theory of sets to assess an indicator, there is a sharp boundary at the level of the limit value. For example, with the ratio recorded as 1.29, how is the financial situation of a company different from the situation in which it reaches a certain level of the critical value (1.3)? This "zero-one" approach (with a "good/bad" indicator for a company) seems to be heavily outdated and unfit to current economic conditions. Numerous phenomena in economics are "fuzzy" and are currently treated by economists as if they were "sharp," or bivalent. With fuzzy sets, we can formally define vague and ambiguous terms, such as the "high risk of bankruptcy," "low risk of bankruptcy," "good financial standing,", etc. While the classic set theory assumes that any item (company) belongs or does not belong to a given set (a "bad" or "good" financial situation), in the fuzzy set theory, an item can partially belong to a set, and this belonging can be expressed by a real number from the interval [0,1]. In other words, using fuzzy logic, a company's financial situation can be assessed as partially "good" or partially "bad". This study is one of the world's first attempts to combine ratio analysis with fuzzy logic to predict the financial situations of companies.

In the studies of this paper, the following were examined:

- The effectiveness of the 13 fuzzy logic models developed for individual financial ratios compared to the traditional ratio analysis **(due to the limited length of this article, only two of these models are presented)**,
- The behavior of these models, along with the extension of the period of analysis from one year to two years prior to the announcement that the company was in a bad financial situation,
- The effectiveness of the discussed models in three different test samples composed of companies from different regions of the world, which made it pos-

sible to draw conclusions about the universality of the fuzzy logic models and compare the aspects of these models with the versatility of the traditional financial ratios.

Based on a literature review and the conclusions of the author's research from over 14 years of academic study on the issue of forecasting the financial standing of companies, the author puts forward the following research hypothesis. The use of fuzzy logic in ratio analysis

- allows for a more effective assessment of the financial condition of enterprises than that of the traditional financial analysis,
- ensures the stability of forecasts by extending the analysis period to two years,
- increases the usefulness of individual financial ratios in the assessment of companies' financial standing,
- increases the universality (i.e., the predictive properties for a diverse population of companies) of ratio analysis.

The paper is organized as follows. Section 2 presents the major drawbacks of the traditional ratio analysis. Section 3 recalls the technical background of the fuzzy logic model. Section 4 presents the research assumptions of this study. Section 5 proposes forecasting models for two financial ratios: the current liquidity and the coverage of fixed assets by long-term capital. Section 6 concludes the paper.

2. Major drawbacks of financial analysis

In its most classic form, financial analysis is based on a set of financial ratios that allow four key aspects of company operations to be examined: liquidity, debt, efficiency of using assets, and profitability.

The use of ratio analysis to assess the financial situation of enterprises brings several disadvantages and limitations. A discussion of these disadvantages and limitations is necessary to understand the validity of the proposal of using fuzzy logic in this paper.

Three major objections are generally raised regarding ratio analysis:

1) *The obsolescence of optimal values of financial indicators over time.* While the methods for calculating ratios have remained virtually unchanged with the passage of time, there are new indicators in the literature that explore new areas of business. However, the optimal ranges of the ratio values become obsolete as a result of various factors, including changes in the business cycle or changes in economic conditions.
2) *The need for determination and interpretation of the standards.* More specifically, there is a need for the designation of optimal ranges of values for various financial ratios. This issue is obviously related to the problem raised earlier, namely, the obsolescence of these standards. The calculation of financial ratios may be rendered useless and may lead to a wrong decision if the calculation lacks proper interpretation. The determination of the standards of values is more difficult in the case of financial ratios that are nominants. In practice, there is no single best value of an indicator. An indicator depends on the business strategy (liquidity, market position, etc.), the industry and the country in which a company operates, as well as external factors, such as rising energy costs.
3) *The static nature of ratio values.* Most financial ratios are calculated based on static values at a given moment (usually at the end of the year under review) from the balance sheet and the income statement. Such an analysis lacks a dynamic view of the indicators. The question arises of whether changes in indicators are relevant predictors of a company's coming financial crisis because declines or increases in values do not immediately mean the deterioration of the economic situation of the company. Nevertheless, by observing changes, we can distinguish between a company that has a low economic indicator values that improve each year and a company that has indicators at a similarly low level that become worse each year. The static model will not detect the difference between such companies. The dynamic model adds an element that differentiates companies with poor financial situations from companies that do not necessarily have good financial situations but have improving financial situations.

The author conducted literature studies on the financial ratios used in credit scoring. After studying approximately 600 research papers on this subject, he chose 55 of them based on the three following criteria: the popularity of the authors and their research in the

Table 1. Overview of the most common financial ratios used in credit-scoring models

No.	Financial ratio	Used in studies
1.	Share of working capital in total assets (working capital / total assets)	[Ahn, Cho and Kim, 2000] [Back, Laitinen and Sere, 1996] [Baek and Ch 2003] [Ignizio and Soltyas, 1996] [Karels and Prakash, 1987] [Lacher, Co Sharma and Fantc, 1995] [Lee, Han and Kwon, 1996] [Lee, Booth and Alam, 2005] [Leshno and Spector, 1996] [Lin and McClean, 2001] [Altm 1993] [Lin and Piesse, 2004] [Hadasik, 1998] [Bandyopadhyay, 2006] [Galvão, Becerra and Abou-Seada, 2004] [Altman, Baidya and Ribeiro D 1979] [Ginoglou, Agorastos and Hatzigagios 2002] [Boritz and Kenne 1995] [Serrano-Cinca, 1996] [Michaluk, 2003] [Wilson and Sharda, 199 [Zapranis and Ginoglou, 2000] [Zhang, Hu, Patuwo and Indro, 1999] [Becerra, Galvao and Abou-Seada, 2005] [Rahimian and Singh, 1993]
2.	Encumbrance of cash surplus with liabilities [(net profit + depreciation) / total liabilities or EBIT / total liabilities]	[Ahn, Cho and Kim, 2000] [Bian and Mazlack, 2003] [Back, Laitinen and Sere, 1996] [Maczynska, 2004]
3.	Quick liquidity [(current assets - inventories) / current liabilities]	[Dimitras, Zanakis, & Zopounidis, 1996] [Fletcher and Goss, 1993] [Lee, Han and Kwon, 1996] [Leshno and Spector, 1996] [Lin and McClean, 2001] [Hadasik, 1998] [Emel, Oral, Reisman and Yolalan, 2003] [Park and Han, 2002] [Piramuthu, Ragavan and Shaw, 1998] [Sikora and Shaw, 19 [Eklund, Back, Vanharanta and Visa, 2003]
4.	Current liquidity (current assets / current liabilities)	[Ahn, Cho and Kim, 2000] [Bian and Mazlack, 2003] [Bryant, 1998] [Dimitras, Zanakis, & Zopounidis, 1996] [Fletcher and Goss, 1993] [Back Laitinen and Sere, 1996] [Lee, Han and Kwon, 1996] [Leshno and Spec 1996] [Maczynska, 2004] [Hadasik, 1998] [Hołda, 2001] [Boritz and Kennedy, 1995] [Kuruppu, Laswad and Oyelere, 2003] [McKee, 2003] [Pendharkar and Rodger, 2004] [Piramuthu, Ragavan and Shaw, 1998] [Shah and Murtaza, 2000] [Sikora and Shaw, 1994] [Witkowska, 2002] [Anandarajan, Lee and Anandarajan, 2001] [Zhang, Hu, Patuwo and In 1999]
5.	Cash liquidity [(current assets - inventories - accounts receivables) / current liabilities]	[Back, Laitinen and Sere, 1996] [Lin and McClean, 2001] [McKee, 2003] [Witkowska, 2002] [Michaluk, 2003] [Laitinen and Kankaanpaa, 1999]
6.	Return on assets (net profit / total assets)	[Ahn, Cho and Kim, 2000] [Bian and Mazlack, 2003] [Bryant, 1998] [Dimitras, Zanakis, & Zopounidis, 1996] [Back, Laitinen and Sere, 1996] [Ignizio and Soltyas, 1996] [Lacher, Coats, Sharma and Fantc, 1995] [Lee Han and Kwon, 1996] [Lee, Booth and Alam, 2005] [Leshno and Specto 1996] [Lin and McClean, 2001] [Altman, 1993] [Lin and Piesse, 2004] [Gajdka and Stos, 1996] [Hołda, 2001] [Yim and Mitchell, 2004] [Galvão, Becerra and Abou-Seada, 2004] [Ginoglou, Agorastos and Hatzigagios 2002] [Boritz and Kennedy, 1995] [McKee, 2003] [Min and Lee, 2005] [Pendharkar and Rodger, 2004] [Piramuthu, Ragavan and Shaw, 1998] [Serrano-Cinca, 1996] [Sikora and Shaw, 1994] [Witkowska, 2002] [Serra Cinca, 1997] [Michaluk, 2003] [Wilson and Sharda, 1994] [Zapranis and Ginoglou, 2000] [Anandarajan, Lee and Anandarajan, 2001] [Eklund, Ba Vanharanta and Visa, 2003] [Zhang, Hu, Patuwo and Indro, 1999] [Becer Galvao and Abou-Seada, 2005] [Rahimian and Singh, 1993]

ble 1. Overview of the most common financial ratios used in credit-scoring models (Continued)

. Financial ratio	Used in studies
Relation of equity to total liabilities [equity / total liabilities]	[Ignizio and Soltyas, 1996] [Lee, Booth and Alam, 2005] [Altman, 1993] [Galvão, Becerra and Abou-Seada, 2004] [Altman, Baidya and Ribeiro Dias, 1979] [Ginoglou, Agorastos and Hatzigagios 2002] [Serrano-Cinca, 1996] [Sikora and Shaw, 1994] [Michaluk, 2003] [Wilson and Sharda, 1994] [Zapranis and Ginoglou, 2000] [Zhang, Hu, Patuwo and Indro, 1999] [Becerra, Galvao and Abou-Seada, 2005] [Rahimian and Singh, 1993]
Period of repayment of short-term liabilities or rotation of liabilities [(current liabilities / operating costs) * 365 or operating costs / current liabilities]	[Lee, Han and Kwon, 1996] [Lin and McClean, 2001] [Gajdka and Stos, 1996] [Prusak, 2005] [Hołda, 2001] [Emel, Oral, Reisman and Yolalan, 2003]
Inventory turnover [(inventories / sales) * 365 or sales / inventories]	[Ahn, Cho and Kim, 2000] [Bryant, 1998] [Back, Laitinen and Sere, 1996] [Karels and Prakash, 1987] [Lee, Han and Kwon, 1996] [Lin and McClean, 2001] [Hadasik, 1998] [Min and Lee, 2005] [Witkowska, 2002]
Turnover of short-term receivables [(receivables/sales) * 365 or sales / receivables]	[Karels and Prakash, 1987] [Hadasik, 1998] [Kuruppu, Laswad and Oyelere, 2003] [Shah and Murtaza, 2000] [Witkowska, 2002] [Eklund, Back, Vanharanta and Visa, 2003]
Turnover of total assets (sales / total assets)	[Bian and Mazlack, 2003] [Bryant, 1998] [Andres, Landajo and Lorca, 2005] [Baek and Cho, 2003] [Ignizio and Soltyas, 1996] [Lacher, Coats, Sharma and Fantc, 1995] [Lee, Han and Kwon, 1996] [Lee, Booth and Alam, 2005] [Leshno and Spector, 1996] [Lin and McClean, 2001] [Altman, 1993] [Gajdka and Stos, 1996] [Hołda, 2001] [Bandyopadhyay, 2006] [Galvão, Becerra and Abou-Seada, 2004] [Altman, Baidya and Ribeiro Dias, 1979] [Kuruppu, Laswad and Oyelere, 2003] [McKee, 2003] [Min and Lee, 2005] [Park and Han, 2002] [Serrano-Cinca, 1996] [Witkowska, 2002] [Michaluk, 2003] [Wilson and Sharda, 1994] [Zhang, Hu, Patuwo and Indro, 1999] [Becerra, Galvao and Abou-Seada, 2005] [Rahimian and Singh, 1993]
Relation of gross profit or EBIT to total assets [EBIT / total assets or gross profit / total assets]	[Bryant, 1998] [Dimitras, Zanakis, & Zopounidis, 1996] [Atiya, 2001] [Baek and Cho, 2003] [Ignizio and Soltyas, 1996] [Lacher, Coats, Sharma and Fantc, 1995] [Lee, Booth and Alam, 2005] [Leshno and Spector, 1996] [Altman, 1993] [Altman, Baidya and Ribeiro Dias, 1979] [Ginoglou, Agorastos and Hatzigagios 2002] [Pendharkar and Rodger, 2004] [Serrano-Cinca, 1996] [Michaluk, 2003] [Wilson and Sharda, 1994] [Zhang, Hu, Patuwo and Indro, 1999] [Becerra, Galvao and Abou-Seada, 2005] [Rahimian and Singh, 1993]
Share of total debt in total assets (total liabilities / total assets)	[Ahn, Cho and Kim, 2000] [Bryant, 1998] [Dimitras, Zanakis, & Zopounidis, 1996] [Karels and Prakash, 1987] [Leshno and Spector, 1996] [Lin and McClean, 2001] [Pang-Tien, Ching-Wen and Hui-Fun, 2008] [Gajdka and Stos, 1996] [Hadasik, 1998] [Gruszczyński, 2003] [Hołda, 2001] [Bandyopadhyay, 2006] [Boritz and Kennedy, 1995] [Kuruppu, Laswad and Oyelere, 2003] [Piramuthu, Ragavan and Shaw, 1998] [Shah and Murtaza, 2000] [Sikora and Shaw, 1994] [Witkowska, 2002] [Michaluk, 2003] [Zapranis and Ginoglou, 2000] [Anandarajan, Lee and Anandarajan, 2001] [Laitinen and Kankaanpaa, 1999] [Charalambous, Charitou and Kaourou, 2000]

Table 1. Overview of the most common financial ratios used in credit-scoring models (Continued)

No.	Financial ratio	Used in studies
14.	Share of equity in total assets (equity / total assets)	[Ahn, Cho and Kim, 2000] [Leshno and Spector, 1996] [Sandin and Porporato, 2007] [Maczynska, 2004] [Yim and Mitchell, 2004] [Emel, Or Reisman and Yolalan, 2003] [Kuruppu, Laswad and Oyelere, 2003] [Min and Lee, 2005] [Park and Han, 2002] [Shah and Murtaza, 2000] [Eklund, Back, Vanharanta and Visa, 2003]
15.	Net return on sales (net profit / total revenues)	[Ahn, Cho and Kim, 2000] [Bryant, 1998] [Lee, Han and Kwon, 1996] [Pang-Tien, Ching-Wen and Hui-Fun, 2008] [Min and Lee, 2005] [Piramuthu, Ragavan and Shaw, 1998] [Shah and Murtaza, 2000] [Sikor and Shaw, 1994]
16.	Operating profit margin or gross profit margin [operating profit / sales or gross profit / sales]	[Bian and Mazlack, 2003] [Karels and Prakash, 1987] [Leshno and Spect 1996] [Lin and McClean, 2001] [Sandin and Porporato, 2007] [Gajdka a Stos, 1996] [Eklund, Back, Vanharanta and Visa, 2003]
17.	Return on equity (net profit / equity)	[Bian and Mazlack, 2003] [Karels and Prakash, 1987] [Kuruppu, Laswad and Oyelere, 2003] [Shah and Murtaza, 2000] [Witkowska, 2002] [Serra Cinca, 1997] [Eklund, Back, Vanharanta and Visa, 2003]
18.	Coverage of fixed assets with long-term capital or equity [(equity + non-current liabilities) / fixed assets or equity / fixed assets]	[Min and Lee, 2005] [Park and Han, 2002]

scientific community, the degree of innovation of the research (duplications of studies showing only adaptations of existing models of low importance were avoided), and the diversification of the methods used. Table 1 shows the results of the query. The query contains the 18 financial ratios that were most frequently used in the research on forecasting the financial situations of companies worldwide.

Based on the results of the query, the frequency of use of each indicator in the 55 aforementioned studies was calculated. Table 1 shows that the following six financial ratios occurred in at least 30% of the studies: the share of working capital in total assets, current liquidity, net return on total assets, turnover of total assets, return on assets measured by profit before taxation and repayment of interest and the share of total debt in total assets. Two of these ratios are liquidity ratios, two are profitability ratios, one is an indicator of debt and one is an indicator of efficiency. The most common (occurred in 63.6% of studies) was the net return on total assets. The second and third most common ratios were the total turnover of assets (50.9%) and the share of working capital in total assets (47.3%), respectively.

3. Application of fuzzy logic to ratio analysis

With regard to the impressive development of forecasting models for companies' financial situations and to the development of ratio analysis itself, the inadequacy of most models and financial indicators for the phenomena occurring in the current business environment should be recognized. This inadequacy is expressed in the use of bivalent logic to describe and evaluate fuzzy, vague and ambiguous phenomena.

The use of statistical methods to forecast a company's risk of experiencing bankruptcy, such as multivariate discriminant analysis, does not change the ituation. When the value of the discriminant function for the studied company is less than the limit, the ompany is at risk of bankruptcy. Here, too, an analyst aces three similar problems, as follows, as in the case f ratio analysis:

- First, even though the assessment of a company's financial condition should be based on a simultaneous calculation of a series of often indirectly related financial ratios without individual interpretations, statistical models are based on the use of traditional financial indicators (both static and using classic logic),
- Second, the threshold of the discriminant function is the value of bivalent logic (the company situation is classified as "good" when the value of the function is above the estimated limit [for example, for the Altman model the limit is 2.99] and "bad" when it is less than this value),
- Third, the term "bankruptcy risk" is ambiguous from both a legal and an economic standpoint (for example, a company may be at risk of bankruptcy, but its situation steadily improves, so it cannot be classified as a future bankruptcy; even defining the situation as "bad" would be inaccurate because the condition of the company is improving steadily).

Vith fuzzy sets, we can formally define vague and amiguous terms, such as the "high risk of bankruptcy" nd "low risk of bankruptcy." Fuzzy set A in a certain on-empty space X ($A \subseteq X$) can be defined as follows Wu, Zhang, Wu & Olson, 2010):

$$\text{A} = \{(x, \mu_A(x)) | x \in X\} \quad (1)$$

vhere $\mu_A: X \rightarrow [0,1]$ is a function that specifies the xtent to which each element in X belongs to set A. 'unction μ_A is the so-called membership function of uzzy set A.

While the classic set theory assumes that any item company) belongs or does not belong to a given set a "bad" or "good" financial situation), in fuzzy set heory, an item can partially belong to a set, and this elonging can be expressed by a real number from he interval [0,1]. Thus, the membership function $\mu_A(x)$: U⇒ [0,1] is defined as follows:

$$\forall_{x \in U} \mu_A(x) = \begin{cases} f(x), x \in X \\ 0, x \notin X \end{cases} \quad (2)$$

where $\mu_A(x)$ is a function specifying the membership of x in set A, which is a subset of U, and f (x) is a function of values in the range [0,1]. The values of this function are called degrees of membership.

The membership function of each element $x \in X$ assigns a degree of membership to fuzzy set A, in which we can distinguish three situations:

- ☐ $\mu_A(x) = 1$ means full membership of element x in fuzzy set A,
- ☐ $\mu_A(x) = 0$ means no membership of element x in fuzzy set A,
- ☐ $0 < \mu_A(x) < 1$ means partial membership of element x in fuzzy set A.

Membership functions are usually presented in graphical form (Nakandala, Samaranayake, & Lau, 2013). The trapezoid function $\mu_A(x)$ is frequently used; the graph of this function is shown in Figure 1. This figure also includes the accepted standards for the current ratio, as reported in the literature. The correct value of this index is a value in the range [1.2; 2]; the incorrect value belongs to the range $(0; 1{,}2) \cup (2; \infty)$. When this ratio is less than 1.2, the company's current liquidity is considered to be too low. Conversely, when this value is greater than 2.0, it is said that the company has excess liquidity (in the case of excess liquidity, such companies may have too much inventory, indicating inefficient management of the company), which is also considered a negative phenomenon.

In such a situation, when using the classic set theory to assess this indicator, there is a sharp boundary between the two sets for the ratio values of 1.2 and 2.0. If one company reported a current ratio, for example, at 1.19, it would be classified as an invalid value, or negative, while if the second company reported this ratio of 1.2, it would be considered as a valid, positive value in an assessment of the company's risk of bankruptcy, even though the values of the two firms differ by only 0.01. The interpretation of the values of these indicators (e.g., liquidity) is further complicated by the fact that different literature sources give different reference limits for each indicator.

The application of fuzzy sets changes the assessment of this problem. A current ratio with a value of 1.19 is considered partially correct and partially invalid. The degree of membership in the two sets depends on the shape of the membership function.

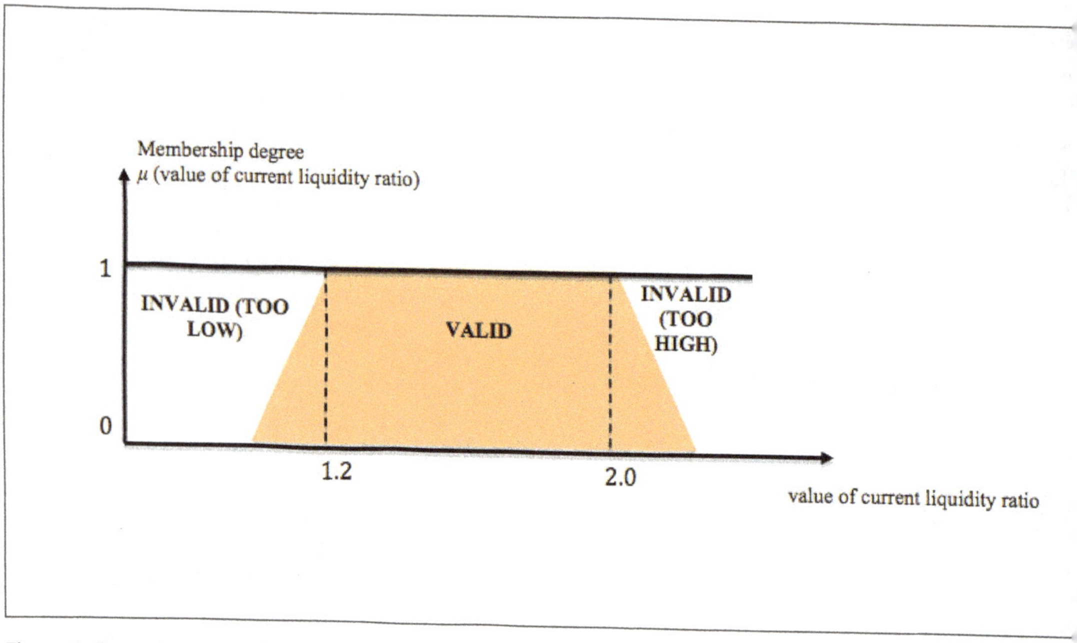

Figure 1. Example trapezoid membership function for current liquidity ratio

4. Assumptions of this study

In this study, the author developed a population of 166 companies from the service and manufacturing sectors. This study disregarded companies from the financial sector (banks and insurance companies) due to their different characteristics and the different financial indicators used in the ratio analysis of these companies.

Within this population of companies, the following characteristics were identified:

- ✓ Test sample no. 1 consisted of 60 Polish joint stock companies listed on the Warsaw Stock Exchange, wherein 30 of them were at risk of bankruptcy. The remaining 30 companies were enterprises in good financial condition. The surveyed companies came from different sectors, such as construction, the metal industry, food processing, chemicals, telecommunications, etc.;
- ✓ Test sample no. 2 consisted of 60 companies from Latin America. The sample was also a balanced sample, including 30 "good" and 30 "bad" companies. These companies came from different sectors of the economy, in such countries as Mexico, Argentina, Brazil, Chile, Peru, and Venezuela;
- ✓ Test sample no. 3 was comprised of 46 international and/or global companies (e.g., Coca-Cola). The test sample included 23 "bad" companies that were at risk of bankruptcy and 23 companies with impeccable financial records. The locations of these companies include countries such as the USA, Germany, France, Great Britain, Sweden, Japan, Finland, Taiwan, South Korea, and the Netherlands.

No training sample was used in this work, as the author tested the fuzzy logic models developed on the basis of his knowledge and previous 14 years of work experience. Models based on the use of fuzzy logic do not require any assumptions about the learning process, as they are developed on the basis of expertise.

For all 166 companies, the author calculated and used 34 financial variables (Table 2) to be analyzed for the period of one year and two years before the recognition of a company as "good" or "bad." However, the study used financial statements for three years (498 balance sheets and 498 income statements) because some of the variables in the dynamic approach were studied between the first and second year and then between the second and third year. In test sample no. 1 the financial data were from 1999-2007; in test sampl

ble 2. Financial variables used in the study

Variable symbol	Description of financial variable
CA	Current assets
INV	Inventory
STL	Short-term liabilities
STR	Short-term receivables
CSH	Cash and cash equivalents
STI	Short-term investments
GP	Gross profit
OP	Operating profit
TRS	Revenues from sales
TR	Total revenues
(TRS / TA) *100%	Turnover of total assets
(STLt / STLt-1)* 100%	Dynamics of short-term liabilities
(LTLt / LTLt-1)*100%	Dynamics of long-term liabilities
[(NPt + At)/ (NPt-1 + At-1) *100%	Dynamics of cash surplus (net profit and depreciation)
(NP + A) / TA	Share of cash surplus in total assets
STL / (NP + A)	Number of years of repayment of short-term liabilities
LTL / (NP + A)	Number of years of repayment of long-term liabilities
(TAt / TAt-1)*100%	Dynamics of total assets
(EQt / EQt-1)*100%	Dynamics of equity
(LTCt / LTCt-1)*100%	Dynamics of long-term capital (equity + long term liabilities)
(FAt / FAt-1)*100%	Dynamics of fixed assets
(FA / TA)*100%	Share of fixed assets in total assets
(CA / TA)*100%	Share of current assets in total assets
(EQ / TA)*100%	Share of equity in total assets
(INV / CA)*100%	Share of inventories in current assets
(STR / CA)*100%	Share of short-term receivables in current assets
LTC / EQ	Ratio of fixed capital to equity
(TRSt / TRSt-1)*100%	Dynamics of revenues from sales
(INVt / INVt-1)*100%	Dynamics of inventories
TRS / INV	Inventory turnover ratio
(STRt / STRt-1)*100%	Dynamics of short-term receivables
TRS / STR	Short-term receivables turnover ratio
TRS / STL	Short term liabilities turnover ratio
CA / STL	Current liquidity ratio

no. 2, the data were from 2000-2009; and in test sample no. 3, the data were from 1999-2009.

In addition, each company was described with a zero-one output variable, which grouped the populations in the two groups of companies as those with bad financial situations (variable = zero) and those with good economic conditions (variable = one).

In total, the author tested 13 models within the time periods of one year and two years prior to the categorization of the company as "good" or "bad," with three test samples (a total of 78 tests). Due to the limited length of this article, only two of these models are presented, which are the disaggregated current liquidity ratio model and the disaggregated ratio of coverage of fixed assets with long-term capital model.

The quality of the classification of all the models was evaluated based on the overall performance as well as Type I and Type II errors. Thus, the following formulas were used:

- ❑ Type I error: $E_1 = (D_1 / BR) \bullet 100\%$
  where D_1 represents the number of companies with bad financial situations classified by the model or ratio as "good," and BR represents the number of companies in the test sample with poor economic conditions;
- ❑ Type II error: $E_2 = (D_2 / NBR) \bullet 100\%$
  where D_2 represents the number of companies with impeccable financial records classified by the model or ratio as "bad,", i.e., at risk of bankruptcy, and NBR represents the number of "good" companies in the test sample;
- ❑ Overall model effectiveness: $S = \{1 - [(D_1 + D_2) / (BR + NBR)]\} \bullet 100\%$.

5. Forecasting financial ratios

In this study, the author proposes the use of fuzzy logic for disaggregated financial ratios. The disaggregation of the indicators was aimed at not only the method of calculating the value of the index but also, and above all, the correct assessment of the factors affecting its level. Due to the limited length of this article, the author will present only two of the 13 models to show the development and operation of these models.

The first sample model is based on the disaggregation of the current liquidity ratio carried out by the author. In the author's opinion, in assessing the liquidity of companies, one should focus more on establishing the critical factors affecting the level of liquidity and less on fixing their limits. This disaggregation was as follows:

$$CR = \frac{CSH}{STL} x \frac{STI}{CSH} x \frac{(CA - INV)}{(CA - INV - STR)} x \frac{CA}{(CA - INV)} \qquad (3)$$

Based on this disaggregation, we can conclude that the current ratio (CA / STL) is dependent on the quick ratio [(CA - INV) / STL] and the ratio of long-term current assets to medium-term current assets, i.e., exchangeable to cash in reasonable time [CA / (CA - INV)]. On the other hand, the quick ratio is dependent on two other measures, i.e., the ratio of the value of medium-term current assets to the value of short-term current assets [(CA - INV) / (CA - INV - STR)] and cash liquidity [(CA - INV - STR) / STL], which can be further disaggregated into the ratio of short-term investments to cash held by the company (STI / CSH) and the ratio of cash to short-term liabilities (CSH / STL).

The model developed by the author consists of the following:

- ✓ Six input variables: current assets (CA), inventories (INV), short-term receivables (STR), short-term investments (STI), cash (CSH) and short-term liabilities (STL). The model for each input variable identifies three fuzzy sets (which are subsets of the set field of values of a given input) and the corresponding membership functions:
  - "small" for low-level variables tested,
  - "medium" for medium-level variables,
  - "high" for high-level variables;
- ✓ Five decision centers, K1, K2, K3, K4 and K5, which are shown in Figure 2;
- ✓ One output, which represents the assessment of the current liquidity ratio on the basis of four factors affecting its level: the ratio of long-term current assets to medium-term current assets, i.e., exchangeable to cash within a reasonable time (K1 decision center), the ratio of the value of medium-term current assets to short-term current assets (K2 decision center), the ratio of short-term investments to cash held by the company (K3 decision center) and the ratio of cash to current liabilities (K4 decision center). Because this indicator is a nominant, the final assessment of the current liquidity ratio (K5 decision cent-

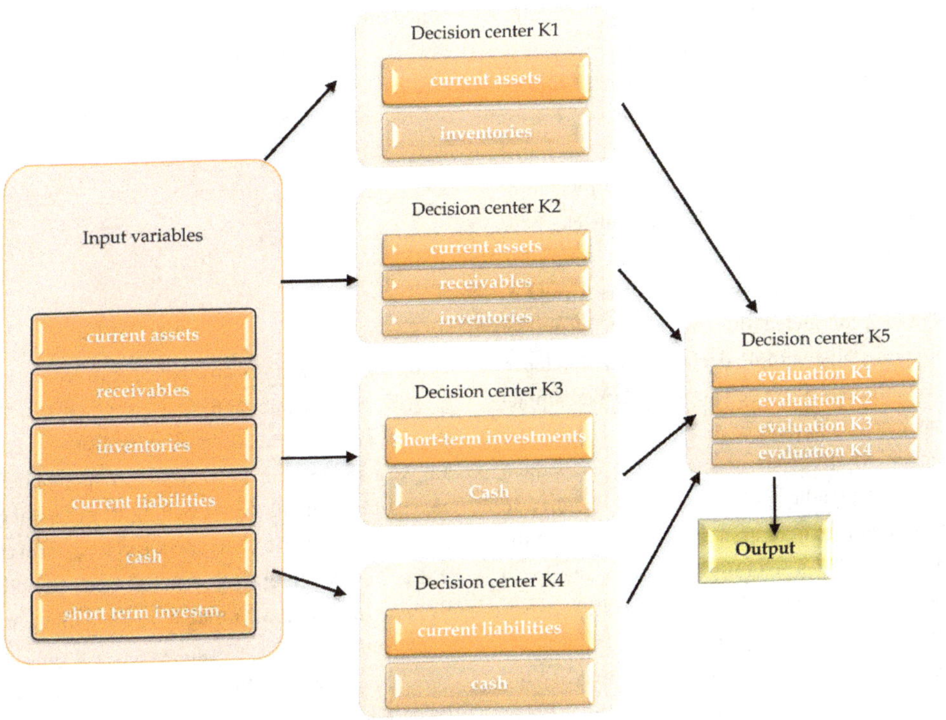

‑ure 2. Structure of the fuzzy logic model for the disaggregated current liquidity ratio

is presented on a scale of 0 to 5, with five membership functions, as shown in Figure 3:

- "neg_low," representing information about negative (dangerously low) levels of current liquidity,
- "low," representing information about a low but safe level of this indicator,
- "medium," indicating the optimal level of the indicator,
- "high," representing a high, but still within optimal range, level of current liquidity,
- "neg_high," describing a situation of too high a degree of liquidity of a company (indicating its mismanagement, affecting the decrease in company efficiency).

The levels of input variables are fuzzy values. Fuzzy sets and the shape of the membership function have been ar‑itrarily set by the author. The rating of the CA and STL variables ("small," "medium" or "high") is based on an analysis of their share in total assets (from 0% to 100%). On the other hand, the variables INV and STR are presented as a percentage of current assets from 0% to 80%, and the CSH and STI variables are presented as a percentage of current assets from 0% to 50%, as shown in Figure 4. These variables have to be presented in relative form. If they are presented in the monetary form, these values, such as a value of assets of one million USD, could be high for one company but low for another.

The outputs of the decision centers K1, K2, K3 and K4 are also inputs of the K5 decision center. In other words, the assessment of the current liquidity ratio is based on the partial evaluation of the various factors affecting liquidity. The assessment of these disaggregated factors takes one of three states: a low score, a medium score, or a high score.

Table 3 shows the developed decision rules for the decision blocks K1, K2, K3 and K4. The decision centers K1, K3 and K4 consist of 9 decision rules, and block K2 consists of 27 rules. For example, when the share of short-term investments in current assets is at a high level (membership function "high"), and the share of cash in current assets is at a low level (membership function "small"), the assessment generated for this disaggregated current liquidity factor will be of a high value ("high"), which is decision rule No. 7 for block K3. This high rating is also an input of decision block K5, where the final assessment of the current liquidity ratio is conducted (due to the limited length of this paper, the table with 81 decision rules developed for decision block K5 can be sent to readers as supplementary data).

Based on 81 decision rules, the final assessment of the current liquidity ratio ("result") is assigned to one of five membership functions (Figure 3) from the situation indicating a liquidity shortage ("neg_low") through optimal conditions, low, medium, high, or excess financial liquidity ("neg_high").

Figure 4 shows the fuzzy sets with membership functions for the sample variable, cash. The share of cash in current assets in excess of 36% is classified as absolutely high (membership function "high"). The share of this variable in current assets less than 13% is considered absolutely low (membership function "small"). Values between 13% and 36% partially belong to individual states from low to high through medium.

The second sample model is developed for the ratio of the coverage of fixed assets (FA) by long-term capital to equity and noncurrent liabilities (LTC). The model uses the following input variables:

- dynamics of the equity in the current period t ($EQ_t / EQ_{(t-1)}$),
- dynamics of long-term capital in the current period t ($LTC_t / LTC_{(t-1)}$),
- dynamics of fixed assets in the current period t ($FA_t / FA_{(t-1)}$),
- dynamics of total assets in the current period t ($TA_t / TA_{(t-1)}$),
- share of fixed assets in total assets in the previous period (t–1) ($FA_{(t-1)} / TA_{(t-1)}$),
- share of equity in financing total assets in the previous period (t–1) ($EQ_{(t-1)} / TA_{(t-1)}$),
- ratio of long-term capital to equity in the previous period (t–1) ($LTC_{(t-1)} / EQ_{(t-1)}$).

With such disaggregation of the ratio, the author obtained the following formula:

$$\frac{LTC}{FA} = \frac{\left(\frac{EQ_{(t-1)}}{TA_{(t-1)}} x \frac{\frac{EQ_t}{EQ_{(t-1)}}}{\frac{TA_t}{TA_{(t-1)}}} \right) x \left(\frac{LTC_{(t-1)}}{EQ_{(t-1)}} x \frac{\frac{LTC_t}{LTC_{(t-1)}}}{\frac{EQ_t}{EQ_{(t-1)}}} \right)}{\frac{FA_{(t-1)}}{TA_{(t-1)}} x \frac{\frac{FA_t}{FA_{(t-1)}}}{\frac{TA_t}{TA_{(t-1)}}}} \quad (4)$$

Using disaggregation, an analyst can compare the growth rate of equity and long-term capital with the growth rate of fixed assets and total assets. For example, a situation in which equity is maintained at a constant level and the value of long-term capital grows may mean that there is an increase in long-term capital due to the growth of long-term liabilities. In addition, by analyzing the growth rate of the dynamics of fixed assets and total assets, we can assess the degree of danger of a situation in which assets are not fully financed by long-term, stable capital.

For each input variable in the dynamic aspect, three membership functions were developed representing the decline in value ("decrease" membership function) and the relative stability ("stable" membership function) or an increase in value ("increase" membership function). For the input variables in the static aspect, the same conditions were used (low, medium, high). It should also be noted that each of these variables has a different course in the membership function. A comparison of Figures 5 and 6 shows that for the share of fixed assets in total assets, a wider range of values of functions was used that belonged to the "medium" fuzzy set, representing the average state of this variable in the case of the share of equity in total assets. The author proceeded on the basis that the proportion of equity, with an average value of 50% and fluctuations from 30% to 70% (depending on the sector of the economy and the business cycle), represents the average level of the index, whereas in the case of the share of fixed assets, it is much more difficult to determine the level of this variable as medium ("medium" membership function) because it depends heavily on the type of business. Therefore, the set of values equival

e 3. The set of decision rules for individual decision centers of the current liquidity ratio model (K1, K2, K3, K4)

Decision center K1

If "CA" is:	If "INV" is:	Then "K1" is:
Small	Small	Low
Small	Medium	Low
Small	High	Medium
Medium	Small	Low
Medium	Medium	Medium
Medium	High	High
High	Small	Medium
High	Medium	High
High	High	High

Decision center K3

If "STI" is:	If "CSH" is:	Then "K3" is:
Small	Small	Low
Small	Medium	Low
Small	High	Low
Medium	Small	High
Medium	Medium	Medium
Medium	High	Low
High	Small	High
High	Medium	High
High	High	Medium

Decision center K4

If "CSH" is:	If "STL" is:	Then "K4" is:
Small	Small	Medium
Small	Medium	Low
Small	High	Low
Medium	Small	Medium
Medium	Medium	Low
Medium	High	Low
High	Small	High
High	Medium	Medium
High	High	Low

Decision center K2

No.	If "CA" is:	If "STR" is:	If "INV" is:	Then "K2" is:
1.	Small	Small	Small	Medium
2.	Small	Small	Medium	Medium
3.	Small	Small	High	Medium
4.	Small	Medium	Small	Medium
5.	Small	Medium	Medium	Medium
6.	Small	Medium	High	Low
7.	Small	High	Small	Medium
8.	Small	High	Medium	Low
9.	Small	High	High	Low
10.	Medium	Small	Small	High
11.	Medium	Small	Medium	Medium
12.	Medium	Small	High	Medium
13.	Medium	Medium	Small	Medium
14.	Medium	Medium	Medium	Medium
15.	Medium	Medium	High	Medium
16.	Medium	High	Small	Medium
17.	Medium	High	Medium	Medium
18.	Medium	High	High	Low
19.	High	Small	Small	High
20.	High	Small	Medium	High
21.	High	Small	High	High
22.	High	Medium	Small	High
23.	High	Medium	Medium	High
24.	High	Medium	High	Medium
25.	High	High	Small	Medium
26.	High	High	Medium	Medium
27.	High	High	High	Low

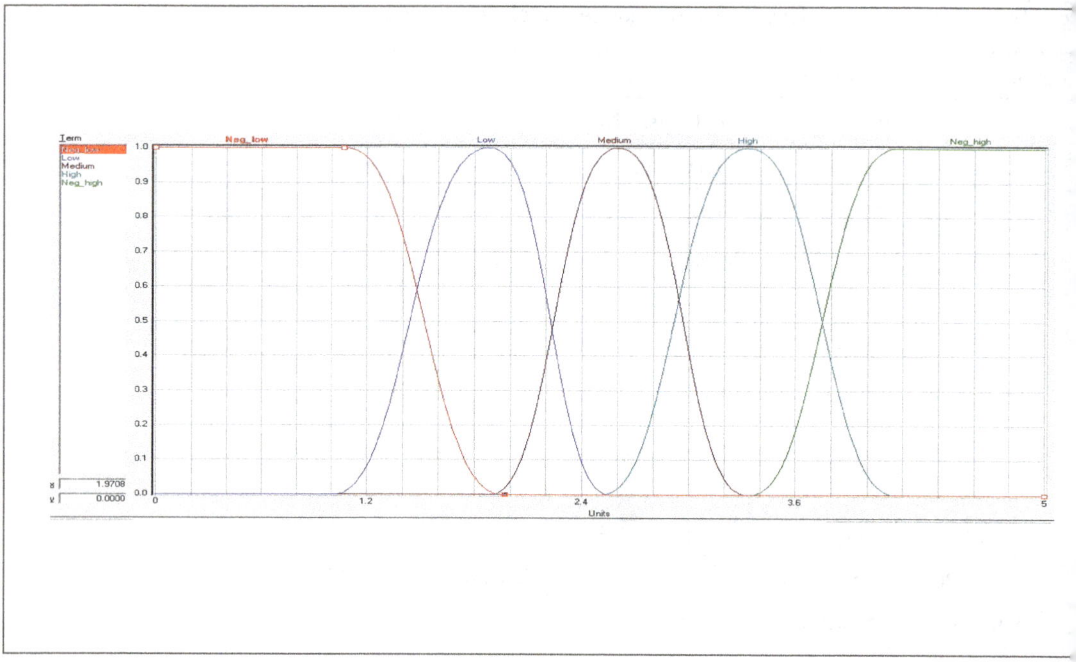

Figure 3. Membership functions for the disaggregated current liquidity ratio
Source: The author's own study (FuzzyTech software).

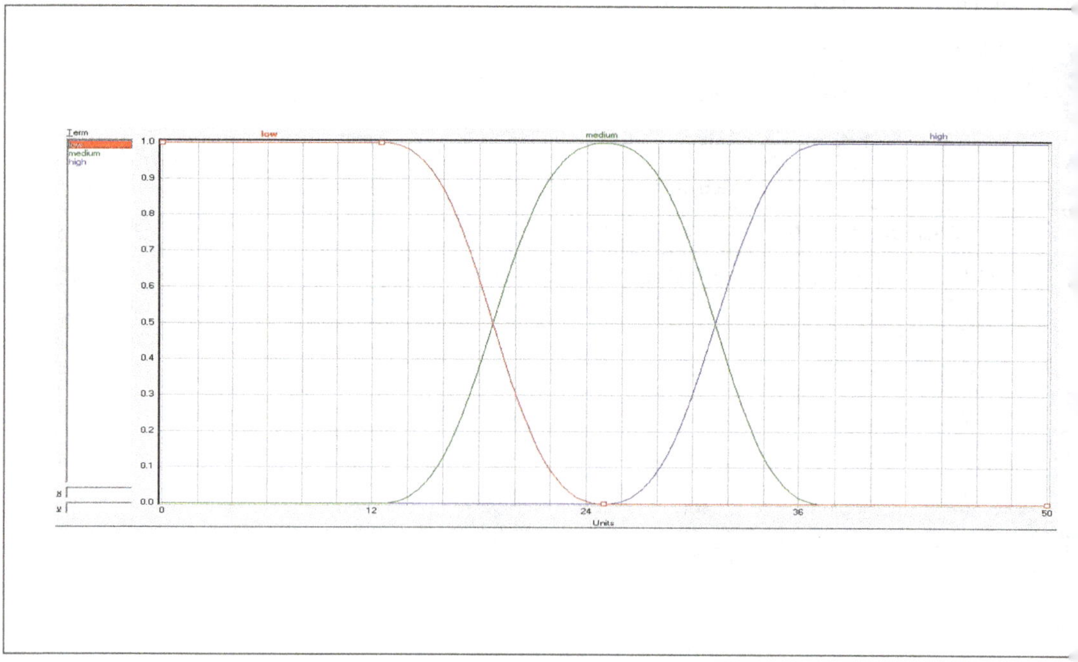

Figure 4. Fuzzy sets for the input variable "cash" with the membership functions
Source: The author's own study (FuzzyTech software).

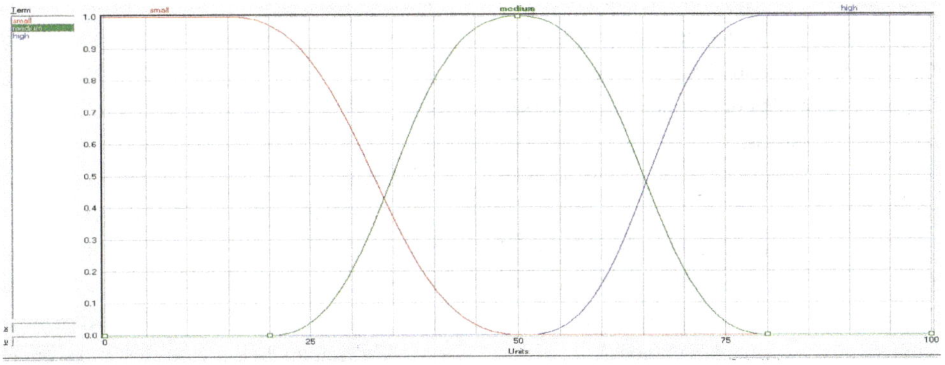

re 5. Membership functions for the input variable "share of fixed assets in total assets" (FuzzyTech software)
ce: The author's own study (FuzzyTech software).

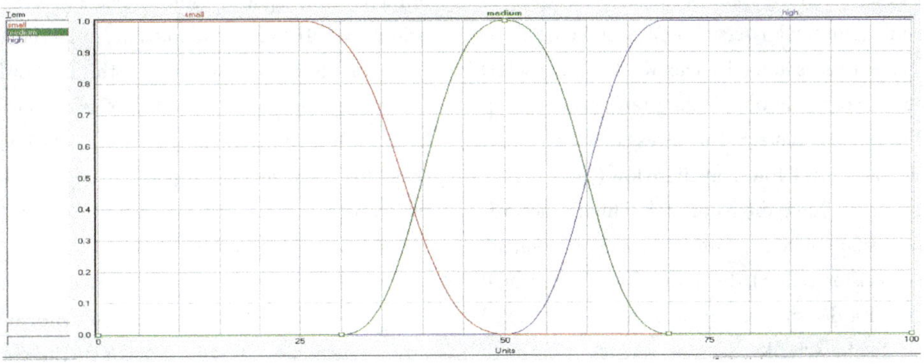

re 6. Membership functions for the input variable "share of equity in the financing of total assets" (FuzzyTech software)
ce: The author's own study (FuzzyTech software).

to the medium level was fuzzified, assuming a range of values from 20% to 80% (Figure 5).

For the last variable (ratio of long-term capital to equity), it was assumed that a value below 115% fully represents a low level (100 percent belonging to the set of values) because the ratio does not take values lower than 100%. When this variable has a value above 170%, it is classified as possessing full membership in the set, showing a high-ratio status.

The decision process of this model also consists of three stages.

In the first stage, the decision centers K1, K2 and K5 allow the assessment of the variables in the dynamic aspect. More specifically, block K1 compares the dynamics of equity to the dynamics of total assets, block K2 evaluates the dynamics of long-term capital in relation to the dynamics of equity, and in block K5, the dynamics of fixed assets are assessed against the background of the dynamics of total assets. These centers generate four different evaluations: the state of decline ("decrease"), the state of slow decline ("stable_dec"), the state of slow growth ("stable_inc") and the state of growth ("increase"), depending on the rate of increase or decrease in the numerator and denominator in the disaggregation formula of the fixed assets coverage ratio by long-term capital.

The second stage assesses the impact of a decrease, slow decrease, slow increase, or increase in the individual variables on the value of the share of equity in the financing of total assets (K3 decision center), the share of fixed assets in total assets (K6 decision center) and the ratio of the amount of long-term capital to equity (K4 decision center). This assessment takes four possible states: low ("low"), medium low ("low_med"), medium high ("high_med") or high ("high"), according to the share of equity in the financing of total assets (K3 decision center), the ratio of long-term capital to equity (K4 decision center) and the share of fixed assets in total assets (K6 decision center). It is worth noting that in this model, the higher the rating of K3 and K4 and the lower the level of assessment of K6, the lower the risk for the company resulting from the structure of financing of fixed assets through relative stability, i.e., safe, long-term capital.

This assessment is made in the K7 decision center in the third and final stage. For example, according to decision rule No. 4 (in block K7), when the share of equity in the financing of the total assets and the ratio of fixed capital to equity remain at a low level ("low" rating) and the share of fixed assets in total assets remains at a high level ("high" rating), then the entire ratio of the coverage of fixed assets by long-term capital receives a "low" score, which indicates the low share of long-term capital in the financing of illiquid assets, such as fixed assets. This situation is synonymous with a company's high risk of liquidity problems in financing these assets. Another example involves decision rule No. 41 presenting a situation in which the company has a medium high share of equity and a medium ratio of long-term capital to equity (both ratings "high_med") and the share of fixed assets in total assets was rated as low ("low" rating). In this case, the ratio score is high ("high" rating), which is equivalent to a high level of coverage of fixed assets through long-term capital (low risk of bad financing of the company).

The evaluation of the two above models is shown below in Tables 4 and 5.

The model examining the current liquidity of the company generates an assessment of the ratio from the range of values from 0 to 5. The membership function informing the too low level ("Neg_low") of this measure ranges from 0 to 1.9, whereas values from 0 to 1.2 indicate full (100%) belonging to the set "Neg_low," and values above 1.9 (it should be noted that this is the scope of the generated ratio rating and not the value of the current liquidity ratio) indicate zero affiliation with the set. The author adopted the intersection point (value of 1.5) of the "Neg_low" with the "Low" function, representing a low but safe level of current liquidity, as the limit point, ranking companies as "good" and "bad" for all three test samples, i.e., regardless of the region of the enterprise's operations, the classification criterion was set the same.

Table 4 shows the resulting overall one-year and two-year efficiencies of the fuzzy logic model for the three test samples ("fuzzy" S1 and S2). These efficiencies were compared with the results obtained from the tests of the examined population of companies using the traditionally calculated current liquidity ratio ("traditional" S1 and S2). In all three test samples for the two-year analysis, the application of a model based on fuzzy logic clearly had a positive impact on improving the efficiency of the assessment of the companies' current liquidity. The greatest improvement le 4. Overall efficiency of the current liquidity model one year (S1) and two years (S2) prior to the classification of the panies' financial condition, including Type I (E1) and Type II (E2) errors

	ONE-YEAR ANALYSIS			TWO-YEAR ANALYSIS		
zy"	Central European	Latin America	Global companies	Central European	Latin America	Global companies
	90.0%	88.33%	76.09%	88.33%	81.67%	71.74%
	6.67%	10.0%	21.74%	10.0%	16.67%	26.09%
	13.33%	13.33%	26.09%	13.33%	20%	30.43%
ditional"	Central European	Latin America	Global companies	Central European	Latin America	Global companies
	81.67%	81.67%	67.39%	80.0%	75.0%	60.87%
	20.0%	20.0%	34.78%	23.33%	26.67%	39.13%
	16.67%	16.67%	30.43%	16.67%	23.33%	39.13%

n performance was observed in test sample no. 3 with global companies in the two-year analysis (from 60.87% to 71.74%). The smallest increase in efficiency due to the use of fuzzy logic can be seen in test sample no. 2 (companies from Latin America). For the two-year analysis, the effectiveness increased by approximately 6 percentage points. The highest efficiency of the fuzzy logic model was observed in test sample no. 1 with Polish companies in the one-year analysis (90% efficiency).

Another element that is worth noting is the level of Type I and II errors generated by the fuzzy logic model and by the traditional ratio analysis. In both years analyzed, not only did the use of fuzzy logic result in a reduction in both types of errors but in addition, when applying the traditional ratio analysis, Type I errors were greater than Type II errors. Using fuzzy logic, the situation is reversed, i.e., Type I errors are reduced much more than Type II errors, which means that the level of Type I error was less than the level of Type II error. This positive trend occurred for both years in all three test samples analyzed. In the literature, a Type I error is considered more expensive than a Type II error. This conclusion is based on the classification of companies with a poor financial situation as a company with a positive financial situation. In this case, the purchase of the "bad" company's shares (Type I error) indicates future losses initially resulting from a decline in trading of that company and ultimately from the company's bankruptcy. On the other hand, a Type II error indicates the loss of potential profits when resigning from the purchase of the "healthy" company's shares when believing that the company is "bad."

The highest Type I and Type II errors in both analyzed years in the traditional and fuzzy approaches were reported for the test sample containing global companies from different countries. These errors were at a level over 30% using the traditional ratio and over 20% with the use of fuzzy logic. On the other hand, the lowest errors were generated when testing the sample of companies from Central Europe.

For the ratio of the coverage of fixed assets by long-term capital, the membership function representing a high financial risk due to the low level of funding for these assets by long-term capital is in the range of 0 to 0.5. Ratings for the values of this ratio below 0.3 indicate full belonging to the set; therefore, these values were considered the companies' classifying values. However, for the traditional ratio analysis, the value of 100% was adopted for all three test samples. The value of 100% indicates a situation in which assets are fully financed by equity and long-term liabilities. Table 5 shows the efficiency obtained from the present model with Type I and Type II errors.

Table 5. Overall efficiency of the model of coverage of fixed assets with long-term capital one year (S1) and two years (S2) prior to the classification of the companies' financial condition, including Type I (E1) and Type II (E2) errors

	ONE-YEAR ANALYSIS			TWO-YEAR ANALYSIS		
"Fuzzy"	Central European	Latin America	Global companies	Central European	Latin America	Global companies
S	83.33%	80.0%	73.91%	83.33%	73.33%	63.04%
E1	16.67%	23.33%	21.74%	13.33%	26.67%	39.13%
E2	16.67%	16.67%	30.43%	20.0%	26.67%	34.78%
"Traditional"	Central European	Latin America	Global companies	Central European	Latin America	Global companies
S	81.67%	76.67%	67.39%	78.33%	71.67%	58.70%
E1	20.0%	26.67%	26.09%	20.0%	26.67%	43.48%
E2	16.67%	20.0%	39.13%	23.33%	30.0%	39.13%

The highest model efficiency was achieved with test sample no. 1, which consisted of companies from Central Europe, and the lowest efficiency was achieved with the sample of multinationals (test sample no. 3). All three test samples noted improvements in the accuracy of the assessment with the use of fuzzy logic (the greatest improvement was shown in the one-year analysis of test sample no. 3, with 6.52 percentage points).

A positive aspect of the fuzzy logic model is also a reduction in the number of errors of both types for the one-year and two-year analysis in all the test samples. In the one-year analysis of companies, the greatest improvement was observed for Type II errors in test sample no. 3 (from 39.13% to 30.43%). In the analysis covering two years, the largest decrease in the number of Type I errors was reported in test sample no. 1 (from 20% to 13.33%).

To enrich the conclusions of this research, the author presented additional information from the study application portion (Table 6). In Table 6, there is information about the mean and median values of two analyzed ratios (CR and LTC/FA) for nonbankrupt and bankrupt enterprises (separately) in all three test samples for the two-year period and one-year period of analysis. The data shows that Central European nonbankrupt enterprises were characterized with much higher current ratio (CR) values than companies from Latin America and global enterprises. However, in the case of companies at risk of bankruptcy in all three test samples, the values were similarly low, which means that Polish firms recorded a much higher decrease in current liquidity with an increasing risk of bankruptcy than the enterprises from other parts of the world.

In the case of the ratio of the coverage of fixed assets by long-term capital (LTC/FA), it can be noted that Latin American companies and global enterprises were characterized by higher values of this ratio than the firms from Central Europe (both "good" and "bad" companies). It can be seen that the companies with high risk of bankruptcy in Poland registered negative values of this ratio, which means that the firms generated profound losses causing negative values in stockholders' equity.

6. Conclusions and recommendations

This paper presents the efficiency problems related to the oldest and most popular method of financial analysis, i.e., ratio analysis. In the introduction, questions were raised about the topicality and, thus, the effectiveness of traditional ratio analysis in the current environment of the increasing globalization and computerization of enterprises. In addition, the global financial crisis that began in mid-2008 resulted in in-

e 6. Historical data for the analyzed ratios (CR, LTC/FA)

)	CR							
ᴐD	ONE-YEAR ANALYSIS				TWO-YEAR ANALYSIS			
	Median		**Mean**		**Median**		**Mean**	
ral ɔean	NON	BANKR.	NON	BANKR.	NON	BANKR.	NON	BANKR.
	1.647	**0.569**	**2.838**	**0.779**	**2.309**	**0.701**	**3.041**	**0.744**
	Median		**Mean**		**Median**		**Mean**	
rican	NON	BANKR.	NON	BANKR.	NON	BANKR.	NON	BANKR.
	1.321	**0.452**	**1.853**	**0.644**	**1.541**	**0.65**	**1.975**	**0.843**
	Median		**Mean**		**Median**		**Mean**	
al ɔanies	NON	BANKR.	NON	BANKR.	NON	BANKR.	NON	BANKR.
	1.454	**0.502**	**2.035**	**0.705**	**1.884**	**0.818**	**2.273**	**0.85**
)	LTC/FA							
ᴐD	ONE-YEAR ANALYSIS				TWO-YEAR ANALYSIS			
	Median		**Mean**		**Median**		**Mean**	
ral ɔean	NON	BANKR.	NON	BANKR.	NON	BANKR.	NON	BANKR.
	1.123	**0.407**	**1.243**	**-3.517**	**1.101**	**0.804**	**1.251**	**-0.184**
	Median		**Mean**		**Median**		**Mean**	
rican	NON	BANKR.	NON	BANKR.	NON	BANKR.	NON	BANKR.
	1.508	**0.557**	**1.352**	**0.275**	**1.621**	**0.712**	**1.452**	**0.595**
	Median		**Mean**		**Median**		**Mean**	
al ɔanies	NON	BANKR.	NON	BANKR.	NON	BANKR.	NON	BANKR.
	1.735	**0.571**	**1.825**	**0.459**	**1.795**	**0.592**	**1.894**	**0.655**

reased uncertainty and complexity of the phenomena ccurring in the global economy. Events such as the mergence of countries' bankruptcy risk (e.g., Greece) r the mass decline of their credit ratings directly and ndirectly influenced companies' financial situations. The author hopes that these studies will be of interest o economic analysts, entrepreneurs, students and re-earchers in economic sciences because of the follow-ng contributions:

. **The proposal of disaggregation, which allows not only the calculation of a financial indicator but also the further assessment of the impact of various financial measures on the size of the indicator. For example, by introducing a dynamic approach, an analyst can compare the dynamics of the factors (e.g., dynamics of selected liabilities in relation to the dynamics of selected assets) and evaluate them on the basis of their values from the previous period, specifically, how much an increase or decrease in these components affects the current state of the examined ratio. Thus, for example, breaking down the ratio of the cover-**

age of fixed assets by long-term capital into the factors of the dynamic and static approaches allowed the author to clearly indicate the risks resulting from an inadequate capital structure in a studied company. Importantly, these risks were observed two years prior to the analysis. In the traditional approach (i.e., in the static approach and without the use of fuzzy sets), this indicator remained at a high, safe level; therefore, an analyst could not have noticed the warning signs of imminent risk.

2. The ranking of financial ratios in order of their most frequent use. This query was based on the literature studies involving 600 articles.
3. The presentation of the theoretical basis of the method, taking fuzzy logic into account.
4. The development of 13 fuzzy logic models for the most popular financial indicators with which companies' financial conditions were assessed.
5. The testing of the fuzzy logic models with three different test samples involving companies from the following countries: Poland, Germany, France, Japan, Taiwan, Sweden, Finland, South Korea, United Kingdom, Mexico, Argentina, USA, Brazil, Chile, Peru, and Venezuela.
6. The verification of the models' universality, i.e., the predictive properties of the proposed models based on a diverse population of 166 companies.
7. A check of the behavior of the models through an extension of the analysis period to two years.
8. The comparison of the effectiveness of ratio analysis based on fuzzy sets with the effectiveness of traditional (zero-one) ratio analysis.

References

Ahn, B. S., Cho, S. S., & Kim, C. Y. (2000). The integrated methodology of rough set theory and artificial neural networks for business failure prediction. *Expert Systems with Applications, 18*(2), 65–74.

Altman, E. (1993). *Corporate Financial Distress and Bankruptcy*. New York, NY: John Wiley & Sons.

Altman, E. I., Baidya, T. K. N., & Ribeiro Dias, L. M. (1979). Assessing potential financial problems for firms in Brazil. *Journal of International Business Studies, 10*(2), 9–24.

Anandarajan, M., Lee, P., & Anandarajan, A. (2001). Bankruptcy prediction of financially stressed firms: An examination of the predictive accurac of artificial neural networks. *Intelligent System in Accounting, Finance and Management, 10(2)*, 69–81.

Andres, J., Landajo, M., & Lorca, P. (2005). Forecasting business profitability by using classification techniques: A comparative analysis based on a Spanish case. *European Journal of Operational Research 167*(2), 518–542.

Asgharian, H. (2003). Are highly leveraged firms more sensitive to an economic downturn? *The European Journal of Finance, 9*(3), 219–241.

Atiya, A. (2001). Bankruptcy prediction for credit risk using neural networks: A survey and new results *IEEE Transactions on Neural Networks, 12(4)* 929–935.

Back, B., Laitinen, T., & Sere, K. (1996). Neural network and genetic algorithm for bankruptcy prediction. *Expert Systems with Applications, 11(4)* 407–413.

Baek, J., & Cho, S. (2003, March). *Bankruptcy prediction for credit risk using an auto-associative neural networks in Korean firms*. Paper presented at the IEEE International Conference on Computational Intelligence for Financial Engineering, Hong Kong.

Bandyopadhyay, A. (2006). Predicting probability of default of Indian corporate bonds: Logistic and Z-score model approaches. *The Journal of Risk Finance, 7(3)*, 255–272.

Becerra, V., Galvao, R., & Abou-Seada, M. (2005). Neural and wavelet network models for financial distress classification. *Journal of Data Mining and Knowledge Discovery, 11*(1), 35-55.

Bhattacharjee, A., Highson, C., Holly, S., & Kattuman P. (2003). Business failure in UK and US quoted firms-impact of macroeconomic instability and the role of legal institutions (Working Paper No 0420). Department of Applied Economics, Cambridge University. Retrieved from http://www.econ.cam.ac.uk/research-files/repec/cam/pdf/cwpe0420.pdf

Bian, H., & Mazlack, L. (2003). Fuzzy-rough nearest neighbour classification approach. Paper presented at the *22nd International Conference on the North American Fuzzy Information Processing Society*, Chicago, IL.

Boritz, J. E., & Kennedy, D. B. (1995). Effectiveness of neural network types for prediction of business failure. *Expert Systems with Applications, 9(4),* 503–512.

Bryant, S. M. (1998). A case-based reasoning approach to bankruptcy prediction modeling. *Intelligent Systems in Accounting, Finance and Management,* 6(3), 195–214.

Charalambous, C., Charitou, A., & Kaourou, F. (2000). Comparative analysis of artificial neural network models: Application in bankruptcy prediction. *Annals of Operations Research, 99,* 403–425.

Dimitras, A. I., Zanakis, S. H., & Zopounidis, C. (1996). A survey of business failures with an emphasis on prediction methods and industrial applications. *European Journal of Operational Research, 90*(3), 487-513.

Dyrberg Rommer, A. (2005). A comparative analysis of the determinants of financial distress in French, Italian and Spanish firms (Working Paper No. 26). Danmarks National Bank.

Eklund, T., Back, B., & Vanharanta, H., Visa, A. (2003). Using the self-organizing maps as a visualization tool in financial benchmarking. *Information Visualization, (3)2,* 171–181.

Emel, A. B., Oral, M., Reisman, A., & Yolalan, R. (2003). A credit scoring approach for the commercial banking sector. *Socio-Economic Planning Sciences, 37*(2), 103–123.

Everett, J., & Watson, J. (1998). Small business failure and external risk factors. *Small Business Economics Journal, 11*(4), 371-390.

Fletcher, D., & Goss, E. (1993). Forecasting with neural networks: An application using bankruptcy data. *Information and Management, 24*(3), 159–167.

Gajdka, J., & Stos, D. (1996). *Wykorzystanie analizy dyskryminacyjnej w ocenie kondycji finansowej przedsiębiorstw [The use of discriminant analysis in evaluation of financial standing of enterprise].* Krakow: Wydawnictwo Akademii Ekonomicznej w Krakowie.

Galvão, R. K. H., Becerra, V. M., & Abou-Seada, M. (2004). Ratio selection for classification models. *Journal of Data Mining and Knowledge Discovery,* 8(2), 151–170.

Ginoglou, D., & Agorastos, K., & Hatzigagios, T. (2002). Predicting corporate failure of problematic firms in Greece with LPM logit probit and discriminant analysis models. *Journal of Financial Management and Analysis, 15(1),* 1–15.

Gruszczyński, M. (2003). Modele mikroekonometrii w analizie i prognozowaniu zagrożenia finansowego przedsiębiorstw [Econometric models in forecasting the risk of bankruptcy]. *Zeszyty Polskiej Akademii Nauk, 34,* 17-18.

Hadasik, D. (1998). *Upadłość przedsiębiorstw w Polsce i metody jej prognozowania [Business bankruptcies in Poland and methods of forecasting].* Poznań: Wydawnictwo Akademii Ekonomicznej w Poznaniu.

Hołda, A. (2001). Wstępna weryfikacja skuteczności funkcji dyskryminacyjnej Zh w warunkach gospodarki polskiej [Preliminary verification of effectiveness of discriminant function Zh in conditions of the Polish economy]. *Rachunkowość, 10,* 625-626.

Hunter, J., & Isachenkova, N. (2006). Aggregate economy risk and company failure: An examination of UK quoted firms in the early 1990s. *Journal of Policy Modeling, 28*(8), 911–919.

Ignizio, J. P., & Soltyas, J. R. (1996). Simultaneous design and training of ontogenic neural network classifier. *Computers Operations Research, 23(6),* 535–546.

du Jardin, P., & Severin, E. (2012). Forecasting financial failure using a Kohonen map: A comparative study to improve model stability over time. *European Journal of Operational Research, 221*(2), 378-396.

Karels, G. V., & Prakash, A. J. (1987). Multivariate normality and forecasting of business bankruptcy. *Journal of Business Finance and Accounting, 14*(4), 573-593.

Kash, T., & Darling, J. (1998). Crisis management-prevention, diagnosis and intervention. *Leadership and Organization Development Journal, 19*(4), 179-186.

Kuruppu, N., Laswad, F., & Oyelere, P. (2003). The efficacy of liquidation and bankruptcy prediction models for assessing going concern. *Managerial Auditing Journal, 18,* 577–590.

Lacher, R. C., Coats, P. K., Sharma, S. C., & Fantc, L. F. (1995). A neural network for classifying the financial health of a firm. *European Journal of Operational Research, 85*(1), 53–65.

Laitinen, T., & Kankaanpaa, M. (1999). Comparative analysis of failure prediction methods: The Finnish case. *The European Accounting Review, 8(1)*, 67–92.

Lee, K., Booth, D., & Alam, P. (2005). A comparison of supervised and unsupervised neural networks in predicting bankruptcy of Korean firms. *Expert Systems with Applications, 29*, 1–16.

Lee, K. C., Han, I., & Kwon, Y. (1996). Hybrid neural network models for bankruptcy predictions. *Decision Support Systems, 18*(1), 63–72.

Leshno, M., & Spector, Y. (1996). Neural networks prediction analysis: The bankruptcy case. *Neurocomputing, 10*(2), 125–147.

Lin, F. Y., & McClean, S. (2001). A datamining approach to the prediction of corporate failure. *Knowledge Based Systems, 14*, 189–195.

Lin, L., & Piesse, J. (2004). Identification of corporate distress in UK industrials: A conditional probability analysis approach. *Journal of Applied Financial Economics, 14*(2), 73–82.

Mączyńska, E. (2004). Biznes a ryzyko: Systemy wczesnego ostrzegania [Business and the risk: Early warning systems]. *Nowe Zycie Gospodarcze, 12*, 4-9.

McKee, T. E. (2003). Rough sets bankruptcy prediction models versus auditor signaling rates. *Journal of Forecasting, 22*(8), 569–586.

Michaluk, K. (2003). Efektywność modeli prognozujących upadłość przedsiębiorstw w polskich warunkach gospodarczych [Effectiveness of bankruptcy forecasting models in Poland]. In L. Pawłowicz & R. Wierzba (Eds.), *Finanse przedsiębiorstw wobec procesów globalizacji [Corporate finance in the face of globalization processses]* (pp. 116-127). Warszawa: Wydawnictwo Gdańskiej Akademii Bankowej.

Min, J. H., & Lee, Y. C. (2005). Bankruptcy prediction using support vector machine with optimal choice of kernel function parameters. *Expert Systems with Applications, 28*(4), 603–614.

Nakandala, D., Samaranayake, P., & Lau, H. C. W. (2013). A fuzzy-based decision support model for monitoring on-time delivery performance: A textile industry case study. *European Journal of Operational Research, 225(3)*, 507-517.

Pang-Tien, L., Ching-Wen, L., & Hui-Fun, Y. (2008). Financial early-warning models on cross-holding groups. *Journal of Industrial Management & Data Systems, 108*(8), 1060–1080.

Park, C. S., & Han, I. (2002). A case-based reasoning with the feature weights derived by analytic hierarchy process for bankruptcy prediction. *Expert Systems with Applications, 23*(3), 255–264.

Pendharkar, P. C., & Rodger, J. A. (2004). An empirical study of impact of crossover operators on the performance of nonbinary genetic algorithm based neural approaches for classification. *Computers and Operations Research, 31*(4), 481–498.

Piramuthu, S., Ragavan, H., & Shaw, M. J. (1998). Using feature construction to improve the performance of the neural networks. *Management Science, 44*(3), 416-430.

Rahimian, E., & Singh, S. (1993). Bankruptcy Prediction by Neural Networks. In R. Trippi (ed.), *Neural Networks in Finance and Investing* (pp. 121-124). Chicago: Probus Publishing Company.

Robson, M. T. (1996). Macroeconomic factors in the birth and death of UK firms: Evidence from quarterly VAT registration. *Manchester School, 64*, 57-69.

Sandin, A. R., & Porporato, M. (2007). Corporate bankruptcy prediction models applied to emerging economies: Evidence from Argentina in the years 1991–1998. *International Journal of Commerce and Management, 17(4)*, 295–311.

Serrano-Cinca, C. (1996). Self organizing neural networks for financial diagnosis. *Decision Support Systems, 17*(3), 227–238.

Serrano-Cinca, C. (1997). Feedforward neural networks in the classification of financial information. *The European Journal of Finance, 3*(3), 183–202.

Shah, J. R., & Murtaza, M. B. (2000). A neural network based clustering procedure for bankruptcy prediction. *American Business Review, 18*(2), 80–86.

Sikora, R., & Shaw, M. (1994). A double layered learning approach to acquiring rules for classification: Integrating genetic algorithms with similarity-based learning. *ORSA Journal on Computing, 6*(2), 174–187.

Stokes, D., & Blackburn, R. (2002). Learning the hard way – the lessons of owner/managers who have closed their businesses. *Journal of Small Business and Enterprise Development, 9*(1), 17-27.

Wilson, R. L., Sharda, R. (1994). Bankruptcy prediction using neural networks. *Decision Support Systems, 11*(5), 545-557.

Witkowska, D. (2002). *Sztuczne sieci neuronowe i metody statystyczne [Artificial neural networks and statistical method]*. Warsaw: C. H. Beck.

Wu, D. D., Zhang, Y., Wu, D., & Olson, D. L., (2010). Fuzzy multi-objective programming for supplier selection and risk modeling: A possibility approach. *European Journal of Operational Research,* 200*(3)*, 774-787.

Yim, J., & Mitchell, H. (2004). A comparison of Japanese failure models: Hybrid neural networks, logit models and discriminant analysis. *International Journal of Asian Management, 3*(1), 103–120.

Zapranis, A., & Ginoglou, D. (2000). Forecasting corporate failure with neural network approach: The Greek case. *Journal of Financial Management & Analysis, 13(2),* 11–21.

Zhang, P. G., Hu, M. Y., Patuwo, E., & Indro, D. C. (1999). Artificial neural networks in bankruptcy prediction: General framework and cross-validation analysis. *European Journal of Operational Research, 116*(1), 16–32.

1

Revisiting the Phillips Curve: Visualization from a Multidimensional Graphical Perspective

Mario Arturo Ruiz Estrada[1], Su-Fei Yap[2], Noor Azina Binti Ismail[2]

ABSTRACT This article explores the possibility of visualizing the Phillips curve from a multidimensional persp tive. We use a new multidimensional coordinate space, the mega-dynamic disks multivariable dom coordinate space in vertical position, which visualizes the graphical behavior of the Phillips cu from a multidimensional point of view. We take A. W. Phillips's original paper published in Econon in 1958, "The Relation between Unemployment and the Rate of Change of Money Wage Rates in United Kingdom, 1861-1957," as our main bibliographical reference. The same paper also serve our main database for transforming the original Phillips curve into a multidimensional graphical fc In essence, our paper extends the significance of the Phillips curve beyond mere theory to serv a practical instrument for solving economic problems.

KEY WORDS: Inflation, Unemployment, Phillips curve, Multidimensional coordinate spaces, Econographicology

---

[1] Social Security Research Centre (SSRC) & Centre of Poverty and Development Studies (CPDS), Faculty of Economics a Administration, University of Malaya, Malaysia; [2] Faculty of Economics and Administration, University of Malaya, Malay

1. Introduction

A. W. Phillips's groundbreaking paper was published fifty-five years ago. Now, we are proposing a new graphical model to visualize its great contribution to economics. Therefore, the main inspiration for this paper is based on transforming the original Phillips curve into a multidimensional graphical format that will provide greater understanding about the relationship between unemployment and the rate of chang money wage rates from a multidimensional persp tive. Therefore, this paper aspires to compare grap cally how the Phillips curve behaves from two mensional and multi-dimensional perspectives. C main objective is to propose an alternative mult mensional graphical framework that can enhance understanding of the complex and dynamic relati ship between unemployment and the rate of cha of money wage rates within the same graphical sp at different periods of time. This paper is divided i six sections: (i) the evolution of graphical meth in economics; (ii) how multidimensional coordir spaces work; (iii) the transformation of the Phil curve into a multidimensional graphical form; (iv)

Correspondence concerning this article should be addressed to: **Mario Arturo Ruiz Estrada**, Social Security Research Centre (SSRC) & Centre of Poverty and Development Studies (CPDS), Faculty of Economics and Administration, University of Malaya, Kuala Lumpur 50603, Malaysia.
E-mail: marioruiz@um.edu.my

introduction to the mega-dynamic disks multivariable random coordinate space in the vertical position; (v) the construction of the Phillips curve in a multidimensional graphical form; and (vi) observations about the difference between the two-dimensional and multidimensional graphical models in the visualization of the Phillips curve.

2. The Evolution of Graphical Methods in Economics

Previous research shows a strong link between the introduction of graphical methods in economics and the development of theories, methods and techniques in statistics and mathematics. In the 18th century, for example, several new graphical methods were developed as a result of contemporary advances in mathematics and statistics research. These graphical methods include line graphs of time series data, curve-fitting and interpolation, measurement of error as a deviation from a graphed line, graphical analysis of periodic variation, statistical mapping , bar charts and printed coordinate chapters (Cohn, Cohn, Balch, & Bradley, 2004). Playfair (2005) introduced the application of graphical methods in economic analysis. Playfair constructed a wonderful collection of graphs at the end of the 18th century, which placed him far ahead of other economists at the time in terms of visualizing economic data.

The development of graphical methods in economics can be classified into two distinct phases. The first phase is the *basic graphical method*, which features histograms and scatter-plots. All of these types of graphs are based on the visualization of a single variable (Y) through time (X) in the first quadrant in the two-dimensional Cartesian coordinate system (see Figure 1). The main objective of the *basic graphical method* in economics is to study the behavior of a single economic variable (e.g., exports, unemployment, inflation rate, etc.) within a time frame based on a time series. In fact, Playfair may be considered the pioneer of the *basic graphical method*. The second phase in the development of graphical methods for economics is the *complex graphical method*. In economics, the *complex graphical method* is distinguished by the use of three-dimensional coordinate systems. According to Maas (2005), Jevons first explored the merits of the graphical method for political economy. This is a case of the use of the *complex graphical method* in economics, where the form of the graph gives an idea of the possible representation of functions describing the relationship between the X, Y, and Z variables that suggests a causal interpretation of the relationship between X,Y and Z. Additionally, the uses of the complex graphical method are based on the two and three-dimensional Cartesian plane, introduced in 1637 by Descartes (Wise, 2011), who made substantial contributions to economics. The two and three-dimensional coordinate spaces opened a new era in economic theory by enabling analysis of a complex and dynamic economic phenomenon based on the relationship between two or three variables. However, it is necessary also to mention the major contribution of Cournot (Mirowski, 1991). Cournot derived the first formula for the rule of supply and demand as a function of price in a two-dimensional view. He was also the first economist to draw supply and demand curves from a graphical view. In addition to Cournot and Jevons, other innovative economists that contributed to the analytical graph system in economics over time include Walras (in the field of general equilibrium) and Marshall (in the field of partial equilibrium) (Boland, 1981). In the 20th century, economists' use and application of the *complex graphical method* was often based on sophisticated graphical techniques introduced during the development of new economic modelling. In particular, economists started to deploy advanced geometry in constructing their graphs. In addition, two- and three-dimensional Cartesian coordinate systems were also a part of complex economics research (Cohn, Cohn, Balch, & Bradley, 2001). High technology and sophisticated analytical machines such as the electronic calculator and the computer facilitated the rapid development of the *complex graphical method*. The development of analytical instruments in economics took place in two stages. The first stage, which took place in the 1950s and 1960s, involved *non-sophisticated computational instruments* such as electronic calculators to compute basic mathematical expressions. The second stage, the *sophisticated computational instruments*, began in the mid-1980s when computers with high speeds and large storage capacities using sophisticated software and applications were first introduced. The use of sophisticated software and applications enabled easy information management, the application of difficult simulations and high-resolution graphs in a three-dimensions. These analytical instruments undoubtedly contributed substantially to developing research in economics. High-tech computational instruments, backed by sophisticated hardware, applications and software, were utilized to create graphical representations with high resolution. In fact, the *basic graphical method* and *complex graphical method* can be categorized according to either function or dimension. In terms of function, the two graphical methods are either descriptive or analytical. In terms of dimension, they can be two-dimensional, three-dimensional or multidimensional coordinate systems. The *basic graphical method* shows arbitrary information that is used to observe the historical behavior of data from a simple perspective. Alternatively, the *complex graphical method* is available to generate graphs from a multidimensional and dynamic perspective (Ruiz Estrada, 2011b).

3. How do Multidimensional Coordinate Spaces Work?

The main reason to apply multidimensional coordinate spaces is to study any economic phenomena from a multidimensional perspective. This has its roots in the limitations of two-dimensional coordinate space and the need to capture and generate a multidimensional visual effect of any economic phenomena in the same graphical space. Hence, the multidimensional coordinate space leads to an alternative graphical modeling that is more flexible and innovative than the current two-dimensional coordinate space for observing multivariable data behavior. The study of multidimensional coordinate spaces requires basic knowledge about the "n-dimensional space". Moreover, the application of multidimensional coordinate spaces offers an adaptation for building n-dimensions, sub-dimensions, micro-dimensions, nano-dimensions and ji-dimensions in the visualization of any economic phenomenon. In other words, economists' use of coordinate spaces is based on plotting different points that represent the relationship between two or more variables in the first and fourth quadrants of two-dimensional coordinate space. They then proceed to join all of these points by lines until is possible to visualize histograms, line graphs and scatter-plots (see Figure 1). Hence, it is possible to observe the trend and behavior of different variables of any economic dynamic and complex phenomenon, such as the relationship between unemployment/inflation and interest rate/investment, etc. From our point of view, each point plotted on two-dimensional, three-dimensional and multidimensional coordinate spaces represents a single rigid point (Ruiz Estrada, 2011a). Recently, a few economists have started to use three-dimensional coordinate space with three axes: "X-coordinate" (or exogenous variable), "Y-coordinate" (or exogenous variable) and the "Z-coordinate" (or endogenous variable). This is based on the construction of surfaces or three-dimensional manifolds to visualize multivariable economic data behavior (see Figure 2). According to our research, the use of three-dimensional coordinate space is not popular among economists and policymakers. Based on one thousand (1,000) papers published in ten (10) reputable economics journals[1] between the year 1950 and 2000 from JSTOR), it is possible to observe that the most common types of graphical representations applied in the study of social sciences, especially in economics, were of the two-dimensional coordinate space type. A total of 97% of these chapters utilized the two-dimensional Cartesian coordinate system, and only 3% of them used three-dimensional coordinate spaces. This research will proffer several reasons as to ***why*** economists continue using two-dimensional coordinate space and only sometimes three-dimensional coordinate space in the graphical representation of complex and dynamic economic phenomena. These reasons are as follows:

- The application of two-dimensional coordinate space in the economic graphical analysis has become a **tradition**.
- Two-dimensional space is **easy to use** to visualize basic trends or values in the same graphical space.
- It is difficult to find **alternative and suitable multidimensional graphical models** to transform two-dimensional coordinate space graphical modeling to multidimensional space graphical modeling.

This article introduces a new multidimensional coordinate space that seeks to generate an innovative multidimensional optical effect to visualize complex and dynamic economic phenomena. Multidimensional coordinate spaces can incorporate a large number of exogenous variables that change constantly and directly affect the behavior of endogenous variable(s)

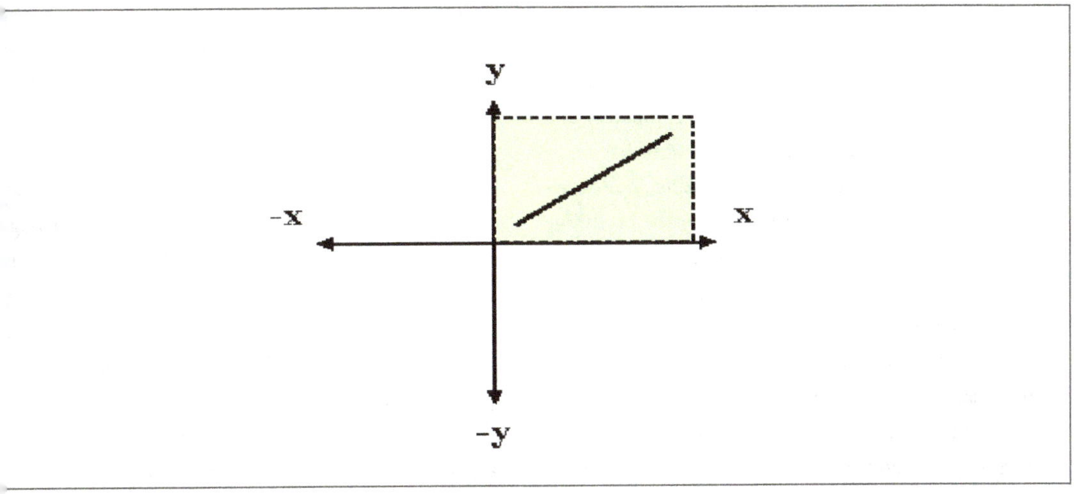

re 1. Two-Dimensional Coordinate Space
ce: Adapted from "Multi-dimensional coordinate spaces", by Ruiz Estrada (2011a) in *International Journal of Physical nces*, 6(3), 340-357.

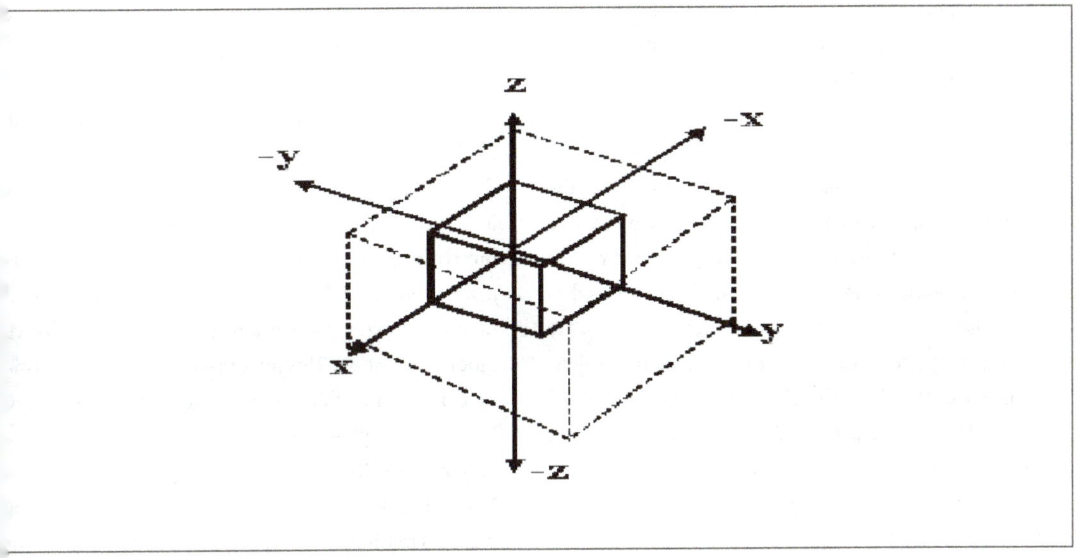

re 2. Three-Dimensional Coordinate Space
rce: Adapted from "Multi-dimensional coordinate spaces", by Ruiz Estrada (2011a) in *International Journal of Physical nces*, 6(3), 340-357.

in the same graphical space. These new types of multidimensional coordinate spaces are based on the mega-dynamic disks multivariable random coordinate space in vertical position. The multidimensional space enables economists, academics and policymakers to analyze economic phenomena from multidimensional perspectives across time and space. The proposed concept is preferred because it offers an immediate multidimensional perspective of the Phillips curve, thus presenting visually what normally would require a lot of data and substantial explanation. When the original Phillips curve was formulated

(Phillips, 1958), it was not possible to capture a structure beyond two-dimensional analysis.

However, the analysis of economics must move in tandem with the advancement of computers and technology. Thus, our primary argument is that a new analytical and visual tool has been created; our development of the Phillips curve is merely the beginning of new and powerful visuals to present economic phenomena to society. Just as the DNA double helix is now immediately recognized as the representation of a biological code, many economic structures, connectivity and imagery can be given a new lease on life through highly impactful images that capture an otherwise lengthy discussion. While both academic arguments and theoretical frontiers remain necessary, new graphics and visuals will convincingly harness ideas in neat and concise representations, thus furthering our objectives as economists to translate concepts to policies.

4. Transformation of the Phillips Curve into a Multidimensional Graphical Form

4.1. Hypothesis of A. W. Phillips (1958)

A. W. Phillips' original hypothesis is based on the argument that the demand for any good or service is high relative to its supply if we expect the price to rise. According to Phillips (1958), if the demand is low relative to the supply of goods and services, we expect the price to fall so that it can generate a deficiency of demand. Finally, the dramatic fall of demand in goods and services can directly affect the change of wage rates. In our case, we can make reference to the labor price. According to Phillips (1958), if the demand for labor is high, then unemployment is low and vice versa. Hence, fast growth in wages attracts more qualified human capital to firms and industries. Finally, Phillips assumes that the relationship between unemployment and the rate of change of wage rates is highly non-linear (Apergis, 2013).

The second argument is that the rate of change of wage rates is directly related to the demand for labor and unemployment. In fact, the business environment (whether a booming economy or an economic crisis) plays an important role in determining labor demand; if it improves, then logically, unemployment shrinks and vice versa. Therefore, any economic crisis leads to a weaker position to push for higher wage rates. At the same time, the average unemployment rate is always directly affected by the labor demand (Carrasco & Ferreiro 2011; Josifidis, Beker Pucar, Srdić, & Ivan, 2014).

The third argument is that the rate of change of wages is directly connected to the changes of retail prices and the cost of living that is reflected in wage rates. According to Phillips (1958), "The cost of living adjustments will have little or no effect on the rate of change of money wage rates except at times when retail prices are forced up by a very rapid rise in import prices." However, the third argument also mentions that productivity has a strong direct relationship with aggregate demand and unemployment.

Additionally, the third argument is concerned about productivity and aggregate demand having a strong relationship that directly affects unemployment. Phillips presents illustrative examples using simple arithmetic to study the cause and effect of a series of variables such as productivity, aggregate demand, unemployment, import process and retail prices. Phillips' main contribution is based on calculating the rate of change of factor costs minus the rate of change of productivity. Finally, Phillips (1958) said that, "The introduction of cost of living adjustments in wage rates will have no effect, for employers will merely be giving under the name of cost of living adjustments part of the wage increases which they would in any case have given as a result of their competitive bidding for labor." This hypothesis is based on statistical evidence that the rate of change of wage rates in the UK can be explained by the rate of change of unemployment for three periods of analysis, namely 1861-1913, 1913-1948 and 1948-1957. In addition, Phillips includes in his analysis the average price of imports to demonstrate his hypothesis.

Phillips' paper presents (1958) a total of eleven figures based on the use of two-dimensional scatter diagrams to represent the relationship between average unemployment rate (X-axis) and average rate of change of wage rates (Y-axis). The calculation of the average rate of change of wage rates is based on the application of Brown and Hopkins (Pencavel, 2011). In summary, this index uses simple growth rates between two periods (past year and present year). Hence, Phillips' paper (1958) mentions that "The tendency for the rate of change of money wage rates to be high when unemployment is low and to be low or negative when unemployment is high." This trend is observed in Figures 5 and 15. In fact, Phillips' main contribution is based on the argument that "There is also a clear tendency for the rate of change of money wage rates at any given level of unemployment to be above the average for that level of unemployment when unemployment is decreasing during the upswing of a trade cycle and to be below the average for that level of unemployment when unemployment is increasing during the downswing of a trade cycle." Moreover, the mathematical modeling that Phillips uses in his paper is based on a non-linear equation that is shown by equations 1, 2, 3 and 4.

$$y = - a + bx^{c} \quad (1)$$

$$y + a = bx^{c} \quad (2)$$

$$\log (y + a) = \log b + c \log x \quad (3)$$

$$\log (y + a) = c \log bx \quad (4)$$

According to Phillips (1958), the rate of change of wage rates is represented by "y" and the percentage unemployment by "x". The constants b and c were estimated by least squares using the values of y and x corresponding to the crosses in the four intervals between 0 and 5 percent, respectively. The variable of unemployment that is a constant is chosen by random error to make the curve pass or be as close as possible to the remaining two crosses in two intervals between 5 and 11 percent, respectively. Finally, the equation of the fitted curve is represented by:

$$y + 0.900 = 9.638x^{-1.394} \quad (5)$$

$$\log (y + 0.900) = \log 9.638 + \log x^{-1.394} \quad (6)$$

$$\log (y + 0.900) = 0.984 - 1.394 \log x \quad (7)$$

Therefore, Phillips supports the construction of the fitted curve based on a simple multiple regression of y on the variables x and the differentiation between dx/dt. He clearly described the difficulty of finding a suitable linear multiple regression equation to evaluate the relationship between unemployment and the rate of change of money wage rates. From a geometrical point of view, all of Phillips's visualizations presented a peculiar fitted curve together with a large series of plotted points representing the relationship between average rates of unemployment and the average rate of change of wage rates. In our opinion, many academicians confuse the fitted curve and try to show that if the unemployment rate is low, then the rate of change of wage rates is high. We can observe that the fitted curve moves from quadrant one (+X, +Y) to quadrant four (+X, -Y) in the two-dimensional Cartesian plane (see Figure 2). Hence, if the unemployment rate is equal to 5.5, then the rate of change of wage rates is zero. The same fitted curve maintains the rate of change of wage rates trend between 10 and -3 in the case of the Y-axis. According to our observations, the unemployment range goes up to 11 for all figures in the same paper. Finally, Phillips assembles all of these points in a logical order around the fitted curve through the use of straight lines. In fact, we can observe that the visualization of all of these lines reveals chaos in the relationship between the unemployment and wages rates in the same graphical space and time. Therefore, Phillips' accuracy from the fitted curve demonstrates the relationship among these two variables. Therefore, we conclude that Phillips never used inflation, as many economists have assumed. In fact, the Phillips curve only shows the relationship between the change of wages and unemployment rate. He never applies inflation rates based on the CPI; rather, he tries to illustrate labor market behavior in certain periods of time according to his observations.

4.2. Modern Approaches in the Construction of the Phillips Curve: The New Keynesian Phillips Curve (NKPC)

The New Keynesian Phillips Curve (NKPC) is based on the relationship between marginal cost and the output gap. This new curve is based on two basic assumptions: (i) optimal price setting by monopolistically competitive firms; and (ii) constant frictionless markup μ. According to the NKPC, the inflation dynamics are represented by equation 8:

$$\pi_t = \beta E_t \{\pi_{t+1}\} + \lambda f'C_{Tt} \quad (8)$$

Therefore, the marginal cost and the output gap are represented in equations 9 and 10.

$$f'C_{Tt} = (\sigma + \varphi)\, y_t \quad (9)$$

The income gap is equal to:

$$y_t = y_{t-} y_t \quad (10)$$

We assume that everything produced is consumed in this model.

$$y_{t=} C_t \quad (11)$$

$$K = \lambda\, (\sigma + \varphi) \quad (12)$$

Finally, the New Keynesian Phillips Curve (NKPC) is represented in equation 13.

$$\pi_t = \beta\, E_t\, \{\pi_{t+1}\} + K\, y_t \quad (13)$$

Accordingly, the New Keynesian Phillips Curve (NKPC) is consistent with rational expectations. The NKPC rests on three basic conditions: (i) inflation leads measure the output gap without trade-off between inflation and output gap stabilization; (ii) disinflation can be achieved without cost; and (iii) inflation is purely forward-looking, and past inflation is irrelevant. A number of studies utilize NKPC, such as Ball and Mazumder in "What Determines the Sacrifice Ratio?" (2011) and Fuhrer and Moore in "Inflation Persistence" (1995). Moreover, Friedman is a sharp critic of the ability to apply rational expectations with the NKPC (Lucas & Sargent, 1981). According to Friedman (1968), "The Keynesian model implicitly relied on the idea that low unemployment could be sustained by allowing high inflation to erode real wages and thus boost labor demand. Friedman pointed out that if policy tried to keep output above its 'potential' or 'equilibrium' level, then wage-bargainers would get used to the higher level of inflation and adjust their nominal wage demands upwards. The result would be higher inflation without the sustainable low unemployment." Finally, Friedman (1968) mentioned that the traditional Phillips curve was an inadequate model for rational expectations because they are based on neoclassical micro-foundations such as sticky prices (without some type of rigid prices) for macroeconomic modeling. From a visual perspective, the NKPC continues to use a two-dimensional coordinate system, which does not permit us to depict completely the real behavior between inflation and unemployment together in the same graphical modeling. Therefore, the next section tries to propose a new multidimensional graphical modeling that it is based on mega-dynamic disks multivariable random coordinate space in vertical position.

5. Mega-Dynamic Disks Multivariable Random Coordinate Space in Vertical Position

This paper proposes a unique multidimensional coordinate space called the mega-dynamic disks multivariable random coordinate space in vertical position (Ruiz Estrada, 2014). The mega-dynamic disks multivariable random coordinate space in vertical position captures n-dimensions in the same graphical space at the same time. Therefore, this new special coordinate space creates the possibility of visualizing a large number of endogenous and exogenous variables that are interconnected and moving in different graphical spaces with different time frameworks without any restriction. It facilitates the observation of how endogenous variables and exogenous variables work together simultaneously. At the same time, one can see how all of these variables interact together through the visualization of an asymmetric spiral-shaped figure with n-faces that constantly moves in real time. This asymmetric spiral-shaped figure with n-faces can show an expansion or contraction that is based on different changes among all variables at different graphical spaces with different time frameworks.

Initially, the mega-dynamic disks multivariable random coordinate space in vertical position proposes a new graphical modeling to visualize a large amount of data. First, this specific coordinate space shows one single vertical straight axis that captures endogenous variable behavior. Hence, we plot our endogenous variables on this single vertical straight axis that is represented by α. Second, each exogenous variable in an analysis is represented by its specific sub-coordinate system such as $\beta_{<SSi:Dj>}$, where "SS_i" represents the sub-space level in analysis, in this case either from sub-space level zero ($SS_0°$) to sub-space level infinite ($SS_{360}°$), and "D_j" represents the disk level in analysis at the same quadrant of exogenous variables (in our case, from disk level 1 = D_1, disk level 2 = D_2, disk level 3 = D_3,..., to disk level D_∞). In fact, we as-

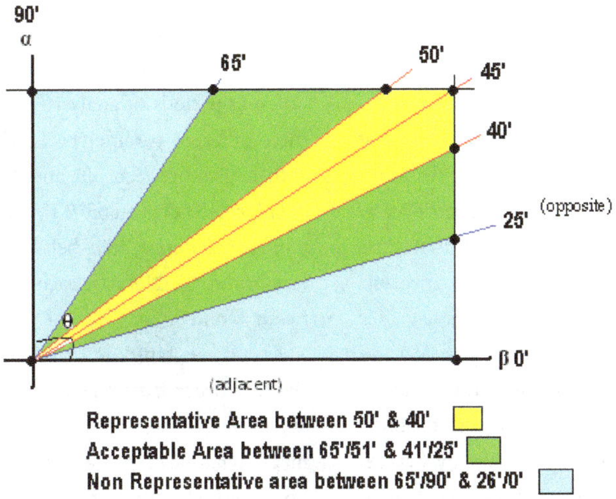

re 3. tan(β/α)[-1]

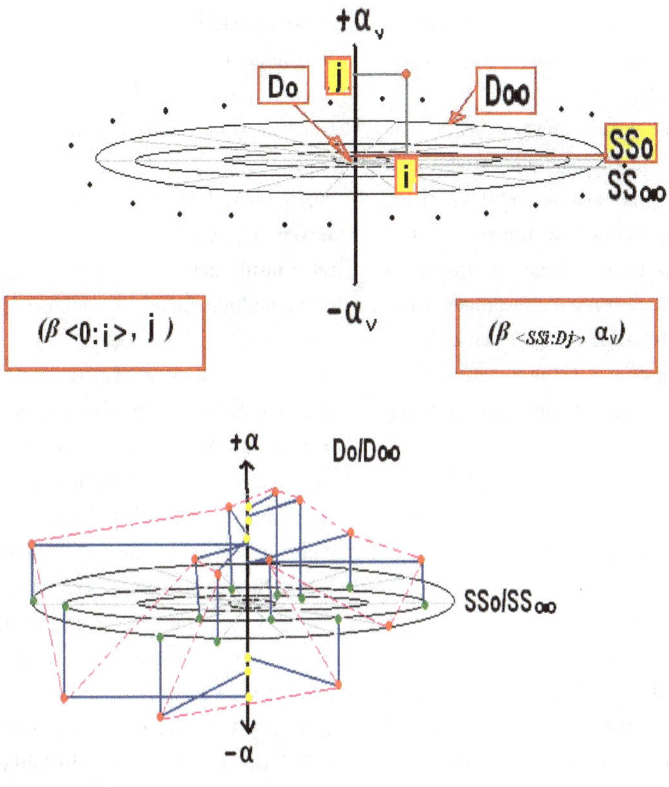

re 4. The Mega-Dynamic Disks Coordinate Space in Vertical Position
ce: Adapted from "An introduction to the mega-dynamic disks coordinate space in vertical and horizontal position", uiz Estrada (2014) in *Malaysian Journal of Sciences*, 33(2), 105-109.

sume that all exogenous variables use only real positive numbers (R_+). To plot different exogenous variables in the mega-dynamic disks multivariable random coordinate space in vertical position, each value needs to be plotted directly on its radial subspace in analysis (SS_i) and disk level in analysis (D_j). Each *i* is a radius that emanates from the origin and is defined by the angle that can range from 0 to just under 360°, a theoretically infinite range. Each disk is a concentric circle that starts from the origin moving outward toward a theoretical infinite value. At the same time, all of these values plotted in different subspace levels in analysis (SS_i) and disk levels in analysis (D_j) need to be joined with its endogenous variable "α" until we build a series of coordinates. These coordinates need to be joined by straight lines until they yield an asymmetric spiral-shaped geometrical figure with n-faces (see Figure 4). It is important to mention at this juncture that the endogenous variable "α" is fixed according to any change associated with its corresponding exogenous variables in $\beta_{<SSi:Dj>}$, where $i = \{0°, 1°, 2°,...,360°\}$ and $j = \{0, 1, 2,...,\infty...\}$, α. Hence, we can imagine a large number of exogenous variables moving constantly in different positions within its radius in real time. We can simultaneously visualize how all of these exogenous variables directly affect the behavior of the endogenous variable *(α)*. Moreover, the endogenous variable *(α)* can fluctuate freely (see Figure 4). In our case, the endogenous variables *(α)* can show positive/negative properties according to our multidimensional coordinate space. In the case of exogenous variables, these can only experience non-negative properties. The mega-dynamic disks multivariable random coordinate space in vertical position is represented by:

$(\beta_{<SSi:Dj>}, \alpha)$

where $\beta \geq O;\ i = \theta°;\ j = R_+ \geq O;\ \alpha = R_{+/-}$ (1)

$\alpha = f\,(\beta_{<SSi:Dj>})$ (2)

Hence, we are interested in applying a specific trigonometry function such as the tangent /tan(β/α)/ and inverse tangent $\tan(\beta/\alpha)^{-1}$. Initially, the calculation of the tangent /tan(β/α)/ is equal to β (adjacent) divided by α (opposite). We apply the absolute value to eliminate negative values in the construction of our Phillips curve. The main objective of calculating the inverse tangent $\tan(\beta/\alpha)^{-1}$ is to find each angle that is located in the mega-dynamic disks coordinate space in vertical position. Therefore, the $\tan(\beta/\alpha)^{-1}$ can help us study the relationship between α (opposite) and β (adjacent) in different periods of analysis. In fact, we can establish three different parameters: (i) *the representative area* with angles between 50° and 40°; (ii) *the acceptable area* located between 65°/51° and 41°/25°; and (iii) *the non-representative area* between 65°/90° and 26°/0 (see Figure 3). Notably, each $\tan(\beta/\alpha)^{-1}$ *is located between* 0° and 90°.

Finally, all $\tan(\beta/\alpha)^{-1}$ results are organized in ascending order from the smallest angle to the largest angle. Finally, we transfer all of these results to the mega-dynamic disks coordinate space in vertical position to visualize the behavior of all angles that help us to appreciate clearly the behavior of the multidimensional Phillips curve.

6. The Transformation of the Phillips Curve into a Multidimensional Visualization

We intend to observe the non-linear behavior between unemployment and the rate of change of wage rates from two-dimensional and multidimensional perspectives. The analysis of the relationship between unemployment and the rate of change of wage rates is observed in Figure 4, which clearly shows the non-linear relationship between these two variables. In the case of the multidimensional graphical form of the Phillips curve, the non-linear behavior is clear through a descendent spiral curve that is displayed in the mega-dynamic disks multivariable random coordinate space in vertical position (see Figure 5). We can visualize its entirety from a multidimensional graphical space and time and note that the behavior of unemployment in relation to the rate of change of wage rates is non-linear. Before we start the construction of the Phillips curve in multidimensional graphical form, we refer to Phillips' original manuscript(1958), "The Relation between Unemployment and the Rate of Change of Money Wage Rates in the United Kingdom, 1861-1957." This paper is our main bibliographical source and database to build the Phillips curve from a multidimensional perspective using the mega-dynamic disks multivariable random coordinate space in vertical position. In Phillips' paper (p. 285), we observe

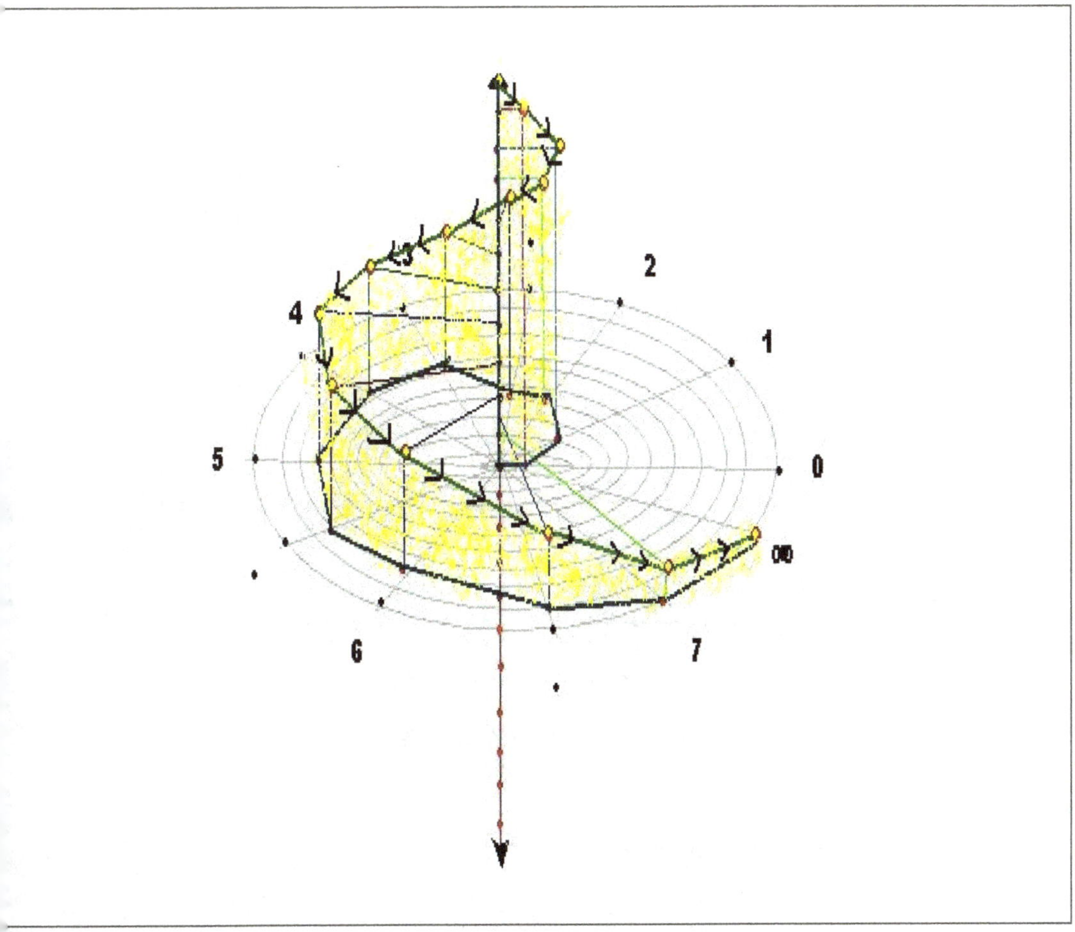

ure 5. Relationship between the Average Rates of Change of Money & Average Unemployment
rce: Adapted from "The relation between unemployment and the rate of change of money wage rates in the United gdom, 1861-1957", by Philips (1958) in *Economica*, 25(100), 283-299.

a simple scatter diagram that shows a large amount of data (points) spread between the first and fourth quadrant in the two-dimensional Cartesian plane. In fact, the large amounts of points represent different groups of coordinates reflecting the relationship between unemployment rates and wage rates. According to Phillips (1958), "Each dot in the diagrams represents a year, the average rate of change of money wage rates during the year being given by the scale on the vertical axis and the average unemployment during the year by the scale on the horizontal axis."

Moreover, in Figure 5, we also observe a curve that is based on a logarithmic equation in Phillips' paper (1958, p. 290). Phillips tries to show graphically the relationship between the average rate of change of money wage rates during the year represented by the scale on the vertical axis (Y-axis or endogenous variable) and the average unemployment rate during the year represented on the horizontal axis (X-axis or exogenous variable). The unemployment rates can only be positive average rates. Hence, the unemployment average rates restriction is equal to $U = \{x|x: 0 \geq x \leq \mathbb{R}_+\}$. The average rate of change of money wage rates has both positive and negative values. Therefore, the average rate of change of money wage rates restriction is equal to $W = \{x|x: \mathbb{R}_- \leq x \geq \mathbb{R}_+\}$. In Figure 5, we observe that Phillips plots 52 results showing the relationship between the average rate of change of money wage rates

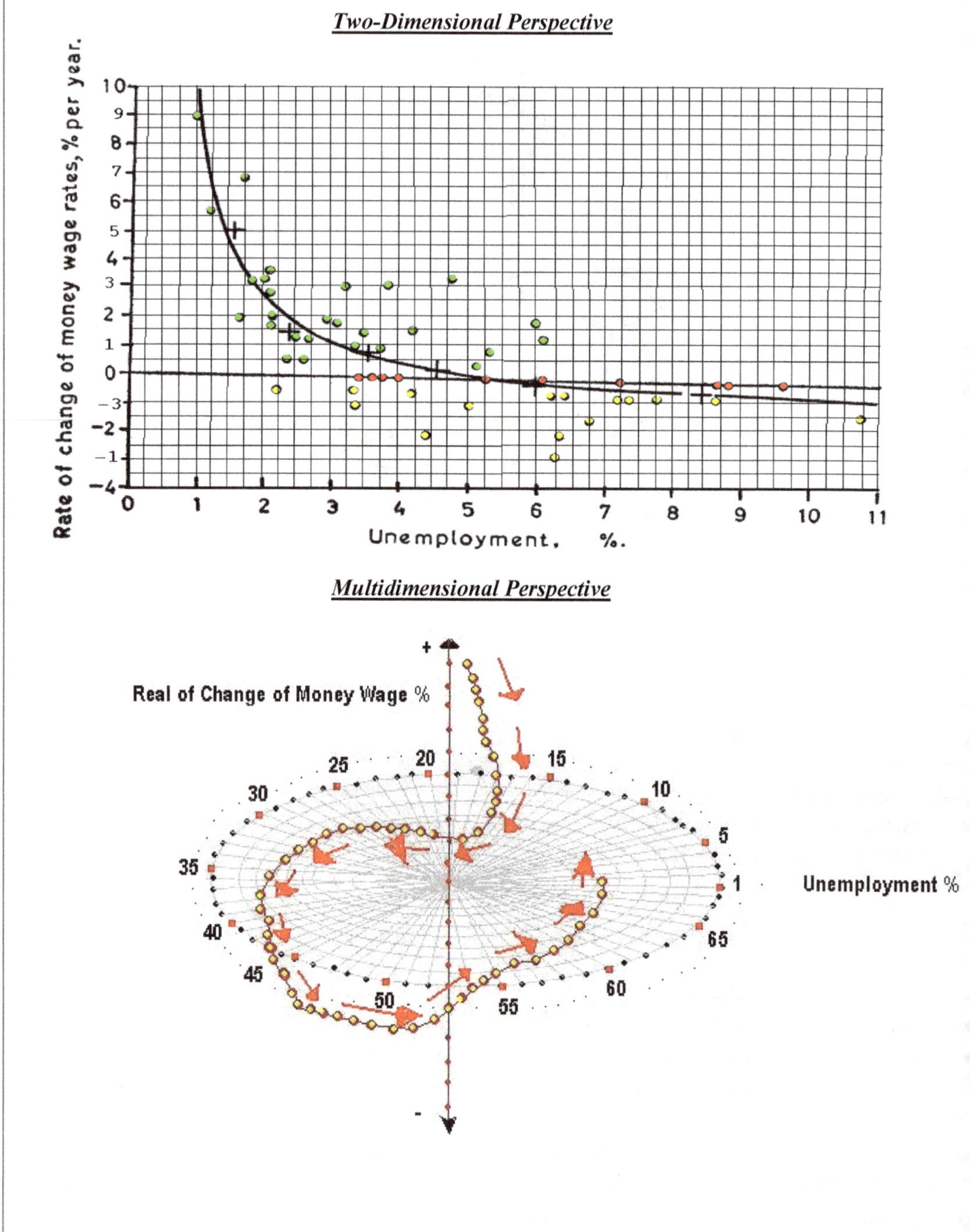

Figure 6. Relationship between the Average Rates of Change of Money & Average Unemployment
Source: Adapted from "The relation between unemployment and the rate of change of money wage rates in the United Kingdom, 1861-1957", by Philips (1958) in *Economica*, 25(100), 283-299.

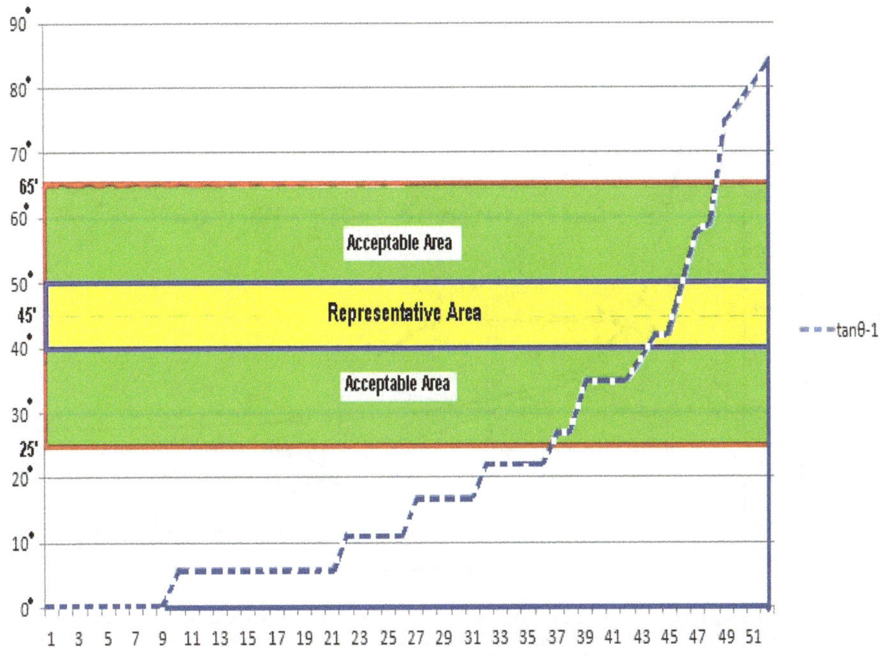

re 7. Multidimensional Phillips Curve Diagram

and the average unemployment rates from 1861 to 1913. Additionally, in Figure 6, we observe a perfect Phillips curve from a multidimensional perspective: when the average rate of change of money is high, there are low unemployment rates in the case of perfect competition. Hence, vertically higher positions (with higher money wage rates) are linked to the horizontal inner disk (lower unemployment).

7. Observations about the Difference between the Two-Dimensional and Multidimensional Graphical Models in the Visualization of the Phillips Curve

Figures 8, 9, 10, 11, 12, 13, 14, 15, 16 and 17 present the visualization of the Phillips curve from a multidimensional perspective. Each set of figures in this paper shows the two-dimensional and multidimensional graphical models of the Phillips curve. Therefore, we clearly can appreciate the multidimensional graphical approach of the Phillips curve, which produces a multidimensional graphical optical effect compared to the two-dimensional perspective. Additionally, we can observe that the average rate of change of money wage rates and the average unemployment rates from 1861 to 1913 (see Figures 7, 8, 9 and 14) have a stronger interconnectivity. The advantage of using the multidimensional graphical approach for the Phillips curve is based on the location of the coordinates that are displayed and follow a logical trajectory in different spaces and time within the same multidimensional coordinate space. Moreover, we can observe how the Phillips curve displayed in different spaces generates a floating effect in the same graphical space. According to Figures 10, 11, 12, 13, and 14, we can observe a non-linear spiral-shape

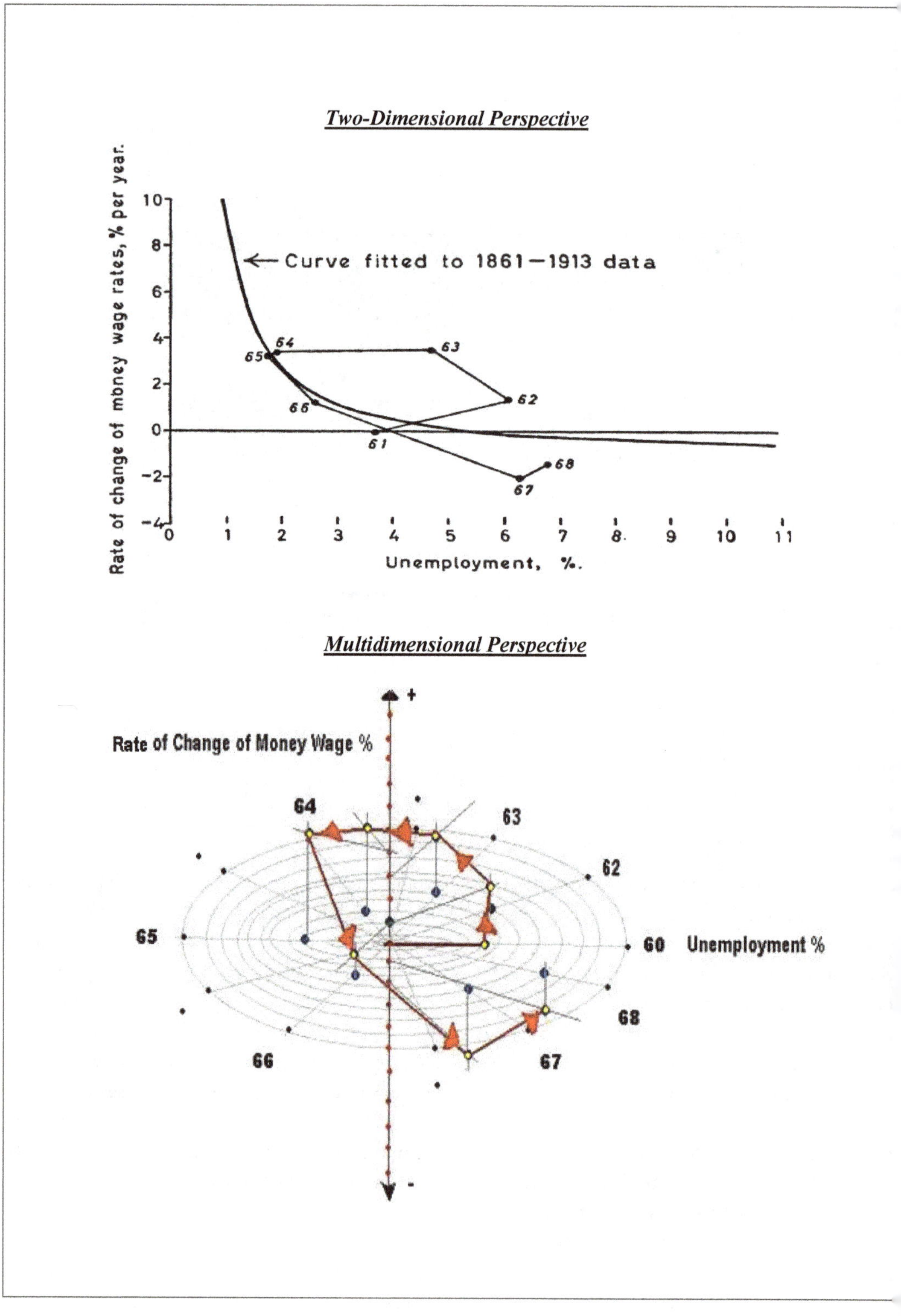

Figure 8. 1861-1913

Source: Adapted from "The relation between unemployment and the rate of change of money wage rates in the United Kingdom, 1861-1957", by Philips (1958) in *Economica*, 25(100), 283-299.

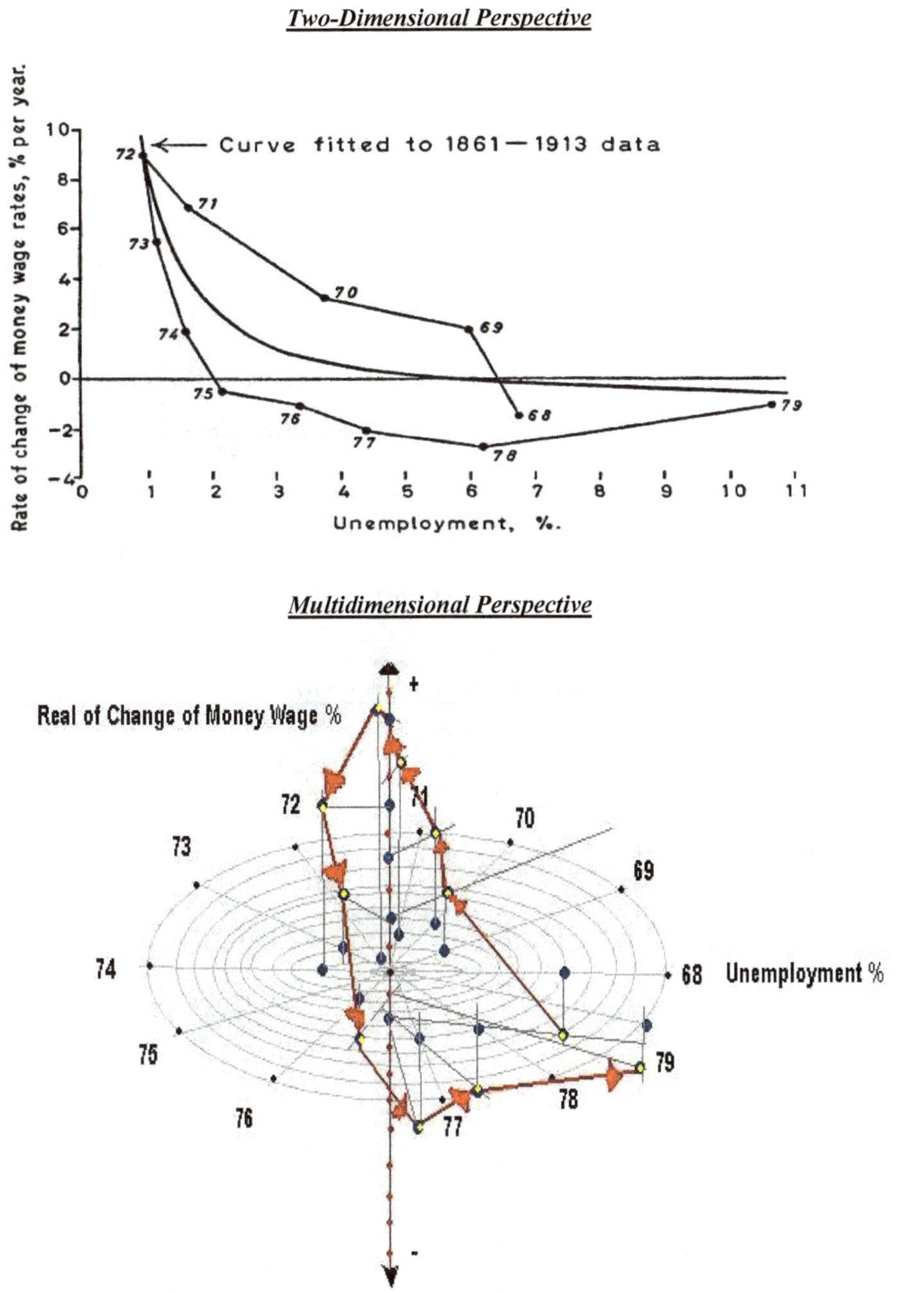

igure 9. 1868-1879

ource: Adapted from "The relation between unemployment and the rate of change of money wage rates in the United ingdom, 1861-1957", by Philips (1958) in *Economica*, 25(100), 283-299.

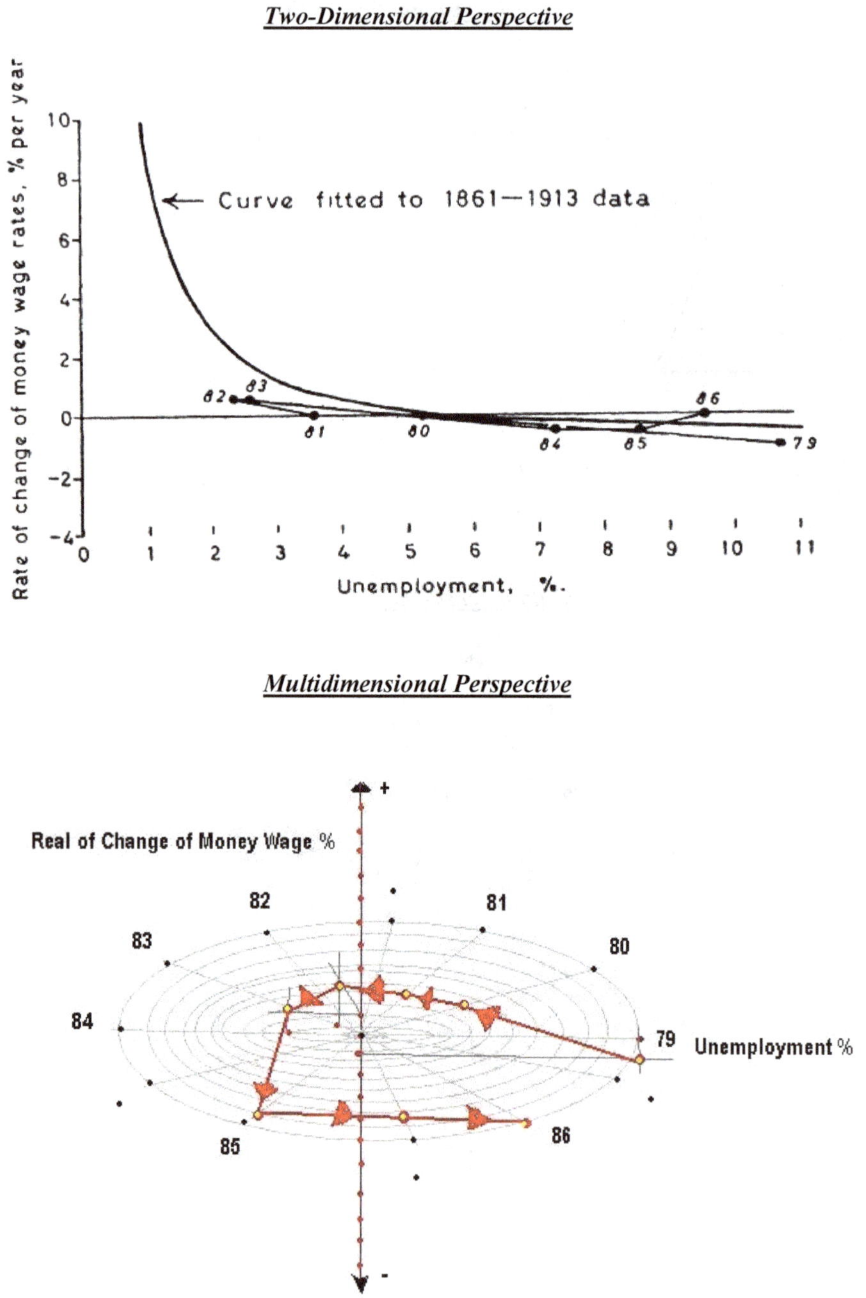

Figure 10. 1879-1886

Source: Adapted from "The relation between unemployment and the rate of change of money wage rates in the United Kingdom, 1861-1957", by Philips (1958) in *Economica*, 25(100), 283-299.

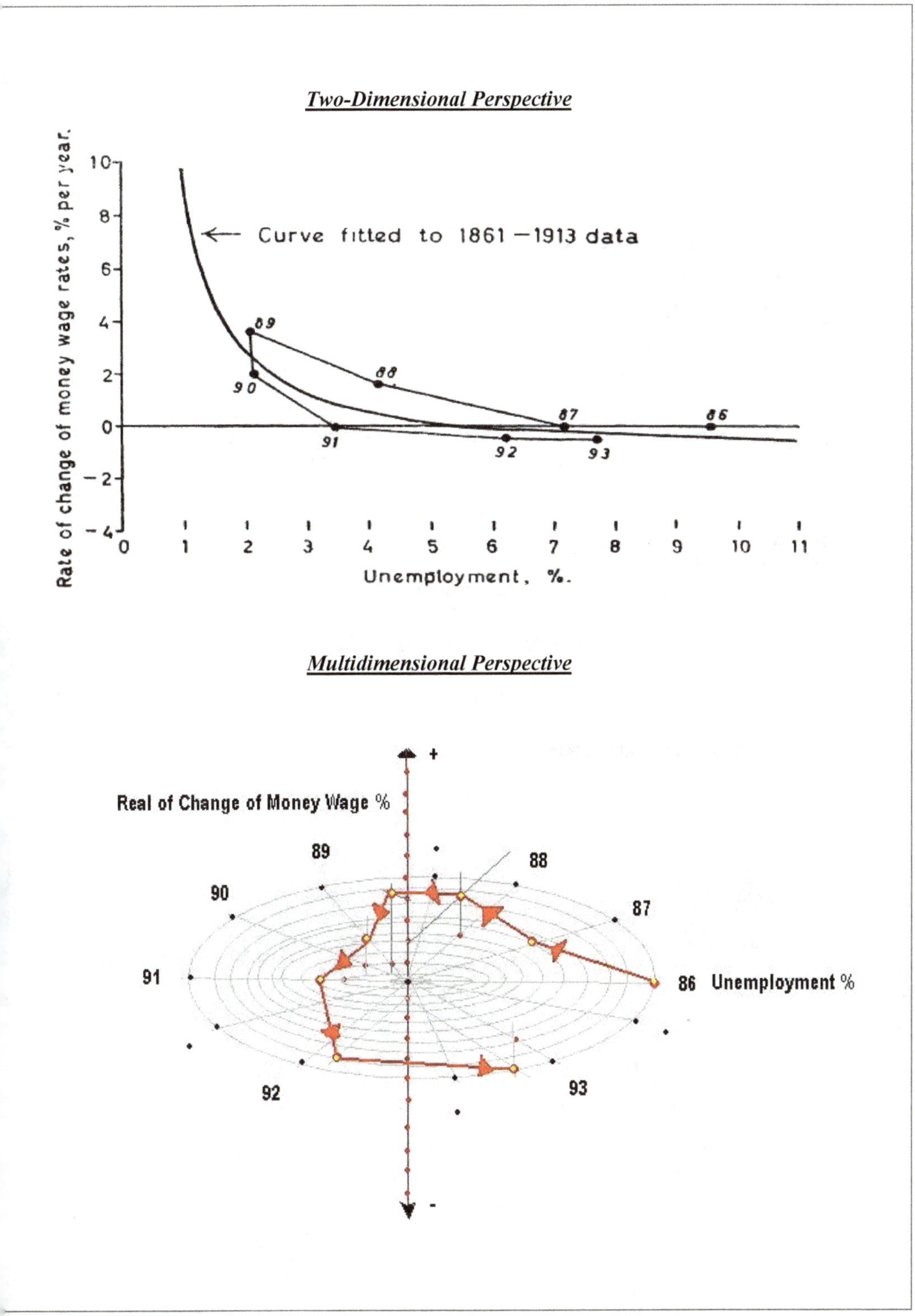

igure 11. 1886-1893

ource: Adapted from "The relation between unemployment and the rate of change of money wage rates in the United ngdom, 1861-1957", by Philips (1958) in *Economica*, 25(100), 283-299.

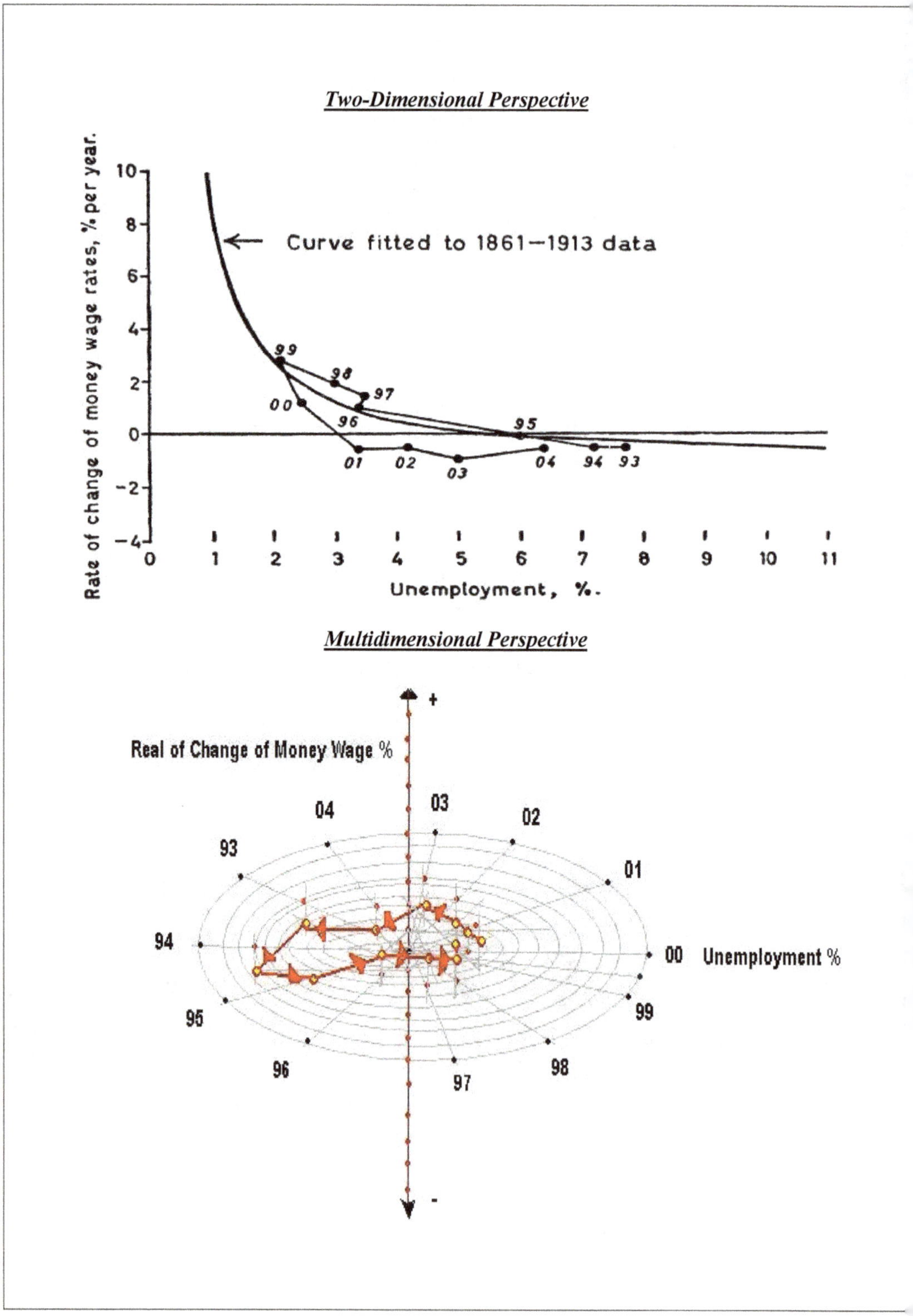

Figure 12. 1893-1904

Source: Adapted from "The relation between unemployment and the rate of change of money wage rates in the United Kingdom, 1861-1957", by Philips (1958) in *Economica*, 25(100), 283-299.

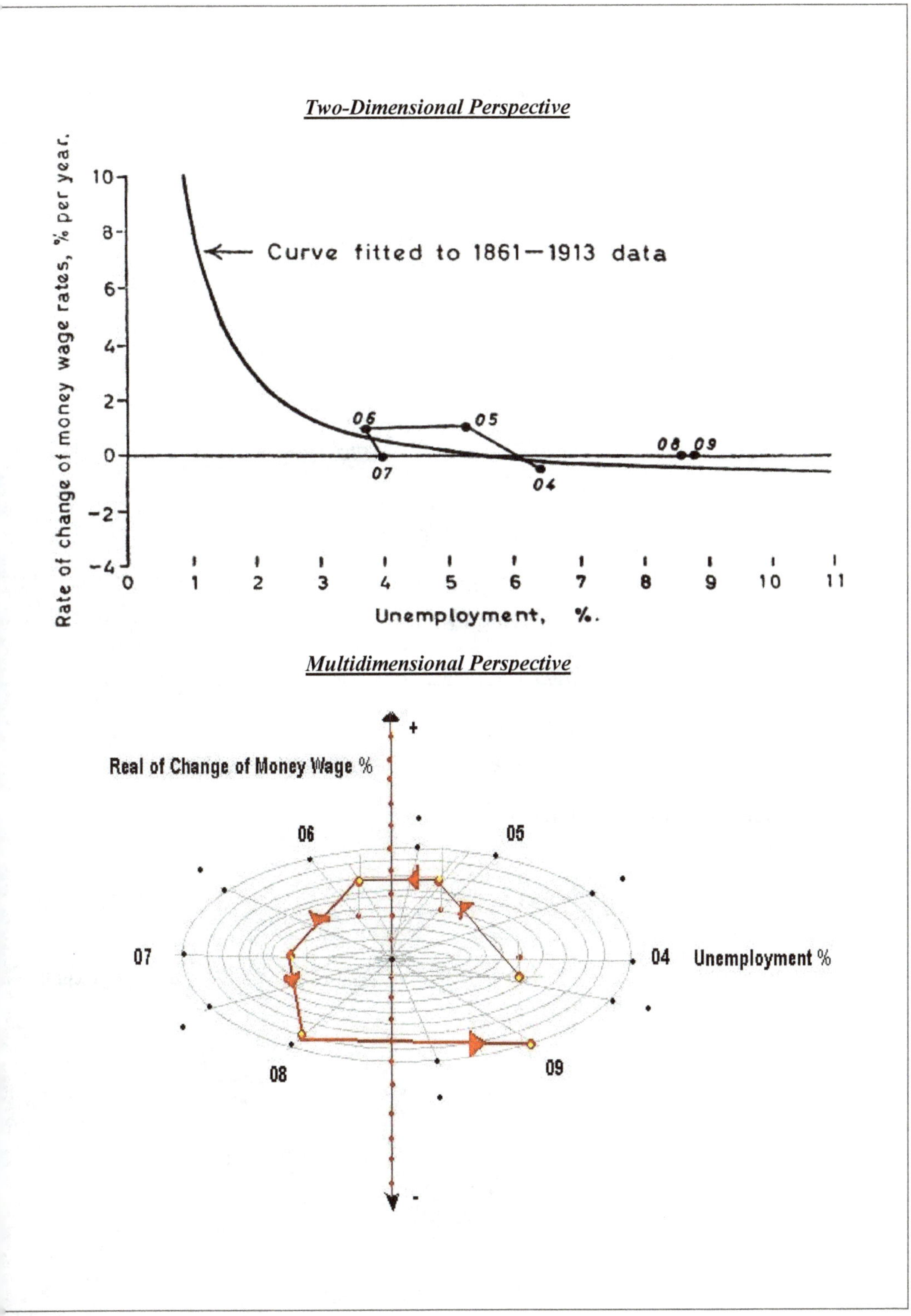

gure 13. 1904-1909

ource: Adapted from "The relation between unemployment and the rate of change of money wage rates in the United ngdom, 1861-1957", by Philips (1958) in *Economica*, 25(100), 283-299.

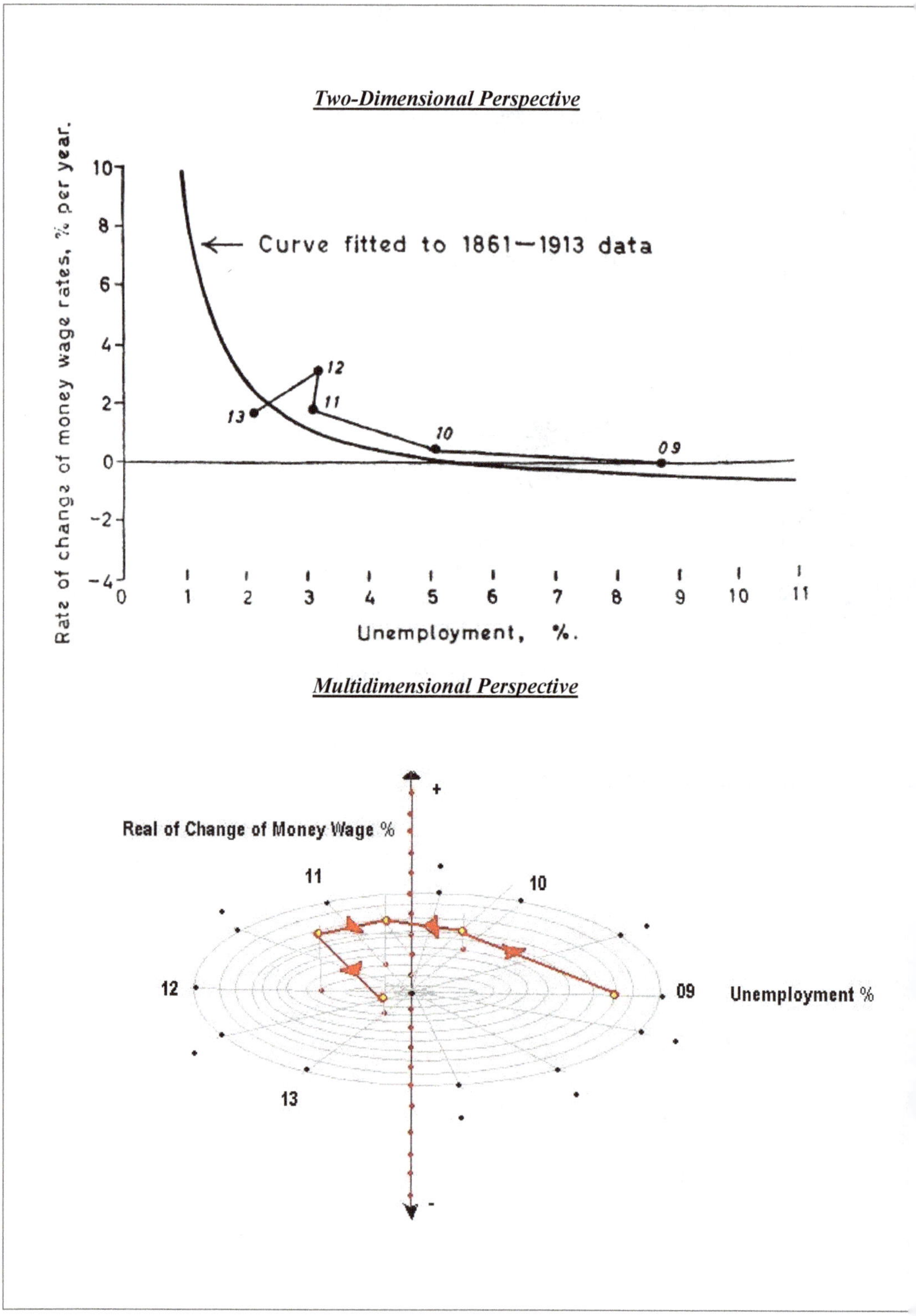

Figure 14. 1909-1913

Source: Adapted from "The relation between unemployment and the rate of change of money wage rates in the United Kingdom, 1861-1957", by Philips (1958) in *Economica*, 25(100), 283-299.

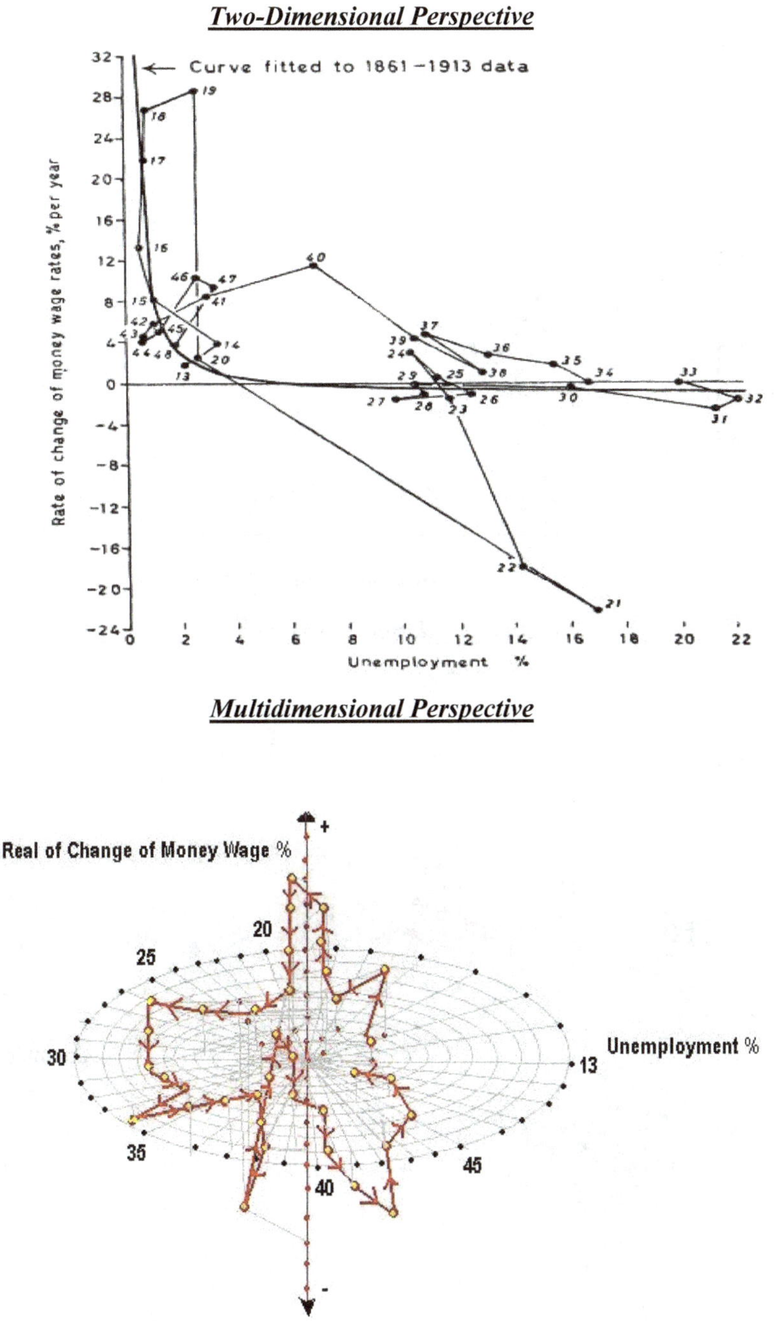

gure 15. 1913-1948

urce: Adapted from "The relation between unemployment and the rate of change of money wage rates in the United ngdom, 1861-1957", by Philips (1958) in *Economica*, 25(100), 283-299.

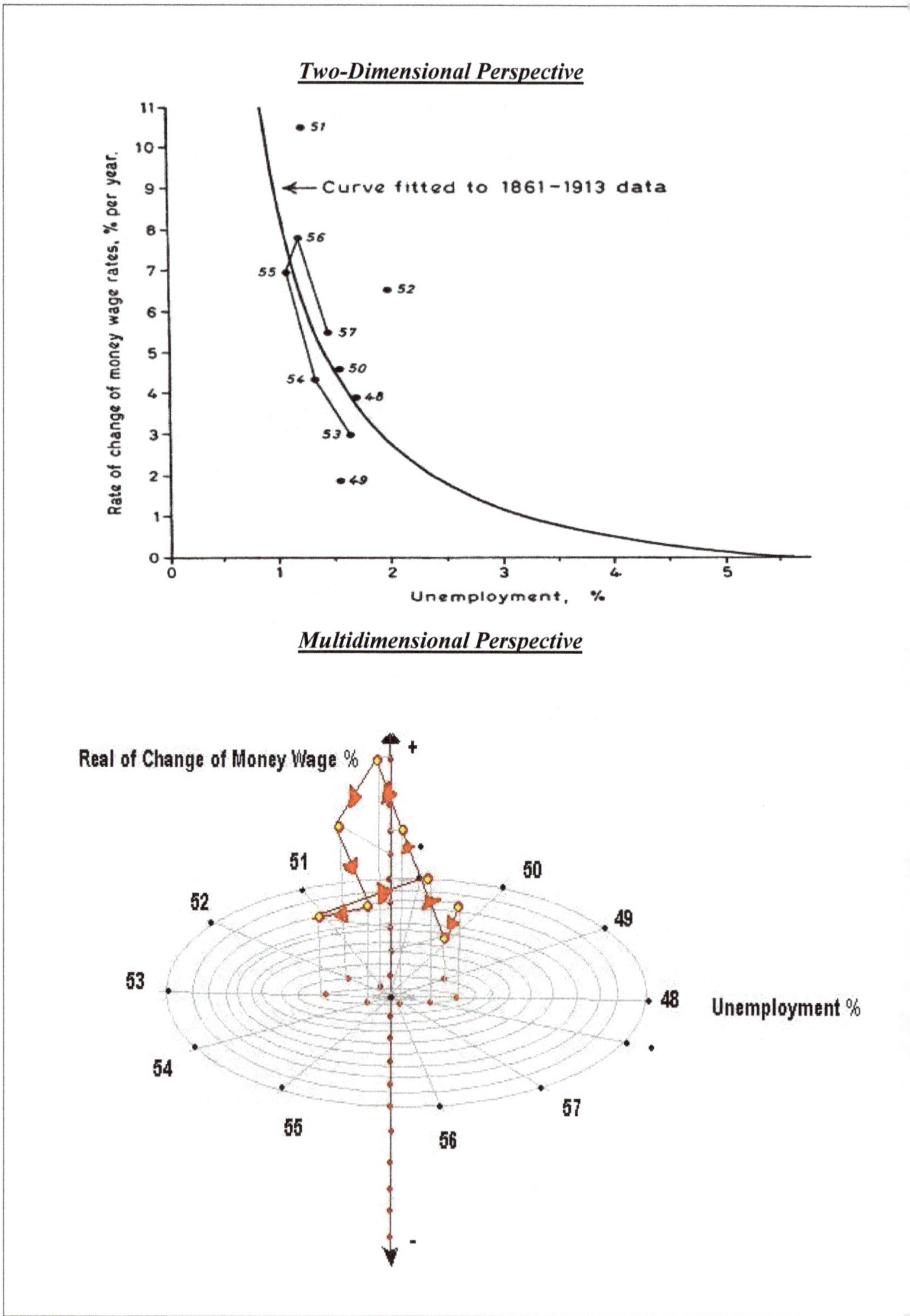

Figure 16. 1948-1957

Source: Adapted from "The relation between unemployment and the rate of change of money wage rates in the United Kingdom, 1861-1957", by Philips (1958) in *Economica*, 25(100), 283-299.

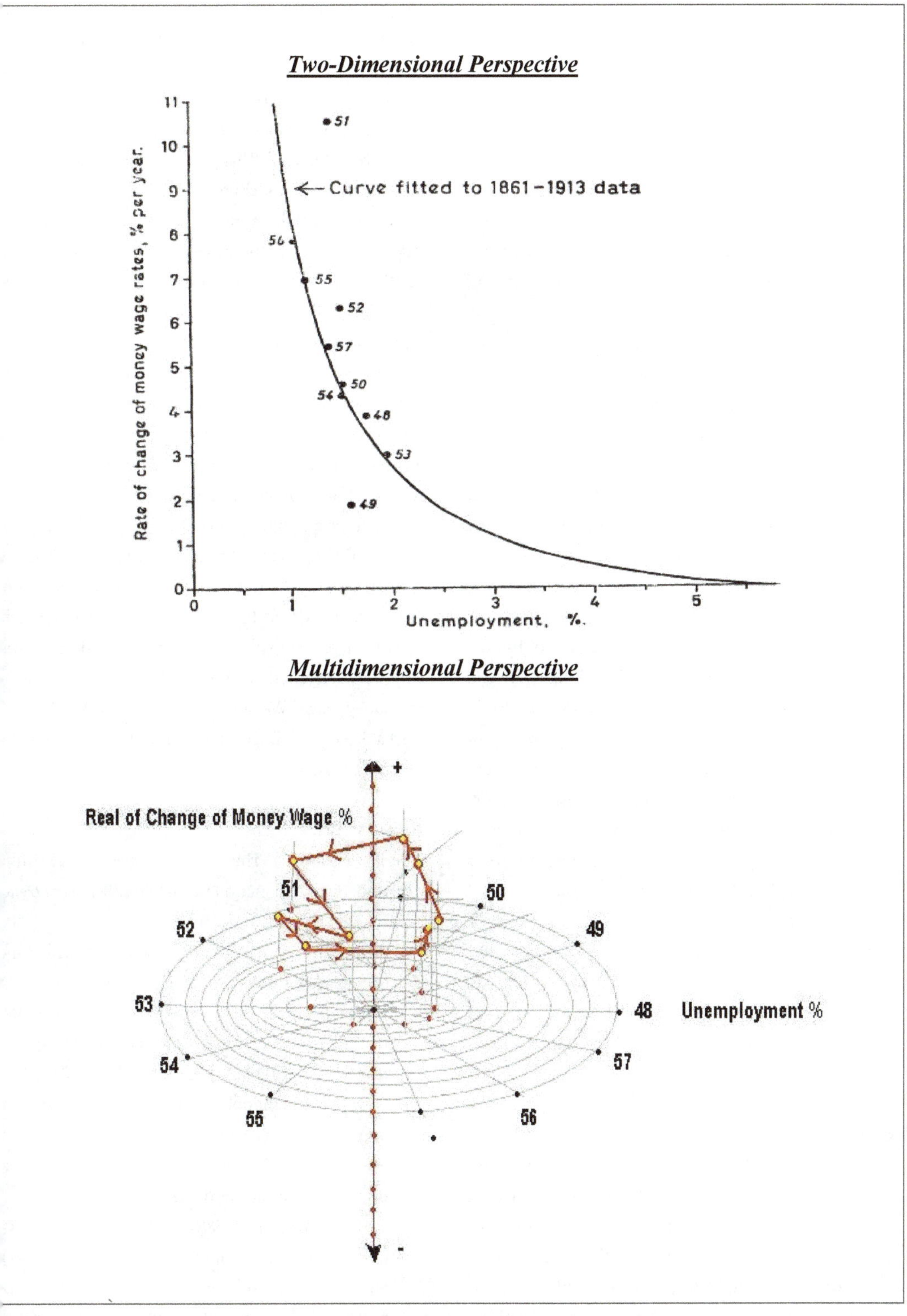

gure 17. 1948-1957

ource: Adapted from "The relation between unemployment and the rate of change of money wage rates in the United ngdom, 1861-1957", by Philips (1958) in *Economica*, 25(100), 283-299.

graphical form with a logical trajectory showing the tendency of the rate of change of money wage rates to be high when unemployment is low and to be low or negative when unemployment is high. Figure 15 confirms Phillips' proposition (1958) that "The clear tendency for the rate of change of money wage rates at any given level of unemployment to be above the average for that level of unemployment when unemployment is decreasing during the upswing of a trade cycle and to be below the average for that level of unemployment when unemployment is increasing during the downswing of a trade cycle." According to Phillips(1958), the results shown in Figure 8 are obtained given the typical relation between the rate of change of wage rates and the level and rate of change of unemployment. In fact, as Phillips (1958) concluded, "The rate of change of money wage rates can be explained by the level of unemployment and the rate of change of unemployment, except in or immediately after those years in which there is a sufficiently rapid rise in import prices to offset the tendency for increasing productivity to reduce the cost of living." This is observed in Figures 16 and 17. Finally, we can observe in Figure 7 that when we applied $/\tan(\beta/\alpha)/$ and $\tan(\beta/\alpha)^{-1}$ in each result between the change of money wage rates and the average unemployment rates progressed from 1861 to 1913 in descending order, we can observe that the fifty-two inverse tangent results $\tan(\beta/\alpha)^{-1}$ were plotted in descending order (from smallest angles to largest angles). It is possible to observe that a conic helix figure is displayed perfectly from the bottom to the top of the mega-dynamic disks coordinate space in vertical position. We are assuming that there are not any negative tangent result $\tan(\beta/\alpha)^{-1}$ in the process for building the multidimensional Phillips curve.

8. Conclusion

We can confirm that A. W. Phillips' research (1958) shows a strong relationship between unemployment and wage rates. Phillips' major contribution is the innovative graphical framework and the application of basic statistics to build a fitted curve for different periods of time. He also plots different points around the curve to fit and interconnect these coordinates with straight lines. At first glance, each figure looks chaotic and non-logical, lacking interconnectivity among these coordinates. According to Phillips (1958), "Each dot in the diagrams represents a year, the average rate of change of money wage rates during the year being given by the scale on the vertical axis and the average unemployment during the year by the scale on the horizontal axis." This paper captures multidimensional graphical modeling based on the mega-dynamic disks multivariable random coordinate space in vertical position that we proposed. We clearly observe the relationship between unemployment and wage rates in a logical and systematic order. Hence, we demonstrate how a non-linear, spiral-shape graphical representation construction can be plotted from the top to the bottom of the mega-dynamic disks multivariable random coordinate space in vertical position. From a multidimensional perspective, the Phillips curve is displayed and follows a consistent behavior to prove that there is a strong relationship between unemployment and wage rates. We affirm A. W. Phillips' great contribution in economics, but as his graphical modeling was restricted to a two-dimensional approach it was unable to explore more than a basic relationship between unemployment and the rate of change of money wage. We conclude that A. W. Phillips left a great legacy; his huge contribution to economics still persists today.

References

Apergis, N. (2013). The stylized facts of Greek inflation: New evidence on persistence. *Panoeconomicus, 60*(1), 51-71.

Ball, L., & Sandeep, M. (2011). Inflation dynamics and the great recession (Working Papers No. 11/121). National Bureau of Economic Research, Inc. Retrieved from https://www.imf.org/external/pubs/ft/wp/2011/wp11121.pdfBoland, L. (1981). Satisficing in methodology: A Reply. *Journal of Economic Literature, 19*(1), 84-86.

Carrasco, C. A., & Ferreiro, J. (2011). Inflation targeting and economic performance: The case of Mexico. *Panoeconomicus, 58*(5), 675-692.

Cohn, E., Cohn. S., Balch, D. C., & Bradley, J. (2001). Do graphs promote learning in principles of economics? *The Journal of Economic Education,* 32(4), 299-310.

Cohn, E., Cohn, S., Balch, D. C., & Bradley, J. (2004). The relation between student attitudes toward graphs and performance in economics. *The American Economist, 48*(2), 41-52.

Friedman, M. (1968): The Role of Monetary Policy. *American Economic Review*, 58(1), 1-17.

Fuhrer, J. & Moore, G. (1995). Inflation persistence. *The Quarterly Journal of Economics, 110* (1), 127-159.

Iosifidis, K., Pucar, E. B., Srdić, S., Ivan, G. (2014). Inflation targeting in advanced vs. emerging economies before and after the crisis. *Panoeconomicus, 61*(1), 79-106.

Lucas, R. E., & Sargent, T. J. (1981). *Rational Expectations and Econometric Practice*. Minneapolis, MN: The University of Minnesota Press.

Maas, H. (2005). *William Stanley Jevons and the making of modern economics*. Cambridge, UK: Cambridge University Press.

Mirowski, P. (1991). The when, the how and the why of mathematical expression in the history of economics analysis. *The Journal of Economic Perspectives, 5*(1), 145-157.

Pencavel, J. (2011). Real wage index numbers. *The American Economic Review, 101*(3), 565-570.

Phillips, A. W. (1958). The relation between unemployment and the rate of change of money wage rates in the United Kingdom, 1861-1957. *Economica, 25*(100), 283-299.

Playfair, W. H. (2005). *Commercial and political atlas and statistical breviary*. Cambridge, UK: Cambridge University Press.

Ruiz Estrada, M. A. (2011a). Multi-dimensional coordinate spaces. *International Journal of Physical Sciences, 6*(3), 340-357.

Ruiz Estrada, M. A. (2011b). Policy modeling: Definition, classification, and evaluation. *Journal of Policy Modeling, 33*(4), 523-536.

Ruiz Estrada, M. A. (2014). An introduction to the mega-dynamic disks coordinate space in vertical and horizontal position. *Malaysian Journal of Sciences, 33*(2), 105-109.

Wise, M. N. (2011). What (good) is historical epistemology? *Erkenntnis, 75*(3), 349-376.

1

Sustainable profitability of ethical and conventional banking

Ricardo Costa-Climent[1], Carla Martínez-Climent[2]

ABSTRACT

In recent years, social movements have echoed calls for greater social and environmental responsib Although financial institutions promote development, consumers have lost confidence in banks. As enter the Fintech era, banks have the opportunity to use new tools that enable greater transpare for customers. Corporate social responsibility (CSR) plays a key role in increasing social awarenes regulators, society, shareholders, and employees—in short, stakeholders. This study therefore focuse banks that have designed their activities and investments to contribute to sustainability. The princ contribution of this paper is to show the existence of a range of business models that arise follow different responses by different types of banks. These different responses occur because the primary jective of sustainable banks is to meet the needs of stakeholders and contribute to sustainable deve ment, whereas conventional banks simply apply and execute CSR policies. It is possible to different between ethical banks and commercial banks. To ensure economic progress and achieve sustainab it is fundamental to balance economic profitability with people's social and environmental aspirati

KEY WORDS: ethical banking; sustainable banking; corporate social responsibility; CSR; fintech

[1] Linnaeus University, Sweden
[2] Universitat de València, Spain

1. Introduction

Economic development over the last century has led to prosperity on the one hand yet the abuse of society and the environment on the other. Accordingly, there is a major need to set society on a sustainable course. At a macro level, the involvement of banks is crucial because of their role as intermediaries around the world and their influence on economic development and progress (Barbu & Vintila, 2007; Caldarelli, Fiondella, Maffei, & Zagaria, 2016; Chang, Jang, Li, & Kim, 2017; De la Cuesta-González, Muñoz-Torres, & Fernánd Izquierdo, 2006).

The most recent financial crisis led to the fai of banks that provided irresponsible loans, opera with little transparency, and crossed numerous eth boundaries (Božović, 2007; Phuong, Fisher, & M taba, 2014; Safakli, 2007). The financial crisis of 2 brought into question the entire banking model, sh ing how the crisis was more structural than cycl and revealing critical defects with the existing finan and economic models (Karyotis & Onochie, 2016). nancial institutions are therefore becoming more aw of the risks they face. Financial, social, and environm tal risks are present in operations with customers in investments (Bing, Yan, & Jun, 2011; De la Cue

Correspondence concerning this article should be addressed to: **Carla Martínez-Climent**, Universitat de València, Spain. E-mail: Carla.Martinez-Climent@uv.es

González et al., 2006; Nandy & Lodh, 2012; Shen, Shuai, Jiao, Tan & Song, 2016). However, non-financial risks are rarely estimated when calculating overall risk, even though doing so would help banks become more efficient and establish a more accurate price based partly on these social and environmental risks.

The banking sector has traditionally played a key function in regional financial development. To use finance to its advantage, a country needs a sound structural framework in terms of macroeconomic performance and solid economic institutions (Bittencourt, 2012; Santiso, 2006; Singh & Cerisola, 2006). Numerous cases prove that the banking sector has contributed massively to countries' economic development and growth. One such example is Bangladesh, despite the problems it faces as a result of its geography and environment (Masud, Bae, & Kim, 2017).

So although financial institutions promote development, consumers have lost confidence in banks (Pérez, Martínez, & Del Bosque, 2013; Pineiro-Chousa, Vizcaíno-González, López-Cabarcos, & Romero-Castro, 2017). Corporate social responsibility (CSR) plays a key role in increasing social awareness of regulators, society, shareholders, and employees—in short, stakeholders. Accordingly, policies are needed to contribute to sustainable development (Shen et al., 2016). Regulation must evolve to keep pace with growth in the financial sector. Otherwise, it contributes to environmentally unsustainable development, which has negative consequences because financial markets are globally interlinked and the way they function can affect the surroundings. As Richardson (2009) affirms, the long-term socially responsible investment (SRI) movement has set standards for the financial sector. But an orientation toward SRI in the financial sector is necessary because a greater number of firms that embrace social responsibility in their investments is needed to achieve sustainable development within the financial sector.

This study therefore focuses on banks that have designed their activities and investments to contribute to sustainability. In recent years, social movements have called for greater social and environmental responsibility. This has alerted banks to the value that consumers place on these issues as well as the traditional functions of the banking sector because banks are able to lay the foundations for sustainable development through their lending policies (Harvey, 1995; Masud et al., 2017).

Modern corporate governance in the form of sustainable management, and particularly corporate social responsibility (CSR) reporting, is relevant in bank management (Dienes & Velte, 2015). The reason is that banks can target price differentiation in the services they offer their clients depending on their CSR practices. By doing so, firms applying CSR can get attractive loans with lower interest rates than those that do not contribute to sustainable development. Another reason why banks apply sustainable management is that it allows them to offer their clients sustainable products that promote socially responsible investment (Jeucken, 2001).

Sustainable development can be achieved through stakeholder-oriented policies. Any investment that marries the financial efficiency pursued by investors with responsible behavior in terms of the environment, society, and governance is deemed sustainable and responsible investment by the European Sustainable Investment Forum (Barnett & Salomon, 2006; Renneboog, Ter Horst, & Zhang, 2008a; Salzmann, 2013). The cited studies report that the key areas of sustainable investment are social fairness, corporate governance, and the environment (Salzmann, 2013).

It is helpful to consider whether moral conscience affects the financial sector. Carrasco (2006) found that sustainably managed firms that consider ethical issues are judged by stakeholders in terms of social as well as economic performance.

Considering both economic and social aspects is generally viewed positively by some stakeholders. Thus, investors and financial intermediaries increasingly consider these issues in their practices, and capital markets reward socially and environmentally responsible policies, encouraging ethical action across the full range of policies.

The environment and the economy are more than just closely related; they are mutually dependent. The government plays a key role by using instruments to internalize environmental effects into market prices so that companies and consumers make more sustainable production and consumption decisions. More sustainable consumer purchasing behavior will encourage companies to make more sustainable production decisions. In addition to these push (government) and pull (consumer) factors, companies can also foster more sustainable development themselves because they may have their own ideological or business reasons for striving for sustainability. Crucially, these measures should not undermine the long-term continuity of these companies; consumers should actually buy the more sustainable products, and governments should support these companies with subsidies and tax concessions.

Interest in non-profit banks has grown among academics and legislators. This interest has been heightened since the recent global financial crisis. The characteristics of cooperative banks could help mitigate the effects of such a crisis in various countries (Becchetti, Garcia, & Trovato, 2011; Segura & Martínez, 2018). Aside from these cooperative banks, which represent a small minority and which, despite their market relevance, have been the subject of relatively little research, commercial and non-profit banks resemble one another in certain ways in terms of credit rationing and attitude toward risk (Becchetti et al., 2011).

2. The banking sector

The need for banks arises because of friction in capital markets (Freixas & Rochet, 1998; Hubbard, 1994; Saunders, 2000). This friction is due to the lack of information that enterprises and families have about the deficits and surpluses of money in the market. The role of banks as intermediaries consists of bringing together lenders and borrowers by channeling surpluses of money towards deficits of money.

There is also information asymmetry between lenders and borrowers of capital. In credit operations, banks have a larger amount of key information on regulations, market trends, development in the strongest sectors, and so on. Furthermore, this knowledge enables banks to establish acceptable economic and environmental risk thresholds, and they are able to reduce information asymmetries in the market. Being aware of these risks allows banks to establish different interest rates considering sustainability issues such as risk perspectives and thus contribute to sustainable financial development.

The role of banks is determined by the effect that the risks taken by banks have on economic growth and the fluctuations in the business and economic cycle in general (Laeven & Levine, 2009). Banks play a key role, and regulations exert pressure on banks because of their considerable impact. The nature of the impact of regulations on risk-taking depends on the bank's capital structure. The capital structure of banks is sometimes overlooked, and conclusions regarding the effect of capital regulations on banks' risk-taking are reached based on insufficient evidence (Laeven & Levine, 2009).

Because banks largely depend on both reputation and performance (Brickley, Smith, & Zimmerman, 2002; Phuong et al., 2014), some financial institutions have signed up to internationally recognized standards such as the Equator Principles, the Principles for Responsible Investment (Chew, Tan, & Hamid, 2016) and enterprise risk management (Caldarelli et al., 2016).

The Equator Principles are a set of principles that provide a risk management framework for financial institutions that finance industrial projects and macro-level infrastructures (Finger, Gavious, & Manos, 2018; Macve & Chen, 2010; Scholtens & Dam, 2007). The objective of the Equator Principles is to safeguard sound environmental management practices for projects financed by affiliated institutions to contribute to socially responsible investment (Finger et al., 2018). In contrast, enterprise risk management enables organizations to effectively manage risks and seize opportunities associated with good performance and the capacity to absorb losses (Committee of Sponsoring Organisations of the Treadway Commission [COSO], 2004; Caldarelli et al., 2016).

The banking sector has experienced a revolution as a result of globalization, disintermediation, financial innovation, deregulation, and technological change, while financial scandals and accounting manipulation through dubious practices have led consumers to distrust banks' financial products and services (Ferreira, Jalali, & Ferreira, 2018; Flavián, Guinaliu, & Torres, 2005; Pérez, Martínez, & Del Bosque, 2013).

The interaction of banks with the environment is noteworthy for several reasons. Banks are key stakeholders that influence governments and other companies. Moreover, banks are an integral part of investment for sustainable development. Thus, banks can offer innovative financial products and influence the environment through their internal processes and their use of resources (Jeucken, 2001).

Financial institutions are a prominent part of today's society, yet the banking sector's image has been tarnished by unethical practices and the influence of customer perception. Mandel, Lachman, and Orgler (1981) cite the importance of managing the image of the banking sector because of the intangible nature of its products, dwindling contact with consumers, and the need to build trust among stakeholders (Mandel et al., 1981; Pérez et al., 2013). The banking sector should thus maintain a balance between social and economic issues.

3. The evolution of banking due to fintech

As mentioned earlier, banks have been heavily influenced by technological progress Financial technology, or *fintech*, refers to the application of technology to tackle issues in finance and thereby obtain new forms of technological tools for finance (Arner, Barberis, & Buckley, 2015; Martínez-Climent, Zorio-Grima, & Ribeiro-Soriano, 2017; Zalan & Toufaily, 2017). Fintech affects private equity, crowdfunding, and numerous other kinds of financing that rely on technology (Arner et al., 2015). Technological institutions that are not banks can now offer financial services.

As reported by Martínez-Climent et al. (2017), fintech refers to the use of a range of technological tools to offer financial services that consumers find more accessible and more efficient (Ma & Liu 2017; Zalan & Toufaily, 2017). Fintech is associated with technological innovation and therefore entails process disruption. We offer the following reasons for this disruption:

1. Mainstream products will be digitalized and commercialized through technological platforms. This will lead to a new fintech approach in the industry.
2. Blockchain will expand beyond its cryptocurrency applications. Artificial intelligence (AI), robotics, and public cloud services will play a prominent role in the distribution of financial services. This will make services more localized. Cybersecurity will pose an even greater risk to financial services than fraud or money laundering.
3. Customer intelligence could be described as the most important incentive for a firm to perform financially. Regulators are expected to be highly active in response to fintech innovations (Gomber, Kauffman, Parker, & Weber, 2018).
4. Fintech reduces transaction costs as processes become optimized. Moreover, by incorporating technology, banks will potentially be more sustainable because they can reduce physical infrastructures with a large ecological footprint while granting users greater access to all information and thereby increasing transparency (Boskov & Drakulevski, 2017).
5. Banks can interact with feedback because users are easily connected with banks' investments. Thus, users can also contribute their point of view and participate in decisions.

4. Corporate social responsibility (CSR)

Three reasons lead companies to adopt CSR practices: strategy, altruism, and greenwashing (Baron, 2009; Finger et al., 2018; McWilliams, Siegel, & Wright, 2006; Wu & Shen, 2013). CSR is seen as strategic because it leads to a competitive advantage by linking the strategic management of a firm to activities that benefit stakeholders, generating value, and improving the image of the business (Pérez & Del Bosque, 2012). Companies engaged in greenwashing portray themselves, their products, and their strategy as being based on a concern for the environment without actually committing to the cause (Finger et al., 2018).

The definition of CSR has changed numerous times since the 1950s. Caroll (1979) proposed a theoretical framework for CSR based on four pillars: economic, legal, ethical, and philanthropic (Pérez et al., 2013). The current approach is the triple bottom line, which consists of the economic, environmental, and social dimensions (Elkington, 1997). The key assumption of the triple bottom line is discretionary adoption, which leads to competitive advantage for sustainable firms (Hussain, Rigoni, & Orij, 2018; Porter, 1991).

Another argument for the ability of CSR to yield a competitive advantage is that CSR contributes to reducing transaction costs and improves access to resources. The resource-based view posits that each firm is a combination of unique resources (Penrose, 1995). According to the resource-based view, firms use key resources to develop a competitive advantage over other firms. Firms with high transactions costs are unable to acquire key resources. Therefore, reducing transaction costs with CSR helps firms achieve a competitive advantage (El Ghoul, Guedhami, & Kim, 2017).

Banks face different kinds of risk because they interact with the environment. The financial, environmental, and reputation risk that banks tend to minimize is huge (De la Cuesta-González et al., 2006). To reduce these risks and boost performance, banks increasingly include CSR in their practices (Viganò & Nicolai, 2009). CSR and social investing have become popular practices in recent years (Finger et al., 2018; Jo & Kim, 2008; Renneboog et al., 2008a). Firms that implement CSR in their practices report that they perform their tasks in a sustainable way, taking into account the social, ethical, and environmental dimensions of society (McWilliams & Siegel, 2001; Porter & Kramer, 2011; Sen & Bhattacharya, 2001). Examples of CSR practices implemented by firms include developing products of a social nature, going beyond legal requirements in human resources programs, reducing pollution, and supporting the local community (El Ghoul et al., 2017; McWilliams & Siegel, 2001). Attention from the business community has risen as CSR has helped firms manage conflicts (Heal, 2005) and increase their capacity to compete effectively in the market (Aupperle, Carroll, & Hatfield, 1985; Finger et al., 2018) by considering all stakeholders' interests rather than just those of shareholders.

Banks that apply CSR are aware of the moral and legal responsibility that firms have to their stakeholders (Margolis & Walsh, 2003) and SRI (Renneboog et al., 2008b). This reflects a shift from banks' traditional passive role when conducting transactions and pursuing opportunities to obtain efficiency (De la Cuesta-González et al., 2006).

One goal of financial institutions is to reduce information asymmetries. To do so, banks evaluate different risks. Sustainability reports such as the report proposed by the Global Reporting Initiative should reduce information asymmetries and transaction costs between stakeholders and organizations (Botosan, 1997; De la Cuesta-González et al., 2006; Dienes & Velte, 2015; Shankman, 1999). From a sustainability approach, banks should consider non-financial risks to estimate overall risk. To do so, banks require more efficient management to correctly set prices. From a bank management perspective, the use of sustainability reports represents an opportunity because it helps alleviate the undervaluation of capital markets and thereby benefits shareholders and stakeholders (Dienes & Velte, 2015). For example, from a CSR perspective, customers that represent a greater social and environmental risk should pay more. A positive correlation between environmental performance and financial performance has been reported (Dasgupta, Laplante, Wang, & Wheeler, 2002; Dowell, Hart, & Yeung, 2000). Weber, Scholz, and Michalik (2010) concluded that sustainability criteria such as CSR can predict traditional financial performance only if complementary assets drive the financial performance relationship.

Other relevant arguments relate to the real cost involved in adopting the Equator Principles because economic investment is required to make periodic reports and reject feasible projects if they fail to meet the required ethical standards (Finger et al., 2018). Preston and O'Bannon (1997) argue that the lack of knowledge regarding the implementation of CSR projects could damage the firm's financial performance.

International institutions such as the OECD promote corporate governance to create an environment of trust, transparency, long-term investment, financial stability, and integrity in business (OECD, 2015).

5. Ethical and sustainable banking

The banking sector can be divided into the social banking and conventional banking sectors. Social banking refers to cooperative banks and ethical banks, which are also sustainable banks (Segura & Martínez, 2018). The main difference between social banking and conventional banking is that social banking has social and economic objectives, although these economic objectives are essential to meet these social objectives. Conventional banking only pursues economic ends. Thus, commercial banks seek profit maximization, whereas ethical banks seek to maximize the volume of performing loans that have the specific characteristics they seek. The main similarity is that social and commercial banks have the same capital constraints to increase reserves when parties default (Becchetti et al., 2011; Segura & Martínez, 2018).

In this context, commercial banks can ration credit and set a non-compensating loan rate that creates excessive credit demand because a higher interest rate might create a moral hazard or adverse selection, thereby increasing risk and generating profits that are not maximized because bank profits do not increase directly with risk (Becchetti, et al., 2011).

Scholars have described the optimal policy for ethical banking as equality between the number of loans and deposits, taking into account the market rate, risks, and costs borne by business. There are therefore some analogies with commercial banks (Canning, Spencer, & Jefferson, 2003).

Ethical banks avoid getting involved in financial practices with dishonest intentions and foster the idea of creating value for the community. The social and economic aim of ethical banking (San-Jose, Retolaza, & Gutierrez-Goiria, 2011) is reflected by the preference for distributing lower returns in favor of investing the money in social projects.

Sustainable banks therefore voluntarily go a step further. The environmental perspective, the firm's purpose, and the role played in the community are crucial for the development of sustainable banking. Sustainable banks are prepared to accept lower margins and/or higher risks to encourage certain activities—they apply non-risk-related premium differentiation—that would have no chance of survival in the current system because the risk is considered too great, the margins too small, and the period of payment too long.

According to Ayadi, Llewellyn, Schmidt, Arbak, and De Groen (2010), the first credit cooperative was conceived in 1865 in Madrid. It was the predecessor of the rural credit cooperatives that were created in the 20th century. These new institutions were promoted by Catholic unions and numbered 1,000 in 1936. Most vanished in the Spanish Civil War. In the 1960s, credit cooperatives once again flourished, and in 1977, there were 200 registered rural and popular credit cooperatives (Ayadi et al., 2010).

A sustainable bank promotes sustainability among stakeholders in the internal and external activities performed by the bank (Bouma, Jeucken & Klinkers, 2017). This modus operandi includes environmental, social, or cultural concerns in selecting ethical investments and supports activities to improve the community.

The first step toward bank sustainability is its view of the environment, the purpose of the firm, and the desired social role. Another key characteristic is that sustainable banks prefer lower margins and take more risk if the activities performed are rewarding.

Comparatively, by definition, ethical investment funds could be described as funds that base their principles on social, cultural, and environmental issues. This means that this type of fund seeks the involvement and support of corporate activities such as cooperation between groups and encouragement of equality. They are therefore reluctant to invest in alcohol, tobacco, gambling, and the like (Bouma et al., 2017).

The philosophy behind sustainable banking is based on not compromising the chances of future generations. This philosophy covers a range of angles: economic interests, the aspirations of society, and environmental impacts. This ensures economic progress for today's society.

This paper focuses on sustainable banking, so it is important to clarify what this term actually means. Sustainable banking institutionalizes socially responsible investments. Socially responsible investments fulfill ethical and economic criteria so that investments meet certain financial conditions as well as conditions regarding the use of funds (Barbu & Vintila, 2007; Caldarelli et al., 2016; Cowton & Thompson, 2001; San Emeterio & Retolaza, 2003; San-Jose et al., 2011). Environmental and ecological problems are a fact of modern life. The financial industry should therefore take responsibility for this issue and channel economic and financial activity toward environmentally friendly pursuits. Although these investments may be less profitable than traditional investments, the aim of achieving sustainable development should be a priority (Richardson, 2009).

This viewpoint is conducive to the emergence of responsible investment funds and the development of the concept of CSR. The term embraces the concept of ethics applied to banking, funds, investments, and social responsibility in banking (Salzmann, 2013; San Emeterio & Retolaza, 2003).

Three principles that govern ethical banking can be extrapolated to sustainable banking. These are affinity, responsibility, and integrity (Caldarelli et al., 2016; Cowton, 2010; San-Jose et al., 2011; Viganò & Nicolai, 2009). The principle of affinity is based on the premise that actions taken by banks meet the requirements of shareholders and depositors in terms of the purpose of the funds. The second principle of responsibility refers to ethical banks' reporting on the consequences of their actions. Integrity relates to avoiding the financial exclusion of segments in risk such as the young, the elderly, immigrants, or women (Caldarelli et al., 2016; Cowton, 2010).

The first ethical bank was created in 1976. The Bangladeshi *Grameen Bank* offered micro-credits to poor people to fight inequality. This bank and its creator, Muhammad Yunus, are global pioneers in ethical banking, and from this project, other similar experiences have sprung up throughout the world. Women are one of the target groups of customers because they are generally poorer and face greater credit restrictions that men do. The bank thereby makes a long-term contribution to women's role in society (Coleman, 2004; Yunus, Moingeon, & Lehmann-Ortega, 2010).

The Global Alliance for Banking on Values (GABV) is an international network that creates a broad, transparent global banking environment. At the beginning of 2017, the GABV comprised 7 strategic partners and 43 sustainable independent banks, 10 of which were European: Alternativa Bank Switzerland and Freie Gemeinschaftsbank Genossenschaft (Switzerland), Banca Popolare Ética (Italy), Credit Coopératif (France), Culture Bank (Norway), Ekobanken (Sweden), GLS Bank (Germany), Magnet Bank (Hungary), Merkur Resource Bank (Denmark), and Triodos Bank (Netherlands) (Segura & Martínez, 2018).

We chose Banco Santander as the conventional bank to examine in this study because it is the biggest bank in Spain in terms of assets. Banco Santander is much larger than Banca Popolare Ética or any of the ethical banks mentioned earlier.

From a theoretical perspective, we differentiate between the two contrasting concepts of conventional banking and ethical banking. In reality, a spectrum of practices prevails in financial institutions and all sectors. It is therefore difficult to label banks because growing attention is paid to social issues in both types of banking.

Banco Santander won the Best Bank in the World 2008 award thanks to its sustainable competitive advantage for its diversified investment and robust balance sheet. Moreover, Banco Santander has been able to create value as a group even in challenging markets (Grupo Santander, 2009). As Xifra and Ordeix (2009) report, in 2008, Santander invested 126 million Euros in CSR "to be in the vanguard in CSR, through … creating wealth and jobs, and fostering the development of society and the environment … and promoting sustainable growth" (Grupo Santander, 2009, p. 8; Xifra & Ordeix, 2009). Banco Santander's CSR policy is based on identifying relevant stakeholders and addressing their needs. This suggests that Santander is not a purely commercial bank because it shows concern for customers, shareholders, employees, suppliers, and society.

In 2008, Banco Santander purchased Abbey National and Alliance and Leicester in the United Kingdom. These transactions were notable in that both companies were building societies. Despite not being considered cooperative banks because they did not offer a complete range of banking services, there was some overlap in their features. A UK law passed in 1986 enabled the conversion of building societies to banks with public limited company form (Ayadi et al., 2010). In short, Banco Santander is a conventional bank that has nonetheless shown an interest in banks with some ethical banking characteristics.

6. Conclusions

This article explores the essential characteristics of commercial banks and ethical, sustainable, and social banks. Traditionally, these have been considered opposing concepts, and scholars have examined the similarities and differences between these models. In reality, however, the range of possibilities is much broader. The principal contribution of this paper is to show the existence of a range of business models that arise following different responses by different types of banks. These different responses occur because the primary objective of sustainable banks is to meet the needs of stakeholders and contribute to sustainable development, whereas conventional banks simply apply and execute CSR policies. Nevertheless, it is possible to differentiate between ethical banks and commercial banks. Whereas ethical banks are driven by an awareness of the destination of their funding activities and a willingness to forgo profit in favor of social causes, conventional or commercial banks' primary interest is to maximize profits.

Some key facts have affected the expansion of ethical banks. First, the financial crisis led to the expansion of ethical banks because of a worsening in customers' perceptions of the image of banks. The financial crisis also revealed the unethical practices of financial institutions, which led to greater social unrest. As a result of the crisis, the needs of different stakeholders must be met. This influences banks' decisions regarding how to rebuild consumer trust (Segura & Martínez, 2018)

Another key observation is that the effects of fintech are positive for ethical banks. Fintech provides banks with tools, enabling greater transparency for customers.

Moreover, technology tends to reduce transaction costs, which has increased the volume of transactions involving new financial securities (Karyotis & Onochie, 2016).

The third observation is that ethical banking is also sustainable banking because the concern for social projects is also a characteristic of sustainability in terms of the sustainable development of society.

After the global financial crisis, CSR strategies had to play a complementary role associated with modern business reporting in conventional banking. To measure the performance of traditional firms, some financial indicators were used. Today, however, environmental, social, and corporate governance are also considered relevant measures (Dienes & Velte, 2015). The implementation of relevant well-known standards such as the Equator Principles, the Principles for Responsible Investment, and enterprise risk management, together with the implementation of CSR in companies, is proof that the banking sector is moving toward a more sustainable model. Conventional banking will become ethical banking in the near future. The reasons for this transformation are society's demands for transparency and guarantees for consumers. The financial sector will be affected by the need to meet certain requirements, which will ultimately lead to ethical banking models.

This study echoes previous studies in showing that private firms and banks have a strong motivation to include CSR practices in their business strategies because of the potential benefits for both macro and micro performance. Whereas macro performance refers to the improvement of environmental practices and promotion of social equality, micro performance refers to the enhancement of the firm's reputation, the ability to recruit and retain high quality workers, and the ability to charge a premium for services. If companies include CSR practices in their strategies, the financial benefits may outweigh the costs, which can result in considerable improvement in long-term firm performance. Consequently, CSR practices have the potential to benefit both corporate shareholders and stakeholders, creating a win-win situation for all (Wu & Shen, 2013). Furthermore, CSR and sustainability reports promote the reduction of asymmetries in transactions and information between stakeholders and companies (Botosan, 1997; De la Cuesta-González et al., 2006; Dienes & Velte, 2015; Shankman, 1999).

Finally, it is worth mentioning that conventional banks embrace fintech solutions and technology in their strategies. This implies a reduction in the number of branches. Thus, traditional banks must consider CSR practices to meet the demands of customers to fully satisfy their needs. The business model of cooperative banks is based on lean governance, employing a small number of workers to minimize costs (Tarantola, 2009). Furthermore, cooperative banks do not offer several senior management positions and do not select a specific person to manage risk issues. Nevertheless, these banks implement efficient enterprise risk management practices. They achieve this success by involving all employees working in the area of risk management at every level of the organization (Caldarelli et al., 2016).

To make the financial system more sustainable, it is necessary to apply CSR practices, invest in social projects, and deal with enterprise risk management. Current social and environmental issues can thus be effectively addressed. The existence of sustainable banks does not restrict the choices facing future generations. However, balancing economic profitability with people's social and environmental aspirations is fundamental to ensure economic progress.

References

Arner, D. W., Barberis, J., & Buckley, R. P. (2015). The evolution of Fintech: A new post-crisis paradigm. Georgetown Journal of International Law, 47, 1271.

Aupperle, K. E., Carroll, A. B., & Hatfield, J. D. (1985). An empirical examination of the relationship between corporate social responsibility and profitability. *Academy of Management Journal, 28*(2), 446–463.

Ayadi, R., Llewellyn, D. T., Schmidt, R. H., Arbak, E., & De Groen, W. P. (2010). *Investigating diversity in the banking sector in Europe: Key developments, performance and role of cooperative banks.* Brussels, Belgium: Centre for European Policy Studies.

Barbu, T., & Vintila, G. (2007). The emergence of ethic banks and social responsibility in financing local development. *Theoretical and Applied Economics, 12*, 29–34.

Barnett, M. L., & Salomon, R. M. (2006). Beyond dichotomy: The curvilinear relationship between social responsibility and financial performance. *Strategic Management Journal, 27*(11), 1101–1122.

Baron, D. P. (2009). A positive theory of moral management, social pressure, and corporate social performance. *Journal of Economics & Management Strategy*, *18*(1), 7–43.

Becchetti, L., Garcia, M. M., & Trovato, G. (2011). Credit rationing and credit view: Empirical evidence from an ethical bank in Italy. Journal of Money, Credit and Banking, 43(6), 1217-1245.

Bing, Z., Yan, Y., & Jun, B. (2011). Tracking the implementation of green credit policy in China: top-down perspective and bottom-up reform. Journal of Environmental Management, *92*, 1321–1327.

Bittencourt, M. (2012). Financial development and economic growth in Latin America: Is Schumpeter right? *Journal of Policy Modeling*, *34*(3), 341–355.

Boskov, T., & Drakulevski, L. (2017). Addressing the Role of Risk Management and Digital Finance Technology on Financial Inclusion. *Quality - Access to Success*, *18*(161), 113–115.

Botosan, C. A. (1997). Disclosure level and the cost of equity capital. *Accounting Review*, *72*(3), 323–349.

Bouma, J. J., Jeucken, M., & Klinkers, L. (2017). *Sustainable banking: The greening of finance*. Abingdon, UK: Routledge.

Božovic⊠, J. (2007). Business ethics in banking. *Facta Universitatis-Series: Economics and Organization*, *4*(2), 173–182.

Brickley, J. A., Smith, C. W., & Zimmerman, J. L. (2002). Business ethics and organizational architecture. *Journal of Banking and Finance*, *26*(9), 1821–1835.

Caldarelli, A., Fiondella, C., Maffei, M., & Zagaria, C. (2016). Managing risk in credit cooperative banks: Lessons from a case study. *Management Accounting Research*, *32*, 1–15.

Carrasco, I. (2006). Ethics and banking. International Advances in Economic Research, 12(1), 43-50.

Carroll, A. B. (1979). A three-dimensional conceptual model of corporate performance. *Academy of Management Review*, *4*(4), 497–505.

Canning, D., Spencer, J., & Jefferson, C. (2003). Optimal Credit Rationing in Not-for-Profit Financial Institutions. *International Economic Review*, *44*, 243–261.

Chang, M., Jang, H. B., Li, Y. M., & Kim, D. (2017). The Relationship between the Efficiency, Service Quality and Customer Satisfaction for State-Owne Commercial Banks in China. *Sustainability*, *9*(12 2163.

Chew, B. C., Tan, L. H., & Hamid, S. R. (2016). Ethical banking in practice: a closer look at the Co operative Bank UK PLC. *Qualitative Research i Financial Markets*, *8*(1), 70–91.

Coleman, I. (2004). The payoff from women's right *Foreign Affairs*, *83*(3), 80–95.

COSO. (2004). Enterprise risk management—Integrated Framework, Executive Summary & Framework. Retrieved from https://www.coso.org/Documents/COSO-ERM-Executive-Summary.pdf

Cowton, C., & Thompson, P. (2001). Financing th social economy: a case study of Triodos Bank. *International Journal of Nonprofit Voluntary Secto Marketing*, *6*(2), 145–155.

Cowton, C. (2010). Banking. In J. Boatright (Ed.), *Finance Ethics: Critical Issues in Financial Theor and Practice*. Kolb Series in Finance (pp. 325-337). Hoboken, NJ: Wiley.

Dasgupta, S., Laplante, B., Wang, H., & Wheeler, D (2002). Confronting the environmental Kuznet curve. *Journal of Economic Perspectives*, *16*(1 147–168.

De la Cuesta-González, M., Muñoz-Torres, M. J., & Fernández-Izquierdo, M. Á. (2006). Analysis o social performance in the Spanish financial industry through public data. A proposal. *Journal o Business Ethics*, *69*(3), 289–304.

Dienes, D., & Velte, P. (2016). The impact of supervisory board composition on CSR reporting. Evidence from the German two-tier system. *Sustainability*, *8*(1), 63.

Dowell, G., Hart, S., & Yeung, B. (2000). Do corporat global environmental standards create or destro market value? *Management Science*, *46*(8), 1059-1074.

El Ghoul, S., Guedhami, O., & Kim, Y. (2017). Country-level institutions, firm value, and the role o corporate social responsibility initiatives. *Journa of International Business Studies*, *48*(3), 360–385.

Elkington, J. (1997). *Cannibals with forks: The tripl bottom line of twentieth century business*. Oxford UK: Capstone.

Ferreira, J. J., Jalali, M. S., & Ferreira, F. A. (2018). Enhancing the decision-making virtuous cycle o ethical banking practices using the Choquet integral. *Journal of Business Research, 88*, 492–497.

Finger, M., Gavious, I., & Manos, R. (2018). Environmental risk management and financial performance in the banking industry: A cross-country comparison. *Journal of International Financial Markets, Institutions and Money, 52*, 240–261.

Flavián, C., Guinaliu, M., & Torres, E. (2005). The influence of corporate image on consumer trust: A comparative analysis in traditional versus internet banking. *Internet Research, 15*(4), 447–470.

Freixas, X., & Rochet, J. C. (1998). Fair pricing of deposit insurance. Is it possible? Yes. Is it desirable? No. Research in Economics, 52(3), 217-232.

Gomber, P., Kauffman, R. J., Parker, C., & Weber, B. W. (2018). On the Fintech Revolution: Interpreting the Forces of Innovation, Disruption, and Transformation in Financial Services. *Journal of Management Information Systems, 35*(1), 220–265.

Grupo Santander. (2009). *Annual report 2008*. Madrid: Banco Santander.

Harvey, B. (1995). Ethical Bank: The Case of the Co-Operative Bank. *Journal of Business Ethics, 14*(12), 1005–1013.

Heal, G. (2005). Corporate social responsibility: an economic and financial framework. *The Geneva Papers on Risk and Insurance: Issues and Practice, 30*(3), 387–409.

Hubbard, R. G. (1994). Money, the financial system, and the economy. Reading, MA: Addison-Wesley.

Hussain, N., Rigoni, U., & Orij, R. P. (2018). Corporate governance and sustainability performance: Analysis of triple bottom line performance. *Journal of Business Ethics, 149*(2), 411–432.

Jeucken, M. (2001). *Sustainable finance and banking: The financial sector and the future of the planet*. Abingdon, UK: Routledge.

Jo, H., & Kim, Y. (2008). Ethics and disclosure: a study of the financial performance of firms in the seasoned equity offerings market. *Journal of Business Ethics, 80*(4), 855–878.

Karyotis, C., & Onochie, J. (2016). Ten Challenges to Have a Sustainable Financial System. In S. Alijani & C. Karyotis (Eds.), *Finance and Economy for Society: Integrating Sustainability* (pp. 179–198). Bingley, UK: Emerald Group Publishing Limited.

Laeven, L., & Levine, R. (2009). Bank governance, regulation and risk taking. *Journal of Financial Economics, 93*(2), 259–275.

Ma, Y., & Liu, D. (2017). Introduction to the special issue on Crowdfunding and FinTech. *Financial Innovation, 3*(8). https://doi.org/10.1186/s40854-017-0058-9.

Macve, R., & Chen, X. (2010). The "equator principles": a success for voluntary codes? *Accounting, Auditing & Accountability Journal, 23*(7), 890–919.

Mandel, L., Lachman, R., & Orgler, Y. (1981). Interpreting the image of banking. *Journal of Bank Research, 12*(2), 96–104.

Margolis, J. D., & Walsh, J. P. (2003). Misery loves companies: Rethinking social initiatives by business. *Administrative Science Quarterly, 48*(2), 268–305.

Martínez-Climent, C., Zorio-Grima, A., & Ribeiro-Soriano, D. (2017). Financial return crowdfunding: literature review and bibliometric analysis. *International Entrepreneurship and Management Journal, 14*(3), 527–553.

Masud, M. A. K., Bae, S. M., Kim, J. D. (2017). Analysis of Environmental Accounting and Reporting Practices of Listed Banking Companies in Bangladesh. *Sustainability, 9*(10), 1717.

McWilliams, A., & Siegel, D. (2001). Corporate social responsibility: A theory of the firm perspective. *Academy of Management Review, 26*(1), 117–127.

McWilliams, A., Siegel, D., & Wright, P. (2006). Corporate social responsibility: International perspectives. Available at SSRN: https://ssrn.com/abstract=900834 or http://dx.doi.org/10.2139/ssrn.900834

Nandy, M., & Lodh, S. (2012). Do banks value the eco-friendliness of firms in their corporate lending decision? Some empirical evidence. International Review of Financial Analysis, *25*, 83–93.

OECD. (2015). *G20/OECD Principles of Corporate Governance*. OECD. Available at http://www.oecd.org/corporate/principles-corporate-governance.htm

Penrose, E. T. (1959). The theory of the growth of the firm. New York, NY: Sharpe.

Pérez, A., & Del Bosque, I. R. (2012). The role of CSR in the corporate identity of banking service providers. *Journal of Business Ethics, 108*(2), 145–166.

Pérez, A., Martínez, P., & Del Bosque, I. R. (2013). The development of a stakeholder-based scale for measuring corporate social responsibility in the banking industry. *Service Business*, *7*(3), 459–481.

Phuong, N. T., Fisher, G., & Mujtaba, B. G. (2014). Ethical decision-making of banking and finance professionals and students. *Asian Journal of Business Ethics*, *3*(2), 141–153.

Pineiro-Chousa, J., Vizcaíno-González, M., López-Cabarcos, M. **Á.**, & Romero-Castro, N. (2017). Managing reputational risk through environmental management and reporting: An options theory approach. *Sustainability*, *9*(3), 376.

Porter, M. E. (1991). Towards a dynamic theory of strategy. *Strategic Management Journal*, *12*(S2), 95–117.

Porter, M. E., & Kramer, M. R. (2011). The big idea: Creating shared value. *Harvard Business Review*, *89*(1), 2-17.

Preston, L. E., & O'Bannon, D. P. (1997). The corporate social-financial performance relationship: A typology and analysis. *Business & Society*, *36*(4), 419–429.

Renneboog, L., Ter Horst, J., & Zhang, C. (2008a). Socially responsible investments: Institutional aspects, performance, and investor behavior. *Journal of Banking & Finance*, *32*(9), 1723–1742.

Renneboog, L., Ter Horst, J., & Zhang, C. (2008b). The price of ethics and stakeholder governance: The performance of socially responsible mutual funds. *Journal of Corporate Finance*, *14*(3), 302–322.

Richardson, B. J. (2009). Keeping ethical investment ethical: Regulatory issues for investing for sustainability. *Journal of Business Ethics*, *87*(4), 555–572.

Safakli, O. V. (2007). Ethical perceptions of customers towards the services of foreign branch banks in Northern Cyprus. *Journal of Applied Sciences*, *7*(2), 294–297.

Salzmann, A. J. (2013). The integration of sustainability into the theory and practice of finance: an overview of the state of the art and outline of future developments. Journal of business economics, 83(6), 555-576.

San Emeterio, J., & Retolaza, J. L. (2003). ¿Existe Espacio para una Banca Ética? [Is There Space for an Ethical Banking?]. Lan Harremanak: Revista de relaciones laborales, 9, 127-163.

San-Jose, L., Retolaza, J. L., & Gutierrez-Goiria, J. (2011). Are ethical banks different? A comparative analysis using the radical affinity index. *Journal of Business Ethics*, *100*(1), 151-173.

Santiso, J. (2006). *Latin America's political economy of the possible*. Cambridge, MA: The MIT Press.

Saunders, A. (2000). Financial institutions management: A modern perspective. New York, NY: The Irwin/McGraw-Hill

Scholtens, B., & Dam, L. (2007). Banking on the Equator. Are banks that adopted the Equator Principles different from non-adopters? *World Development*, *35*(8), 1307–1328.

Segura, E. A., & Martínez, M. D. C. V. (2018). Análisis estratégico de la Banca ética en España a través de Triodos Bank. Financiación de proyectos sociales y medioambientales [Strategic analysis of Ethical Banking in Spain through Triodos Bank. Financing of social and environmental projects]. *CIRIEC-España: Revista de Economía Pública, Social y Cooperativa*, 2018(92), 87–120

Sen, S., & Bhattacharya, C. B. (2001). Does doing good always lead to doing better? Consumer reactions to corporate social responsibility. *Journal of Marketing Research*, *38*(2), 225–243.

Shankman, N. A. (1999). Reframing the debate between agency and stakeholder theories of the firm. *Journal of Business Ethics*, *19*(4), 319–334.

Shen, L., Shuai, C., Jiao, L., Tan, Y., & Song, X. (2016). A global perspective on the sustainable performance of urbanization. *Sustainability*, *8*(8), 783.

Singh, A., & Cerisola, M. (2006). *Sustaining Latin America's Resurgence: Some Historical Perspectives* (Working Paper No. 06/252). International Monetary Fund. Retrieved from https://www.imf.org/external/pubs/ft/wp/2006/wp06252.pdf

Tarantola, A. M. (2009, February 27). Cooperative Banks and Competition: Local Vocation and Governance Issues. Bank of Italy: Taormina.

Viganò, F., & Nicolai, D. (2009). CSR in the European banking sector: evidence from a survey. In R. Barth & F. Wolff (Eds.), *Corporate Social Responsibility in Europe: Rhetoric and Realities* (pp. 95–108). Cheltenham, UK: Edward Elgar.

Weber, O., Scholz, R. W., & Michalik, G. (2010). Incorporating sustainability criteria into credit risk management. *Business Strategy and the Environment*, *19*(1), 39–50.

Wu, M. W., & Shen, C. H. (2013). Corporate social responsibility in the banking industry: Motives and financial performance. *Journal of Banking & Finance*, *37*(9), 3529–3547.

Xifra, J., & Ordeix, E. (2009). Managing reputational risk in an economic downturn: The case of Banco Santander. *Public Relations Review*, *35*(4), 353–360.

Yunus, M., Moingeon, B., & Lehmann-Ortega, L. (2010). Building social business models: Lessons from the Grameen experience. *Long Range Planning*, *43*(2), 308–325.

Zalan, T., & Toufaily, E. (2017). The Promise of Fintech in Emerging Markets: Not as Disruptive. Contemporary Economics, 11(4), 415-430.

1

Working Capital Management through the Business Cycle: Evidence from the Corporate Sector in Poland

Paweł Mielcarz[1], Dmytro Osiichuk[1], Paweł Wnuczak[2]

ABSTRACT The paper examines the influence of the business cycle on working capital management strate based on evidence from the Polish corporate sector. By exploring the interrelation between w ing capital investment and profitability ratios, we attempt to define the respective transmis mechanisms and summarize the principles of sound financial management across the econo cycle. We found that more profitable companies tend to implement a more conservative worl capital management strategy during recessions and that underperforming firms may be ur to cut working capital in response to plummeting cash flows. The accumulation of precautior cash reserves appears to help firms navigate through times of economic turmoil. The paper h lights the importance of working capital management for optimizing a firm's profitability. Rese outcomes may point to the redistributive function of trade finance under conditions of finan constraints, which become particularly acute during troughs aggravated by a credit market cru

KEY WORDS: working capital, business cycle, profitability

[1] Akademia Leona Kozminskiego - Department of Finance, Poland; [2] Akademia Leona Kozminskiego, Poland

1. Introduction

Efficient working capital management represents an important tool for optimizing a firm's liquidity and exploiting its value-creating potential (Ferrando & Mulier, 2013). We investigate the influence of economic slump on the working capital management strategy by analyzing the interrelation between a firm's profitability ratios and working capital investment dynamics.

Theoretical and empirical evidence suggests that capital market imperfections may have important consequences for corporate decision-making (F zari, Hubbard, Petersen, Blinder, & Poterba, 1 Moyen, 2004; Myers & Majluf, 1984). In the contex financing constraints theory, the analysis of econo crisis settings represents a case of particular inte as troughs may considerably limit access to ex nal finance and exacerbate the deficiency in inte sources of cash flows. In turn, impaired financing pacity may significantly alter the patterns of work capital investment, which may be used to tempora improve liquidity and even substitute for other sou of finance (Fazzari & Petersen, 1993).

The 2008 financial crisis became a natural econo experiment allowing deeper insights into corpo practices under conditions of an overall downt

Correspondence concerning this article should be addressed to: **Paweł Mielcarz**, Akademia Leona Kozminskiego - Department of Finance, Jagiellonska 57/59, Warszawa 03-301, Poland. E-mail: pmielcarz@kozminski.edu.pl

The research literature barely discusses the problems of working capital management through the business cycle. This paper attempts to fill this research gap by presenting findings for the Polish corporate sector. The paper is structured as follows: first, we offer an overview of existing research; second, we elaborate research hypotheses and present empirical results accompanied by a discussion of implications for operational and tactical decision-making at the firm level.

2. Theoretical Overview

Several studies (e.g., Chiou, Cheng, & Wu, 2006; Ng, Smith, & Smith, 1999) have explored the determinants of working capital investment in an attempt to formulate the postulates of an optimal management strategy allowing one to secure a company's solvency and ensure the smooth workflow of business operations. Existing empirical literature suggests that financing constraints and phases of the business cycle are among the key factors influencing the modes of working capital finance.

Aktas, Croci, and Petmezas (2015) studied the value relevance of working capital management strategy in a sample of US companies and reported the existence of an optimal level of working capital investment. Gradual transition to the optimum allows one to secure superior operating performance and gains in shareholder value. Additionally, spare resources released by optimization of working capital management may be used to finance positive-NPV projects such as acquisitions.

2.1. *Impact of Financing Constraints on Working Capital Management*

Petersen and Rajan (1997) suggest that trade finance may perform a redistributive function by channeling credit resources from less financially constrained companies, which have a better access to capital markets, to more vulnerable firms. Hence, trade credit substitutes for external finance in companies facing information asymmetry problems. Additionally, financially sound companies were found to grant relatively more trade credit, which may be attributed to their willingness to secure future business, lower degree of information asymmetry and reliance on secured credit backed by goods purchased. Similar findings are reported by Cuñat (2007) for UK companies: in order to preserve customer relationships, firms may be willing to relax trade credit conditions, thereby effectively cushioning the cash flow constraints faced by their customers and alleviating the problem of limited access to capital markets.

Nilsen (2002) reports findings that may question the redistributive function of trade credit, since both small and large firms are reported to increase reliance on trade finance during negative monetary shocks accompanied by a credit crunch. On the other hand, the postulates of financing constraints theory hold with large companies recurring to external borrowing to a greater extent than small companies experiencing a cash shortage. Yang (2011) concludes that during the periods of monetary contraction companies tend to substitute trade credit for bank loans due to the increased cost of external capital, while during monetary expansion trade finance and bank loans appear to exhibit a complementarity effect. The same study reports a high sensitivity of inventory investment to exchange rate fluctuations for financially constrained companies.

Casey and O'Toole (2014) analyzed the lending patterns of SMEs in the Eurozone and concluded that financially constrained companies were more likely to rely on trade finance, recur to intercompany credit financing and apply for grants.

Opler, Pinkowitz, Stulz, and Williamson (1999) examined the cash holding patterns based on US firm-level data. Companies with significant growth potential and volatile cash flows tended to hold larger stocks of cash. These companies were more likely to experience financing constraints. On the other hand, firms with investment credit rating tended to hold relatively smaller amounts of cash. Evidence suggests that the principal cash-holding motive of constrained companies may be that of compensating for potential operating losses. Since an economic downturn may induce a considerable fall in sales, holding precautionary cash reserves appears to be a sound decision.

2.2. *Influence of Working Capital Management on Profitability*

Deloof (2003) analyzed the influence of working capital management on the profitability of Belgian companies. The reduction of receivables and inventory turnover periods were found to improve companies' operating performance. The study also found a negative relationship between operating profit and account payables, which may be explained by reversed causality: underperforming companies short of funds require more time to pay their suppliers.

For a set of Finnish companies, Enqvist, Graham, and Nikkinen (2014) found a negative relationship between a firm's profitability, measured by gross operating income and return on assets, and the cash conversion cycle, with the effect being particularly pronounced during an economic crisis. A negative relationship was also found between profitability and accounts payable days as well as between profitability and inventory levels. The effects were more pronounced during an economic slump. The results suggest that in order to alleviate the negative consequences of unfavorable conjuncture, management should try to minimize receivables and inventories and extend accounts payable days.

Garcia-Teruel and Martinez-Solano (2007) report a negative relationship between cash conversion cycle and profitability: a reduction of inventories and accounts receivable appears to improve KPIs. Based on data from the Portuguese corporate sector, Pais and Gama (2015) conclude that an application of a more aggressive working capital management strategy by SMEs may enhance their operating performance. Additionally, reduction in accounts payable days was found to positively influence profitability, which resonates with previously cited evidence.

By examining the data for the food industry in Poland and in Eurozone countries, Bieniasz and Gołaś (2011) corroborated a negative relationship between cash conversion cycle and profitability. Large companies in the Polish food industry were manifesting the highest efficiency in managing their working capital and were concomitantly the best performers in terms of profitability. Based on data from the Polish stock market, Bolek (2013) concluded that there was no correlation between working capital management policy and profitability ratios.

2.3. Working Capital Management under Conditions of Economic Turmoil

Campello, Graham, and Harvey (2010) used qualitative research methodology to determine the influence of financing constraints on corporate decision-making during the 2008 financial crisis. The companies labeled as financially constrained were more prone to cut investment expenditures, deplete precautionary cash reserves, rely on credit lines and external financing, and sell assets in order to compensate for internal funds deficiency. Additionally, due to restricted access to external finance, constrained companies reported having missed attractive investment opportunities.

Love, Preve, and Sarria-Allende (2007) studied the influence of credit contraction during the 1997 crisis in Asia on the dynamics of trade finance in emerging economies. Crisis outbreak was found to be accompanied by a trade credit expansion followed by subsequent gradual decay. The authors conclude that the contraction had a supply-side origin whereby financial constraints forced the companies to slash trade finance in order to preserve liquidity. The same study reports that companies which experienced a cash flow shortage and largely depended on short-term debt financing were more likely to cut back on trade credit and increase trade payables.

Gertler and Gilchrist (1994) found that large and small companies react differently to monetary policy shocks. Large companies tend to be heavily dependent on short-term debt financing, which gradually increases through the phase of economic growth and subsequently falls following the outbreak of an economic slump. Small companies exhibit more conservatism and start slashing short-term debt before the recession begins. Small firms are also found to disproportionately reduce inventory expenditures compared to large companies. In line with findings by Fazzari and Petersen (1993), this may suggest that financially constrained companies may use working capital as a reserve of liquidity, which may temporarily make up for the internal cash flow deficiency.

The advent of a financial crisis may cause substantial shifts in a firm's strategic positioning, with the more financially sound companies benefitting at the expense of the more fragile ones. Baskin (1987) argues that companies may hold additional amounts of cash as a deterrent for potential entrants. The cash reserves may become a worthy argument in the competitive rivalry.

The problematics of working capital management through the business cycle in the emerging market settings appear to have been insufficiently explored. The Polish market is dynamically developing and may exhibit features divergent from the patterns generally bserved in mature markets. Additionally, empirical vidence suggests that Polish companies may be con-onted with significant financing constraints (Jackow-z, Kozłowski, & Mielcarz, 2016), which may exercise negative impact on their investment policy during conomic turmoil (Jackowicz & Mielcarz, 2015). The aper, therefore, contributes to the general discussion f working capital management, with a particular fo-us on the impact of economic cycle on managerial ecision-making.

. Hypothesis Development

Vorking capital investment is influenced by three rincipal considerations: maintaining uninterrupted vorkflow of operations, ensuring sufficient liquidity nd solvency, and optimizing profitability of invest-ent. Hence, firms constantly face important tradeoffs regard to determining the structure of working capi-l. Expansion of a company's operations induces an crease in working capital investment. Conservative anagement of inventories allows for the reduction of rdering costs, secure purchase discounts, and elimi-ation of the risk of stock-outs (Corsten & Gruen, 004). On the other hand, aggressive inventory man-gement and implementation of a just-in-time system educes holding costs, the risk of obsolescence and pil-erage. Relaxing terms of trade credit may allow firms increase sales and secure future business by im-roving customer relationships (Summers & Wilson, 002). Simultaneously, the proportion of bad debts and e overall credit risk increase. An increase in trade ayables days may help to improve short-term liquid-y; however, this most certainly jeopardizes a firm's elationship with suppliers. In addition, additional vestment in working capital diverts limited financial esources from other productive uses, which poses the roblem of trade-off between liquidity and profitabil-y. Conservative management sets sufficiency of work-g capital investment as a priority, while aggressive trategies help to maximize profitability (Kieschnick, aplante, & Moussawi, 2013). This line of reasoning al-ows us to formulate the following hypothesis H1.

I1: Conservative working capital management strat-gy reduces a firm's profitability.

H1 will be tested for each element of working capital nvestment separately, i.e., for investment in account receivables (H1.1), trade payables (H1.2), inventories (H1.3) and cash reserves (H1.4).

The situation may look different during economic tur-moil. Due to external shocks (demand-side translating into decreased sales, or supply-side causing production costs to rise), the corporate sector experiences a short-age of internal finance. In an overall economic slump, capital market imperfections and the problem of in-formation asymmetry are amplified by uncertainty, and financing constraints become tighter. Under these circumstances, companies face the following trade-offs. On the one hand, due to restricted access to external fi-nancing, the firm may treat working capital as a liquid-ity reserve and deplete it in order to compensate for the temporary insufficiency of operating cash flows. This implies an implementation of an aggressive working capital management strategy: pressure for receivables collection, sale of excess inventories and withdrawal of outstanding purchase orders, delays in payments to suppliers and depletion of cash reserves to cover discre-tionary spending. This strategy may help to amass nec-essary resources to cover the liquidity gap and finance profitable investment projects (or at least avoid cutting back on investment expenses and R&D). This strategy, however, has important drawbacks. Chasing receiv-ables impairs customer relationships, while failure to pay suppliers in time may negatively influence sup-pliers' business. Similarly, the breach of purchase con-tracts and refusal to reorder inventory may jeopardize counterparty relationships. Depletion of cash reserves may be negatively perceived by the market, as the com-pany faces the probability of a severe liquidity short-age, with solvency risks being particularly high during financial crises. Implementation of a more conservative strategy stressing the importance of long-term business relations may help to secure future business, enhance trust and maintain liquidity (by accumulating cash in-stead of spending it; e.g., to smooth investment). This strategy may, however, severely damage profitability. We attempt to determine which strategy yields the best payoff. Figure 1 summarizes the presented strategies of working capital management.

H2: During an economic downturn, an aggressive working capital management strategy increases a firm's profitability.

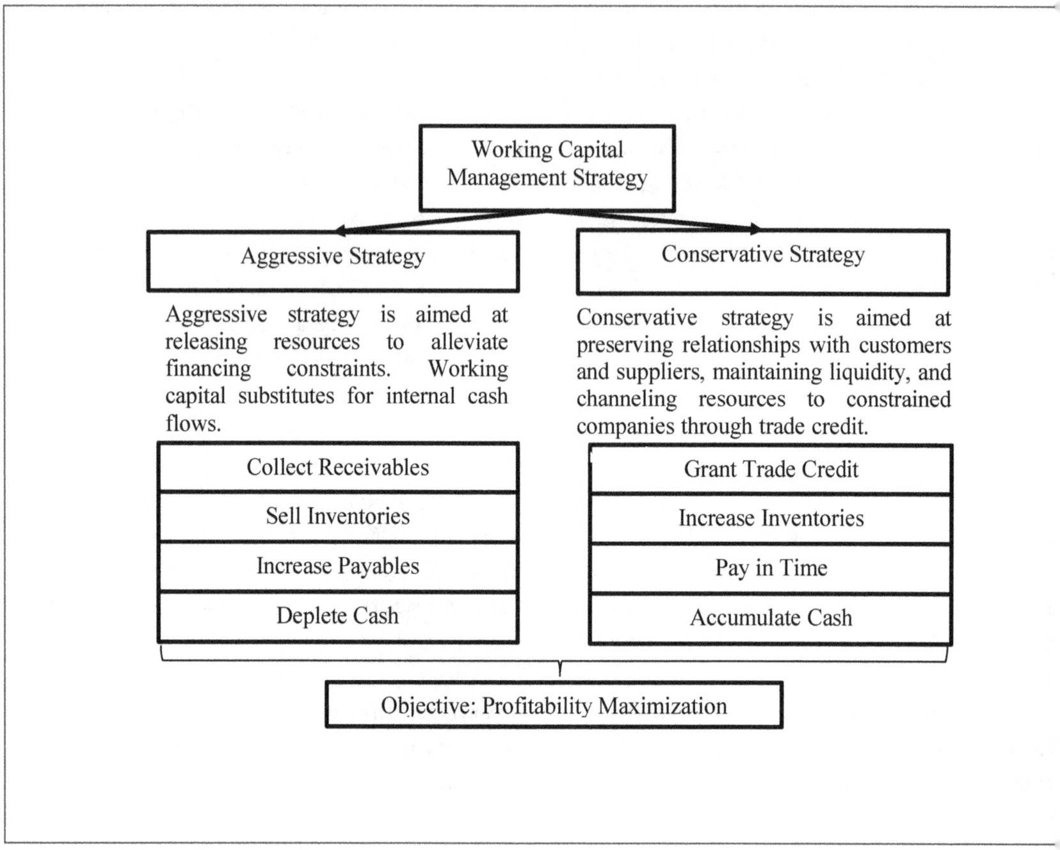

Figure 1. Working Capital Management Strategies During Economic Crises

H2 will be tested for each element of working capital investment separately, i.e., for investment in accounts receivable (H2.1), trade payables (H2.2), inventories (H2.3) and cash reserves (H2.4).

4. Data and Methodology

The sample comprises 719 Polish companies quoted on the Warsaw Stock Exchange, New Connect and OTC market. The resulting unbalanced panel dataset includes yearly firm-level data for the period 1997-2014 retrieved from the Notoria database. Financial companies were excluded from the sample, while those which no longer exist were left in order to account for survivorship bias.

We constructed static panel regression models with random effects. All models incorporate a year dummy variable to account for common macroeconomic and period-specific effects. All nominal vari-ables are scaled by total assets to avoid the heterosce-dasticity problem.

The econometric model used to test the research hy-potheses is presented by Equation 1.

$$Profitability_{it} = \\ = \beta_0 + \beta_1 WCI_{it} + \beta_2 WCI_{it} Crisis + \beta' Control_{it} + \varepsilon_{it} \quad (1)$$

where i encodes the firm, t encodes the observatio time period, $Profitability_{it}$ – dependent variable rep resented by return on assets (ROA), WCI_{it} – workin capital investment including cash scaled by total as sets, *Crisis* – binary dummy variable which is equa to 1 for the period 2008-2010 and 0 for other peri ods; $WCI_{it} x Crisis$ – interaction term used to test H2 $Control_{it}$ – a set of control variables discussed below

ε_{it} – error term. To test H1.1, H1.2, H1.3, and H1.4, the independent variable WCI_{it} is replaced with the respective element of working capital: YoY change in receivables (*Rec*), YoY change in payables (*P*), YoY change in inventory (*Inv*) and YoY change in cash and cash equivalents holdings (*Cash*) scaled by total assets.

Control Variables

Size. A natural logarithm of firms' fixed assets (*Log Fixed Assets*) is used to control for the influence of size on profitability. Empirical evidence demonstrates clear differences in patters of working capital management between small and large companies. Larger companies may be better at managing their working capital (Moss & Stein, 1993). At the same time, they are less likely to be financially constrained and may afford higher working capital investments in order to boost sales and prevent stock-outs or liquidity problems.

Growth opportunities. We use price-to-book value (*P/BV*) as a proxy for growth opportunities (Fazzari et al., 1988). Firms having valuable real options are more likely to face financing constraints and experience a shortage of internally generated cash flow, which may translate into more aggressive working capital management. Concomitantly, growth companies are more likely to accumulate cash in anticipation of attractive investment projects or in order to reduce reliance on more expensive external financing.

Leverage ratio. In addition to potentially boosting return on equity, increased gearing may alleviate the agency problem (Jensen, 1986) and stimulate more efficient working capital management.

Investment. Capital expenditure scaled by total assets (*Capex/Assets*) controls for the influence of investment policy on profitability.

Operating cash flow. Operating cash flows scaled by total assets (*OCF/Assets*) constitute an important determinant of profitability and working capital investment (Chiou et al., 2006). Generating significant OCF allows the firm to implement a conservative working capital management strategy (Fazzari & Petersen, 1993), accumulate cash, and finance value-generating investments.

Dividend payout (*Dividend Payout Ratio*). In accordance with signaling theory (Grullon, Michaely, & Swaminathan, 2002), dividend policy may serve as a predictor of a firm's profitability. Gradual transition from the growth phase to maturity and exhaustion of attractive investment projects pushes the company to pay out dividends.

External finance (*ExF/Assets*). The variable is calculated as a ratio of additional debt incurred to total assets. Braun and Larrain (2005) report that industries which predominantly rely on external financing experience more hardships during economic downturns, with the effect being particularly pronounced during a credit crunch. External finance may also be used to accommodate a conservative working capital management strategy.

Sales and sales growth. Revenue scaled by assets (*Sales/Assets*) is included as an alternative proxy for availability of internal financing. Sales growth (*Sales Growth*) may serve as a proxy for revenue volatility, which, aside from being a determinant of profitability, may also influence working capital management strategy. Being unable to accurately predict future sales, companies may choose to hold additional inventories (Hill, Kelly, & Highfield, 2010). Management may also decide to collect receivables faster or extend payables days in order to accommodate negative sales fluctuations.

5. Empirical Results

Tables 1 to 5 present the results of testing of the research hypotheses. The tested econometric models have satisfactory econometric properties and allow us to derive valid conclusions. The explanatory variables are jointly statistically significant at the conventional levels. Individual regressors preserve statistical significance after introducing additional control variables. The model specification was checked for possible collinearity issues using variance inflation factors diagnostics.

The results presented in Table 1 positively verify H1. We conclude that increased investment in working capital deteriorates a company's profitability measured

Table 1. Results of H1 and H2 Tests

	Regressand: Return on Assets							
Model No	**1**		**2**		**3**		**4**	
no. of observations	4519		4519		4519		4470	
Wald (joint)	1199	***	1205	***	1218	***	1206	***
R^2	0,2248298		0,2256386		0,2273674		0,2289685	
AR(1) test	-2,359	**	-2,385	**	-2,4	**	-2,003	**
AR(2) test	-6,346	***	-6,412	***	-6,452	***	-5,837	***
Constant	-0,0416137		-0,0408299		-0,0743248	*	0,0256946	
	(0.044)		(0.044)		(0.044)		(0.043)	
WCI/Assets	-0,214	***	-0,215	***	-0,221	***	-0,215	***
	(0.021)		(0.021)		(0.021)		(0.021)	
WCIxCrisis	0,129808	***	0,136997	***	0,138785	***	0,137133	***
	(0.040)		(0.040)		(0.040)		(0.039)	
Log Fixed Assets	0,0274494	***	0,0273511	***	0,0290573	***	0,0207579	***
	(0.004)		(0.004)		(0.004)		(0.004)	
P/BV	-0,003	***	-0,003	***	-0,003	***	-0,003	***
	(0.001)		(0.001)		(0.001)		(0.001)	
Leverage Ratio	-0,472982	***	-0,473578	***	-0,473643	***	-0,467534	***
	(0.016)		(0.016)		(0.016)		(0.015)	
Capex/Assets	-0,0456002		-0,0083		-0,0409433		-0,037519	
	(0.037)		(0.041)		(0.039)		(0.037)	
OCF/Assets	-0,038	*	-0,058	**				
	(0.021)		(0.023)					
Dividend Payout Ratio	-2,13918E-05		-2,15312E-05		-0,000021856		-1,99934E-05	
	(000)		(000)		(000)		(000)	
ExF/Assets			-0,0787002	**	-0,0427056		-0,0441457	
			(0.036)		(0.033)		(0.032)	
Sales/Assets					0,0133138	***		
					(0.003)			
Sales Growth							1,10647E-05	
							(000)	

Notes: All models include the time dummies (not reported). This table presents the static panel model estimates. The heteroscedasticity robust standard errors are provided in parentheses. ***, **, and * indicate significance at the 1%, 5%, and 10 levels, respectively.

ble 2. Results of H1.1 and H2.1 Tests

	Regressand: Return on Assets							
odel No	1		2		3		4	
. of observations	4233		4225		4254		4118	
ld (joint)	615,4	***	622,7	***	668,1	***	644,4	***
2	0,164772		0,1661608		0,1730705		0,176903	
(1) test	6	***	5,906	***	6,035	***	6,861	***
(2) test	-2,964	***	-3,039	***	-3,094	***	-3,848	***
nstant	0,101114	***	0,102532	***	0,0781989	***	0,156908	***
	(0.022)		(0.022)		(0.023)		(0.023)	
c/Assets	-0,284	***	-0,283	***	-0,290	***	-0,251	***
	(0.025)		(0.025)		(0.025)		(0.025)	
cxCrisis	-0,159514	**	-0,160905	**	-0,163396	**	-0,185399	***
	(0.073)		(0.073)		(0.072)		(0.071)	
g Fixed Assets	0,0043718	**	0,00426371	**	0,00593107	***	3,3376E-05	
	(0.002)		(0.002)		(0.002)		(0.002)	
3V	-0,001	**	-0,001	**	-0,001	**	-0,001	***
	(000)		(000)		(000)		(000)	
verage Ratio	-0,271937	***	-0,271909	***	-0,276187	***	-0,26436	***
	(0.013)		(0.013)		(0.013)		(0.013)	
pex/Assets	0,00036825		0,0282329		0,0251842		0,0140458	
	(0.027)		(0.029)		(0.028)		(0.027)	
F/Assets	0,015		-0,004					
	(0.019)		(0.020)					
idend Payout Ratio	-7,0481E-06		-7,3662E-06		-7,2273E-06		-9,551E-06	
	(000)		(000)		(000)		(000)	
/Assets			-0,0954612	***	-0,0909394	***	-0,0673977	**
			(0.033)		(0.031)		(0.030)	
es/Assets					0,00906905	***		
					(0.002)			
es Growth							0,0199422	***
							(0.004)	

tes: All models include the time dummies (not reported). This table presents the static panel model estimates. The het-
scedasticity robust standard errors are provided in parentheses. ***, **, and * indicate significance at the 1%, 5%, and 10%
els, respectively.

Table 3. Results of H1.2 and H2.2 Tests

	Regressand: Return on Assets							
Model No	**1**		**2**		**3**		**4**	
no. of observations	4152		4144		4174		4053	
Wald (joint)	390,7	***	398,8	***	429,5	***	485,3	***
R^2	0,1269279		0,1285512		0,1339776		0,1500387	
AR(1) test	6,17	***	6,096	***	6,022	***	7,254	***
AR(2) test	-2,617	***	-2,659	***	-2,639	***	-3,168	***
Constant	0,12249	***	0,124394	***	0,104875	***	0,15575	***
	(0.022)		(0.022)		(0.022)		(0.022)	
P/Assets	0,126	***	0,125	***	0,122	***	0,087	***
	(0.034)		(0.034)		(0.034)		(0.033)	
PxCrisis	-0,186037	***	-0,183346	***	-0,177578	***	-0,1527	**
	(0.069)		(0.069)		(0.069)		(0.066)	
Log Fixed Assets	0,00129618		0,001168		0,00242605		-0,00132526	
	(0.002)		(0.002)		(0.002)		(0.002)	
P/BV	-0,001	***	-0,001	***	-0,001	***	-0,002	***
	(000)		(000)		(000)		(000)	
Leverage Ratio	-0,266182	***	-0,266184	***	-0,270418	***	-0,266018	***
	(0.014)		(0.014)		(0.014)		(0.014)	
Capex/Assets	-0,00727065		0,0201015		0,0174573		0,0136623	
	(0.027)		(0.029)		(0.028)		(0.027)	
OCF/Assets	0,013		-0,005					
	(0.019)		(0.020)					
Dividend Payout Ratio	-7,8974E-06		-8,1848E-06		-7,8493E-06		-1,0698E-05	
	(000)		(000)		(000)		(000)	
ExF/Assets			-0,0941861	***	-0,0861712	***	-0,0641513	**
			(0.032)		(0.030)		(0.029)	
Sales/Assets					0,00835911	***		
					(0.002)			
Sales Growth							0,0287324	***
							(0.004)	

Notes: All models include the time dummies (not reported). This table presents the static panel model estimates. The h eroscedasticity robust standard errors are provided in parentheses. ***, **, and * indicate significance at the 1%, 5%, and 10 levels, respectively.

ble 4. Results of H1.3 and H2.3 Tests

	Regressand: Return on Assets							
odel No	**1**		**2**		**3**		**4**	
›. of observations	4319		4311		4341		4199	
ald (joint)	573,7	***	581,8	***	623	***	641,9	***
^2	0,1559928		0,1575083		0,1637621		0,1745289	
R(1) test	5,794	***	5,663	***	5,696	***	6,306	***
R(2) test	-2,337	**	-2,373	**	-2,445	**	-2,822	***
onstant	0,116471	***	0,118595	***	0,0941973	***	0,165085	***
	(0.022)		(0.022)		(0.022)		(0.022)	
v/Assets	-0,402	***	-0,402	***	-0,412	***	-0,369	***
	(0.038)		(0.038)		(0.038)		(0.037)	
vxCrisis	0,425574	***	0,426001	***	0,427504	***	0,360209	***
	(0.065)		(0.065)		(0.065)		(0.064)	
og Fixed Assets	0,0022711		0,00212768		0,00372943	*	-0,00166973	
	(0.002)		(0.002)		(0.002)		(0.002)	
BV	-0,001	**	-0,001	**	-0,001	**	-0,001	***
	(000)		(000)		(000)		(000)	
everage Ratio	-0,274119	***	-0,273966	***	-0,27791	***	-0,266423	***
	(0.013)		(0.013)		(0.013)		(0.013)	
apex/Assets	-0,00165517		0,0258291		0,0210413		0,0127204	
	(0.028)		(0.030)		(0.028)		(0.027)	
CF/Assets	0,007		-0,011					
	(0.020)		(0.021)					
ividend Payout Ratio	-9,7852E-06		-1,0068E-05		-9,8037E-06		-1,1563E-05	
	(000)		(000)		(000)		(000)	
F/Assets			-0,0942663	***	-0,0859152	***	-0,0654962	**
			(0.033)		(0.031)		(0.030)	
ales/Assets					0,00946038	***		
					(0.002)			
ales Growth							0,027015	***
							(0.004)	

otes: All models include the time dummies (not reported). This table presents the static panel model estimates. The het-
oscedasticity robust standard errors are provided in parentheses. ***, **, and * indicate significance at the 1%, 5%, and 10%
vels, respectively.

Table 5. Results of H1.4 and H2.4 Tests

				Regressand: Return on Assets				
Model No	**1**		**2**		**3**		**4**	
no. of observations	4182		4174		4204		4082	
Wald (joint)	486,5	***	491,7	***	519,9	***	544,4	***
R^2	0,1444091		0,1454266		0,1497415		0,1604576	
AR(1) test	5,766	***	5,652	***	5,851	***	7,514	***
AR(2) test	-1,78	*	-1,765	*	-1,821	*	-3,323	***
Constant	0,0926877	***	0,0942514	***	0,0740542	***	0,134438	***
	(0.024)		(0.024)		(0.024)		(0.024)	
Cash/Assets	0,105	***	0,107	***	0,101	***	0,110	***
	(0.036)		(0.036)		(0.036)		(0.035)	
CashxCrisis	0,14614	**	0,144391	**	0,152597	**	0,0903746	
	(0.068)		(0.068)		(0.068)		(0.066)	
Log Fixed Assets	0,00269016		0,0025964		0,00388856	**	-0,00051788	
	(0.002)		(0.002)		(0.002)		(0.002)	
P/BV	-0,001	**	-0,001	**	-0,001	**	-0,001	***
	(000)		(000)		(000)		(000)	
Leverage Ratio	-0,274214	***	-0,274061	***	-0,276438	***	-0,262868	***
	(0.014)		(0.014)		(0.014)		(0.013)	
Capex/Assets	-0,00185726		0,0221766		0,0157842		0,0085085	
	(0.028)		(0.030)		(0.029)		(0.028)	
OCF/Assets	-0,001		-0,016					
	(0.020)		(0.021)					
Dividend Payout Ratio	-1,1613E-05		-1,1907E-05		-1,1288E-05		-1,2386E-05	
	(000)		(000)		(000)		(000)	
ExF/Assets			-0,0807768	**	-0,0677732	**	-0,0571014	*
			(0.033)		(0.031)		(0.030)	
Sales/Assets					0,00733934	***		
					(0.002)			
Sales Growth							0,0300307	***
							(0.004)	

Notes: All models include the time dummies (not reported). This table presents the static panel model estimates. The h eroscedasticity robust standard errors are provided in parentheses. ***, **, and * indicate significance at the 1%, 5%, and 1 levels, respectively.

by ROA. Larger companies are found to perform better, while those having more immediate growth opportunities appear to underperform in terms of profitability ratios. In line with expectations, companies with higher sales have better KPIs, and those relying more on external financing may have a lower ROA. The cost effect of increased working capital investment generally outweighs the benefits of procuring long-term business relationships through granting trade credit, investing heavily in inventory and paying suppliers on short notice. This implies that companies may boost their profitability by reducing cash conversion cycles. As seen in Tables 2 to 4, the same inference holds for particular elements of working capital. Hence, H1.1, H1.2, and H1.3 cannot be rejected. Profitability is inversely related to investment in receivables and inventory, and positively related to outstanding accounts payable. Interestingly, the amount of funds held in cash and cash equivalents is positively correlated with profitability, which rejects H1.4. This may suggest that the cost effect of cash holding may be overridden by precautionary motives. Additionally, profitable high-growth companies which tend to rely on internal funds for financing investment expenditure may accumulate cash in anticipation of value-generating projects. Hence, financing constraints may be the defining determinant of increased cash holdings.

The results look different for the crisis settings. The 2008 turmoil, which began in the financial markets and gradually spread to the real economy, engendered a major negative demand shock for the corporate sector. Firms had to cope with several challenges: slump in aggregate demand (caused by plummeting private consumption, investment spending, and public expenditure), overindebtedness of the corporate sector entailing the need to delay investment projects, and a credit crunch caused by a conservative monetary policy and prevailing uncertainty. Limited access to external financing, amplified by decreasing sales revenues, was an immediate repercussion of the implemented economic policy. Under growing financing constraints, firms may have altered their working capital management strategies.

Table 1 present the results of H2 testing. During the crisis, increased working capital investment was positively correlated with profitability. Thus, we reject H2. This may indicate that the cost effect lost its role as a key determinant of working capital investment, giving priority to financing constraints. Tables 2 to 5 further expand the argumentation by analyzing each element of working capital. The coefficients for the interaction term *ReceivablesxCrisis* are persistently negative and statistically significant, suggesting that chasing receivables may improve corporate performance under economic distress. Hence, we fail to reject H2.1. Negative coefficients at payables may suggest that an attempt to fill the liquidity gap by delaying payments to suppliers may jeopardize customer relationships and worsen the company's financial performance. It may also point to the simple fact that more profitable companies tend to be less reliant on trade credit during a financial crisis. Underperforming companies have to delay payments to suppliers and negotiate extensions of trade credits in order to make up for incurred operating losses. For inventory investments, decision-making also appears to be altered by the crisis settings. More profitable companies may afford a more conservative inventory management policy. They may do so in anticipation of future sales growth or in order to maintain stable relationships with suppliers. Under the latter assumption, the theory supporting the redistributive function of trade finance under conditions of financing constraints may be substantiated. Less constrained companies use trade relationships to channel financial resources to the more vulnerable firms. Limited access to capital markets reverts the criteria of optimal inventory management by shifting the accent from cost considerations to interfirm relations. Less profitable companies which endure severe cash shortages are forced to drastically reduce their working capital investment in order to release resources and cover the internal liquidity gap. This conclusion corroborates findings by Gertler and Gilchrist (1994).

Table 5 shows that firms which hold higher cash reserves during a crisis tend to perform better in terms of profitability ratios. Again, the precautionary motive and anticipation of attractive investment projects may explain the preference for cash. This relationship may also constitute an argument for the presence of financing constraints.

6. Concluding Remarks

The paper proves that financial crisis settings considerably change working capital decisions. Generally, it has been shown that firms may enhance their profitability by optimizing their cash operating cycle, i.e., by improving receivables collection, improving procedures for collecting bad debts, decreasing inventory investments and extensively using trade credit from suppliers. These findings highlight the importance of working capital management as a potential source of efficiency improvement and persistent competitive advantage. There may be a need to elaborate new planning techniques in order to improve working capital management practices.

Under conditions of increased capital constraints, the guidance into the process of working capital management may need additional clarification. More profitable companies appear to implement a more conservative working capital management strategy. It may be an argument in favor of the redistributive function of trade finance during crises. Financially constrained companies may be urged to cut their working capital investment in order to accommodate a reduction in internal cash flows. This paper underlines the importance of working capital management through the business cycle and accentuates the need to make careful projections in anticipation of business fluctuations.

References

Aktas, N., Croci, E., & Petmezas, D. (2015). Is working capital management value-enhancing? Evidence from firm performance and investments. *Journal of Corporate Finance, 30*, 98–113.

Baskin, J. B. (1987). Corporate liquidity in games of monopoly power. *The Review of Economics and Statistics, 69*(2), 312–319.

Bieniasz, A., & Gołaś, Z. (2011). The influence of working capital management on the food industry enterprises profitability. *Contemporary Economics, 5*(4), 68–81.

Bolek, M. (2013). Working capital management, profitability and risk - analyse of companies listed on the Warsaw Stock Exchange. *E-Finanse, 9*(3), 1–10.

Braun, M., & Larrain, B. (2005). Finance and the business cycle: International, inter-Industry evidence. *Journal of Finance, 60*(3), 1097–1128.

Campello, M., Graham, J. R., & Harvey, C. (2010). The real effects of financial constraints: Evidence from a financial crisis. *Journal of Financial Economics, 97*(3), 470–487.

Corsten, D., & Gruen, T. (2004). Stock-outs caus walkouts. *Harvard Business Review, 82*(5), 26–28.

Cuñat, V. (2007). Trade credit: Suppliers as debt collectors and insurance providers. *The Review of Financial Studies, 20*(2), 491–527.

Casey, E., & O'Toole, C. M. (2014). Bank lending constraints, trade credit and alternative financing during the financial crisis: Evidence from Europea SMEs. *Journal of Corporate Finance, 27*, 173–193.

Chiou, J., Cheng, L., & Wu, H. (2006). The determinants of working capital management. *The Journa of American Academy of Business, 10*(1), 149–155

Deloof, M. (2003). Does working capital managemen affect profitability of Belgian firms? *Journal o Business Finance & Accounting, 30*(3-4), 573–588

Enqvist, J., Graham, M., & Nikkinen, J. (2014). Th impact of working capital management on firn profitability in different business cycles: Evidenc from Finland. *Research in International Busines and Finance, 32*, 36–49.

Fazzari, S., Hubbard, G., Petersen, B., Blinder, A. S., & Poterba, J. M. (1988). Financing constraints an corporate investment. *Brookings Papers on Economic Activity, 19*(1), 141–206.

Fazzari, S., & Petersen, B. (1993). Working capital an fixed investment: New evidence on financing constraints. *The RAND Journal of Economics, 24*(3) 328–342.

Ferrando, A., & Mulier, K. (2013). Do firms use th trade credit channel to manage growth? *Journal o Banking & Finance, 37*(8), 3035–3046.

Garcia-Teruel, P. J., & Martinez-Solano, P. (2007). Effects of working capital management on SM profitability. *International Journal of Manageria Finance, 3*(2), 164 - 177.

Gertler, M. L., & Gilchrist, S. (1994). Monetary polic business cycles, and the behavior of small manufacturing firms. *The Quarterly Journal of Economics, 109*(2), 309–340.

Grullon, G., Michaely, R., & Swaminathan, B. (2002) Are dividend changes a sign of firm maturity *Journal of Business, 75*(3), 387–424.

Hill, M. D., Kelly, G. W., & Highfield, M. J. (2010). Ne operating working capital behavior: A first look *Financial Management, 39*(2), 783–805.

Jackowicz, K, Kozłowski, Ł., & Mielcarz, P. (2016). Financial constraints in Poland: The role of size an political connections. *Argumenta Oeconomica, 1*(36), 225–240.

ackowicz, K, & Mielcarz, P. (2015). The Impact of Investment on Operational Performance during the Recent Crisis. *Zeszyty Naukowe Uniwersytetu Ekonomicznego w Krakowie/ Cracow Review of Economics and Management, 2*(938), 31–43.

ensen, M. (1986). Agency costs of free cash flow, corporate finance, and takeovers. *American Economic Review, 76*(3), 323–329.

Kieschnick, R., Laplante, M., & Moussawi, R. (2013). Working capital management and shareholders' wealth. *Review of Finance, 17*(5), 1827–1852.

Love, I., Preve, L. A., & Sarria-Allende, V. (2007). Trade credit and bank credit: Evidence from recent financial crises. *Journal of Financial Economics, 83*(2), 453–469.

Moss, J., & Stein, B. (1993). Cash conversion cycle and firm size. *Managerial Finance, 19*(8), 25–34.

Moyen, N. (2004). Investment-cash flow sensitivities: Constrained versus unconstrained firms. *The Journal of Finance, 59*(5), 2061–2092.

Myers, S. C., & Majluf, N. S. (1984). Corporate financing and investment decisions when firms have information that investors do not have. *Journal of Financial Economics, 13*(2), 187–221.

Ng, C. K., Smith, J. K., & Smith, R. L. (1999). Evidence on the determinants of credit terms used in interfirm trade. *Journal of Finance, 54*(3), 1109–1129.

Nilsen, J. (2002). Trade credit and the bank lending channel. *Journal of Money, Credit, and Banking, 34*(1), 226–253.

Opler, T., Pinkowitz, L., Stulz, R., & Williamson, R. (1999). The determinants and implications of corporate cash holdings. *Journal of Financial Economics, 52*(1), 3–46.

Pais, M. A. & Gama, P. M. (2015). Working capital management and SMEs profitability: Portuguese evidence. *International Journal of Managerial Finance, 11*(3), 341 - 358.

Petersen, M., & Rajan, R. (1997). Trade credit: Theories and evidence. *Review of Financial Studies, 10*(3), 661–691.

Summers, B., & Wilson, N. (2002). Trade credit terms offered by small firms: Survey evidence and empirical analysis. *Journal of Business Finance & Accounting, 29*(3-4), 317–335.

Yang, X. (2011). Trade credit versus bank credit: Evidence from corporate inventory financing. *The Quarterly Review of Economics and Finance, 51*(4), 419–434.

Market reactions to dividends announcemen and payouts: Empirical evidence from the Warsaw Stock Exchange

Urszula Mrzygłód[1], Sabina Nowak[2]

ABSTRACT

The main goal of this paper is the empirical examination of the Polish stock market reactions to dividend nouncements and dividend payouts made by the companies listed on the Warsaw Stock Exchange (WSE). The search sample comprises 56 companies (WIG index constituents) that announced dividend payments and co pleted the payout during 2013. In the analysis, event study methodology is employed including either calculat abnormal returns and cumulative abnormal returns around the event day or testing their statistical significa using parametric and nonparametric tests. The average cross-sectional abnormal return calculated for the en sample is found to be significant on the dividend announcement day ($t = 0$, 0.86%) and on one day after ($t =$ 0.59%) at the 1% and 10% significance levels, respectively. The outcomes of the analysis conducted within three distinguished subsamples are rather more diverse. In the subgroup of the first announced dividends dividends announced after a minimum one-year break), the significant average abnormal return is found on $t = +1$ (0.90%, 5% significance level), whereas in the case of the dividend decreases subsample, the significant av age abnormal returns (at the 10% significance level) occur on days $t = -4$ (-1.44%) and $t = +2$ (-1.15%). The aver abnormal return calculated within the subsample of dividend increases turns out to be positive and signific on day $t = +1$ (1.03%, 10% significance level). The results obtained for the average cumulative abnormal retu corroborate the findings reached for the average cross-sectional abnormal returns in the case of the first divide and dividend increase subsamples. However, the average cross-sectional abnormal returns calculated within eleven-day-long event window around the dividend payment day turn out to be statistically insignificant. obtained results provide evidence that the Polish stock market reaction to dividend announcements is posi and immediate. However, the market does not significantly react to dividend payouts, which may lead to conclusion that the WSE directly incorporates news on dividends into stock prices. Moreover, the reaction of market for dividend announcements is consistent with the sign of the dividend change: dividend-increase (- crease) announcements are interpreted as a positive (negative) signal by the investors. Such results support b the informational content of the dividend hypothesis and the dividend signaling hypothesis. Considering the observed abnormal market behavior disappears within two days at most after the announcement date, results of the study can be useful for financial practitioners only with regard to short-term investment decisior

KEY WORDS: dividends, stock prices, event study, Warsaw Stock Exchange

---

[1] University of Gdansk - Institute of International Business, Poland; [2] University of Gdansk - Department of Econometrics, Pola

Correspondence concerning this article should be addressed to:
Sabina Nowak, University of Gdansk - Department of Econometrics, Armii Krajowej 101, Sopot 81-824, Poland. E-mail: sabina.nowak@ug.edu.pl

1. Introduction

The issue of payout policy is of great importance for companies' managers and remains one of the most interesting problems in theoretical and empirical finance. Since Lintner's (1956) and Miller and Modigliani's (1961) original papers, a number of theories, which often have divergent views on the determinants and consequences of dividend payouts, were developed and empirically investigated. A consensus, however, has not been reached, and we still do not know exactly why companies choose to pay dividends. In prior studies, the problem of stock price responses to dividend announcements has attracted particular attention. Regardless of the predictions of the Miller and Modigliani (1961), dividend irrelevance hypothesis, the previous studies on the developed markets confirm that stock markets do react to dividend announcements. Thus, dividends convey valuable information for shareholders about the future prospects of the companies and can be a valuable tool used by managers to signal the financial condition of the companies.

Although these questions of fact have been the subject of the extensive research on mature markets, less attention has been paid to the emerging stock markets. The literature regarding those markets is rather limited, and the conclusions remain ambiguous. Thus, it is justified to investigate dividend announcement and payout effects on the behavior of the Polish stock market.

The aim of the paper is to investigate the stock market reaction to dividend announcements and dividend payouts made by companies listed on the Polish stock market, namely, the Warsaw Stock Exchange (WSE). The research is based on a sample of 56 companies that announced dividend payments and completed the payouts in 2013. In the analysis, the event study methodology is employed.

In addition to the main goal of the paper, the reactions of the stock market among different groups concerning dividend announcements are investigated. Similar to other studies, groups were distinguished by comparing the dividend level in 2013 to the previous year. Thus, the sample was divided into three groups: a) first dividend announcement or announcement of dividend resumption after a minimum one-year break, b) dividend-decrease announcement, c) dividend-increase announcement.

In the present paper, we make three contributions to the existing literature on the Polish stock market. First, we treat the first official recommendation containing information of the dividend amount as the date of announcement. The present study differs from prior studies that equated the dividend announcement day with the date of the annual shareholders meeting. Second, we concentrate only on the effect of dividend announcements by clearing the dataset and removing the earning announcements. Third, we not only employ common parametric tests to verify the results, but we also recognize the distribution of the stock returns and introduce nonparametric tests when needed.

The remainder of the paper is organized as follows. In section 2, a concise literature review regarding the impact of dividend announcements and payouts on stock prices is presented. In section 3, the Polish stock market is briefly characterized, and results from previous studies conducted on companies listed on WSE are presented. In section 4, the outline of empirical design is described, while in section 5, the results of the research are discussed. In the last section, the conclusions and implications for further research are presented.

2. Literature review

The relevance or irrelevance of dividend policy to the market value of shares has been one of the most discussed topics in the financial literature since the pioneering works of Lintner (1956) and Miller and Modigliani (1961). In the latter paper, the reasoning is conducted under three important assumptions: perfect capital markets, investors' rational behavior and investors' perfect certainty. The authors conduct the analysis for a single type of financial instrument, namely, stocks (Miller & Modigliani, 1961), and prove that with a given investment policy, the dividend policy cannot influence either the company's valuation or the shareholders' total return (the dividend irrelevance hypothesis). In Miller and Modigliani's ideal world, investors are indifferent between receiving dividends (cash payments) or capital gains (the rise in stock prices) as a source of wealth augmentation. In their paper (1961), Miller and Modigliani refer also to the fact that dividend decisions are often accompanied by changes in the share prices and introduce the so called 'informational content of dividends'. However, the authors explain that if the company had conducted stable dividend policy to the date of the announced dividend change, the investors might perceive this shift as a consequence of changing management views of company's future earnings and growth opportunities. Thus, the shift in the dividend ratio provides an opportunity to change the price of shares. Still, the market valuation is entirely based on company's investment policy and growth opportunities.

Contrary to Miller and Modigliani (1961), Lintner (1956; 1962) and Gordon (1959) argue that investors differentiate between capital gains and dividends ('bird in hand fallacy hypothesis'). Dividends are not irrelevant for a firm's value since in investors' perception, dividends tend to be less risky in comparison to 'uncertain' capital gains. Moreover, interviews with managers of 28 companies brought Lintner to the conclusion that dividend policy plays an essential role in managers' decisions. In their responses, managers formed strong beliefs about investors preference over a stable rate of dividend payouts and the positive market reaction for stable or gradual growth in the dividends rate. Managers were also more reluctant to cut than to raise dividends in response to earnings changes and avoided making changes in dividends ratio that were to be soon reversed.

Lintner's findings inspired the discussion among researchers, and his partial-adjustment model of dividends was also under investigation in signaling theories of dividends, which recognize the capital market's imperfections, particularly information asymmetries. As Bhattacharya (1979) indicates, outside investors have imperfect information about a company's profitability and future cash flow. Hence, managers having this 'insider' knowledge can use the dividend as a signal and inform the market about their expectations regarding the financial condition of the company (Dasilas & Leventis, 2011). The dividend-signaling hypothesis implies that an increase (decrease) in dividends positively (negatively) influences stock prices (Baker, Powell, & Veit, 2002). Developments of dividend signaling models can be found in works of Bhattacharya (1979), John and Williams (1985), Miller and Rock (1985), Myers and Majluf (1984), Ofer and Thakor (1987).

Positive investor reactions in response to a dividend increase are also expected in agency theory. Here, dividend payments solve the problem of potential overinvestment since dividends reduce the level of available free cash flow that could be used by managers to invest in less profitable projects. In this view, manager having higher levels of free cash flow at their disposa induce the firm's growth beyond an optimal size (Jensen, 1986). A major contribution in the developmen agency theory comes from the works of Easterbrool (1984), Jensen and Meckling (1976), Jensen (1986) Based on the company's life cycle theory, Grullon, Michaely, and Swaminathan (2002) confirm the occurrence of the negative relationship between the investment level and dividends and eventually conclude tha more mature companies with fewer investment opportunities tend to pay higher dividends. Agency theor implies that by paying dividends, the companies ar exposed to an increased level of market discipline an monitoring (Baker et al., 2002).

The fact that investors are not indifferent betwee receiving dividends or capital gains and reveal stron preference toward dividends is also recognized by th theories of behavioral finance. This theoretical strean goes back to the works of Shefrin and Statman (1984 and is based on the main features of the prospect theory developed by Kahnemann and Tversky (1979), als broadened in their later study (Tversky & Kahnemanr 1992). First prospect theory explains the widely-recognized phenomenon why dividend cuts have large negative impact on stock prices that the positive impac of raise in dividends. In terms of the prospect theory decreasing dividends are perceived as making losse (decreasing investors welfare), as such losses are havin more pronounced effect than gains. The second behavioral approach to dividends recalls that an investor's assessment of the investment opportunity is relative to th chosen benchmark, and the investor undertakes suc cognitive operations as 'coding' (Forbes, 2009, pp. 340 341). Among the theoretical works based on behaviora finance, the catering theory of dividends proposed b Baker and Wurgler (2004) must be mentioned. Withi this theory, managers take decisions to pay dividend accordingly to the investor's sentiments towards dividends. It means that managers payout dividends if investors are prone to pay relatively high price for 'dividend' stocks, and conversely, managers do not initiat dividends if investors prefer 'non-dividend' stocks. A review of the research devoted to the dividend caterin theory and the other streams of dividend theories can b found i.a. in Gajdka (2013) and Kowerski (2011).

In their more recent paper, Baker and Wurgler (2012) also rely on prospect theory findings and argue that investors assess current dividends against past dividends, which serve as a 'psychological reference point'. Furthermore, Baker and Wurgler (2012) develop a multi-period dividend model that is consistent with the empirical findings of dividend announcements (the signaling effect of dividends) and explains the observed managers' behavior of 'dividend smoothing' (Linter partial adjustment model).

The market reactions to dividend announcements were examined in numerous empirical studies, which were mostly focused on large, developed stock markets (e.g., USA). In recent years, less developed stock markets have also received greater attention, and thus, the results have become more diverse.

Most empirical studies confirm the existence of the positive relationship between dividend announcements and stock price movements. The classic Pettit's (1972) study based on a sample of 625 companies listed on the NYSE in the period of 1964-1968 proves that dividends carry valuable information. Pettit divides the dividends dataset into seven categories: omissions, reductions, no change, initial payment, less than 10% increase, 10-25% increase, 25% or higher increase, whereas the initial payment group comprised companies that paid no dividend in the previous period. Pettit confirms that an increase (decrease) in dividends induces positive (negative) abnormal returns. It is pertinent to note that the major conclusions are drawn based on the monthly price data. Pettit additionally examines a much smaller sample of the daily stock returns (approximately equal to 10% of the monthly data sample) and finds that the market discounted the information within one day after the announcement. The author is aware that in such studies, the effect of related market information (i.e., earning announcements) must be excluded or at least considered. However, his proposal for overcoming this problem seems to be somewhat ambiguous and does not prevent the influence of the earnings announcements on the obtained results. Contemporary research devoted to the market price reactions should be conducted basing on time series data of at least daily intervals. The results obtained by Pettit are under discussion in later studies - see i.a. Dasilas and Leventis (2011) or Al-Shattarat, Al-Khasawneh, and Al-Shattarat (2012).

Similar to Pettit's work, Aharony and Swary (1980) also divide dividend announcements into subsequent subsets: no change in dividends, dividend increase, and dividend decrease. The sample covers 149 companies listed on NYSE in the period 1963-1976. Contrary to Pettit's study, the authors concentrate on daily data and introduce a method of grouping the earnings and dividend announcements according to the sign of dividend changes and the number of trading days between both types of announcements. Thus, Aharony and Swary (1980) obtain clear and mutually exclusive groups of announcements. Moreover, cases in which an earnings disclosure preceded (or followed) the dividend announcement are examined separately. In the case of a dividend increase, Aharony and Swary (1980) confirm significant abnormal returns on the day of dividend announcement and the day before. Moreover, in the cases of negative changes in dividends, the authors confirm significant negative abnormal returns whereas stable dividends give mixed and statistically insignificant results.

The effect of the first (initial) dividend announcement and an announcement after a long 'non-dividend' period is investigated by Asquith and Mullins (1983) on a sample of 168 companies listed on the NYSE or ASE for the period 1963-1980. The authors assume that dividend announcements are unexpected by market participants (see also Gurgul, Mestel, & Schleicher, 2003). As Asquith and Mullins report, for almost 70% of companies, there was a positive market reaction to the initial dividend announcement. Asquith and Mullins additionally control for the effects of other important events that might have influenced the results and conclude that dividends convey unique information to investors. The authors also find support for the hypothesis that dividends and earnings announcements can be partial substitutes. However, the results may be disturbed by an unequal division of the announcements into the analyzed subsamples.

The joint impact of dividend announcements on stock and bond prices is investigated by Dhillon and Johnson (1994). The authors aim at distinguishing between two hypotheses, namely: the information content (1) and wealth redistribution (2). Dhillon and Johnson collect data on dividend announcements and bond prices for companies traded on NYSE and AMEX for the period 1978-1987 and introduce the subsequent categories: dividend increases that comprise dividend initiations and large positive changes in dividends (greater than 30%), dividend decreases that comprise dividend omissions, large (greater than 30%) and separately small (less than 30%) dividend decreases. According to the intended purpose of the paper, Dhillon and Johnson reduce the initial sample of 14,349 announcements to a much smaller one of 131 observations. The study reveals a statistically significant 2-day abnormal return for stocks in the case of dividend increase and moderate but an insignificant abnormal return for bonds. However, the effect is significant only for share prices in the subsample of large increases. In the case of dividend cuts, the authors find a significant negative abnormal return on stock prices and a positive abnormal return for bond prices. Large dividend changes have a joint but opposite impact on share and bond prices, thus supporting the wealth redistribution hypothesis. As Dhillon and Johnson acknowledge, the study does not, however, contradict the dividends' information content hypothesis. Again, as in Asquith and Mullins' (1983) paper, one must take note that the number of observations in the examined subsamples is not comparable.

In addition, more recent works confirm the existence of abnormal returns connected with dividend announcements. Yoon and Starks (1995) conduct research on a large set of dividend announcements coming from companies listed on NYSE between 1969-1988. In their work, Yoon and Starks (1995) reveal larger share price reactions to dividend cuts than dividend increases, and Charitou, Lambertides, and Theodoulou (2011) confirm unfavorable market reactions (stock price movements) when dividends are omitted or decreased because of a loss in earnings. Moreover, Charitou et al.'s (2011) study favors the observation that the market reaction becomes more severe if the company had a history of well-established earnings and dividend payouts. It is noteworthy that the authors have a straightforward strategy to select the companies and divide them into the subsamples of well and less-established entities.

All of the above discussed studies are based on US data. The impact of dividend announcements on European stock markets has also been investigated by several authors. In the Lonie, Abeyratna, Power, and Sinclair (1996) study, 620 UK listed companies that announced the level of annual dividend per share between January and June 1991 are investigated. The authors extend the approach implemented in the prior studies and introduce the additional category of the announcements division – the sign of announced earnings in 12 months' time (increased, decreased). The decision of choosing a rather short period in comparison to other studies is based on two main arguments. First, Lonie et al. (1996) indicate that in the first six months of each year, almost all dividends are already announced to market participants. Second, the authors allude to the studies conducted by Chowdhury and Miles (1989) and DeAngelo, DeAngelo, and Skinner (1992) and highlight that mixing events of dividend announcement from different periods might be inappropriate, since the interpretation of dividend signals is influenced by economic conditions. Generally, the results favor the statistically significant positive reaction of share prices in a 2-day window in the case of a dividend increase and negative abnormal returns in the case of dividend cuts (Lonie et al., 1996). Moreover, Lonie et al. (1996) find excess return in the case of stable dividends decisions.

The UK stock market as well as the French and Portuguese stock markets are evaluated by Vieira and Raposo (2007). The authors have a large sample of the dividend announcements of the companies listed on the London Stock Exchange, Euronext Paris and Euronext Lisbon. The results are rather mixed and give weak support for the stock price reaction in response to dividend announcements. In the case of the UK and Portuguese stock markets, no price reaction is observed. In the case of France, as Vieira and Raposo (2007) acknowledge, the results only partially confirm the dividend signaling hypothesis since there are statistically significant positive stock market reactions in response to stable and decreasing dividends.

There are also several studies devoted to the smaller European stock markets located in Austria, Ireland and Greece. Gurgul et al. (2003) investigate the Austrian stock market reaction to dividend change in terms of prices and trading volume. In this paper, there are 181 first dividend announcements recognized, which are defined –contrary to the previous studies – as '*the very first official statement on dividends of the executive board*' (Gurgul et al., 2003). The results confirm increasing stock prices (positive reaction) on announced dividend increases and decreasing prices in the case f dividend cuts. Stable dividends are not followed by ny statistically significant price reaction. Moreover, in he analysis of the German stock market (310 dividend nnouncements), with respect to larger and smaller ompanies, the author confirms abnormal trading volme during the announcement day irrespective of the ividend level (higher, lower, stable) (Gurgul, 2012).

The same definition of dividend announcement as Gurgul et al.'s (2003) is also adopted in the Dasilas and Leventis (2011) study devoted to the Greek stock maret. Additionally, the authors decide to eliminate all vents that could interfere with dividend announcenents, such as news on earnings and stock splits, tc. Thus, based on 231 events, Dasilas and Leventis 2011) confirm significant price reactions to dividend announcements (increases and decreases). The tatistically significant stock price movements on the ividend announcement day are also confirmed on he sample of 50 Irish companies in the 15 years' time pan (McCluskey, Burton, Power, & Sinclair, 2006). Unlike in other studies, the authors solely concentrate n those companies that announced simultaneously on the same day) the earnings and dividend decions. In the conclusion, McCluskey et al. (2006) disover that the earnings news are more important for nvestors than the dividend announcements.

To summarize, in most of the studies discussed bove, the dividend announcement day is defined as he annual shareholders meeting day. In the present paper, we decided to follow the methodology of Gurgul t al. (2003) and adopt the date of the first official recommendation containing information of the dividend mount as the date of the dividend announcement. In ddition, considering the problem of the small sample ize that occurred in several studies, we concentrate olely on the impact of dividend announcements on tock prices and do not introduce a further sample ivision regarding the earnings announcements and ompanies' performance.

3. Evidence from the Warsaw Stock Exchange

The history of the Polish stock market is rather short ince it was only re-established in 1991 together vith market reforms introduced in Poland (Ziarkoiwek, 2008, p. 347). The main motive prevailing in he construction of the WSE was to enable smooth privatization processes to aid in effective capital allocation, as Janicka (2005) notes. Since its establishment, the WSE has experienced growth in terms of capitalization and number of companies listed, and currently is a recognized regional stock market (see also Mrzygłód & Nowak, 2013). However, it is worth noting that the WSE remains a relatively small market in comparison to the highly-developed US, German and UK stock exchanges. Moreover, by some global market players, such as the MSCI (Morgan & Stanley Capital International), the WSE is identified as an emerging stock market.

The short history of the Polish stock market and the fact that the market remains in a developing stage influences, in the authors' opinions, the dividend policy of companies. Gurgul and Majdosz (2005) indicate that generally Polish companies do not follow a formal and transparent dividend policy. In our opinion, while the market is becoming more mature and companies are progressing to the next stage of the life-cycle, the empirical studies devoted to dividend effects are becoming even more justified.

Among prior studies concentrated on the Polish stock market, Gurgul and Majdosz (2005), Tuzimek (2012; 2013), Pieloch-Babiarz (2014) and Czekaj (2014) examine the impact of dividend announcements on stock prices. The stock market reaction is also investigated by Perepeczo (2013; 2014). In those two latter studies however, the time series of cumulative abnormal returns fail to comply with normal distribution. Thus, results being based on parametric tests, although promising, are inconclusive.

Based on 45 dividend announcements within the period 2000-2004, Gurgul and Majdosz (2005) confirm the positive reaction of the stock market (+0.79%) on the day after news release (t+1). Contrary to studies on the US and European markets, Gurgul and Majdosz (2005) assume that any announcement concerning dividend payment should be treated as positive information for investors. Additionally, the authors examine the stock price reaction of the company's rivals coming from the same sector of the economy and reveal that industry rivals also experience positive stock price movements on the second day after announcement (t+2).

The larger sample of dividend events (245) is employed in the Tuzimek's study (Tuzimek, 2013, pp. 275-

315), although the number of dividend announcements is limited to the companies that have been paying dividends for at least 3 consecutive years in the period 2001-2009. The author argues that this three-year timespan restriction excludes from the sample the reckless management decisions that can influence irrational investors' behavior. This study reveals that dividend announcements positively influence stock prices. Positive abnormal returns are statistically significant on the day of the announcement (0.55%) as well as the day before (t-1; 0.35%) and a day after the announcement (t+1; 0.35%) for the entire sample. Moreover, Tuzimek finds statistically significant positive market reactions on the day after dividend announcement in the case of first/resumed (0.1%), increasing (1.35%), and decreasing dividends (0.43%). In the case of stable dividends, the abnormal returns are found to be positive and statistically significant on the day of the announcement (0.76%) (Tuzimek, 2013, p. 279-281). Additionally, the author investigates the effect of dividend announcements on stock prices dividing the companies into selected categories, such as company size, turnover liquidity, P/E ratio, P/BV ratio, ROE, debt ratio.

Positive abnormal returns on the day of the announcement for the events of dividend resumption or initiation (1.17%) and dividend increase (1.08%) are statistically significant in the Czekaj's study based on the dividend announcements in the period 2008-2012 (Czekaj 2014). Moreover, Pieloch-Babiarz (2014) investigates the effect of ex-dividend date on stock prices movements based on 117 dividend payments in the period 2009-2011. The obtained results lead to the conclusion that within the chosen sample, the stock prices decrease less than the level of the dividend payout ratio. The effect of stock prices dropping is smaller for companies that pay dividends not only from the current earnings but also from the reserve or/and supplementary capital.

Although the studies described above already confirm in part the positive relationship between dividend announcements and stock prices, in the authors' opinion, investigating this problem is justified since some methodological issues are not revealed in prior studies devoted to the Polish market. Except for Gurgul and Majdosz (2005), other authors do not clarify whether the type of distribution of abnormal returns is considered. Moreove a majority of the authors do not indicate whether th influence of earnings announcements is someho under control.

4. Data and methodology

The research sample contains companies listed o the WSE selected based on two criteria: (1) the announced dividend payments in 2013 and subsequently conducted the dividend payouts, no matte interim or final, and (2) they were WSE WIG inde constituents in 2013 (WIG – Warszawski Indek Giełdowy, Warsaw Stock Exchange index). Simila to Lonie et al. (1996), the economic cycle effect o stock market behavior is intentionally eliminated The final research sample comprises 56 dividen announcements and 57 dividend payouts made b 56 firms.

The event date is defined in the study twofold:

(1) as the day of publishing by the executive boar of the company the first official recommendatio containing information of the dividend amou for the financial year 2012,

(2) as the day of actual dividend payment by the company.

The database is collected manually from the financia portal Bankier.pl, which covers all the official statements published by the companies listed on the WSE As a result, in the first stage of the research, the sample comprises 137 dividend announcements and 14 dividend payouts made in 2013. Because publishin the official recommendation of the intention to pa the dividends often coincides with other corporat events, particularly earnings announcements, we decide to remove from the sample all the cases when announcing the events could have disturbed the impac of dividend announcement on the stock prices. It reduces the sample size by nearly 60%. The relativel small amount of the final research sample is undoubtedly a limitation of the study. However, one can fin in the literature, other event study research devote to the WSE based on comparably small samples (i.e. Gurgul and Majdosz, 2005), which emerges from th specificity of the Polish stock market.

In addition, the authors are aware of at least on remaining problem related to the second adopte definition of the event day: assuming that the event day and dividend payment day are equal, it does not fulfil any of the four conditions obligatory for event study proposed by Tabak and Dunbar (1999), namely, '*there is no reason to believe that the market anticipated the news*'. However, the decision of analyzing the market response for the dividend payment in itself is dictated by the curiosity of whether the Polish market quickly incorporates the news into stock prices.

In the first stage of the research, the analysis of the abnormal returns and the cumulative abnormal returns performance within the event window (-5, +5) days around the dividend announcement day and the dividend payment day in the entire sample is conducted.

In the next stage of the research, the stock price reactions conditioned on the direction of announced changes in expected dividend payouts are examined. To this end, the entire sample of dividend announcements is divided into four subsamples relating to the a) first dividend announcement or announcement of dividend resumption after a minimum one-year break (sample size: 18), b) dividend-decrease announcement (13), c) dividend-increase announcement (19) and d) constant-dividend announcement (6). Due to the small size of the 4th subsample, it is omitted in further calculations.

In this study, the standard event study methodology is employed. The calculation is conducted based on daily data of stock prices derived from the official WSE website, gpwinfostrefa.pl. The actual daily stock return for i company is calculated as follows:

$$R_{it} = \ln\left(\frac{P_{it}}{P_{it-1}}\right) \tag{1}$$

where P_{it} (P_{it-1}) indicates closing price for i share on day $t\,(t-1)$.

The basic event period comprises 11 days around the dividend announcement (or payment) date, which gives the event window equal to (-5, +5) days around day $t=0$.

The abnormal return AR is defined as the market adjusted return

$$AR_{it} = R_{it} - R_{Mt} \tag{2}$$

where R_{Mt} is the rate of return of market index reflected by WIG index. Adopting the abnormal return as the market adjusted return instead of calculating it based on market model, namely, $AR_{it} = R_{it} - \hat{\alpha} - \hat{\beta}\cdot R_{Mt}$, is related either to the problem with time-varying parameters in the market model or to the high probability of not fulfilling the classical OLS assumptions in the case of using the daily data in estimation of the model parameters. However, computing abnormal returns according to equation (2) does not require using the estimation window, which eventually excludes the possibility to improve the properties of selected parametric tests, which will be discussed in detail below.

The average cross-sectional daily abnormal return is computed as follows:

$$\overline{AR}_t = \frac{1}{N}\sum_{i=1}^{N} AR_{it} \tag{3}$$

where N indicates the number of observations used in the study. The null hypothesis maintains that the abnormal return on day t within the event window is equal to zero:

$$H_0 : E(AR_t) = 0 \tag{4}$$

which means that the considered event has no influence on stock prices behavior. This hypothesis can be tested using the parametric test based on the ratio of cross-sectional mean abnormal returns and the standard deviation

$$t = \frac{\overline{AR}_t}{\hat{\sigma}(AR_t)}\sqrt{N} \tag{5}$$

where $\hat{\sigma}(AR_t) = \sqrt{\frac{1}{N-1}\sum_{i=1}^{N}\left(AR_{it} - \overline{AR}_t\right)^2}$. Assuming that the abnormal returns are independent, identically distributed and normal, the t-statistic has a Student-t distribution with $N-1$ degrees of freedom under the null hypothesis. With a similar procedure of verification, the statistical significance of the average cross-sectional cumulative abnormal returns is subsequently conducted.

The cumulative abnormal return is calculated as follows:

$$CAR_i(t_1, t_2) = \sum_{t=t_1}^{t_2} AR_{it} \tag{6}$$

where t_1 and t_2 are the days chosen within the eleven days long event window. Consequently, the average cross-sectional cumulative abnormal return is equal to

$$\overline{CAR}(t_1,t_2) = \sum_{i=1}^{N} CAR_i(t_1,t_2) \quad (7)$$

where N indicates the number of observations used in the study.

However, daily returns (either actual or abnormal) are, in general, not normally distributed; according to the standard central limit theorem, the cross-sectional mean excess return converges to normality with the increase in the number of securities. Otherwise, the usage of statistic (5) has a different limitation: the event occurrence on day t usually leads to the contemporaneous changes of the numerator and denominator of the expression (5). Thus, it can lead to the situation when the t-statistic remains statistically insignificant, although the event considerably determines the stock prices (Gurgul, 2012, p. 51). Regrettably, equating abnormal returns to market adjusted returns instead of excessive returns over the market model impedes either employing the standard deviation of abnormal returns computed for estimation window (Gurgul, 2012, p. 51) or calculating the standardized abnormal returns and using parametric test proposed by Boehmer, Masumeci and Poulsen (1991).

Taking the asymmetry of the cross-sectional abnormal return distribution into account, the nonparametric Corrado's rank test (Corrado, 1989) and the generalized sign test are conducted. The first one is based on the statistic

$$T(u) = \frac{\frac{1}{N}\sum_{i=1}^{N}(K_{it} - \overline{K})}{s(K)} \quad (8)$$

where K_{it} denotes the rank of the abnormal return of i security in period t, $t = 1,2,...,T$, $\overline{K}$ is the average rank calculated as $\overline{K} = \frac{1+T}{2}$, $s(K)$ denotes the standard deviation of ranks computed expressed as

$$s(K) = \sqrt{\frac{1}{T}\sum_{t=1}^{T}\left[\frac{1}{N}\sum_{i=1}^{N}\left(K_{it} - \overline{K}\right)\right]^2}. \quad (9)$$

Under the null hypothesis expressed as (4), statistic $T(u)$ is distributed asymptotically as unit normal $T(u) \sim N(0,1)$.

The generalized sign test is used to check whether the abnormal returns are independent across stocks. Under the null hypothesis of no abnormal performance, the number of positive and negative abnormal returns equals to 50 percent in the event window. The number of non-negative values of abnormal returns has a binomial distribution with parameter p (Brown & Warner, 1980; Cowan, 1992). The statistic for the sign test is defined as follows:

$$z = \frac{p_0 - p}{\sqrt{p(1-p)N}} \quad (10)$$

where p_0 denotes the observed fraction of positive returns in the event period. Under the null hypothesis $z \sim N(0,1)$.

5. Results

The results describing abnormal returns performance within the event window (-5, +5) days around the dividend announcement day in the entire sample are summarized in Table 1.

The mean cross-sectional abnormal returns are positive and significantly different from zero either on the dividend announcement day ($t = 0$; 0.86%) or the day after the announcement ($t = +1$; 0.59%). Shapiro-Wilk statistics reveal that the daily stock returns on days $t = -3$, $t = -2$, $t = -1$, $t = 0$, $t = +3$ and $t = +4$ within the event window are not normally distributed.

Table 2 contains the summary of abnormal returns behavior within the event window around the dividend payment day.

In this case, mean cross abnormal returns are found to be statistically insignificant for all 10 days around the day the dividend was paid. The results of the Shapiro-Wilk test represent significant departures from normal distribution of majority abnormal returns within the event window. The cumulative abnormal return (CAR), which is calculated in the event window around the dividend announcement day, is approximately 3.5 times as large as the CAR calculated around the dividend payment day.

The results obtained for the average abnormal returns calculated within the entire sample are con-

e 1. Summary statistics for cross-sectional daily abnormal returns around dividend announcement day

ay *t*	**min** AR_t	**max** AR_t	$\overline{AR}_t$	$\hat{\sigma}(AR_t)$	**t stat.**	**skewn.**	**kurtosis**	**SW stat.**	**p-value**
-5	-0.0686	0.0792	0.0035	0.0265	1.0032	0.3251	1.3395	0.9484	0.0180
-4	-0.0758	0.0773	-0.0042	0.0279	-1.1240	-0.1091	1.2035	0.9641	0.0936
-3	-0.0467	0.0748	0.0016	0.0212	0.5541	1.0967	3.2196	0.9213	0.0013
-2	-0.0583	0.0485	-0.0019	0.0220	-0.6579	0.1797	1.0318	0.94	0.0078
-1	-0.0718	0.1025	0.0008	0.0263	0.2252	0.5529	3.9329	0.9254	0.0019
0	-0.0294	0.0934	0.0086***	0.0223	2.8741	1.1700	2.6928	0.9318	0.0035
1	-0.0725	0.0572	0.0059*	0.0251	1.7558	-0.2364	0.8626	0.9741	0.268
2	-0.0502	0.0514	-0.0017	0.0200	-0.6455	-0.1463	0.7689	0.9741	0.2702
3	-0.048	0.0744	0.0006	0.0244	0.1912	1.1880	2.4397	0.8921	0.0001
4	-0.0552	0.0411	-0.0014	0.0209	-0.5047	-0.7515	0.4938	0.9383	0.0066
5	-0.0539	0.0478	-0.0015	0.0190	-0.5778	0.1335	1.5055	0.9594	0.0569
CAR	–	–	0.00697						

: *, *** – significance at the 10%, 1% significance level.

e 2. Summary statistics for cross-sectional daily abnormal returns around dividend payment day

ay *t*	**min** AR_t	**max** AR_t	$\overline{AR}_t$	$\hat{\sigma}(AR_t)$	**t stat.**	**skewn.**	**kurtosis**	**SW stat.**	**p-value**
-5	-0.0809	0.0735	-0.0005	0.0271	-0.1477	0.0321	2.6646	0.9038	0.0003
-4	-0.1267	0.0708	0.0014	0.0287	0.3673	-1.6244	7.4620	0.8378	0.0000
-3	-0.0943	0.0687	-0.0028	0.0288	-0.7275	-0.5454	1.7503	0.9603	0.0586
-2	-0.0576	0.0491	-0.0013	0.0210	-0.4831	-0.3887	0.5168	0.9824	0.5705
-1	-0.0489	0.1184	-0.0002	0.0255	-0.0574	1.7334	7.2616	0.8772	0.0000
0	-0.0874	0.0565	-0.0009	0.0244	-0.2777	-0.2677	2.5614	0.9346	0.0042
1	-0.0543	0.1010	0.0043	0.0251	1.2875	0.8844	4.0279	0.9145	0.0007
2	-0.0637	0.0933	0.0009	0.0268	0.2607	0.7234	2.8391	0.9342	0.0040
3	-0.0666	0.0670	0.0043	0.0273	1.1965	0.1286	0.9117	0.9613	0.0655
4	-0.0790	0.0654	0.0025	0.0238	0.7916	-0.4173	2.3122	0.9404	0.0074
5	-0.0910	0.0456	-0.0028	0.0224	-0.9538	-1.2011	3.5796	0.9319	0.0032
CAR	–	–	0.00204						

Table 3. Statistical significance of the average cross-sectional cumulative abnormal returns ($C\bar{A}Rs$) around the divider announcement and dividend payment day

	dividend announcement day			dividend payment day		
(t_1, t_2)	$C\bar{A}R$	$\hat{\sigma}(CAR_t)$	**t stat.**	$C\bar{A}R$	$\hat{\sigma}(CAR_t)$	**t stat.**
(-5,0)	-0.0002	0.0587	-0.0280	-0.0034	0.0645	-0.4032
(-4,0)	-0.0038	0.0497	-0.5672	-0.0029	0.0598	-0.3680
(-3,0)	0.0004	0.0384	0.0828	-0.0043	0.0491	-0.6635
(-2,0)	-0.0011	0.0357	-0.2393	-0.0015	0.0351	-0.3297
(-1,0)	0.0008	0.0263	0.2252	-0.0002	0.0255	-0.0574
0	0.0086***	0.0223	2.8741	-0.0009	0.0244	-0.2777
(0,1)	0.0144***	0.0343	3.1478	0.0034	0.0353	0.7240
(0,2)	0.0127**	0.0395	2.4084	0.0043	0.0455	0.7149
(0,3)	0.0133**	0.0430	2.3194	0.0086	0.0503	1.2958
(0,4)	0.0119*	0.0507	1.7591	0.0111	0.0499	1.6841
(0,5)	0.0105	0.0495	1.5831	0.0083	0.0472	1.3265

Note: *, **, *** – significance at the 10%, 5%, 1% significance level.

firmed by the findings reached for the average cumulative abnormal returns.

The average cross-sectional cumulative abnormal returns ($C\bar{A}R$) around dividend announcement day turns out to be statistically significant in the daily intervals (0,1), (0,2), (0,3) and (0,4), whereas all the average cross-sectional cumulative abnormal returns calculated within the eleven days long event window around the dividend payment day are statistically insignificant.

The behavior of the cumulative abnormal returns in the window (-5, +5) days around the dividend announcement day and the dividend payment day are illustrated on Graph 1 and Graph 2, respectively.

Considering the frequent occurrence of non-normal distribution of abnormal returns, the significance of obtained results is verified by conducting the nonparametric Corrado rank test and the generalized sign test. The summary of findings is presented in Table 4.

The results of the Corrado test generally corroborate the previous findings. Abnormal returns significantly different from zero occur on the days $t = 0$ in the case of the dividend announcement and do not occur in an case of the dividend payment. All abnormal returns i the event window around the dividend payment da are independent across the stocks examined. The proportion of positive returns is found to be significantl lower than 50% on the day $t = -2$ in the event windo around the dividend payment day.

Table 5 contains the values of abnormal return calculated for the three subsamples described i section 4. The values of Shapiro-Wilk statistics wit p-values indicate the legitimacy of using either parametric or nonparametric significance tests.

In the case of the average cross-sectional abnorma returns for the 18 first announced dividends (or dividends announced after a minimum one-year-break the only one significant average abnormal return i found on the day $t = +1$ (0.90%, 5% level, nonparametric test). Since the series of abnormal returns for all th days of the event window turn out not to be normall distributed, the usage of the Corrado test is justified.

In the case of the 13 dividend decreases, the significant average abnormal returns (at the 10% level

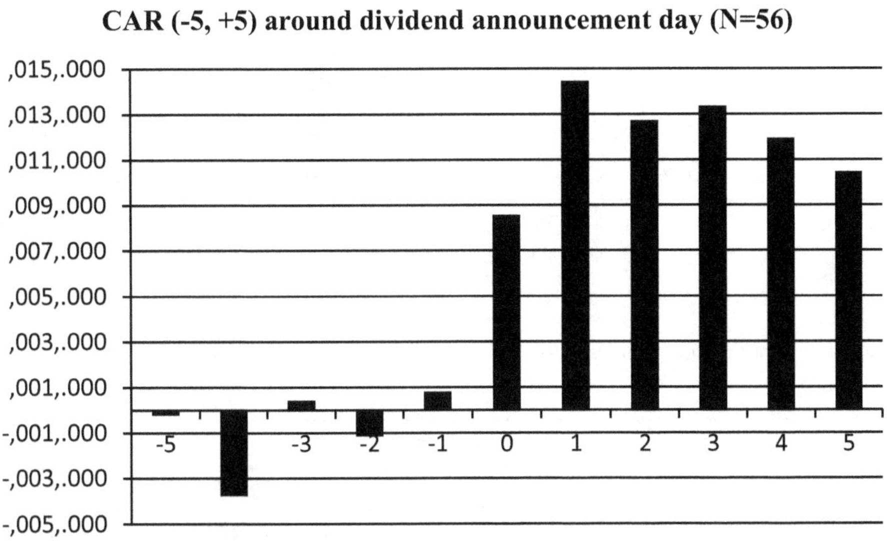

ph 1. Cumulative abnormal returns in the window (-5, +5) days around the dividend announcement day

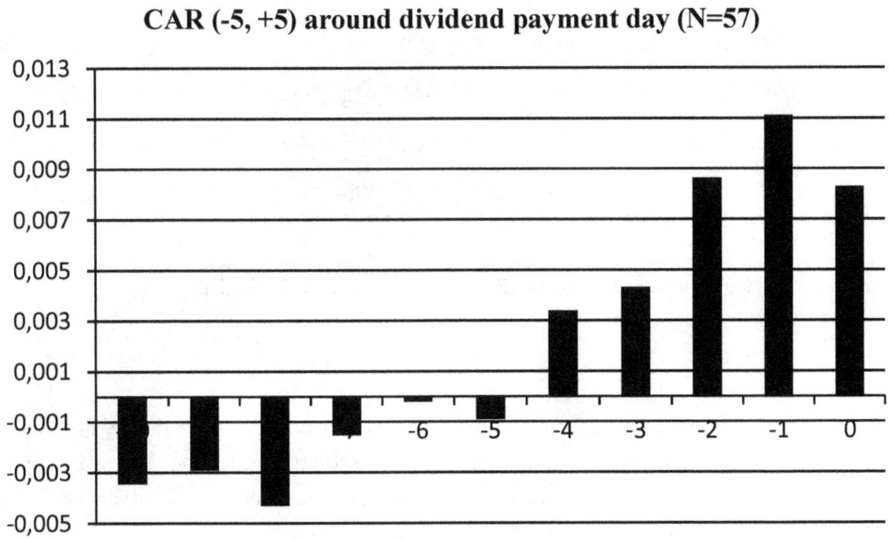

ph 2. Cumulative abnormal returns in the window (-5, +5) days around the dividend payment day

Table 4. Results of Corrado test and the generalized sign test

day t	-5	-4	-3	-2	-1	0	1	2	3	4	5
T(u) [a]	0.46	-1.56	0.08	-1.28	1.01	2.32**	1.35	-0.55	-0.89	-0.17	-0.8
T(u) [b]	-0.80	1.17	-0.42	-0.46	-0.67	-0.42	0.50	-0.17	1.26	0.96	-0.9
z [a]	0.27	-0.53	0.80	-2.14**	0.80	1.07	0.80	0.27	-1.07	0.80	-0.5
z [b]	-1.19	-0.13	0.13	-0.13	-1.46	-0.66	0.92	-0.13	1.46	0.13	-0.6

Note: ** – significance at the 5% significance level, T(u) – statistic for Corrado test (equation 6), z – statistic for generalized test (equation 8), [a] – event day equals to dividend announcement day, [b] – event day equals to dividend payment day.

Table 5. Average daily abnormal returns around the dividend announcement day in three subsamples – the results of parametric and nonparametric tests

	A					B					C				
day t	$\overline{AR}_t$	SW stat.	p-value	t stat.	T(u)	$\overline{AR}_t$	SW stat.	p-value	t stat.	T(u)	$\overline{AR}_t$	SW stat.	p-value	t stat.	T(
-5	0.0022	0.267***	0.000	0.2979	-0.5217	0.0063	0.905	0.155	0.8124	0.6139	0.0049	0.970	0.770	0.9048	1.04
-4	-0.0048	0.266***	0.000	-0.8278	-0.7454	-0.0144*	0.874*	0.059	-1.8838	-1.6664	0.0006	0.944	0.307	0.0738	-0.6
-3	-0.0015	0.273***	0.000	-0.2487	-0.5963	0.0001	0.901	0.138	0.0212	0.0000	0.0044	0.874**	0.017	0.8502	0.22
-2	0.0023	0.301***	0.000	0.3184	-0.2981	-0.0029	0.827**	0.015	-0.7209	-0.7894	-0.0021	0.892**	0.034	-0.5108	-0.3
-1	0.0000	0.396***	0.000	-0.0031	0.1491	-0.0004	0.961	0.763	-0.0760	0.6139	0.0010	0.854***	0.008	0.2299	0.74
0	0.0092	0.835***	0.004	1.4170	1.2671	0.0065	0.916	0.222	1.1721	0.7016	0.0077	0.972	0.811	1.5617	0.52
1	0.0090**	0.354***	0.000	1.3093	2.2361	0.0019	0.940	0.463	0.3320	0.5262	0.0103*	0.885**	0.027	1.9544	0.29
2	0.0027	0.287***	0.000	0.4753	0.0745	-0.0115*	0.952	0.626	-2.0571	-1.7541	-0.0018	0.858***	0.009	-0.4896	-0.2
3	-0.0010	0.275***	0.000	-0.1523	-1.0435	0.0045	0.877*	0.066	0.5367	0.9648	0.0004	0.857***	0.009	0.0691	-1.2
4	-0.0038	0.262***	0.000	-0.7526	-0.5217	-0.0029	0.939	0.443	-0.5373	-0.2631	0.0026	0.943	0.300	0.4956	1.26
5	0.0027	0.259***	0.000	0.5387	0.0000	0.0023	0.849**	0.027	0.4290	1.0525	-0.0053	0.832	0.832	-1.5221	-1.5
N			18					13					19		

Note: A – first dividend/dividend resumes after a break, B – dividend decreases, C – dividend increases, *, **, *** – significa at the 10%, 5%, 1% significance level.

are found on the days $t = -4$ (-1.44%) and $t = +2$ (-1.15%). The decision of the statistical significance is made based on either parametric or nonparametric significance test due to the normality of distribution of analyzed abnormal returns time series.

The average abnormal returns for the 19 announced dividend increases turn out to be positive and significant on the day $t = +1$ (1.03%, 10% level, parametric test). However, this result should be treated with caution, since the abnormal returns on the day $t = +1$ are not normally distributed at the 10% significance level.

Table 6 contains summarized values of the average cumulative abnormal returns around the dividend announcement day calculated for the three selected subsamples.

e 6. Statistical significance of the average cumulative abnormal returns ($\bar{CA}Rs$) around the dividend announcement n three subsamples

	A			B			C		
t_2)	$\bar{CA}R$	$\hat{\sigma}(CAR_t)$	t-stat	$\bar{CA}R$	$\hat{\sigma}(CAR_t)$	t-stat	$\bar{CA}R$	$\hat{\sigma}(CAR_t)$	t-stat
,0)	0.0089	0.0741	0.5208	-0.0113	0.0437	-0.9317	-0.0017	0.0593	-0.1244
,0)	0.0039	0.0653	0.2608	-0.0176**	0.0269	-2.3559	-0.0040	0.0515	-0.3280
,0)	0.0033	0.0404	0.3600	-0.0032	0.0306	-0.3754	0.0009	0.0483	0.0755
,0)	-0.0011	0.0274	-0.1768	-0.0033	0.0278	-0.4277	0.0023	0.0523	0.1879
,0)	0.0010	0.0182	0.2299	-0.0004	0.0181	-0.0760	0.0000	0.0402	-0.0031
)	0.0077	0.0214	1.5617	0.0065	0.0199	1.1721	0.0092	0.0277	1.4170
1)	0.0179**	0.0348	2.2467	0.0084	0.0316	0.9573	0.0183*	0.0387	2.0053
2)	0.0162**	0.0311	2.2654	-0.0032	0.0352	-0.3231	0.0210*	0.0499	1.7835
3)	0.0165	0.0448	1.6086	0.0014	0.0299	0.1667	0.0200	0.0521	1.6282
4)	0.0191	0.0553	1.5036	-0.0015	0.0349	-0.1574	0.0162	0.0606	1.1327
5)	0.0138	0.0540	1.1141	0.0008	0.0320	0.0873	0.0189	0.0581	1.3799
N	18			13			19		

: A – first dividend/dividend resumes after a break, B – dividend decreases, C – dividend increases,
- significance at the 10%, 5% significance level.

The results of the average cumulative abnormal eturns' analysis confirm – in most cases – the findngs obtained for the average cross-sectional abnormal eturns. The reaction of the market is statistically sigaificant in the daily intervals (0,1) and (0,2), either in he case of the first dividend (dividend resumes after break) announcement (1% significance level) or in he case of dividend-increase announcements (10% ignificance level). In the case of dividend-decrease nnouncements the average cumulative abnormal reurns remain statistically insignificant. Therefore, the esults obtained for cumulative abnormal returns in he subgroup of dividend decreases stay in contrast to he findings reached for the average abnormal returns compare Table 5).

The presented results generally stay in line with the ther studies conducted on the Polish stock market. n comparison to Gurgul and Majdosz (2005), a posiive and statistically significant market reaction apears already on the day of the dividend announcement. However, unlike Tuzimek (2013), the authors do not obtain significant mean cross-sectional abnormal returns on the day before the announcement. The effects of the announcements in the distinguished subsamples, namely, first dividend announcement or dividend resumption, dividend cut and dividend increase, stay in line with the theoretical predictions. The average abnormal returns for dividend initiations and increases are positive in sign, and the results are comparable with Czekaj (2014) and Tuzimek (2013). Unlike Tuzimek (2013), the present findings indicate the expected negative impact on stock prices in the case of dividend cuts. However, as in the Tuzimek study (2013), the findings obtained for dividend decreases are statistically significant at the 10% significance level.

The obtained results are generally in line with US and European studies (Dasilas & Leventis, 2011; i.e., Gurgul et al., 2003; Lonie et al., 1996), which proves the existence of the dividend announcement signaling effect not only in the case of the news release that promises investors an increasing dividend.

6. Summary and conclusions

The results obtained based on 56 dividend announcements among companies listed on the WSE in the year 2013 are mixed. Based upon the sample of 56 firms, the market reaction turns out to be statistically significant and positive only on the dividend announcement day and one day after the announcement. The mean cross abnormal returns are found to be insignificantly different from zero for all ten days around the dividend payment day. Thus, the effect of dividend announcement is reflected in stock prices immediately.

Considering the direction of changes in the expected dividend payouts, in the case of increasing dividends and dividends paid for the first time (or dividend resumes after a break), the impact of the news release on stock prices is statistically significant, positive and noticed on the first day after the announcements. Furthermore, in the case of dividend decrease announcements, their impact on stock prices is negative and noticeable on the second day after the announcement.

The outcomes of the study allow us to confirm that the effect of dividend announcements is in line with the informational content of the dividend hypothesis as well as with dividend signaling models. The reaction of the market is consistent with the direction of the dividend change: dividend-increase (-decrease) announcements are interpreted as a positive (negative) signal by the investors. Moreover, the stock market reaction on the news release turns out to be rather quick. Thus, the prices seem to 'digest' the information immediately. Based on the employed sample the authors cannot confirm that behavioral models of dividends have a good explanatory power in the case of the Polish stock market. The reaction of the stock prices, although correct in sign, has not been stronger in the case of dividend cuts compared to dividend increases.

Finally, the authors would like to add two general remarks. First, the Polish stock market is not semi-strong informationally efficient in a given period. However, it is pertinent to note that the observed abnormal market behavior disappears within two days at most after the announcement date. Second, the obtained results can be useful for financial practitioners. The statistical significance of abnormal returns in response to dividend announcements can be used to build portfolios wit dividend companies. However, the profitability of suc portfolios should be checked in a long-term perio which is beyond the scope of this study.

References:

Aharony, J., & Swary, I. (1980). Quarterly dividen and earning announcements and stockholder returns: An empirical analysis. *The Journal of Fi nance, 35*(1), 1-12.

Al-Shattarat, W. K., Al-Khasawneh J. A., & Al-Shatta rat, H. K. (2012). Market reaction to changes i dividend payments policy in Jordan. *The Journa of Applied Business Research, 28*(6), 1193-1210.

Asquith, P., & Mullins, D. W. (1983). The impact o initiating dividend payments on shareholder wealth. *The Journal of Business, 56*(1), 77-96.

Baker, H. K., Powell, G. E., & Veit, E. T. (2002). Revisit ing the dividend puzzle: Do all the pieces fit now *Review of Financial Economics, 11*(4), 241-261.

Baker, M., & Wurgler, J. (2004). A catering theory o dividends. *The Journal of Finance, 59*(3), 1125 1165.

Baker, M., & Wurgler, J. (2012). Dividends as referenc points: A behavioral signaling approach (Workin Paper Series No. 18242). National Bureau of Eco nomic Research. Retrieved from http://www.nbe org/papers/w18242.pdf

Bhattacharya, S. (1979). Imperfect information, divi dend policy, and 'the bird in the hand' fallacy. *Th Bell Journal of Economics, 10*(1), 259-270.

Boehmer, E., Masumeci, J., & Poulsen, A. B. (1991 Event-study methodology under conditions o event-induced variance. *Journal of Financial Eco nomics, 30*(2), 253-272.

Brown, S. J., & Warner, J. B. (1980). Measuring securit price performance. *Journal of Financial Econom ics, 8*(3), 205–258.

Charitou, A., Lambertides, N., & Theodoulou, G (2011). Losses, dividend reductions, and marke reaction associated with past earnings and divi dends patterns. *Journal of Accounting, Auditin and Finance, Forthcoming, 26*(2), 351-382.

Chowdhury, G., & Miles, D. K. (1989). Modelling com panies' debt and dividend decisions with com pany accounts data. *Applied Economics, 21*(11 1483-1508.

Corrado, Ch. J. (1989). A nonparametric test for abnormal security-price performance in event studies. *Journal of Financial Economics, 23*(2), 385-395.

Cowan, A. R. (1992). Nonparametric event study tests. *Review of Quantitative Finance and Accounting, 2*(4), 343-358.

Czekaj, J. (2014). Efektywność półsilna [Semi-strong efficiency]. In J. Czekaj (Ed.), *Efektywność giełdowego rynku akcji w Polsce z perspektywy dwudziestolecia [The efficiency of the stock market in Poland in the perspective of twenty years]* (pp. 91-134). Warszaw: Polskie Wydawnictwo Ekonomiczne.

Dasilas, A., & Leventis, S. (2011). Stock market reaction to dividend announcements: Evidence from the Greek stock market. *International Review of Economics and Finance, 20*(2), 302-311.

DeAngelo, H., DeAngelo, L., & Skinner, D. J. (1992). Dividends and losses. *The Journal of Finance, 47*(5), 1837-1863.

Dhillon, U. S., & Johnson, H. (1994). The effect of dividend changes on stock and bond prices. *The Journal of Finance, 49*(1), 281-289.

Easterbrook, F. H. (1984). Two agency costs explanations of dividends. *American Economic Review, 74*(4), 650-659.

Forbes, W. (2009). *Behavioral finance.* Chichester, UK: John Wiley & Sons.

Gajdka, J. (2013). *Behawioralne finanse przedsiębiorstw. Podstawowe podejścia i koncepcje [Behavioral corporate finance. Basic approaches and concepts].* Łódź: Wydawnictwo Uniwersytetu Łódzkiego.

Gordon, M. (1959). Dividends, earnings and stock prices. *The Review of Economics and Statistics, 41*(2), 99-105.

Grullon, G., Michaely, R., & Swaminathan, B. (2002). Are dividends changes a sign of firm maturity? Journal of Business, *75*(3), 387- 424.

Gurgul, H. (2012). *Analiza zdarzeń na rynkach akcji. Wpływ informacji na ceny papierów wartościowych [Event study on stock markets. Impact of information on the securities prices]* (2nd ed.). Warszaw: Wolters Kluwer Polska.

Gurgul, H., & Majdosz, P. (2005). Effect of dividend and repurchase announcement on the Polish stock market. *Badania Operacyjne i Decyzje, 1*, 25-41.

Gurgul, H., Mestel, R., & Schleicher, Ch. (2003). Stock market reactions to dividend announcements: Empirical evidence from the Austrian stock market. *Financial Markets and Portfolio Management, 17*(3), 332-350.

Janicka, M. (2005). Polski rynek kapitałowy – powstanie rozwój i perspektywy w strukturach jednolitego rynku finansowego Unii Europejskiej [Polish capital market – foundation, development and prospects within the structures of the single European financial market]. *Ekonomista, 5*, 673-689.

Jensen, M. C. (1986). Agency costs of free cash flow, corporate finance and takeovers. *The American Economic Review, 76*(2), 323-329.

Jensen, M. C., & Meckling, W. H. (1976). Theory of the firm: Managerial behavior, agency costs and ownership structure. *Journal of Financial Economics, 3*(4), 305-360.

John, K., & Williams J. (1985). Dividends, dilution, and taxes: A signalling equilibrium. *The Journal of Finance, 40*(4), 1053-1070.

Kahneman, D., & Tversky, A. (1979). Prospect theory: An analysis of decision under risk. *Econometrica, 47*(2), 263-292.

Kowerski, M. (2011). *Ekonomiczne uwarunkowania decyzji o wypłatach dywidend przez spółki publiczne [The economic determinants of the dividend payout decisions of public companies].* Kraków-Rzeszów-Zamość: Wydawnictwo Konsorcjum Akademickie.

Lintner, J. (1956). Distribution of incomes of corporations among dividends, retained earnings, and taxes. *The American Economic Review, 46*(2), 97-113.

Lintner, J. (1962). Dividends, earnings, leverage, stock prices and the supply of capital to corporations. *The Review of Economics and Statistics, 44*(3), 243-269.

Lonie, A. A., Abeyratna, G., Power, D. M., & Sinclair C. D. (1996). The stock market reaction to dividend announcements: A UK study of complex market signals. *Journal of Economic Studies, 23*(1), 32–52.

McCluskey, T., Burton, B. M., Power, D. M., & Sinclair, C.D. (2006). Evidence on the Irish stock market's reaction to dividend announcements. *Applied Financial Economics, 16*(8), 617-628.

Miller, M. H., & Rock, K. (1985). Dividend policy under asymmetric information. *The Journal of Finance, 40*(4), 1031-1061.

Miller, M. H., & Modigliani, F. (1961). Dividend policy, growth, and the valuation of shares. *The Journal of Business, 34*(4), 411-433.

Mrzygłód, U., & Nowak, S. (2013). Stock exchanges go public: The case of Warsaw stock exchange. *Journal of International Studies, 6*(2), 111-123.

Myers, S. C., & Majluf, N. S. (1984). Corporate financing and investment decisions when firms have information that investors do not have. *Journal of Financial Economics, 13*(2), 187-221.

Ofer, A. R., & Thakor, A. V. (1987). A theory of stock price responses to alternative corporate cash disbursement methods: Stock repurchases and dividends. *The Journal of Finance, 42*(2), 365-394.

Perepeczo, A. (2013). Reakcja akcjonariuszy na decyzje o wypłacie dywidendy w spółkach publicznych - wyniki badań empirycznych [Market reactions to dividend announcements in public companies - empirical evidence]. In K. Jajuga, W. Ronka- Chmielowiec (Eds.), *Prace Naukowe Uniwersytetu Ekonomicznego we Wrocławiu, Inwestycje finansowe i ubezpieczenia - tendencje światowe a rynek polski [Research Papers of Wrocław University of Economics, Financial Investments and Insurance - Global Trends and the Polish Market]* (pp. 253-264). Wrocław: Wydawnictwo Uniwersytetu Ekonomicznego we Wrocławiu.

Perepeczo, A. (2014). Reakcja inwestorów na decyzje o wypłacie dywidendy a kryzys finansowy [The reaction of investors to changes in the dividend policy and the financial crisis]. In A. Kopiński, A. Bem (Eds.), *Prace Naukowe Uniwersytetu Ekonomicznego we Wrocławiu, Zarządzanie finansami firm - teoria i praktyka [Research Papers of Wrocław University of Economics, Financial Management - Theory and Practice]* (pp. 184-195). Wrocław: Wydawnictwo Uniwersytetu Ekonomicznego we Wrocławiu.

Pettit, R. R. (1972). Dividend announcements, security performance, and capital market efficiency. *The Journal of Finance, 27*(5), 993-1007.

Pieloch-Babiarz, A. (2014). Wysokość pieniężnych wypłat dywidendy a kształtowanie się kursu giełdowego akcji spółek w pierwszym dniu notowań 'bez dywidendy' [Amount of cash dividend payments and the 'ex-dividend' day return's formation]. In A. Kopiński, A. Bem (Eds.), *Prace Naukowe Uniwersytetu Ekonomicznego we Wrocławiu, Zarządzanie finansami firm - teoria i praktyka [Research Papers of Wrocław University of Economics, Financial Management - Theory and Practice]* (pp. 196-208). Wrocław: Wydawnictwo Uniwersytetu Ekonomicznego we Wrocławiu.

Shefrin, H. M., & Statman M. (1984). Explaining investors preferences for cash dividends. *Journal of Financial Economics, 13*(2), 253-282.

Tabak, D. I., & Dunbar, F. C. (1999). Materiality and magnitude: Event studies in the courtroom (Working Paper No. 34). National Economic Research Associates. Retrieved from http://www.nera.com/content/dam/nera/publications/archive1/3841.pdf

Tversky, A., & Kahneman, D. (1992). Advances in prospect theory: Cumulative representation of uncertainty. *Journal of Risk and Uncertainty, 5*(4), 297-323.

Tuzimek, R. (2012). Wpływ wypłat dywidendy na wartość akcji spółek notowanych na Giełdzie Papierów Wartościowych w Warszawie [Effect of dividend payments on the value of shares listed on the Warsaw Stock Exchange]. In K. Jajuga, W. Ronka- Chmielowiec (Eds.), *Prace Naukowe Uniwersytetu Ekonomicznego we Wrocławiu, Inwestycje finansowe i ubezpieczenia - tendencje światowe a rynek polski [Research Papers of Wrocław University of Economics, Financial Investments and Insurance - Global Trends and the Polish Market]* (pp. 333-346). Wrocław: Wydawnictwo Uniwersytetu Ekonomicznego we Wrocławiu.

Tuzimek, R. (2013). Efektywność decyzji dotyczących wypłat na rzecz właścicieli [The effectiveness of decisions regarding distribution to owners]. In R. Tuzimek (Ed.), *Decyzje finansowe w spółkach giełdowych a wartość akcji [Financial decisions of companies listed on the stock exchange and the value of shares]* (pp. 275-315). Warszaw: Oficyna Wydawnicza Szkoły Głównej Handlowej.

Yoon, P. S., & Starks, L. T. (1995). Signaling, investment opportunities, and dividend announcements. *The Review of Financial Studies, 8*(4), 995-1018.

Vieira, E. S., & Raposo, C. C. (2007). Signalling with dividends? New evidence from Europe. Available at http://ssrn.com/abstract=1004523

Ziarko-Siwek, U. (2008). Giełda papierów wartościowych w Polsce – Giełda Papierów Wartościowych w Warszawie S.A [Stock exchange in Poland – The Warsaw Stock Exchange]. In U. Ziarko-Siwek (Ed.), *Giełdy kapitałowe w Europie [Stock exchanges in Europe]* (pp. 347-374). Warszaw: CeDeWu Sp. z o.o.

15

Financial Performance Measurement of Hungarian Retail Food Companies

Veronika Fenyves[1], Zoltán Bács[1], Laura Karnai[2], Adrián Nagy[2], Tibor Tarnóczi[1]

ABSTRACT

The comparison of company performances, i.e., benchmarking, is becoming more and m critical. Presently, companies mostly use traditional financial ratios to evaluate their financial p formance. We also use financial ratios to measure and compare company performances, f which we create complex efficiency coefficients using Data Envelopment Analysis. Using D Envelopment Analysis, we analyzed the efficiency of retail food companies in Hungary's No ern Great Plain region from 2009 to 2014 using their financial reports. To improve the resu the performance measurement, we used the bootstrap method, the Hamiltonian Monte C simulation, and Bayesian statistics. We transformed the primarily deterministic DEA method i a stochastic DEA model. The primary target of this extension is to enhance statistical infere in DEA and to integrate it with a stochastic mechanism of Bayesian techniques. To develop stochastic DEA model, we use Stan Stochastic Modelling Language within the framewor the R Statistics. Analyzing the results, we can state that the DEA method can be used for ana ing efficiency, and the additions shown can make the evaluation much more accurate. We conclude that the best results were produced by the combined method, during a simultane application of the input orientation.

KEY WORDS: performance measurement, principal components analysis, data envelopment analysis, bayesian statistics, stan stochastic programming language

[1] University of Debrecen, Faculty of Economics and Business, Institute of Accounting and Finance, Hungary
[2] University of Debrecen, Faculty of Economics and Business, Institute of Business Administration, Hungary

1. Introduction

Company leaders are under enormous pressure to increase their company's performance. Performance assessment or benchmarking is a widely used method for corporate development and profitability enhancement. Benchmarking is becoming an increasingly important activity for companies in today's globalized world. Business enterprises need to perform t operations efficiently to survive the market com tition and achieve the expected level of profitabi Efficiency is a significant indicator in the compar activities analysis, and it is one of the fundamental most frequently used performance indicator. To m sure, monitor and improve efficiency is a vital task enterprises in the 21st century (Andrejic, Bojovic Kilibarda, 2013).

It is essential for every company to be able to p itself in the corporate rankings of its industry. termining the ranking of a company within indu

Correspondence concerning this article should be addressed to: **Veronika Fenyves**, University of Debrecen, Faculty of Economics and Business, Institute of Accounting and Finance, Egyetem tér 1., Debrecen 4032. E-mail: fenyves.veronika@econ.unideb.hu requires to measure corporate performance using a composite indicator. Company experts attempt to measure company performance using scores assigned to corporate financial indicators in general. However, to transform financial ratios into a composite indicator is quite complicated. One of the ways to create corporate industry rankings can be to use Data Envelopment Analysis (DEA), which creates a company ranking using multiple performance indicators. The DEA method allows using various input and output variables to determine a performance indicator (efficiency coefficient). However, it is essential to bear in mind that accurate performance measurement is possible only if the conditions for calculating the DEA are met (Sarkar, 2017).

The primary goal of this study is to use the DEA method to rank and compare the retail food companies of the Northern Great Plain region while defining a complex performance indicator that allows an accurate assessment of the investigated companies. The objective of the research was to achieve a correct assessment by extending the DEA method using the principal component analysis (PCA) and the Stan probabilistic programming language. Principal component analysis can help us to reduce the dimensions of input and output variables. PCA is a data reduction tool that removes redundant information, shows hidden features and essential relationships existing between observations (Putri, Chetchotsak, & Jani, 2017). The classical DEA model cannot be applied in our case because it does not have sufficient discriminatory power.

We chose the food retail sector as the subject of analysis because it is an important sector within the Hungarian economy and no similar study has been made regarding the Northern Great Plan region in the past.

The rest of this paper is organized as follows:

- The section on 'Methodology' presents the database investigated and the methods used: data envelopment analysis, principal component analysis and Stan stochastical programming language based on Bayesian statistics.
- The next section 'Results', presents the results and discussion of the analysis.
  - *Checking the number of variables and the outliers.*
  - *Determining the efficiency coefficients using PCA-DEA.*
  - *Determining the interval of DEA efficiency coefficients using Stan stochastic modeling tool.*
- Conclusions are given in the last section.

2. Methodology

2.1. Investigation database

The enterprises that were included in the study database are situated in the Northern Great Plain region of Hungary and are selected if their main activity was indicated as a "Food retail mixed store" which was established before January 1, 2009, and which have six financial years closed with an annual report (2009-2014). The enterprises were selected from the OPTEN company database, and their annual reports were downloaded from the Hungarian Electronic Reporting Portal (e-beszamolo). There were 887 companies fitted the conditions determined above in the region, 563 of which are part of the database analyzed. During the period examined, 86 enterprises were liquidated, and 238 enterprises did not produce annual reports in several years of the period examined, or the items needed to the analysis of the annual report contained zero values. The number of enterprises involved in the investigation in the region, were, by county:

- Szabolcs-Szatmár-Bereg County 131
- Hajdú-Bihar County 250
- Jász-Nagykun-Szolnok County 182
- Total Northern Great Plain Region 563

The great majority of enterprises in the database prepared a simplified annual report, and so the analysis was performed upon the data found in those simplified reports. For the analysis, we used the accounting items shown in Table 1 as input and output variables.

2.2. Data envelopment analysis

In this study, Data Envelopment Analysis was used to measure corporate performance, which was developed from mathematical programming used in operations research. DEA is, in essence, a linear programming model which allows us to rank the enterprises (decision-making units – DMU) involved in the examination by a joint utilization of different input and output characteristics. Cook and Zhu (2005) comment in their study that DEA is a data-oriented

Table 1. Accounting parameters used for performance measurement

Input variables		Output variables	
Number	**Name of variables**	**Number**	**Name of variables**
1	Fixed assets	1	Revenue
2	Inventories	2	Operating profit
3	Receivables	3	Profit before tax
4	Cash	4	Profit after tax
5	Equity		
6	Reserves		
7	Non-current liabilities		
8	Current liabilities		
9	Material costs		
10	Employee costs		
11	Depreciation		
12	Other costs		
13	Financial expenses		
14	Corporate taxes		

approach to performance evaluation and improvement and they then present the various authors' research on DEA. In several professional contexts, DEA models are also called nonparametric deterministic models, where the word 'deterministic' can be applied only to the basic model and its extensions because it is also possible to create stochastic DEA models (Huang & Li, 2011; L. Li & M. Li, 2014). This study does not deal in detail with the DEA method because many authors had dealt with it during the past 60 years what was described by Farell initially (1957). However, the real "birth" of the method is calculated from 1978 when Charnes and his co-authors published their DEA article (Charnes, Cooper, & Rhodes, 1978). Thousands of publications have been published on DEA since 1978 (Tavares 2002; Emrouznejad, Parker, & Tavares, 2008).

DEA is a useful tool for evaluating the relative performance efficiency of companies (Putri et al., 2017). The advantage of the DEA method is that it can take into account more input and output variables at the same time, using a relative efficiency measurement coefficient. Efficiency is defined as the proportion of outputs to inputs. The DEA method focuses on limit values instead of central tendencies. Researchers from various research fields quickly realized that DEA is an excellent method to model operational processes in any segment of the economy (Cooper, Seiford, & Tone, 2007).

When using DEA, the following considerations should be made:

- DEA is sensitive to low numbers of investigated units;
- DEA is sensitive to outliers;
- DEA is sensitive to a large number of input and output variables;
- DEA is sensitive to the degree of statistical noise (measurement errors).

2.3. *Combining the data envelopment analysis and the principal component analysis*

All the analysis of this study was performed in the R statistical system which is free and public software environment for statistics and graphics: it is free to use, and the source code can be modified free as well (www.r-project.org). R is different from other statistical software because R is a programming language or a programming environment because it uses command scripts instead of menus. R has thousands of software packages to solve various problems (currently over 12,000). The R packages are extensions of the basic R system. For the calculations, we used the BERT tool (https://bert-toolkit.com/) that connects R and Excel, so we could work in Microsoft Excel, taking advantage of both systems' possibilities.

Using a relatively large number of input and output variables during the DEA analysis, it can cause a problem in discriminating between the efficient and the inefficient units, that is, the discrimination power decline. The Principal Component Analysis (PCA) can help both reduce the number of variables and increase the discrimination between efficient and inefficient units (Põldaru & Roots, 2014; Putri et al., 2017). The PCA is a multivariate method what can help to reduce the dimensionality of multivariate analysis (Fu & Ou, 2013; Adler & Golanyi, 2017). The PCA-DEA method is widely used in economic analysis, and it can also be seen in the portfolio analysis (Jothimani, Shankar, & Yadav, 2017). Dong, Mitchell, Knuteson, Wyman, Busman, and Conley (2016) investigate the farm sustainability in agricultural sectors using PCA-DEA method.

We strive to minimize the loss of information using the PCA method reducing the number of model variables (Jolliffe 2002). We want to achieve this objective by transforming original variables into principal components that are linear combinations of these variables. The principal components are uncorrelated, and the first few of them contain most of the variance of the original variables (Everitt & Hothorn, 2011). PCA decomposes some correlated variables into some uncorrelated principal components using linear transformation in a multidimensional database. The extracted principal components are estimated as the projections on the eigenvectors of the covariance or correlation matrix of the database (Faed, Chang, & Saberi, 2016). The variance of the variables is an indicator describing the range of the data. The larger deviation means that the principal components include more information. The PCA ensures that the first few components will contain most of the variance of the original variables (Everitt & Hothorn, 2011). We chose the principal components which have an eigenvector value greater than 1. The remaining components can be rejected without significant loss of information. (Fu & Ou, 2013). The complete information of input and/or output variables is not lost until the principal component weights representing variables are eliminated. This procedure minimizes information loss (Andrejic et al., 2013).

The steps of the PCA-DEA analysis follow:

- Standardization of the original data (using "scale" function in R).
- Performing the principal component analysis separately for input and output variables (using "principal" function of the psych package in R).
- Determining the number of principal components (using the results of "principal" function).
- Using the principal component scores to perform DEA (using "dea" function of Benchmarking package in R)

2.4. *The interval determination of DEA efficiency coefficients using Stan stochastic modeling tool*

Unsal and Orkcu (2017) used simulation related to PCA-DEA analysis to increase the efficiency of company ranking. We also applied the simulation method using Stan stochastic (probabilistic) modeling tool based on Bayesian statistics. Korner-Nievergelt et al. (2015) explain that there are at least four main reasons why statistical models are used:

1. models support to describe how we think a system works,
2. data can be summarized using models,
3. comparison of model predictions with data helps to understand the system, and
4. models allow for predictions, including the quantification of their uncertainty, and, therefore, they help with making decisions.

Stan is similar to BUGS (Lunn, Thomas, Best, & Spiegelhalter, 2000) and Jags (Plummer 2003) that allow one to write a Bayesian model in a convenient language. The Bayesian approach applies the laws of probability directly to the problem which offers many advantages over the more commonly used frequentist statistical approach (Bolstad 2004). A Stan program defines a statistical model through a conditional probability function p(θ|y;x), where θ is a sequence of modeled unknown values, y is a sequence of modeled observed values, and x is a sequence of unmodeled predictors and constants. Stan is an imperative probabilistic programming language (Stan Development Team 2017). Stan uses Hamilton Monte Carlo (HMC) and No U-Turn Sampling (NUTS) and is implemented by C++ to speed up computation. The Stan project provides the 'rstan' package to call Stan easily from R. Hamiltonian Monte Carlo is a Markov chain Monte Carlo algorithm that avoids the random walk behavior and sensitivity to correlated parameters that plague many MCMC methods. The Hamilton Monte Carlo algorithm allows converging to high-dimensional target distributions much more quickly than simpler methods such as Gibbs sampling (Hoffman & Gelman 2012).

Box (1979) wrote, „no model is perfect, but a good model is useful". This quotation states the obvious that there is no perfect model, but if we can create such a model that reflects reality well, it can help us achieve a better understanding of the real world. The Stan modeling system can help us to build models which help us better describe the real world. The goal of the Stan project is to provide a relatively easy probabilistic programming language for Bayesian statistical modeling to fit robust, scalable, and efficient models (Carpenter et al. 2017).

Kruschke (2010) writes that applying mathematics can be very useful when the data has large variances, and we are highly uncertain as to our knowledge of the situation. Researchers very frequently encounter uncertain parameters contained in data sets with high variance, and only the statistical inference can give precise numerical bounds on our uncertainty in this situation.

3. Results

3.1. Check the number of variables and the outliers

According to Bogetoft and Otto (2011), the number of input and output variables must correspond to either of the two following expressions [(1) – (2)]whose calculated value is larger:

$K > 3 * (m + n)$ or (1

$K > m * n$ (2

This requirement does not cause any problem in ou case as the number of units involved in the investigation significantly exceeds both expected values. Th number of units involved in the investigation (K) i 563 companies, the number of input variables (m) i 15, and the number of output variables (n) is 4. Base on the previous expressions, the expected values ar $3 * (15 + 4) = 57$ or $15 * 4 = 60$, which are considerabl smaller than the number of units investigated (K = 563

The next problem may be the number of outlier To examine the outliers, we created boxplot-diagram that showed that there is a large number of upper sid outliers. Based on the results of the boxplot-diagram it can be concluded that the average number of outlier -taking into account all input and output variables – i 87, with the minimum number of 59 and the maximum number of 151. There is no significant differenc between the average numbers of outliers over the year taking into account all the variables: the average number of outliers range from 84 to 91.

Subsequently, we divided the database into tithe creating deciles. Examining the range of total dat and the deciles of variables, we found that in aver age, 97.06% of the total range was in the tenth decil (the maximum value is 99.44% in the average of th years, and the minimum value is 87.46%). Taking int account the results, we have decided to include onl those companies whose revenue values are not outliers in the last year (2014). To reduce the outliers, w have chosen the sales variable because it includes th highest outlier values based on the boxplot-diagran although the number of outlier values is only averag The number of companies in the tenth decile is 57 i 2014, so the total number of investigated companie is 506. We can significantly reduce the outliers by thi restriction, and this also meets the number of requirement for units which is 60 units.

3.2. PCA-DEA

We used input-orientated and variable return-to-scal (VRS) models in the DEA analysis. We performe the calculation of the traditional DEA efficiency co efficients for 506 companies. Both input and outpu le 2. Results of using traditional DEA

Efficiency ratio	Years						Average of years
	2009	2010	2011	2012	2013	2014	
0.0	466	454	458	452	475	360	444.17
0.1	6	3	3	2	4	4	3.67
1 - 0.2	0	1	0	4	3	2	1.67
2 - 0.3	0	2	0	3	0	5	1.67
3 - 0.4	1	1	2	2	0	6	2.00
4 - 0.5	0	3	2	4	1	7	2.83
5 - 0.6	1	3	0	1	1	8	2.33
6 - 0.7	0	1	1	3	1	10	2.67
7 - 0.8	0	0	1	2	0	9	2.00
8 - 0.9	1	0	2	0	0	15	3.00
9 - 1.0	0	2	1	0	0	11	2.33
1.0	31	36	36	33	21	69	37.67
verage efficiency	0.065	0.085	0.083	0.081	0.046	0.231	0.098

variables have been standardized. Table 2 shows that most of the companies are inefficient. In the first five years, nearly 90% of companies are inefficient, and only slightly more than 5% is efficient. The number of efficient companies has increased considerably in the last year.

Table 2 also shows the annual average of efficiency coefficients, which are very low. We can conclude that the investigated companies are inefficient considering these financial characteristics. However, the question arises whether this is in fact reality? Can this result be improved if classical DEA is combined with principal component analysis? According to the literature, the PCA-DEA combination may increase the discriminatory power of the DEA method and reduces the number of variables. The number of efficient companies in the first four years was nearly the same (≈ 6.5%), it decreased to 2/3 of the previous years in the 5th year, and it is more than doubled in the 6th year. We think that the situation cannot be quite as bad as shown in Table 2. However, we are aware that there are serious problems with the level of corporate efficiency in Hungary, and this is especially true in the case of SMEs.

Table 3 shows the results of the PCA-DEA calculation. Table 3 presents that in the case of the PCA-DEA, there were no inefficient companies, and the efficiency coefficients showed a higher scatter. We used those principal components to determine the efficiency coefficients of the DEA method whose eigenvector value had reached or exceeded 1. Table 3 also shows that instead of the 14 input variables, it was enough to use two principal components what covered approximately 90% of the total variance in the first five years. In the last year, the eigenvector value of 6 principal components was more than 1, but they only covered 82% of the total variance.

Table 3 and Table 2 show the distribution of the efficiency coefficients which significantly differ comparing the classical DEA and the PCA-DEA. We can also discover a better distribution using the PCA-DEA method. For PCA-DEA, there is a higher dispersion of company performances, that is, the efficiency coefficients of corporate performances can be more realistic. We can see

Table 3. Results of PCA-DEA calculation

Efficiency ratio	Years						Average of years
	2009	2010	2011	2012	2013	2014	
Input PCs	1, 2	1, 2	1, 2	1, 2	1, 2, 3	1, 2, 3, 4, 5, 7	
Cummulative proportion	90%	92%	92%	89%	93%	82%	
Output PCs	2, 3	1, 2	1, 2	1, 2	1, 2	1	
Cummulative proportion	76%	98%	100%	100%	100%	79%	
= 0.0	0	0	0	0	0	0	0
< 0.1	3	0	0	3	0	397	66
0.1 - 0.2	2	0	1	2	0	20	4
0.2 - 0.3	5	2	1	9	1	14	5
0.3 - 0.4	29	3	9	18	0	7	11
0.4 - 0.5	72	8	21	23	1	9	22
0.5 - 0.6	278	24	36	45	2	4	65
0.6 - 0.7	97	49	82	89	4	5	54
0.7 - 0.8	5	66	182	142	27	5	71
0.8 - 0.9	0	134	150	153	69	1	68
0.9 - 1.0	4	202	12	13	360	1	99
= 1.0	11	18	12	9	42	43	22
Average efficiency	0.554	0.836	0.738	0.710	0.933	0.147	0.653

from Table 3 that the efficiency coefficients improved significantly, and the average efficiency coefficient (0.653) is more than 6.5 times higher than in the case of traditional DEA. Average efficiency reached the highest value in the 5th year when it was close to 1 (0.933). Based on the PCA-DEA calculation it can be stated that there were no ineffective companies in this case. Figure 1 shows that the distributions of company efficiency coefficients are different, and there is only some similarity in 2010-2012 years.

3.3. *Interval determination of DEA efficiency coefficients*

We determined the DEA efficiency coefficients using the Stan programming language only for the year 2013. The model was executed by the 'rstan' function of the R statistical system, which translates the model into the C ++ programming language. 'RStan' is the R interface to Stan programming language. The model was run in RStudio software (Cirillo, 2016), which makes it easier to use R. Using the C ++ programming language and compiling the program allows for much faster execution. The 'rstan' program performed two thousand iterations in one Markov-chain during the simulation, one half of which was related to the prior, and the other half for the posterior estimation. The 2000-iteration simulation allows for a better estimation of the efficiency values and determines the intervals of the estimated values.

The input values of Stan model (*dea_ec*) were the efficiency coefficients obtained in the PCA-DEA method

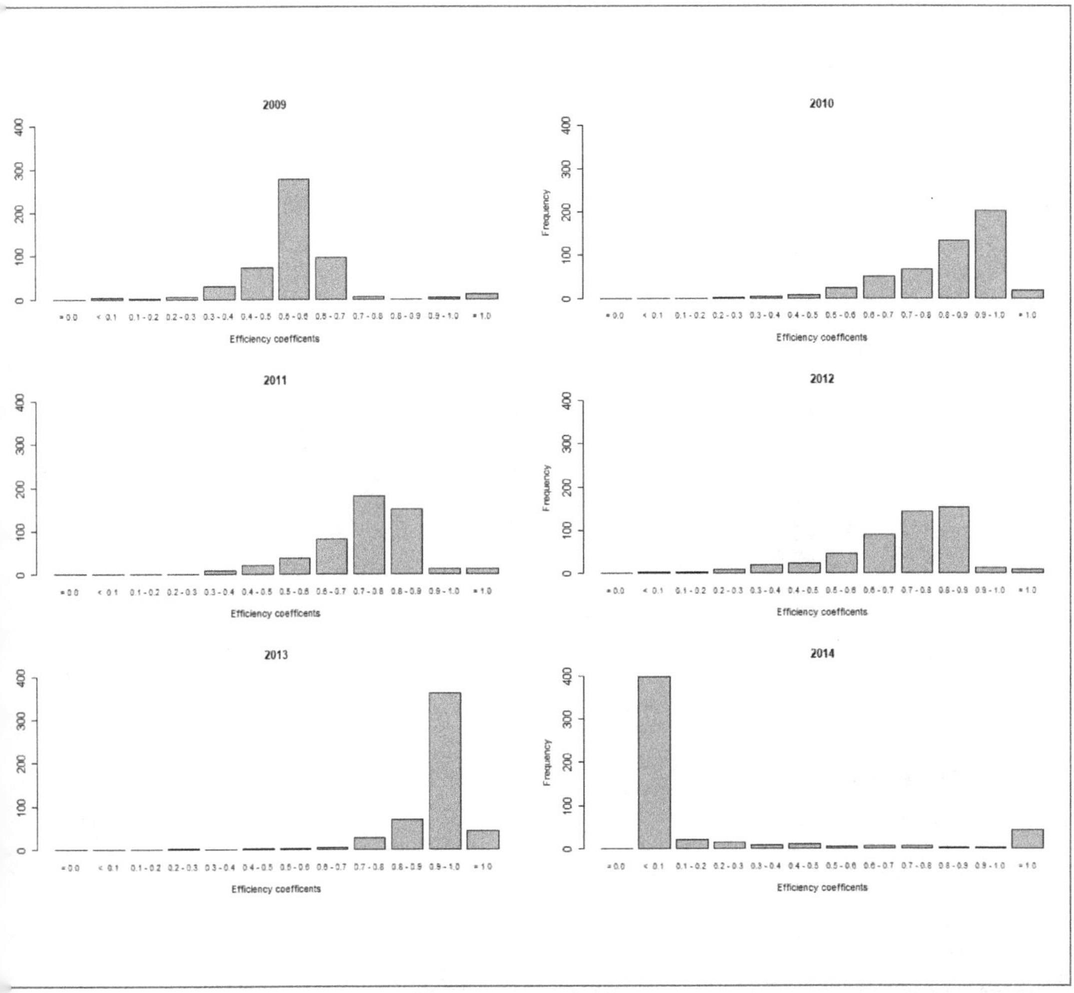

re 1. Results of PCA-DEA calculation

Appendix 1). The Stan model used is necessarily a kind f extension of the DEA model.

Table 4 shows that the Stan model gave different esults than the conventional DEA and the PCA-DEA nethod. Corporate performance indicators calculated y the Stan model have higher dispersion than oberved in the previous two methods and the number f efficient companies increased.

We cannot show the intervals calculated by the Stan nodel in the case of all 506 companies. We present nly the statistical parameters of the results of the Stan nodel (Table 5) in the case of all companies and efcient companies. Table 5 also shows that the average ifference between the lower and the upper limits is large enough to indicate the greater uncertainty of the estimated values. If the difference between the lower and the upper limit is high, the efficiency value is more uncertain because it is in a relatively wide range; its dispersion is also higher. There are no significant differences in the proportions of the different statistical characteristics of differences considering all companies and efficient companies, but the values of efficient companies are higher (Table 5). Based on the results, we can conclude that the PCA-DEA method provided better results than the conventional DEA method, which was further improved by the Stan model. We believe that the results of the Stan model, showing that more than 28% of companies are efficient and the rest

Table 4. Results of the models

Efficiency ratio	Conventional DEA	PCA-DEA	Stan model
= 0.0	475	0	0
< 0.1	4	0	0
0.1 - 0.2	3	0	1
0.2 - 0.3	0	1	0
0.3 - 0.4	0	0	0
0.4 - 0.5	1	1	3
0.5 - 0.6	1	2	16
0.6 - 0.7	1	4	93
0.7 - 0.8	0	27	86
0.8 - 0.9	0	69	89
0.9 - 1.0	0	360	75
= 1.0	21	42	143
Average efficiency	0.046	0.933	0.851
The lower limit of average efficiency			0.827
The lower limit of average efficiency			0.850

of them are not wholly inefficient, is closer to reality than the result of the traditional DEA model.

Figure 2 also shows that while the efficiency values and their upper and lower boundaries are relatively balanced, the differences between the lower and the upper limits are dispersed quite significantly. In the case of differences, there are many outliers. There are many outliers in case of differences, which highlights the wide range between upper and lower limits.

4. Conclusion

First, this study evaluated the performance of retail food companies in Hungary's Northern Great Plain region and is based on their financial statements from 2009 to 2014 via data envelopment analysis and principal component analysis. The Conventional DEA model has been defined including 14 input and four output variables. We used various packages of the R statistical program to solve the problems.

Using the PCA-DEA method we received man different results than in the case of conventiona DEA for the same companies. The PCA-DEA meth od evaluated the companies more extensively, whil in the case of the traditional DEA the extreme value were more pronounced. The results show that th level of information reduction has a considerabl effect on the efficiency classification of companie In the case of the PCA-DEA model, the companie have relatively better distribution than in the case c conventional DEA. That is why the PCA-DEA ap proach is believed to produce a more accurate clas sification outcome.

We can conclude from the results of the Stan mod that it provides us with a more acceptable result an allows a more accurate assessment of company per formance. However, the results of the Stan model als draw attention to the fact that sometimes the uncer tainty of the estimated values is high enough.

le 5. Statistical characteristics of efficiency values and intervals calculated by Stan model

lame of the statistical parameter	Efficiency coefficient	Lower limit	Upper limit	Difference between upper and lower limit
		All companies		
inimum	0.1986	0.1948	0.1982	0.0034
uartile 1	0.7388	0.7149	0.7369	0.0220
edian	0.8803	0.8495	0.8787	0.0292
uartile 3	1.0000	0.9663	0.9972	0.0309
aximum	1.0000	0.9954	0.9997	0.0043
verage	0.8513	0.8266	0.8498	0.0232
		Efficient companies		
inimum	1.0000	0.7247	0.9952	0.2705
uartile 1	1.0000	0.9675	0.9978	0.0302
edian	1.0000	0.9833	0.9984	0.0151
uartile 3	1.0000	0.9900	0.9988	0.0088
aximum	1.0000	0.9954	0.9997	0.0043
verage	1.0000	0.9593	0.9982	0.0389

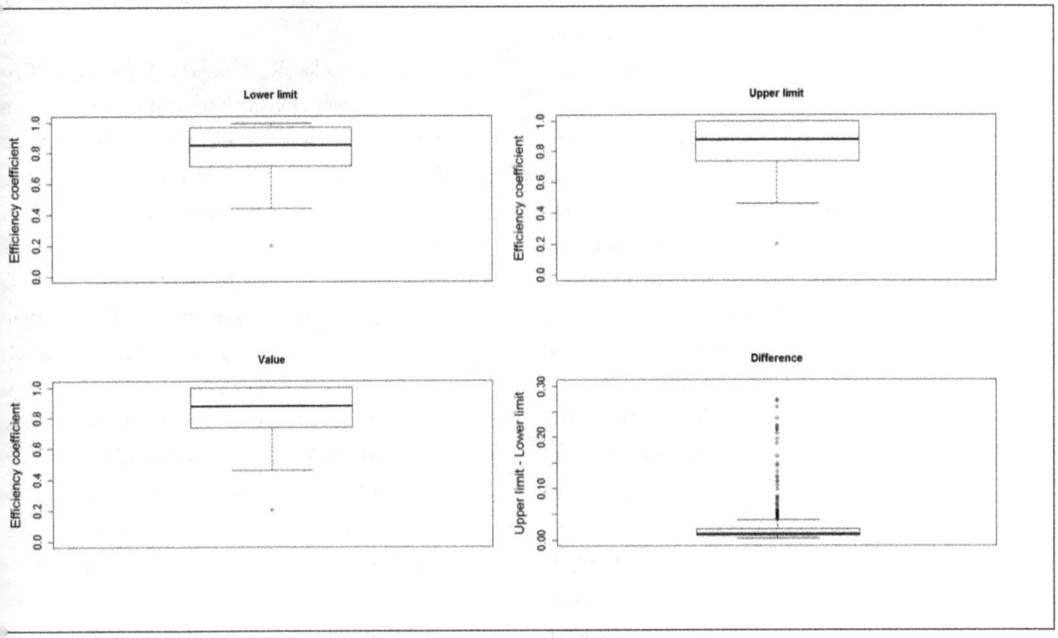

re 2. Box-plot diagrams of results of Stan model

In summary, it can be stated that combining different methods (DEA, PCA and Bayesian statistics) can help to define enterprise performance better. A more accurate definition of performance metrics allows for better evaluation and a well-founded comparison thus ensuring better overall decision making.

References

Adler, N., & Golany, B. (2017). PCA-DEA. In W. Cook, & J. Zhu (Eds.), Modeling Problem Structure and Data Varieties using Data Envelopment Analysis: A Problem-Solving (pp. 139-153). Boston, MA: Springer.

Andrejic, M., Bojovic, N., & Kilibarda, M. (2013). Benchmarking distribution centres using Principal Component Analysis and Data Envelopment Analysis: A case study of Serbia. Expert Systems with Applications, 40(10), 3926-3933.

Bogetoft, P. & Otto, L. (2011). Benchmarking with DEA, SFA, and R. New York, NY: Springer Verlag.

Bolstad, W. M. (2004). Introduction to Bayesian Statistics. Hoboken, NJ: John Wiley & Sons. Inc.

Box, G.E.P. (1979, May). Robustness in the Strategy of Scientific Model Building. Defense (Technical Summary Report No. 1954). Mathematic Research Center. University of Wisconsin.

Carpenter, B., Gelman, A., Hoffman, M. D., Lee, D., Goodrich, B., Betancourt,… Riddell, A. (2017). Stan: A probabilistic programming language. Journal of Statistical Software, 76(1), https://doi.org/10.18637/jss.v076.i01.

Charnes, A., Cooper, W. W., Rhodes, E. (1978). Measuring the efficiency of decision making units. European Journal of Operational Research, 2, 429–444.

Cirillo, A. (2016). RStudio for R Statistical Computing Cookbook. Birmingham, UK: Packt Publishing

Cook, W. D., & Zhu, J. (2005). Modeling performance measurement. Applications and implementation issues in DEA. New York, NY: Springer.

Cooper, W. W., Seiford, L. M., & Tone, K. (2007). Data Envelopment Analysis: A Comprehensive Text with Models, Applications, References and DEA-Solver Software. New York, NY: Springer.

Dong, F., Mitchell, P. D., Knuteson, D., Wyman, J., Bussan, A. J., & Conley S. (2016). Assessing sustainability and improvements in US Midwestern soybean production systems using a PCA-DEA approach. *Renewable Agriculture and Food Systems, 31*(6), 524-539

Emrouznejad, A., Parker, B. R., Tavares, G. (2008). Evaluation of research in efficiency and productivity: A survey and analysis of the first 30 years of scholarly literature in DEA. Journal of Socio-Economic Planning Sciences, 42(3), 151–157.

Everitt. B., & Hothorn, T. (2011). An Introduction to Applied Multivariate Analysis with R. New York NY: Springer.

Faed, A., Chang, E., & Saberi, M. (2016). Intelligent customer complaint handling utilising principal component and data envelopment analysis (PDA) Applied Soft Computing, 47, 614-630.

Farrell, M. (1957). The measurement of productive efficiency. Journal of Royal Statistical Society, Series A, 120(3), 253–281.

Fu, H. P., Ou, J. R. (2013). Combining PCA With DEA to Improve the Evaluation of Project Performance Data: A Taiwanese Bureau of Energy Case Study Project Management Journal, 44(1), 94–106

Hoffman, M. D., & Gelman, A. (2014). The No-U-Turn Sampler: Adaptively Setting Path Lengths in Hamiltonian Monte Carlo. Journal of Machine Learning Research 15, 1593-1623.

Huang, Z., & Li, S. X. (2011). Stochastic DEA Models With Different Types of Input-Output Disturbances. Journal of Productivity Analysis, 15 95–113.

Jothimani, D., Shankar, R., & Yadav, S. S. (2017). A PCA-DEA framework for stock selection in Indian stock market. Journal of Modelling in Management 12(3), 386-403

Jolliffe, I. T. (2002). Principal component analysis. New York, NY: Springer.

Korner-Nievergelt, F., Roth, T., von Felten s, Guèlat, J. Almasi, B., Korner-Nievergelt, P. (2015). Bayesian Data Analysis in Ecology Using Linear Models with R, BUGS, and Stan. London, UK: Elsevier.

Kruschke, J. K. (2010). Doing Bayesian Data Analysis A Tutorial with R and BUGS. London, UK: Elsevier

Li, L., & Li, M. (2014), Evaluation of Energy Production Companies Efficiency Based on the Combination of Principal Component Analysis (PCA) and Data Envelopment Analysis (DEA). Environmental Engineering and Management Journal 13(5), 1147-1154.

Lunn, D., Thomas, A., Best, N., Spiegelhalter, D. (2000). Winbugs – a Bayesian modelling framework: concepts, structure, and extensibility. Statistics and Computing, 10, 325–337.

Plummer, M. (2003, March 20-22). JAGS: A program for analysis of Bayesian graphical models using Gibbs sampling. In K. Hornik, F. Leisch, & A. Zeileis (Eds.), Paper presented at the 3rd international workshop on distributed statistical computing (DSC 2003). Vienna, Austria: Technische Universität Wien. Retrieved from https://www.r-project.org/conferences/DSC-2003/Proceedings/Plummer.pdf

Põldaru, R., & Roots, J. (2014). A PCA-DEA approach to measure the quality of life in Estonian counties. Socio-Economic Planning Sciences, 48, 65-73.

Putri, E. P., Chetchotsak, D., & Jani, M. A. (2017). Performance Evaluation Using PCA and DEA: a Case Study of the Micro and Small Manufacturing Industries in Indonesia. ASR Chiang Mai University Journal of Social Sciences and Humanities, 4(1), 37-56.

Sarkar, S. (2016). Application of PCA and DEA to recognize the true expertise of a firm: a case with primary schools. Benchmarking: An International Journal, 23(3), 740-751.

Stan Development Team (2017). Stan Modeling Language: User's Guide and Reference Manual. Version 2.17.0. Available at http://mc-stan.org/users/documentation/index.html

Tavares, G. (2002, January). A Bibliography of data envelopment analysis (1978-2001) (Research Report No. 01-02). Piscataway, NJ: Rutgers Center for Operations Research, Rutgers University.

Unsal, M. G., & Orkcu, H. H. (2017), Ranking decision making units with the integration of the multidimensional scaling algorithm into PCA-DEA. Hacettepe Journal of Mathematics and Statistics, 46(6), 1187-1197.

Appendix 1.

Interval determination of the DEA coefficients in the Stan programming language

```
data {
   int<lower = 0> n;
   real<lower = 0, upper = 1> dea_ec[n];
}
parameters {
   real x1;
   real x2;
   real alpha01[n];
   real alpha02[n];
}
model {
   x1 ~ gamma(1, 1);
   x2 ~ gamma(1, 1);
   for(i in 1:n)
   {
         alpha01[i] ~ gamma(x1, x2);
         alpha02[i] ~ gamma(x1, x2);
         dea[i] ~ exponential(alpha01[i]);
         dea[i] ~ normal(0, alpha02[i]) T[0, 500];
   }
}
generated quantities {
   real ec1[n];
   real ec2[n];
   for(i in 1:n)
   {
         ec1[i] = (alpha01[i] - 1) / alpha01[i];
         ec2[i] = (alpha02[i] - 1) / alpha02[i];
   }
}
```

ᐩermissions

l chapters in this book were first published in CE, by University of Finance and anagement, Warsaw; Vistula University; hereby published with permission under the eative Commons Attribution License or equivalent. Every chapter published in this book ıs been scrutinized by our experts. Their significance has been extensively debated. The pics covered herein carry significant findings which will fuel the growth of the discipline. ıey may even be implemented as practical applications or may be referred to as a beginning ›int for another development.

ıe contributors of this book come from diverse backgrounds, making this book a truly ternational effort. This book will bring forth new frontiers with its revolutionizing research formation and detailed analysis of the nascent developments around the world.

e would like to thank all the contributing authors for lending their expertise to make the ok truly unique. They have played a crucial role in the development of this book. Without eir invaluable contributions this book wouldn't have been possible. They have made vital forts to compile up to date information on the varied aspects of this subject to make this ok a valuable addition to the collection of many professionals and students.

ıis book was conceptualized with the vision of imparting up-to-date information and vanced data in this field. To ensure the same, a matchless editorial board was set up. ery individual on the board went through rigorous rounds of assessment to prove their ırth. After which they invested a large part of their time researching and compiling the ost relevant data for our readers.

ıe editorial board has been involved in producing this book since its inception. They have ent rigorous hours researching and exploring the diverse topics which have resulted in e successful publishing of this book. They have passed on their knowledge of decades rough this book. To expedite this challenging task, the publisher supported the team at ery step. A small team of assistant editors was also appointed to further simplify the iting procedure and attain best results for the readers.

ıart from the editorial board, the designing team has also invested a significant amount their time in understanding the subject and creating the most relevant covers. They rutinized every image to scout for the most suitable representation of the subject and eate an appropriate cover for the book.

ıe publishing team has been an ardent support to the editorial, designing and production ım. Their endless efforts to recruit the best for this project, has resulted in the complishment of this book. They are a veteran in the field of academics and their pool knowledge is as vast as their experience in printing. Their expertise and guidance has oved useful at every step. Their uncompromising quality standards have made this book exceptional effort. Their encouragement from time to time has been an inspiration for eryone.

ıe publisher and the editorial board hope that this book will prove to be a valuable piece knowledge for researchers, students, practitioners and scholars across the globe.

List of Contributors

Agnieszka Springer and Karolina Oleksa
WSB University in Poznan, the Institute of Management, Poland

Víctor M. González Sánchez
Department of Applied Economy, UNED – National University of Distance Education, Spain

S. S. Vinokurov
SPb State University of Economics (UNECON), Russia HSE, Russia

A. A. Medved and L. A. Mierin
SPb State University of Economics (UNECON), Russia

Willem K. M. Brauers
Department of Economics, University of Antwerp, Belgium
Vilnius Gediminas Technical University, Lithuania

Monika Mačiulienė
Mykolas Romeris University, Lithuania

Aelita Skaržauskienė
Vilnius Gediminas Technical University, Lithuania

Dick Botteldooren
Ghent University, Belgium

Mahsa Gorji
Faculty of Finance, University of Raja, Iran

Rasoul Sajjad
Faculty of Finance, University of Essex, Colchester, United Kingdom

Yetunde Anibaba and Godbless Akaighe
Lagos Business School, Nigeria

Małgorzata Baran
Collegium Civitas, Poland

Arturo Orea Rocha, Carmelo García Pér Fernando Crecente Romero and Ma Teresa del Val Núñez
University of Alcalá, Spain

Tomasz Korol
Politechnika Gdanska - Faculty Management and Economics, Poland

Mario Arturo Ruiz Estrada
Social Security Research Centre (SSR & Centre of Poverty and Developm Studies (CPDS), Faculty of Economics a Administration, University of Mala Malaysia

Su-Fei Yap and Noor Azina Binti Ismail
Faculty of Economics and Administrati University of Malaya, Malaysia

Ricardo Costa-Climent
Linnaeus University, Sweden

Carla Martínez-Climent
Universitat de València, Spain

Paweł Mielcarz and Dmytro Osiichuk
Akademia Leona Kozminskiego - Departm of Finance, Poland

Paweł Wnuczak
Akademia Leona Kozminskiego, Poland

Urszula Mrzygłód
University of Gdansk - Institute International Business, Poland

Sabina Nowak
University of Gdansk - Department Econometrics, Poland

ronika Fenyves, Tibor Tarnóczi and ltán Bács
iversity of Debrecen, Faculty of Economics d Business, Institute of Accounting and ance, Hungary

Laura Karnai and Adrián Nagy
University of Debrecen, Faculty of Economics and Business, Institute of Business Administration, Hungary

Index